the
law of nations
and the
new world

the
Law of nations
and the
new world

L.C. Green

Olive P. Dickason

with an introduction by
Timothy J. Christian

 THE UNIVERSITY OF ALBERTA PRESS

First published by
The University of Alberta Press
Athabasca Hall
Edmonton, Alberta
Canada T6G 2E8

Copyright © The University of Alberta Press 1989
Paper edition issued in 1993.
ISBN 0–88864–257–1

Canadian Cataloguing in Publication Data

Green, L.C. (Leslie Claude), 1920–
    The law of nations and the New World

    ISBN 0–88864–257–1

    1. Indians of North America – Claims.
    2. Indians of North America – Land tenure.
    3. Indians of North America – Land transfers.
    4. Indians of North America – Canada – Claims.★
    5. Indians of North America – Canada – Land tenure.★
    6. Indians of North America – Canada – Land
    transfers.★ I. Dickason, Olive Patricia, 1920–
    II. Title.
    E98.C6G74 1989   346.704'32   C88-091069-0

Typesetting by The Typeworks, Vancouver, British Columbia, Canada

Printed by Hignell Printing Ltd., Winnipeg, Manitoba, Canada

Contents

Introduction

TIMOTHY J. CHRISTIAN

C anada's new Constitution "recognizes and affirms" the "exist-ing aboriginal and treaty rights of the aboriginal peoples of Canada."[1] Constitutional force has thus been given to rights which are difficult to define and have been of doubtful legality.[2] One of the issues that the courts may have to address is whether the aboriginal rights enshrined in the Constitution preserve the sovereignty and right of self-government possessed by Amerindians before the age of European discovery and colonial expansion. *The Law of Nations and the New World* will help to place any such argument in historical con-text.

When one reflects upon the rights set out in our Constitution, fun-damental questions arise about the European occupation of the New World. What were the philosophical and legal justifications of colo-nial expansion? What were the arguments advanced to defend the subjection of the Amerindians and the creation of European hege-mony? Were any voices raised in opposition and, if so, what was the basis for such opposition? Were the actions of the colonizers lawful when viewed from the perspective of developing international law? What was the method of claiming title in the New World and was this method lawful? What is the basis for a claim that surviving aboriginal peoples possess the attributes of sovereignty? Did theologians defend the rights of the Amerindians or rationalize the claims of the colonists?

In answering these questions *The Law of Nations and the New World* explores the ideology of European colonial expansion into the New World, describing and evaluating the legal, theological and philo-sophical justifications of the colonizers and their sponsors. Consistent with their academic interests, Professor Green deals with the legal, and Professor Dickason with the theological and philosophical arguments from a historical perspective. The result is an interdisciplinary analysis of these three components of the ideology of colonialism.

In "Claims to Territory in Colonial America," Professor Green begins with the fundamental assumption that the lawfulness of an action must be determined according to the law in force at the time of the act, as opposed to the law in force when a subsequent dispute arises.[3] Therefore, he asks whether the discovery of the New World and the subjection of its peoples to European control was lawful according to the rules of international law in force during the age of discovery. This inquiry leads to an examination of state practice, a consideration of the views of the classical writers, and a review of the leading cases. Having treated these sources of law, Professor Green then assesses the legal validity of the claim that Canada's native people have a sovereign status that has survived the period of colonial expansion.

To document state practice a review is made of the commissions which authorized the earliest voyages of discovery, and of the contemporary accounts of various expeditions. This study discloses that the accepted methods of asserting sovereignty over newly discovered lands varied from the French practice of planting crosses bearing royal coats of arms to the Russian custom of burying coins or kettles or beads. It is clear from the survey that the explorers and their patrons considered that these rather simple devices were effective to convey territorial title—to the exclusion, not only of other European rulers, but of the original inhabitants as well. The indigenous people were not consulted and the Europeans made no attempts to conclude treaties or other formal arrangements with them, assuming them to be incapable of ownership. As a contemporary writer stated, the native population did not enjoy property rights but only had a general residence ". . .as wild beasts in a forest."[4]

The later colonizing efforts of the sixteenth and seventeenth centuries also proceeded on the premise that there was no need to consult or obtain the consent of the native inhabitants. While letters of commission sometimes spoke of the missionary motives of expeditions, the documents indicate that the primary purposes were the acquisition of territory. Further, contemporary treaties evidence a general agreement as to the proper method of asserting title and a general recognition of the legal effects of title so acquired. This leads Professor Green to conclude that at the time of discovery ". . .it was a well established practice, amounting to law. . ."[5] that rule over the newly discovered lands passed to the sovereign in whose name a territory was claimed, regardless of any proprietary claims of the original inhabitants. Did contemporary legal theory support this approach?

Perhaps not surprisingly, the classical writers, Spanish, German, and English, agreed that European dominion over the New World and its peoples was legally justified. This conclusion was reached by different writers in different ways but the three main arguments can be framed as claims in the alternative. Where one argument failed, another arose in its stead. First, some contended that the New World was unoccupied and that Europeans had a right to claim the lands. This involved diminishing the status of the original inhabitants by characterising them as barbarians who, since they did not live in civilized society, were incapable of enjoying legal rights of ownership. A second, related argument was that Europeans, as Christians, had a duty to spread the word of the gospel and a right to engage in trade and to cultivate unoccupied land without interference. Conversely, the peoples of the New World had an obligation to receive the ambassadors of the pope, the trade expeditions and the colonists, and any resistance or hostility to the European presence could be met with force of arms. This right of self-defence authorized the establishment of fortifications and taking such pre-emptive military actions as were necessary to ensure the safety of the Europeans. Alternatively, it was argued that the Christian rulers of Europe had a moral and legal obligation to end the cannibalism and human sacrifice practiced by some tribes. There was a legal right to wage war to protect afflicted persons and to vanquish those New World rulers who condoned barbaric practices and prevented their subjects from converting to Christianity. Third, even if it were conceded that the campaigns which the Europeans had undertaken to establish themselves in the New World were unjust wars, the victors could not be deprived of their spoils because the doctrines of usucaption or prescription by long usage served to legitimize the reality of effective occupation. Professor Green traces the reasoning of the leading scholars who, while often mounting different arguments, arrived at the same conclusion—that European occupation was lawful according to the law of nations.

This analysis places in context the decisions of various international tribunals and courts of the United States and Canada to the effect that aboriginal peoples do not possess the attributes of sovereignty in international law. Indeed, it would be odd if international law did not authorize the expansionist activities of the leading, colonial powers, for the law of nations was little more than a self-serving, crystallization of state practice. One might be forgiven for concluding that a legal analysis of questions of this magnitude is predictably circular, for if it was done it was lawful. After being conquered and subjected to the rule of the colonizing powers, it is difficult to see, from a legal point of view, how anything resembling sovereignty could have endured in the Amerindians.

Professor Dickason in "Concepts of Sovereignty at the Time of First Contacts" examines the theological and philosophical perspectives on colonialism in the New World. While her contention is that colonial expansion could not be justified according to natural or divine law, it is clear from her analysis that the majority of contemporary, influential scholars had little difficulty defending European hegemony.

While there was some theological controversy over the status of the Amerindians, the prevailing view was that they were savages living in an infant culture who ought not to be accorded the same status as Christians or even infidels who at least were civilized enough to have developed a religion—albeit non-Christian and inferior. The status accorded infidels and that bestowed upon Amerindians is usefully compared by Professor Dickason. While it was generally conceded that infidels were capable of *dominium*—the lawful possession of property and political power—leading scholars regarded the Amerindians as subhumans who were incapable of it.

In the thirteenth century Pope Innocent IV held that all rational creatures, Christian or pagan, had the right under natural law to own property and to govern themselves. Accordingly, not even the pope could seize the possessions or displace the jurisdiction of heathen without just cause. This view was contested by Hostiensis who asserted that the rights of infidels were subject to those of Christians. Only those infidels who recognized the lordship of the church were to be tolerated by it—being permitted to own possessions and exercise jurisdiction over Christians. Any ill-treatment of Christian subjects could lead to a revocation of authority by the pope and a justifiable expropriation of the land, possessions and jurisdiction or lordship of the infidel. Hostiensis held that Christ had assumed all power on His coming and that those who failed to recognize Him had forfeited their rights. The views of Hostiensis prevailed and applying his reasoning, the possessions of the Amerindians could be seized with impunity.

Further support for the subjugation of the Amerindians was found by adopting Aristotle's doctrine of natural servitude. It was argued that the Amerindians were naturally inferior and could not qualify for the same rights as Europeans. Thus, European domination was consistent with the natural order of things and the slave trade and exploitation of native labour could be justified.

The ascendancy of these views coincided with the loss of influence of a universal Catholic church and the creation of national monarchies. Concerns about pervasive standards of justice, as disclosed in natural law, were replaced by the need to justify and regulate the activities of particular monarchs in the New World. The law of nations displaced natural law as the critical standard. While the overriding importance of the principles of justice were theoretically affirmed, on a practical level, short-term, expansionist considerations prevailed.

The predominant view, and that which justified colonial expansion, was that Amerindians were beyond the reach of natural law. However, not all theologians, especially those who had actually spent time in the New World, agreed with this disposition of the Amerindian's interests, even on a theoretical basis. Chief among those who championed the cause of the Amerindian was the Spanish Dominican, Las Casas. Professor Dickason examines his writings, pointing out that his arguments "did not deflect the course of empire, but restated basic principles effectively enough that they are still being heard today."[6]

Las Casas contested each of the propositions relied upon by conventional theologians to justify the dehumanization and exploitation of the Amerindians. First, he argued that natural law did apply to the Amerindians as it did to all human beings. Thus, he attacked the Aristotelian notion of natural servitude, pointing out that Aristotle was himself not a Christian and that his doctrine which allowed for the subjection of some to servitude was inconsistent with the Christian object of uniting mankind. Further, he contended that the views of Hostiensis were heretical. Second, he argued that true conversion could only take place among free people. Infidels could not be forced to accept Christianity—rather, the power of rational argument, which he was confident would ultimately succeed, had to be trusted.

Thus the obligation to spread the gospel did not create a right to force unbelievers to listen. Third, based on his personal observation, he disputed the contention that the Amerindians were barbarians, arguing that merely because some had not adopted a government on European lines did not mean that they lacked the reason to be brought into an orderly domestic and political society. Indeed, he was of the view that the cultural attainments of some of the New World peoples were on a level with those of the Greeks and Romans. Fourth, Las Casas accepted that European monarchs were obliged to protect the innocent living in those cultures where human sacrifice was practiced. However, he was of the view that this duty could not justify the conquest and enslavement of the New World peoples nor the appropriation of their lands and possessions. It was the prerogative of God to impose punishment for the sins of an infidel committed "within the borders of the territory of his own masters and his own unbelief."[7] Finally, and as a logical result of his argument that the Amerindians were under natural law, Las Casas argued that the Amerindians were entitled to make war against, and kill, the Spaniards, in self-defence.

Professor Dickason traces the influence of these arguments on contemporary theologians and on the development of legislation purporting to restrict oppressive colonial practices in the New World. This analysis provides a refreshing indication that not all scholars were swept up in rationalizing expansion, but it also is a depressing reminder that, ultimately, the views of Las Casas were superseded by arguments supportive of the material interests of the colonial regimes.

In her account of French expeditions of discovery and colonization, Professor Dickason emphasizes the alliances formed between the Europeans and their Amerindian allies. She argues that while the historical evidence indicates that the Amerindians believed the alliances were a *de facto* recognition of their sovereign rights, the French never wavered in their view of the Amerindians as "hommes sauvages" living out of society and incapable of enjoying legal rights. The English, likewise, were preoccupied with the prospects of New World wealth and little concerned about the rights of the inhabitants. By the time of Elizabeth I the natural right to engage in trade was routinely claimed in commissions authorizing expeditions—just as the possible rights of the Amerindians were routinely ignored.

Whether regarded from the legal, theological, or philosophical perspective, the prevailing ideology of the age of European discovery and colonization gave no credence to the humanity of the Amerindians. As subhumans they were incapable of possessing rights—legal, natural or divine. It will be interesting to see what effect this historical reality has on the definition of aboriginal rights in the new Constitutional guarantee—particularly if it is regarded as an attempt to ameliorate ancient and longstanding injustices. *The Law of Nations and the New World* provides a fascinating insight into the thinking of those who were responsible for and who opposed the subjugation of the Amerindians. It will be of special interest to those who want to examine the assumptions which permitted it to be done.

Notes

1. S. 35(1), *The Constitution Act, 1982*.
2. Some recent consideration of these questions from a legal perspective can be found in: Gagne, "The Content of Aboriginal Title at Common Law" (1982-83) 47 *Sask. L. Rev.* 309; L.C. Green, "Aboriginal Peoples, International Law and the Canadian Charter of Rights and Freedoms" (1983) 61 *Can. Bar. Rev.* 339; N. Lyon "The Teleological Mandate of the Fundamental Freedoms Guarantee: What to do with Vague but Meaningful Generalities" (1982) 4 *Sup. Ct. L. Rev.* 57; Lysyk, "The Rights and Freedoms of the Aboriginal Peoples of Canada" in Tarnopolsky and Beaudoin (eds.), *The Canadian Charter of Rights and Freedoms* (1982); McNeil, "The Constitutional Rights of the Aboriginal Peoples of Canada" (1982) 4 *Sup. Ct. L. Rev.* 255; Shaun Nakatsuru, "A Constitutional Right of Indian Self-Government" (1985) 43 *U. T. Fac. L. Rev.* 72-99; Sanders, "The Rights of the Aboriginal Peoples of Canada" (1983) 61 *Can. Bar Rev.* 314; B. Slattery, "The Constitutional Guarantee of Aboriginal Rights and Freedoms" (1983) 8 *Queen's L. J.* 232; B. Slattery, "The Hidden Constitution: Aboriginal Rights in Canada" (1984) 32 *Am. J. Comp. L.* 361-91.
3. In adopting this approach, Professor Green used the same method of analysis as was employed by Judge Huber, a sole arbitrator dealing with competing claims by the United States and the Netherlands over the sovereignty of an East Indian Island, in *The Island of Palmas* (1928) 2 *U.N., Reports of Int'l Arb. Awards,* 831. He held that the effect of the discovery of the Island by Spain was ". . .to be determined by the rules of international law in force in the first half of the 16th century."
4. Green at p. 18.
5. Green at p. 38.
6. Dickason at p. 199.
7. Dickason at p. 210.

claims to territory in colonial america

L. C. GREEN

Detail from Clouet's *Carte d'Amerique,* 1782. Reprinted with permission from the Public Archives Canada, National Map Collection, NMC 11879.

I t has become increasingly common since the end of the Second World War for aboriginal peoples in a variety of countries, including Canada, to assert that they are the true and sovereign owners of the territories they occupy, regardless of the fact that they may constitute a minority of the population. Frequently they put forward claims for a return of the land, despite the presence of nonaboriginals who may have been there a century or more. On occasion these claims have been met by land grants by the local government or by compensation, but there have been instances when the aboriginal peoples have demanded self-government or independent statehood. Aboriginal groups and their sympathisers often suggest that the ruling majority are alien interlopers lacking any true title to the country they govern. These groups tend to ignore the fact that in the modern world title to statehood depends not on local custom or morality, but on international law. In assessing the claims of Canada's aboriginal peoples, especially the Indians, it is necessary to look at the history of Western settlement and the legal basis of claims to territory and sovereignty in international law.

In considering the validity of claims to titles to territory in international law, it must be remembered that international law is a vital and progressive rather than a sterile system. That is to say, what may have been sufficient to establish title in the sixteenth century might not necessarily be sufficient today. Equally, claims of an indigenous people which might be recognised today, might well have been unknown then. It is necessary, therefore, to examine the validity of the acquisition of current titles in accordance with the principles and customs that were valid at the time when the title was claimed to have been established, and not now when its validity may be challenged.[1]

Further, it must be borne in mind that international law as we know it today is the development of the practice of the European Christian states and it is important to examine that practice in order to ascertain what the law was in that developmental period before it became the universal system it now is. This is necessary when examining any alleged rule of law, and even more so in the case of title to territory as may be seen if one looks at the manner in which the Latin American states in the nineteenth century, and equally the new states of Africa today have insisted on maintaining the old colonial boundaries which were established either to delimit the jurisdictional limits of local administrators or to define the extent of competing imperialist expansionist policies.

The Pope and the Papal Bulls

At the time of the era of discovery, from the early part of the fourteenth century, it was generally accepted that the entire globe was the property of God and, as such, distributable by the Pope as His delegate on earth. At the same time, it was the practice of the European states to seize for themselves territories which had not yet been claimed by other Christian states, regardless of the attitude or presence of aboriginal inhabitants, who, for the main part, were described as "savages" or "barbarians." Many of these seizures were based on a series of Papal Bulls, whereby the yet undiscovered world—that is to say, undiscovered by the European powers—was divided by the Pope primarily between Portugal and Spain. Insofar as the Western hemisphere is concerned, the Bull of 4th May 1493, issued after Columbus returned from his first voyage, is the most significant. By it, the Pope granted to Ferdinand and Isabella and their descendants all lands lying west of a line joining the North and the South Poles, 100 leagues west of the Azores, including regions discovered and unknown, so long as they had not already been seized by any other Christian Prince. The subjects of other states were not allowed to enter this domain without the consent of the Spanish King. Lands east of the line were awarded to Portugal:

> . . .on one of the chief of these aforesaid islands [discovered by Columbus] the said Christopher has caused to be put together and

built a fortress fairly equipped, whereon he has stationed as garrison certain Christians. . .who are to make search for other remote and unknown islands and mainlands. . . .Wherefore,. . .you have purposed. . .to bring under your sway the said mainlands and islands with their residents and inhabitants and to bring them to the Catholic faith. . . .And in order that you may enter upon so great an undertaking with greater readiness and heartiness endowed with the benefit of our apostolic favour, we, of our own accord, not at your instance nor the request of anyone else in your regard, but of our own sole largess and certain knowledge and out of the fullness of our apostolic power by the authority of Almighty God conferred upon us in blessed Peter and of the vicarship of Jesus Christ, which we hold on earth, do by tenor of these presents, should any of said islands be found by your envoys and captains, give, grant, and assign to you and your heirs and successors,. . .forever, together with all their dominions, cities, camps, places and villages, and all rights, jurisdictions, and appurtenances, all islands and mainlands found and to be found, discovered and to be discovered towards the west and south, by drawing and establishing a line from the Arctic pole. . .to the Antarctic pole. . ., no matter whether the said mainlands and islands are found in the direction of India or towards any other quarter, the said line to be distant one hundred leagues from any of the islands commonly known as the Azores and Cape Verde. With this proviso however that none of the islands and mainlands, found and to be found, discovered and to be discovered, beyond the said line, towards the west and south, be in the actual possession of any Christian king or prince up to the birthday of our Lord Jesus Christ just past from which the present year one thousand four hundred and ninety-three begins. And we make, appoint and depute you and your said heirs and successors lords of them with full and free power, authority, and jurisdiction of every kind: with this proviso however, that by this our gift, grant, and assignment no right required by any Christian prince, who may be in actual possession of said islands and mainlands prior to the said birthday of our Lord Jesus Christ, is hereby to be understood to be withdrawn or taken away. . . .Furthermore, under penalty of excommunication *late sententie* to be incurred *ipso facto,* should anyone thus contravene, we strictly forbid all persons of whatsoever rank, even imperial or royal, or of whatsoever estate, degree, order, or condition, to dare, without your special permit or that of your aforesaid heirs and successors, to go for the purpose of trade or any other reason to islands or mainlands, found and to be found, discovered and to be discovered. . .apostolic constitutions and ordinances and other decrees whatsoever to the contrary notwithstanding. . . .Let no one, therefore, infringe, or with rash boldness contravene, this our recommendation, exhortation, requisition, gift, grant, assignment, constitution, deputation, degree, mandate, prohibition, and will. Should anyone presume to attempt this, be it known to him that he will incur the wrath of Almighty God and of the blessed apostles Peter and Paul. . . .[2]

It is clear from the wording of this Bull that the Pope, and presumably the Christian kings and princes who owed him allegiance, believed that the world belonged to God and that the administration thereof was within the jurisdiction of the Pope as His representative. Moreover, the language makes it clear that the Pope regarded his award as a legal grant giving the Spanish and Portuguese monarchs full power of sovereignty and jurisdiction over the territories concerned, with the primary objective of spreading Christianity. That the rulers of Spain and Portugal considered the Pope's grant as being completely effective is evidenced by the Treaty of Tordesillas, 1494,[3] whereby they shifted the one hundred league line demarcating their spheres of ownership to three hundred and seventy leagues west of the Cape Verde Islands. While dividing the seas between them, they recognised the right of each to cross into the territory of the other to the extent that this should be necessary, but affirmed the exclusive ownership of each within its area. This alteration of the Bull *Inter caetera* was confirmed by the Bull *Ea quae* of 1506,[4] issued after Vasco da Gama had rounded the Cape. This Bull reiterates and recognises the right of the King of Portugal "to navigate the ocean sea, [and] seek out the islands, ports, and mainlands lying within the said sea, and to retain those found for himself, and to all others it was forbidden under penalty of excommunication, and other penalties. . . from presuming to navigate the sea in this way against the will of the aforesaid king, or to occupy the islands and places found there." In none of the documents cited is there any reference to the possessory rights of any local inhabitants who might be found in the territories concerned when the latter were discovered by explorers commissioned by the rulers of Spain or Portugal. In this connection it is interesting to note that whereas the earliest Bull issued to the Portuguese referred to the enemies of Christ as "infidels," it nevertheless named them as "Saracens,"[5] and authorised the Portuguese king "to reduce their persons to perpetual slavery." However, the Bulls regarding the discoveries in the New World talked of "barbarous nations—*barbare nationes*," without attempting to accord any distinctive name to them or their inhabitants.

Within a generation of the Bull *Inter caetera* Protestantism made its appearance in Europe and the Protestant countries, England, The Netherlands and Russia, could not be expected to acquiesce in this allotment. Even Francis I of France, the "Most Christian King," 1515-1547, asked to be shown the will of Adam whereby he had been deprived of the right to acquire territory in the New World.[6] However, even the opponents of such Papal largesse, when issuing commissions to their own explorers/land-grabbers, instructed them not to seize land already claimed in the name of another Christian prince, although in practice the Papal disposition seems not to have been regarded by these dissenters as sufficient warrant of title and some other evidence, often in the form of a cross with the royal arms superimposed thereon, was regarded as sufficient.

Symbolic Acts of Possession

The practice of putting up crosses as a sign of a claim of title was in general use during the period of early exploration, and these crosses were often adorned with the arms of the sovereign. Insofar as Columbus was concerned, on his 1492 voyage, he "planted the cross, hoisted the royal standard of Spain: and. . .took possession of these new countries, and was immediately acknowledged as Admiral of the Ocean, Viceroy and Governor of the islands and main land discovered and to be discovered, in the name of the monarchs of Spain."[7] In his letters,[8] we find Columbus (or his scribes) writing:

In all the countries visited by your Highnesses' ships, I have caused a high cross to be fixed upon every headland, and have proclaimed, to every nation I have discovered, the lofty estate of your Highnesses, and of your court in Spain. . . .[T]he princes of Spain have never gained possession of any land out of their own country, until now that your Highnesses have become the masters of another world. . . .[T]he Admiral landed with the royal banner in his hands and took formal possession on behalf of their Majesties. . . . I took possession of all these islands in the name of our invincible King, and the government of them is unreservedly committed to his said Majesty. . . .Your Highnesses are as much lords of this place as they are of Xeres or Toledo, and your ships that may come here will do so with the same freedom as if they were going to your own palace. . . .

The lands in this part of the world, which are now under your Highnesses' sway, are richer and more extensive than those of any other Christian power, and. . .I had, by the Divine will, placed them under your high and royal sovereignty. . . .

That the placing of marks in this way was not merely the whim of the explorer but was regarded as essential for the assertion of sovereignty is illustrated by the patent [asiento] given to Alonso de Hojedo in 1500 and 1501:[9]

. . .that you set up marks with the arms of their Majesties or with other signs that may be understood, such as may be fitting to you, so that it may be known that you have discovered that land in order that you may stop discoveries of the English in that direction.

The early adventurers to North America pursued the same practice. Thus, Cartier records:[10]

On the 24th of July [1534] we had a cross made. . .which was put together in the presence of a number of the Indians [in his own French text Cartier uses the term "sauvages"], under the cross-bar of which we fixed a shield with three fleurs-de-lys in relief, and above it a wooden board, engraved in large Gothic characters, where was written "Long Live the King of France". . . .We explained to them by signs that the Cross had been set up to serve as a landmark and guide-post on coming into the harbour, and that we would soon come back. . . .On May 3rd 1536 [during the second voyage]. . .the Captain. . .had a beautiful Cross erected some thirty-five feet high, under the cross-bar of which was attached an escutcheon, embossed with the arms of France, whereon was printed in Roman characters "Long Live Francis I By God's Grace King of France."

That these crosses were in fact more than signs and landmarks for the future is shown by the record of the second voyage in 1536:[11]

The Second Voyage undertaken by the command and wish of the Most Christian King of France, Francis the First. . .for the completion of the discovery of the western lands. . .as the territories and kingdom of that prince. . . .One sees the princes of Christendom and the true pillars of the Catholic church. . .striving day by day to extend and enlarge the same, as the Catholic King of Spain has done in the countries discovered to the west of his lands and kingdoms, which before were unknown to us, unexplored and without the pale of our faith, as New Spain,. . .where innumerable peoples have been found, who have been baptized and brought over to our holy faith. And now through the present expedition undertaken at your royal command for the discovery of the lands in the west formerly unknown to you. . .with the sure hope of the future mercies of our most holy faith and of your possessions and most Christian name.

That Cartier and his King regarded these efforts as sufficient to create a territorial title is clear from comments concerning the third voyage in 1541[12] on which occasion cattle, goats and hogs were carried "for breede in the countrey," while Francis I appointed John de la Roche "his Lieutenant and Governour in the Countreys of Canada and Hochelaga," by the Lachine Rapids.

This practice was still being followed more than half a century later when Champlain was making his voyages to New France:[13]

Of this wood I made a Cross which I set up at one end of the island, on a high and prominent point, with the arms of France, as I had done in the other places where I had stopped. I named this place Saint-Croix Island. . . .Before I left, I built a Cross, bearing the arms of France, which I set up in a prominent place on the shore of the lake, and begged the Indians to be kind enough to preserve it, as well as those they would find along the trails by which we had come. I said that if they broke these down harm would befall them, but that if they preserved them, they would not be attacked by their enemies.

It should be noted that, as with Cartier before him, Champlain does not in his French text use the word "Indians." This is an innovation of his translators, for he refers to the native inhabitants as "sauvages,"[14] and occasionally by their tribal names,[15] while his comments about them and their customs are frequently highly uncomplimentary.[16] By attaching the French arms to the Cross, enjoining the Indians to preserve them with threats against them should they destroy his Crosses, and guarantees of protection against enemies in return for preservation of his markers, Champlain clearly indicates that he regarded the installation of such markers as an act entailing acquisition of sovereignty, with an indication to the indigenous people that they would, as a consequence, be placed under French protection.

The English explorers did not always raise a cross in the places where they landed and which they claimed for their monarch, but they did nevertheless consider it necessary to indulge in some formal ceremony, which often involved a symbolic taking of part of the realty. Thus, of Cabot, the Milanese envoy to Westminster informed the Duke of Milan[17]

> . . .he hoisted the royal standard and took possession for the King here; and after taking certain tokens he returned,

while another Italian version states[18] he

> planted on his new-found land a large cross, with one flag of England and another of St. Mark, by reason of his being a Venetian, so that our banner has floated very far afield.

Insofar as Drake's circumnavigation of 1577 was concerned,[19] disregarding the Spanish claims based on the crosses planted by Magellan:

> formall possession was then and there taken of the said Straits and Territories, with Turfe and Twigge, after the English manner:

Captain Drake delivering the said possession in the name and to the use of Queen Elizabeth and her successors.

When Mendoza, the Spanish Ambassador, protested at Drake's activities, Elizabeth replied[20] in terms that were somewhat reminiscent of the sarcasm of Francis I:[21]

> she would not persuade herself that [the Indies] are the rightful property of Spanish donation of the Pope of Rome in whom she acknowledged no prerogative in matters of this kind, much less authority to bind Princes who owe him no obedience, or to make that New World as it were a fief for the Spaniard and clothe him with possession: and that only on the ground that the Spaniards have touched here and there, have erected shelters, have given names to a river or promontory: acts which cannot confer property. So that this donation of *res alienae* which by law *(ex jure)* is void, and this imaginary proprietorship, ought not to hinder other princes from carrying on commerce in these regions and from establishing colonies where Spaniards are not residing, without the least violation of the law of nations, since without possession prescription is of no avail *(haud valeat)*, nor yet from freely navigating that vast ocean since the use of the sea and air is common to all men; further that no right of the ocean can inure to any people or individual since neither nature nor any reason of public use permits occupation of the ocean.

Despite Elizabeth's insistence on some act of possession in addition to a mere title based on discovery, her own explorers had been acting in much the same fashion as had those of Spain and France. Drake had proclaimed the Queen's title to islands in the Straits,[22] and had in fact intended claiming Cape Horn itself, for which purpose he had made a "monument of her Majestie, engrauen in metall,"[23] but was prevented from raising it due to lack of a safe harbourage and adverse weather conditions. Frobisher and Gilbert, too, operated in a somewhat similar fashion. Thus Frobisher,[24] at Hudson Bay in 1577, had

> marched through the Countrey with Ensigne displaied, so far as thought needfulle, and now and then heaped up stones on high mountaines, and other places, in token of possession, as likewise to signifie unto such as hereafter may chance to arrive there, that pos-

session is taken in behalfe of some Prince, by those who first found out the Countrey,

while at Frisland[25] he and some of his personnel

went ashore, being the first knowen Christians that we have true notice of that ever set foote upon that grounde; and therefore the Generall tooke possession thereof to the use of our Sovereigne Lady the Queenes Majestie, and discovered there a goodly harborough for the ships, where there were certain little boates of that countrey,

the presence of which did not inhibit Frobisher from his act of annexation. Gilbert's voyage to Newfoundland took place in 1583, that is after Elizabeth's reprimand of Mendoza, and, on landing,[26] there

was openly read and interpreted his commission; by vertue whereof he tooke possession in the same harbour of St. John, and 200 leagues every way, invested the Queenes Majestie with the title and dignities thereof, had delivered unto him (after the instance of England) a rod and a turffe of the same soile, entring also possession for him, his heirs and assignes forever: And signified unto all men, that from this time forward, they should take the same land as a territorie appertaining to the Queen of England, and himself authorised under Her Majestie to possesse and enjoy it.

But Gilbert seemed aware of the need of further acts of a more than symbolic character, and having promulgated a code of laws,

afterward were erected not farre from that place the Armes of England ingraven in lead, and affixed upon a pillar of wood. Yet further and actually to establish this possession taken in right of her Majestie, and to the behalfe of Sir Humphrey Gilbert knight, his heires and assignes forever: the Generall graunted in *fee farme* divers parcels lying by the waterside, both in this harbour and elsewhere.

Further, Elizabeth's assertion of nonownership of the seas did not stop her successor, James I, from instructing Selden to write his *Mare Clausum* asserting British sovereignty over the "narrow seas," and which was published under Charles I in 1635.

English explorers acting for foreign sovereigns tended to introduce the English practice into their own activities, claiming sovereignty for their foreign masters by token possession of the land. In 1605, acting on behalf of the King of Denmark in Greenland, Cunningham[27] and a member of his crew

> went a land, we falling downe on oure knees and thanked God in his goodness; the which done, the Captaine tooke possession of the same in your Majesties behalfe, takinge with him both earth and stones,

there being no trees to provide twigs, and Eskimos brought back from that expedition were being described by the King as "Our Subjects,"[28] although there is nothing to show that these people were consulted in any way as to the disposition of their lands or the acquisition of nationality.

Reference has already been made to the activities of Cartier and Champlain, but it is perhaps of interest to note that just as before so after their expeditions the French were planting markers as sign of French authority. According to Laudonnière,[29] New France was so called because

> in the year, 1524, John Verrazzano, a Florentine, was sent, by King Francis I, and by Madam the Regent, his mother, unto these new regions, where he went on land and discovered all the coast which is from the Tropic of Cancer,. . .and further unto the north. He planted in this country, the ensigns and arms of the King of France, so that the Spaniards themselves, which were there afterward, have named this country, Terra Francesca. . . .

Perhaps one of the clearest expressions of the attitude of France may be seen in the description of Saint-Lusson's acquisition of Sauteurs, now Sault Ste. Marie, in 1671:[30]

> All around the great throng of Indians stood or crouched or reclined at length, with eyes and ears intent. A large cross of wood had been made ready. Dablon, in solemn form pronounced his blessing on it, and then it was reared and planted in the ground, while the French, uncovered, sang the *Vexilla Regis*. Then a post of cedar was planted beside it, with a metal plate attached, engraven

with the Royal Arms; while Saint-Lusson's followers sang the *Exaudiat*, and one of the Jesuits uttered a prayer for the King. Saint-Lusson now advanced, and, holding his sword in one hand, and raising with the other a sod of earth, proclaimed in a loud voice:

"In the name of the Most High Majesty and Redoubted Monarch, Louis, Fourteenth of that name, Most Christian King of France and Navarre, I take possession of this place, Sainte Marie du Saut, as also of Lakes Huron and Superior, the Island of Manitoulin, and all countries, rivers, lakes and streams contiguous thereunto,—both those which have been discovered and those which may be discovered hereafter, in all their length and breadth, bounded on the one side by the seas of the North and the West and on the other by the South Sea: declaring to the nations thereof that from this time forth they are vassals of His Majesty, bound to obey his laws and follow his customs; promising them on his part all succor and protection against the invasions of their enemies; declaring to all other potentates, princes, sovereigns, states and republics,—to them and to their subjects,—that they cannot and are not to seize or settle upon any part of the aforesaid countries, save only under the good pleasure of His Most Christian Majesty, and of him who will govern in his behalf; and this on pain of incurring his resentment and the effort of his arms. VIVE LE ROY."

Despite the publicity, formality and assumption of nationhood, insofar as the indigenous population is concerned, there is no suggestion that the latter played any part in this proceeding or had in fact been consulted as to whether they wished to become vassals of France. Moreover, despite the symbolic taking of earth, it was still considered possible to assume sovereignty over lands that were yet undiscovered and in respect of which no true occupation could have ensued. Even in the middle of the eighteenth century, the French were still erecting wooden crosses with lead plates bearing the Royal Arms attached, and in 1846 the plate asserting such authority and dated 1749 was found at the mouth of the Kanawha River near its confluence with the Ohio,[31] although the purpose of the plate was to reassert an existing possession, rather than serve as an initial claim:

In this year 1749, in the reign of Louis XV, of France, We, Céleron commandant of a detachment sent by the Marquis de la Galissoniere, Captain-General of New France, in order to re-establish tranquillity among some villages of savages [note that the word "Indians," or other form of description, is not used] of these parts, buried this plate at the mouth of the Chi-no-da-hich-e-tha, the 18th August, near the river Ohio. . .as a monument of renewal of possession *[pour monument du renouvellement de possession]*, which we have taken of the said river Ohio, and of all those which empty themselves into it, and of all the lands on both sides, even to the sources of said rivers; as have enjoyed, or ought to have enjoyed, the preceding kings of France, and that they have maintained themselves there by force of arms and by treaties, especially by those of Riswick, of Utrecht, and of Aix-la-Chapelle[32]

not one of which was signed with the local people, but each of which was with another European power.

It is perhaps enough to refer to Russian practice to confirm that the installation of markers, whether or not accompanied by other acts betokening possession, was regarded as a sufficient method of acquiring sovereignty during the early period of exploration. When an expedition reached the Peninsula of Kamchatka in 1696, it erected "a cross upon its banks and built some huts."[33] When exploring Alaska and the Aleutian Islands in 1743 Behring left beads, an iron kettle and some coins as evidence of his visit,[34] and these were apparently accepted by Cook as evidence of Russian possession.[35] The expedition of the Russian-American Company to Kodiak Island in 1788 is indicative to show that the practice of leaving or burying material was still in vogue at the end of the eighteenth century:[36]

. . .They were to explore new islands, and to bring the natives under the Russian dominion, [and] to secure to that Empire the newly discovered parts of America by erecting tokens with Russian coats of arms and inscriptions. In conformity with these instructions, after receiving five copper tables, and five coats of arms. . ., the two pilots sailed. . . .On this day they buried in the earth one of the copper plates, and erected over it a cross with the inscription *Russian Imperial Territory*. . . .At the extremity of the wood, on the right side of the entrance, and near a little island covered with trees, we buried. . .another of the copper plates. . . . Atascha, the brother of the Toion Shenuga,. . . .came. . .and traded with us. As he appeared to be a person of good understanding, we entrusted him with one of the Russian coats of arms and required him to deliver it to his brother. . . .In delivering. . .the coat of arms, we informed him that the Sovereign of All the Russias solemnly bound herself to protect the inhabitants of these distant islands and that the Toion must, on his part, wear the coat of arms on his outer garment, and display it as well to his subjects as to foreigners navigating in these parts, and we assured him that it would prove that the Toion was under Russian protection and prevent all foreigners from injuring him or any of his relatives. Atascha. . .received the coat of arms with extreme satisfaction. . . .As a still further proof that all this part of the American continent and islands enjoyed the protection of the Russian Empire, one of the copper coats of arms was produced;. . .the Troion. . .received the coat of arms with extreme joy. . . .[T]he Troion paid another visit to the ship. . .; he wore on his. . .mantle the coat of arms. . . which he had before received from us. . . .[H]e earnestly declared that in memorial of the great successor to the Imperial throne he might be gratified with one of the portraits which he had seen in the cabin, and as there happened to be on board two engravings of the Grand Duke, one of these was delivered to him. . . .Above was written "In June 1788 the factor of the Company. . .being in the Bay of Yakutat, carried on a considerable traffic with the Troion Ilchak and his subjects, the Koliuski, and finally received them under the protection of the Russian Empire. As a memorial of these events we gave the said Troion a Russian coat of arms on copper, and this engraving of his Imperial Highness, the successor to the Russian throne. Orders are hereby given to all Russian and foreign ships sailing to this place to treat this Troion with cordiality and friendship without omitting the necessary precautions. . ." On the eighteenth we landed and buried another copper plate in a place which was accurately specified. We then expiated on the power and authority of the Sovereign of All the Russias with such effect that the Troion, in the most solemn manner, expressed his full confidence in the protection of the Russians, and his resolution in persevering in his friendly behaviour. We then exhibited a Russian coat of arms and presented it to him with the same ceremonies as we had done to the Koliuski chief, Ilchak.

Clearly, the Russians were of opinion that the presentation of gifts, particularly the coat of arms, accompanied by promises of protection, was sufficient to affirm Russian protection, to an extent that would be recognised and observed by other Europeans. In this manner, they were merely repeating the procedures adopted earlier by Champlain,[37] and neither attempted to enter into treaties or other formal arrangements.

Title by Discovery and Colonisation

From this survey it is clear that between the fifteenth and eighteenth centuries explorers commissioned by the European monarchs were convinced that they were able, in the name of their Monarchs, to take over territories newly discovered by them, so long as there was no evidence that such places had already been acquired by another Christian prince. Insofar as the Protestant countries were concerned, they were not prepared to accept the authority of the Papal disposition of the New World, nor, at least in the case of Drake, was Elizabeth willing to acknowledge Spanish sovereignty based merely on discovery and the placement of markers, in the absence of some concrete evidence of settlement. On no occasion does there seem to have been, at this stage, any thought that it was necessary to secure the agreement of the local inhabitants to the assumption of sovereignty, although attempts were made to assure them that by agreeing to the desires of their visitors they would be protected against their enemies. In view of the respect for symbols, formalities and the written word during this period, there is little doubt that if the explorers or their sovereigns had any thought that a treaty of any kind was necessary, such would in fact have been entered into. In any case, for the most part the general attitude, to some extent flowing from the Papal attitude to non-Christian heathen, was that the indigenous population of the New World lacked any identity that required recognition or rights which were entitled to respect. Rather, these people were looked upon as savages or barbarians who, rightly, could be subjected to the rule of European monarchs, under the ideological pretence that this subjection was, in the first place, for the glory of the Church, and only secondly for the greater aggrandisement of the monarch and country concerned.

That the sixteenth and seventeenth century explorers were aware that their activities were not and were not intended to be in accord with the principles of international law as understood at the time is clear from such statements as that by the French lawyer Lescarbot, who was at Port Royal with Champlain:[38]

> there is here no question of applying the law and polity of Nations, by which it would not be permissible to claim the territory of another. This being so, we must possess it and preserve its natural inhabitants.

This statement was made when the French were already aware of, and repeated among themselves as jokes,[39] the views of the Indians:[40]

> le Pape devoit être très liberal de ce qui appartenoit à autrui. . . puisqu'il donnoit ce qui n'étoit pas sien; et que le Roi étoit quelque pauvre homme, puisqu'il demandoit

their lands as his own.

The Holy See did in fact try to mitigate some of the evil consequences of the European occupation of the American continent. Thus, by the Bull *Sublimis deus sic dilexit*[41] of 1537, Paul III decreed that Amerindians were not to be treated as

> dumb brutes created for our service. . .[but] as true men. . . capable of understanding the Catholic faith. . . .[Moreover,] the said Indians and other people who may be discovered by Christians, are by no means to be deprived of their liberty or the possession of their property, even though they be outside the faith of Jesus Christ. . .nor should they be in any way enslaved,

and a century later Urban VIII found it necessary[42] to threaten excommunication for those who deprived Amerindians of their liberty or property. However, these Bulls did not relate to the territorial property of the Amerindians. In any case, they carried no validity or threat to non-Catholics, and in 1609 in *A Good Speed to Virginia*[43] we find it clearly stated that

> it is likely true that these savages have no particular property or parcell of that country, but only a generall residence there as wild beasts have in the forest.

Since the explorers clearly thought they had the right to acquire the newly-discovered lands for their monarchs, it is necessary to examine some of the commissions and patents authorising their expeditions.

As early as May 1493 Ferdinand and Isabella were issuing documents describing Columbus as Admiral of the Ocean and Governor and Viceroy of the islands and mainland in that ocean on the route to India, language which clearly indicates their belief that a result of his discoveries would be an affirmation of Spanish authority and their power to instruct him to govern in their name, while at the same time enjoining him from encroaching upon the territories claimed by Portugal.[44] More significant, perhaps, are the letters patent issued by Henry VII to John Cabot and his sons in 1496:[45]

> . . .we have giuen and granted. . .full and free authoritie, leaue, and power, to sayle to all partes, countreys, and seas, of the East, of the West, and of the North, under our banners and ensignes,. . . to seeke out, discouer, and finde, whatsoeuer iles, countreyes, regions or prouinces, of the heathen and infidelles, whatsoeuer they bee, which before this time haue heen vnknowen to all Christians. We haue granted to them also,. . .and haue giuen them licence to set up our banners and ensignes in euery village, towne, castel, yle, or maine land, of them newely founde. And that the aforesaid John and his sonnes. . .may subdue, occupie, and possesse, all such townes, cities, castles, and yles, of them founde, which they can subdue, occupie, and possesse, as our vassailes and lieutenantes, *getting vnto vs the rule, title, and iurisdiction* of the same villages, townes, castles, and firme lands so founde. . . .And, moreouer, wee haue giuen and graunted to them. . .all the firme landes, Iles, Villages, Townes, Castles, and places, whatsouer they be, that they shall chaunce to finde, may not of any other of our subiectes bee frequented or visited without the licence of the foresayd John [and] his sonnes. . ., under payne of forfayture as well of their shippes as of all and singuler goods of all of them that shall presume to sayle to those places so founde. . . .

That other countries did not question Henry's acquisition of Cabot's discoveries is clear from the despatch of the Duke of Milan's ambassador at Westminster informing his prince "how his majesty here has acquired a portion of Asia without a stroke of his sword."[46] Soncino further pointed out that while Cabot was granted the profits of whatever he discovered, "the sovereignty was reserved to the crown."

A somewhat similar patent issued by King Emmanuel of Portugal to Gaspar Corte-Real in 1500,[47] after referring to Real's earlier voyages, stated

> . . .taking into consideration how greatly it will redound to our service and honour, and to *the increase of our kingdoms and domains, if such islands and mainlands should be discovered by subjects of ours,.* . . .it is our pleasure, and we are pleased of our own motion, royal and absolute power, should he discover and find an island or islands, or mainland, to grant and give him. . .the governorship of any islands or mainlands he may thus discover or find afresh with the following privileges, to wit: civil and criminal jurisdiction, both high and low, with full power and authority without appeal or redress. . . .; and it is our wish that he and his heirs, both in our name and in that of our successors hold, govern and rule the mainland or islands so found, freely and without any hindrance whatsoever. . .agreeing only in regard to ourselves, that whenever it may seem to us necessary, we may send thither one of our people to learn how the said Gaspar Corte-Real is exercising the said jurisdiction and government of the mainland, and to bring us information thereof, in order that, should we find he does not rule or govern the said islands and mainland as is fitting to God's service and our own, we may punish him as we think proper, in his person alone, without taking from him or relieving him of the said jurisdiction. Nevertheless should he not conduct himself properly, and should we order him to appear before us to receive in his person the punishment he deserves,. . .he may and shall leave in the said islands and each of them, or on the mainland, one of his people to exercise and advance and carry on the administration of justice and government in his name and as he himself would if present, such person being nevertheless one agreeable to ourselves. . . .

In this patent there is clear evidence that Emmanuel intended to acquire sovereignty and that Corte-Real should establish a colonial settlement with himself as governor and possessing full powers to rule in the name of his King. It was also made perfectly clear that while Corte-Real was to enjoy the powers of governorship, he was in no way to regard himself as a sovereign, so much so that any successor he might be required to appoint *ad interim* had to be one of whom the King approved.

A similar intent to colonise is evidenced in the patent granted by Henry VII in 1501 to Richard Warde and others, including some "of the Islands of the Azores in the dominions of the king of Portugal":[48]

> . . .we grant full and unrestricted authority, faculty and power to sail and transport themselves to all parts, regions and territories of the eastern, western, southern, arctic and northern seas, under our banners and ensigns. . .to find, recover, discover and search out whatsoever islands, countries, regions or provinces of heathens and infidels, in whatever part of the world they may lie, which before this time were and at present are unknown to all Christians,[49] and to set up our banners and ensigns in any town, city, castle, island or mainland by them thus newly found, and to enter and *seize* these same. . .*for us and in our name,* and as our vassals and governors, lieutenants and deputies *to occupy, possess and subdue these, the property, title, dignity and suzerainty of the same being always reserved to us.* And furthermore whenever henceforth such islands, countries, lands and provinces shall be acquired, recovered and found by [those] before-named, then. . .all and singular as well men as women, of this our kingdom and the rest of our subjects, wishing and desiring to visit these lands and islands thus newly found, and to inhabit the same, shall be allowed and have power to go freely and in safety to the same countries, islands and places with their ships, men and sevants, and all their goods and chattels, and to dwell in and inhabit the same under the protection and government of the. . .aforesaid, and to acquire and keep the riches, fruits and profits of the lands, countries and places aforesaid; giving furthermore. . .to the aforesaid. . .full power and authority to rule and govern all and singular the men, sailors and other persons removing and making their way for the aforesaid purpose to the islands, countries, provinces, mainlands and places before-mentioned,. . .and to make, set up, ordain and appoint laws, ordinances, statutes and proclamations for the good and peaceful rule and government of the said men, masters, sailors and other per-

sons. . ., and also to issue proclamations to chastise and punish according to the laws and statutes set up by them in that region all and singular those they may find there hostile and rebellious and disobedient to the laws, statutes and ordinances aforesaid, and all who shall commit and perpetrate theft, homicide or robberies or who shall rape and violate against their will or otherwise any woman of the islands or countries aforesaid. . . .

The King then provided that for a period of ten years no subject could visit the places discovered by this group, for trading purposes without a licence from them, but after ten years such licence had to be granted both by the patentees and the King, and anyone visiting without such licence was liable to forfeiture, with half the proceeds going to the monarch and half to the patentees.

An interesting feature of this grant is the reference to offences against the "women of the islands or countries aforesaid," whereby Henry made it clear that he was taking the inhabitants under his protection, in itself a sovereign act carrying as a concomitant a duty of allegiance.[50] Moreover, as if to make clear that any places discovered by the patentees really were under Henry's sovereignty,

. . .if afterwards any strangers or other persons should presume against the wish of the said [patentees] to sail to these said regions for the purpose of enriching themselves, and to enter the same by violence, and. . .to conquer and expel them, or otherwise to disturb them, then we. . .grant power to the same subjects of ours, to expel and resist with all their force, as well by land as by sea and fresh water, these strangers, even though they be subjects and vassals of some prince in league and friendship with us, and to wage and carry on war against them, and to arrest, bind and place them in prison, there to remain until they shall have made fine and redemption to our said subjects; or otherwise to chastise and punish them according to [their] sober discretion. . . .And also. . . we grant full power to our aforesaid subjects. . .to make, constitute, nominate and appoint under them. . .any captains, lieutenants and deputies whatsoever in each of the states, cities, towns and places aforesaid for the administration and government of all and singular the persons in those parts, under the rule and authority of our said subjects there dwelling, and for the due execution and ad-

ministration of justice in the same, according to the tenour and import of the ordinances, statutes and proclamations aforesaid. . . .
And furtheremore. . .we make, constitute, ordain and appoint. . .
the said [patentees, including the Portuguese],. . .conjointly and
separately, our Admirals in the same parts. . .full power and authority to do, exercise and carry out all and singular the things
which pertain to the office of Admiral, according to the law and
naval custom obtaining in this our realm of England. . . .

Finally, by these letters patent Henry naturalised the Portuguese
members of the group and their descendants, conferring upon them
all the rights and protection that pertained to his own subjects,

> provided always that. . .each of them does liege homage to us, and
> that they each and each one of them aids with lot and scot[51] with
> the other dues payable and customary everywhere in our aforesaid
> realm, as our lieges who are born within our said kingdom. Pro-
> vided also that. . .each of them pays to us and to our heirs so many
> and such customs, subsidies and other dues for their goods and
> merchandise as foreigners are held to pay and give to us. . .

Henry thus made sure that insofar as the Portuguese were not trading
or functioning as his representatives they remained liable to the
normal burthens of aliens.

At no time in this very lengthy patent does Henry make any reference to a need to confer with the local inhabitants or to make them
party in any way to the act of acquisition. The sole reference is to the
protection of women, if that may be construed as applying to indigenous females as well as those coming as settlers.

Somewhat similar provisions with regard to the administration of
justice appear in the letters patent issued by Queen Joanna of Spain to
Juan de Agramonte in October 1511:[52]

> . . .you are to go. . .to discover and find a land called Newfound-
> land [Terranova]. . .and. . .you shall be and are our captain over
> the said people, as well by sea and on the land that you discover
> there, and until you return with news of what you have found and
> discovered. . .: And. . .I command all and whatsoever persons
> you thus take with you. . ., who may go and settle in the said

Newfoundland, and who may be there until your return and dis-
embarkation with the said news, to hold and consider you as our
captain over all, and to obey you. . ., and by yourself or your
lieutenants to execute justice for us as well by sea as on land for the
whole of the said period; and that you. . .do hear and despatch and
determine all the lawsuits and cases, as well civil as criminal, which
may arise on the said sea or land during the said period. . .; and
that as such captain you may find and do hold all kinds of investi-
gations permitted in law-cases, and perform all other things belonging to the said office, and which in your opinion are fitting for
our service, for the execution of our justice and for the welfare of
the said voyage. . . .

In this case it may be considered that the authority to exercise justice
was restricted to the personnel who accompanied him and only during the voyage and until he returned again to Newfoundland. In this
instance, there is no indication that the local inhabitants were protected by or subjected to Spanish law, nor is there any reference to the
assumption of sovereignty. This omission is repaired, however, in
the patent granted by Charles V to Stephen Gomez in 1523:[53]

. . .[Having made an] offer to go and discover Eastern Cathay, of
which you have notice and information, where you hope to discover as far as our Molucca islands, which all falls and lies within
our limits and sphere of influence; and seeing that along this said
route to Eastern Cathay there are many islands and provinces
hitherto undiscovered, very rich in gold, silver, spices and drugs, I
accepted under the following conditions and terms: First of all I
give you licence to make the said voyage and discovery on condition you do not enter the limits of the sphere of influence of the
Most Serene king of Portugal, my very dear and much beloved
cousin and brother, nor approach any of his possessions, but only
within our limits; because our wish is that the agreement and covenant between the royal crown of our kingdoms and that of Portugal be observed and carried out in full. . . .[W]e do appoint you
our captain, and give you power and authority to use. . .the said
office. . .during the period of the said voyage,. . .both on sea and
on land, by yourself and by your lieutenant, in the cases and matters belonging to and connected with the said office, and which

you may consider as belonging to the execution of our justice and
to the welfare and utility of the lands and islands you may discover. . .; and. . .we command the. . .people who may sail in the
said expedition and any persons who may visit or reside in the said
lands and islands by you discovered. . .to consider and receive and
regard you as our captain, and to acknowledge you as such, and to
carry out your orders, on pain of the punishment. . .which in our
name you may inflict and may order to be inflicted, which we by
these presents inflict and hold to be inflicted on them, and we give
you power and authority to carry out these on their persons and
goods. . . .And. . .we command that should any lawsuits and differences arise during the time you are absent on the said expedition, either at sea or on land, you may decide and settle them and
cause justice to be done in each case quickly and summarily without clamour or formal tribunal. . . .

In the case of the French explorations, the patent issued by or on
behalf of the monarch used the ideology of the expansion of the true
faith and the conversion of the indigenous population as the reason
for authorising the expedition, although it was clear that sovereignty
was as much involved as this, and the habit of the explorers of planting crosses or other markers with the royal arms thereon emphasises
this point.[54] Thus Cartier's commission in respect of his third voyage
reads:[55]

. . .Comme pour le dexir d'entendre et avoir congoissance de
plusieurs pays qu'on dict inhabitez, et aultres estre possedez par
gens sauvaiges vivans sans cognoissance de Dieu et sans visage de
raison, eussions des piecza à grands fraiz et mises, envoyé descouvrir esdicts pays par plusieurs bons pillottes et aultres noz subiectz
de bon entendement, sçavoir et experience, qui d'iceux pays nous
auroient amené divers hommes que nous avons par long temps
tenuz en nostre royaume les faisant instruire en l'amour et craincte
de Dieu et de saincte loy et doctrine chrestienne en intencion de les
faire ramenner esdocts pays en compagnie de bon nombre de noz
subiectz de bonne volonté, affin de plus facilement induire les
aultres peuples d'iceux pays à croire en nostre saincte foy; Et entre
aultres y eussions envoyé nostre cher et bien amé Jacques Cartier,
lequel auroict descouvert grand pays de terres de Canada et

Ochelaga, faisant vn bout de l'Asie du costé de l'occident, lesquelz pays il a trouvez, ainsi qu'il nous a rapporté, garniz de plusieurs bonnes commodittez et les peuples d'iceux bien formez de corps et de membres et bien disposez d'esprit et d'entendement, desquelz il nous a semblement amené aucun nombre que nous avons par long temps faict vivre et instruire en nostredicte saincte foy avecques nosdictz subiectz, En consideracion de quoy et de leur bonne inclinacion, Nous avons advisé et deliberé de renvoier ledict Cartier esdictz pays de Canada et Ochelaga et jusques en la terre de Saguenay, s'il peult y aborder, avecques bon nombre de navires et de nosdictz subiects de bonne volonté et de touttes qualitez, artz et industrie pur plus avant entrer esdictz pays converser avecques lesdictz peuples d'iceux et avecques eux habiter, si besoin est, affin de mieux parvenir à nostredicte intencion et à faire chose aggréable à Dieu nostre createur et redempteur et qui soict à l'augmentacion de son sainct et sacré nom et de nostre mère saincte eglise catholique,. . .

and to assist him in his purpose Cartier was authorized to take up to fifty convicts from the gaols. While these patents did not expressly state that the purpose was to seize territory for France, that this was in fact the case is clear from the letter of the King of Spain to the Cardinal of Toledo:[56]

I have received today letters from my ambassador in France, in which he advises me that in spite of the efforts of the ambassador of the most Serene King of Portugal, there residing, and what he, himself, has told the Council of the King of France respecting the licence that the said King gave to his subjects to proceed to the Indies, a certain Jacques Cartier has received a commission. . .to go to the New Lands. . . .[A]nd my ambassador speaking of this to the Constable of France, that it might be remedied, was given to understand that the Said Cartier has gone to make discoveries in parts not belonging to us nor to the most Serene King of Portugal; saying that to uninhabited lands, although discovered anyone may go. . . .[T]he efforts of our said ambassador and those of the ambassador of Portugal have up to the present not borne fruit. And although I have ordered. . .that he do continue to insist and make fitting instance that the said licence be not proceeded with, being, as it is, in direct contravention of the treaty between us and the said King of France, [57] and contrary to the grace and concession granted by the Apostolic See to the Kings of Castile and Portugal for the said conquest. . .

and he went on to instruct the Cardinal that a Spanish fleet should be prepared

to resist and destroy them. . . .[A]nd let. . .the said fleet. . .unite with the fleet. . .of the said King of Portugal, and let each fleet give help and support to the other. And should they meet with the ships of the said Jacques or any other Frenchman sailing with a fleet bound to the said Indies, let them engage and destroy them, since the intention of these Frenchmen is known; and let all the men taken from their ships be thrown into the sea, not saving any one person, for this is necessary as a warning against the undertaking of similar expeditions. . .

Colonisation or Propagation of the Faith?

That the fears of Spain were not unwarranted is seen in the letters patent issued by Francis to the Sieur de Roberval at the beginning of 1540,[58] from which it would appear that the letter to the Cardinal just referred to was based on both these French instruments. The Roberval document states that the expedition is to

. . .Canada et Ochelaga et aultres circontacens mesmes en tous païs transmarins et maritimes inhabitez et non possédez et donnez par aulcuns princes chrestiens aulcun bon nombre de gentilhommes non subjets et aultres, tant gens de guerre que populle — de chacun sexe et artz libéraulx et mécanique pour plus entrer esdit païs et jusques en la terre de Saguenay et tous aultres païs susd. afin d'en iceulx conserver avec lesd. peuples estrangers sy faire se peulx habiter esd. terres et païs y construire et ediffier villes et forts, temples et eglises pour la communication de nostre ste foye catholique et doctrine chrestienne, constituer et establir loix et par nous ensemble officiers de justice pour les faire vivre par raison et police et en la crainte et amour de Dieu, affin de mieulx parvenir à nostre intention et faire chose agréable à Dieu nostre Créateur, Sauveur et Rédempteur, et qui soit à la satisfaction de son sainct nom et à l'augmentation de nostre foy chrestienne et accroissement de nostre mère la Ste Eglise Catholique de laquelle nous sommes dict et nommé le premier fils. . . .Avons donné. . .pouvoir et mande-mens espécial à nostre Lieutenant Général. . .aller venir èsd. païs estrangers, de descendre et entrer en yceulx et les mettre en nostre main tant par voye d'amitié ou aymables compositions, sy faire ce peulx que par forces d'armes, main forte et touttes aultres voyes d'hostilité, de assailir villes, chasteaulx forts et habitations et d'en construyre et en ediffier ou faire construire et ediffier d'aultres esd. païs et d'y mettre habitations, créer, constituer establir desmettre et destituer capitaines justiciers et généralement tous aultres officier que bon luy semblera de par nous et qui luy semblera nécessaire, pour astraire les peuples d'iceulx à la cognoissance et amour de Dieu et yceulx mettre et tenir nostre obéissance, de faire loix, es-dicts, statuz et ordonnances politiques et aultres ycelles, augmenter ou diminuer, faire garder, observer et entretenir par toutes voyes et manières dues et raisonnables, de pugnir et faire pugnir les déso-béissans rebelles et aultres malfaicteurs tant ceulx qui yront à la dite expédition que aultres des dits païs soit de mort corporelle ou aultre pugnicion exemplaire, de pardonner et remettre les maiffaitz à ceulx qui le requerront. Le tout ainsi qu'il verra bon estre pourvu, toutefoys que ce ne soyt païs tenus, occupez, possédez et dominez et estant sous la subjection et obéissance d'aulcuns princes ou potentats nos alliez et conféderez et mesme de nos très chers amés frères, l'Empereur [d'Espagne] et le Roy de Portugal. . .

The similarities between this commission and those of the English monarch, especially with regard to the establishment of habitations and the law, confirm the view that in the sixteenth century there was no doubt that this was the method by which sovereignty over terri-tory in the Americas was considered proper, without any reference to the consent or views of the local inhabitants.

When in 1608, King Henry granted a monopoly to the Sieur de Monts at the time of Champlain's third voyage, there is no reference to the missionary character of the expedition, other than in the most cursory fashion, although the acquisitive purpose of the expedition was clearly understood:[59]

. . .Acting upon the information which has been given to us by those who have returned from New France, respecting the good quality and fertility of the lands of that country, and *the disposition of the people to accept the knowledge of God,* We have *resolved to continue the settlement* previously undertaken there, in order that our subjects may go there to trade without hindrance. . . .

That Champlain continued to pay at least lip-service to the missionary character of his voyage is shown in the introductory chapter of the 1632 edition of his *Voyages* recounting his discoveries between 1603 and 1629:[60]

. . .In New France are a great number of savage tribes,. . .without any knowledge of God. But there is hope that the friars who have been taken out, and who are beginning to get settled and establishing seminaries, may be able in a few years to make great progress in the conversion of these peoples. This is the principal concern of his Majesty, who raising his eyes heavenward rather than turning them earthwards will. . .sustain these masterbuilders who undertake to transport priests thither to labour at this holy harvest, and whose design it is to found there a colony as the sole and unique means to make known there the name of the true God and of establishing there the Christian religion, compelling the French who may proceed thither to labour first of all at tilling the soil, in order to possess on the spot the basis of their food supply, without being under the necessity of having it brought out from France. . . .the most illustrious palms and laurels that kings and princes can win in this world are in contempt of temporal things, to turn their desires to things spiritual. This cannot be more usefully accomplished than by attracting through their labour and piety an infinite number of savage souls (who live without faith, law, or knowledge of the true God) to profess the Catholic, Apostolic, and Roman religion. For neither the capture of fortresses, nor the winning of battles, nor the conquest of countries is anything in comparison nor of a price with the conquests which prepare crowns in heaven unless it be done against Infidels, where war is not only necessary but just and holy, in that here it is a question of the safety of Christianity, of the glory of God, and of the defence of the faith; and these labours are in themselves praiseworthy and very commendable, in addition to God's commandment which says, *that the conversion of the infidel is of more value than the conquest of a kingdom*. And if all this cannot move us to seek the blessings of heaven as passionately at least as those of the earth, since men's greed for this world's goods is such that the majority pay no heed to the conversion of infidels, provided their wealth corresponds to their desires and that everything comes to them exactly as they wish; yet it is this covetousness which has ruined and ruins entirely the progress and advancement of this holy enterprise which has not yet made much progress and is in danger of failing unless his Majesty brings to it a very holy, charitable, and just direction like himself, and unless he himself takes pleasure in hearing what can be done for the increase of God's glory and for the welfare of his own State, driving back the envy shown by those who should support this enterprise [but] who rather seek its ruin than its accomplishment. It is no new thing for the French to make sea voyages for new conquests. . .

Despite the high-sounding religiosity and other-worldness indulged in by Champlain in describing the purpose of his voyages, he did not disguise the fact that he was fully aware of the political and predatory significance of what he was undertaking. In addresses he submits to the King and his Lords in Council, as well as to the Chamber of Commerce, he emphasises rather the effect his discoveries will have for the greater glory of France:[61]

The Sieur de Champlain. . .has toiled with laborious zeal as well in the discoveries of New France as of divers peoples and nations whom he has brought to our knowledge, who had never been discovered save by him;. . .planting there the divine worship,. . .in addition to the abundance of merchandise from the said country of New France, which would be drawn thence annually through the diligence of the workmen who would go there. Should the said country be given up, and the settlement abandoned,. . .the English or Flemings, envious of our prosperity, would seize upon it, thereby enjoying the fruits of our labours. . . .And considering the advantage and profit to be derived therefrom, as well for the glory of God as for the honour of his Majesty and for the good of his subjects. . . .His said Majesty will establish the Christian faith among an infinite number of souls, who neither hold nor possess any form of religion whatsoever, and nevertheless wish only for the knowledge of divine and human worship. . . .The King will make himself master and lord of a country nearly eighteen hundred leagues in length. . . .

He then goes on to state that all states depend on force, justice, trade and husbandry, and he therefore proposes that fortresses be built, troops sent, as well as families of settlers, to be certain that neither the Flemings nor the English drive them out and destroy the French presence. To the Chamber of Commerce[62] he refers to "the honour and glory of God, the increase of this realm and the establishment of a great and permanent trade in New France."

Moreover, it was clearly understood at the time that the settlements thus created and the grants under which they were established had legal effects in the most complete sense of that term. It is perhaps sufficient to refer to two further documents of 1611. There is a commission[63] from Charles of Bourbon, Grand Master of France and the King's

Lieutenant General in the country of New France,. . .[ordering Champlain] to go represent our person in the said country of New France: and to this end we have ordered him to go and settle with all his servants at. . .Quebec. . .; and at the said place, and in other places where [he] shall think fit, to have constructed and built such other forts and fortresses as shall be expedient. . .which. . .he will maintain for us to the utmost; in order at. . .Quebec and in other places within our authority, and as much and as far as may be possible, to establish, extend, and make known the name, power and authority of His Majesty, and thereto to subject, submit and put in obedience all the peoples of the said land and those adjacent to it, and. . .to maintain, keep and secure the obedience to and under the authority of his said Majesty. And. . .we have, by virtue of our said authority, allowed. . .Champlain to commission, constitute and appoint. . .officers for administration of justice and maintenance of police authority, regulations and ordinances, to negotiate and contract, with the same purpose, peace, alliance and federation, friendly relations and intercourse with the said peoples and their princes or others having authority and rule over them, to maintain, keep and carefully preserve the treaties and alliances which he shall contract with them, provided that they on their part satisfy the terms of these. And in their default to make open war upon them to constrain and bring to such reason as he shall judge needful, for the honour, obedience and service of God, and for the establishment, maintenance and preservation of the authority of His said Majesty among them, at least as far as to live, reside, visit and have intercourse and communication, to have business and to trade with them in amity and peace. . .And where. . .Champlain shall find Frenchmen *and others* trading, bartering and communicating with the savages and peoples from. . .Quebec and inland beyond it, we have authorized. . .him to seize and apprehend them together with their ships, merchandise and everything found therein appertaining to them, and to have them conveyed and brought to France to. . .Normandy [Charles of Bourbon who granted this commission was Governor of Normandy], and put into the hands of justice, to be prosecuted according to the strict terms of the royal ordinances and what has been granted to us by His said Majesty. . . .

There are two points about this commission that require comment. In the first place it is a clear assertion by Charles that the King of France claims full and complete jurisdiction over the territories referred to and the authority delegated to Champlain in regard to the enforcement of law extends even to foreigners—"Frenchmen and others"—who may seek to trade in what is regarded as French territory with individuals considered as being under French sovereignty and trade with whom is a French monopoly. Further, it is evident from Champlain's account of his voyages that the "treaties and alliances" referred to differ from those normally concluded between princes. They were not written, and related to promises made by him to the Indians with whom he dealt that he would assist them against their enemies, and they in return would assist and even protect the settlements particularly while he was away.[64]

This document should be read together with Champlain's account of the attempts made in 1610 and 1611 by Mme. de Guercheville[65] to enter into a partnership agreement with the Sieur de Poutrincourt who had obtained from the Sieur de Monts a grant of lands adjacent to Port Royal:[66]

The partnership contract was executed with this lady under the authority of her husband, Monsieur de Liencour, first equerry to the King and Governor of Paris. By this contract it was provided that she should contribute at once a thousand crowns for the cargo of a vessel and thereby be entitled to a share in the profits returned by the vessel and in the lands which the King had granted to the Sieur de Poutrincourt as set forth in the draft of that contract. The Sieur de Poutrincourt reserved to himself Port Royal and its lands, not intending that these should be held in common with the seignories, capes, harbours and provinces which he held in that country near Port Royal. The lady asked him to exhibit the title-deeds under which these seignories and lands belonged to him, and to show how he came to possess so large a domain. But he excused himself by saying that his title-deeds and papers had remained in New France. When the lady heard this, distrusting what. . .Poutrincourt said, and wishing to guard herself against being caught unawares, she negotiated with the Sieur de Monts for ceding to her all rights, titles and interests that he held or ever had held in New France by reason of the grant made to him by the late Henry the Great. Mme. de Guercheville obtained letters from His Majesty now reigning, in which was renewed to her the grant of all the lands of New France, from the great river [St. Lawrence] as far as Florida, Port Royal only excepted, which was what the Sieur de Poutrincourt originally held, and nothing else.

Perhaps the best example of the view of the day is to be found in the statement of de Monts[67] that there is no better way to serve France

que de s'appliques. . .a descouvrir quelques costes et terres loingtaines despourveues de peuples, ou habités par gens encore Sauvages, Barbares et desnuez de toute religion, loix et civilité, pour s'y loger et fortifier, et tascher d'en amener les nations à profession de la Foy Chrestienne, civilisation de leurs moeurs, reglement de leur vie, pratique et intelligence avec les Français pour l'usage de leur commerce: Et en fin à leur recognoissance et submission à l'authorité et domination de cette couronne de France.

That the intent of the explorers, regardless of the language they used, was to acquire territory for their monarch is shown by the dedication by Champlain to the King of the account of his voyage of 1618 [68] and his later dedication to Richelieu:[69]

> . . .land belongs to you,. . .who. . .will gain an immortal name for carrying the glory and sceptre of the French as far westward as your predecessors carried it eastward, and over the whole habitable earth.
> . . .the settlements and forts that have been built in [New France] in the name of France.

The people of France, too, were convinced that they acquired legal rights in the territories as a result of the discoveries effected by explorers going from their harbours. This may be seen from the attitude of the people of St. Malo commented upon by Champlain:[70]

> . . .the people of St. Malo. . .say that the profit from these discoveries belongs to them, because Jacques Cartier, who first visited Canada and the islands of Newfoundland, comes from their town, as if that town had contributed to the expenses of the said discoveries of Jacques Cartier, who went there at the command, and at the expense, of King Francis I, in the years 1534 and 1535, to explore these lands now called New France. If then Cartier made these discoveries at the expense of His Majesty, all his subjects are entitled to the same rights and liberties therein as the people of St. Malo, and these cannot prevent any who have made discoveries at their own expense. . .from the peaceable enjoyment thereof; wherefore they should not claim a right to anything to which they themselves have not contributed: and their reasons in this respect are poor and weak. And to show more fully to those who would maintain this plea, that they have no ground to stand on, let us take the case of a Spaniard or other foreigner having discovered lands and treasures at the expense of the King of France, would the Spaniards or other foreigners lay claim to these discoveries and treasures, because the discoverer was a Spaniard or other foreigner? No, there is no ground for this; the discoveries would certainly belong to France, so that the people of St. Malo cannot claim these. . .because Cartier came from that town. . .

Treaties Acknowledging Claims to Title

It was not only in the commissions issued by the monarchs and their
delegates, and the reactions to them of the explorers to whom they
were addressed, and the grants of territory that were made in accordance with them, that illustrate the general view of the normal manner in which legal title to territory in the New World could be established. The same understanding is to be found in a number of treaties
of the period, in which we find undertakings not to encroach upon
each other's territory or for the mutual use thereof against a common
enemy, but again there is no reference to any right in the aboriginal
inhabitants, although at times the geographic scope of the treaty is
not clear from the text but only from the occasion that gave rise to it.
An example of this is the Treaty of Lyons of 1536 between France and
Portugal.[71] A clear example is the separate article appended to the 1556
Franco-Spanish Treaty of Vaucelles,[72] in which Philip of Spain, consequent upon his marriage to Mary, is described as the King of England, and whereby it was agreed that French nationals could not
trade with the Spanish Indies without a licence from Philip, and con-
ceding that force might be used against those illegally trading, without any breach of the peace between France and Spain:

> . . .Aussy a este expressment convenu et capitule, que jaçoit ladite
> tresve soit marchande et communicative, sy est ce les subjectz
> dudit seigneur Roy de France ou aultres par leur adveu ne pourront
> naviguer trafficquer, ou negocier aux Indes appartenant audit sieur
> Roy dangleterre, sans son conge et licence. Autrement, faisans le
> contraire, sera licite user contre eulx dhostilite, demeurant toutte
> ffois ladite tresve en sa force et vigeur.

This treaty was soon broken, partly as a result of French activities in
the Indies, and in 1559 there was an oral agreement[73] whereby west of
the prime meridian and south of the Tropic of Cancer might would
constitute right, and violence by either against the other would not be
considered a violation of any treaty. Beyond these "lines of amity,"
treaties were to lose their force. Difficulties arose since the Spanish
placed the prime meridian in the Azores and the French in the west-
ernmost of the Canaries. In fact, the Spanish "line of amity" corre-

sponded with the Portuguese line of demarcation in the Papal Bull of 1455[74] and the Spanish line in that of 1493.[75] It is interesting to note that in 1559 one of the grounds put forward by France to justify the free movement of French vessels was that the sea was held in common, regardless of Papal decree:

> . . .Oultres ce, nous avone longuement debatu pour exclure les Franchois de la navigation des Indes: mais nous ne les avons sceu attraire a ce quilz voulussent exclure leurs subjectz de la ditte navigation, ny que lon leur donnast mettes ou limites: du moins quil ne leur fut permis daller aux lieux que si bien ilz sont descouvertz, toutesfois nobeissent ny au royaulme de Castille ny a celluy de Portugal. Bien consentiroient ilz quilz nallassent aux terres possedées par Vôtre Majesté et par le Roy de Portugal, ou que lon demeurast aux termes des traictez passez, quest quil ne sen fist mention, et a qui si lon les trouve faisant chose quilz ne doibvent que lon les chastye: alleghans les argumens ordinaires que la mer soit commune, et nous au contraire nous servant do fondement de la bulle du pape Alexandre et du pape Julle second, de la sommation que se fit auz princes Cretiens pour scavoir ceulx que vouldriont contribuer aus frais du descouvrement, la demarcation que sen fit, et que ce nestoit raison que aultres vinssent joyr des travaulx et fraiz faictz par aultruy pour descouvrir les dittes Indes. Et que nous leur voulions bien declarer que silz y venoient, encoires quil fur en paix, que lon procureroit de les jecter au fond, sans que par ce nous entendissions que lon peust alleguer davoir contrevenu ausdits traictez en ce quilz traictent de la communication et conversation des subjectz de lung sur les pays de laultre. . . .

The general view at the time as expressed in these and similar treaties was that French voyagers contravening the stipulations embodied therein were to be treated as pirates and robbers,[76] and they are thus described in the Treaty of Joinville, 1585,[77] between the King of Spain, among whose titles is "dominateur en Asie et Affricque," and the Catholic Princes of France:

> Cesseront incontinant touttes pirateries, excumeries de mer, et touttes aultres navigations illicites vers les Indes et Isles comprises

soubz icelle apartenans a Sa Majeste Catolique [Philip], sans quelles puissent estre permises de la en avant.

Finally, it is perhaps sufficient to refer to the instructions issued to the English negotiators participating in the Bourbourg discussions of 1587[78] and in relation to the Treaty of London, 1604,[79] whereby James I tried to restore relations with Spain after the death of Elizabeth:

. . .It is likely allso, that some speciall article will be required to forbyd all trafick of our peoples into the Indias, both of the west belonging to the crowne of Castill and to the Est allso now in the King of Spaynes possession.. . .[O]ur meaning is. . .that ther is no reason to barre our subjects to use trade of marchandise in the Indias, where the Frenche are daily suffred so to doo, so as the same be with the goodwill of the inhabitants of the countryes, and only for lawfull trade of marchandise. And likewise it is no reason by a large naming of the Indias, to barre our marchantes to trade in any places discovered or to be discovered by our own people, being places where neyther in the tyme of the Emperor Charles, nor of the King that now is, any Spanyard, Portingale, or any other Christian people have had any habitation, residence or resorte. . . .
In the argument thereof ye may aledge that the cheefe reasons why the Emperor Charles and the King of Portingale in their tymes did seeke to prohibite all others than their own subjectes to trade into those Indias discovered by their people, was in recompence of the charges sustayned by the discoverers that the proffitt of the riches discovered might recompence the first discoverers and their heirs. A matter agreeable to good reason, but not so to be extended as by the large titles and nomination of the Indias (whereof ther is no certain limitation) all parts of the worlde in the West or in the East, that were not or should not be discovered by the subjects of the said Emperor, or by the kinges of Portingale should still so remayne undiscovered and not to be by any other Christians with their laboure sought out discovered and brought to the knowledge of God, and of Christ the Saviour of the Worlde, for that were all against Christian charitie, and against all humain reason, and directly againste that generall proposition in the holy Scripture: Coelum coeli Domino, terram dedit filiis hominum.
. . .Lastly, it is likely they will forbid us trade into the Indias,

---

wherein you must. . .maintain that it is very disconsonant with trewe amitie to forbid their friends those common liberties. Yea, though the whole Indias were as merely subject to their soveraig-netie as Spaine it selfe is, especiallie when in former treaties there have been contrarie clauses, which have given freedome of trade into all their domynions. And yet because it shall appeare that wee will not be found unreasonable, you shall let them knowe that, to avoyde all inconveniences that may peradventure happen in places so remote, when the subjects of other princes shall fall in companie one with another, where their lawes and discipline cannot be so well executed, wee are contented to prohibite all repaire of our subjects to any places where they are planted, but onely to seeke their traffique by their owne discoveries in other places, whereof there are so infinite dymensions of vast and great territories as themselves have no kind of interest, but do trade with divers great kings of those countryes but as forrayners and strangers, from which to barre ourselves by accord, seeing it is not in his power to do it by force, no not to any pettie prince, were both an unkind-nesse and an indignitie to be offered.

There is little to be gained by referring to further treaties of the six-teenth and seventeenth centuries which merely confirm what has al-ready been indicated, namely that the various princes demanded the right to take for themselves territories which had not yet been settled by any Christian prince, Catholic or Protestant, regardless of any claim that may have been put forward merely on the basis of a papal donation or mere discovery. At the same time, there was general rec-ognition of the right to exclude foreign traders from territories which had been so settled, although claims were put forward which might be compared to most-favoured-nation assertions.

The Papal Bulls, commissions issued to explorers, the actions of the explorers, as well as their personal accounts of their voyages, to-gether with the treaties of the fifteenth to early seventeenth centuries, all tend to confirm the view that at the time of the discovery of the new world it was well established practice, amounting to law, that the state in whose name a settlement was established in territory formerly unsettled by the nationals of any European monarch, be-came sovereign of the territory in question. While there may occa-sionally have been references to arrangements with the "savages/Indians" and even attempts to protect their rights insofar as their person or property was concerned,[80] at no time were they considered as the owners of their land or as being entitled to any role in connection with its disposition.

The Views of the "Fathers" of International Law

Having examined the state practice in this way, it is now necessary to turn to the classical writers in order to ascertain the extent to which the doctrine reflects, confirms or rejects the legal basis of that practice.

Of the classicists, there is one in particular who dealt specifically with the problem of the North American aborigines. In his *De Indis Noviter Inventis*,[81] Vitoria first put forward the view that the Indians of North America were neither chattels nor beasts, but human beings entitled to a modicum of respect as such, even from Catholics carrying the word of God. This Professor of Theology at the University of Salamanca wrote in 1532[82] denying that the Pope possessed civil or temporal powers over the whole world, or even spiritual jurisdiction over unbelievers. For this reason the Pope had no secular power to confer upon princes, while even if he had it would not be possible to convey it, for this would belong in perpetuity to the Papacy and no Pope could be less than his predecessor. Moreover, since the Pope's temporal power was only such as subserves spiritual matters, since he possessed no spiritual power over Indian aborigines, he possessed no temporal power over them either. Therefore, "even if the barbarians refuse to recognize the lordship of the Pope, that furnishes no ground for making war on them and seizing their property."

While it is of value to examine the views of Vitoria as to the claims of Spain to rule the Indians and possess their lands, it should not be overlooked—and this comment is extremely important when confronted with claims the basis of which was completely unknown at the time of the discovery of North America and its inhabitants, especially when the title which the claim confronts is one that has been recognized for generations—that[83]

> it might seem at the very outset that the whole of this discussion is useless and futile. . .because neither the sovereigns of Spain nor

those at the head of their councils are bound to make completely
fresh and exhaustive examination of rights and titles which have
been elsewhere discussed and settled, especially as regards things of
which the sovereigns are in *bona fide* occupation and peaceful possession:. . .and sovereigns. . ., if they had to trace the title of their
rule back to its origin, they could not keep anything they had discovered.

However, even though the title be good, it is perhaps of value to assess whether the circumstances involved were in fact lawful, and he
starts from the premise[84]

that the barbarians in question [the Indians] cannot be barred from
being true owners, alike in public and in private law, by reason of
the sin of unbelief or any other mortal sin, nor does such sin entitle
Christians to seize their goods and lands. . . .[T]he aborigines undoubtedly had true dominion in both public and private matters,
just like Christians, and. . .neither their princes nor private persons could be despoiled of their property on the ground of their
not being true owners. It would be harsh to deny to those, who
have never done any wrong, what we grant to Saracens and Jews,
who are the persistent enemies of Christianity. We do not deny
that these latter peoples are true owners of their property, if they
have not seized lands elsewhere belonging to Christians. . . .
[E]ven if we admit that the aborigines in question are as inept and
stupid as allèged, still dominion can not be denied to them, nor are
they to be classed with the slaves of civil law. True, some right to
reduce them to subjection can be based on this reason and
title. . . .Meanwhile the conclusion stands sure, that the aborigines
in question were true owners, before the Spaniards came among
them, both from the public and the private point of view.

Having asserted the dominionship of the Indians, Vitoria then examined the titles under which they could have come under Spanish sovereignty, dismissing, as has been pointed out, any thought that this
stemmed from Papal grant, whatever view the Spanish monarchs, or
for that matter the Popes, might have taken of this contention. In his
view,[85] "at the time of the Spaniards' first voyages to America they

took with them no right to occupy the lands of the indigenous population." Moreover, any claim based on discovery is also discounted, for one can only acquire title by discovery over what is unowned and, for him, the Indians were true owners.

While the various papal bulls, royal commissions, and accounts of their voyages by the discoverers all proclaimed that one of their purposes was to extend the power and ambit of the Church, implying that this aim justified their overlordship of the Indians, Vitoria contended[86] that so long as the faith had not been preached to them, so that their ignorance was "invincible," there was no basis to assault them, nor did he consider that they were in mortal sin if they did not accept Christianity immediately upon hearing it expounded. However,[87]

If the Christian faith be put before the aborigines with demonstration, that is, with demonstrable and reasonable arguments, and this be accompanied by an upright life, well-ordered according to the law of nature. . .and this be done not once only and perfunctorily, but diligently and zealously, the aborigines are bound to receive the faith of Christ under penalty of mortal sin. . . .[But i]t is not sufficiently clear to me that the Christian faith has yet been so put before the aborigines and announced to them that they are bound to believe it or commit fresh sin. . . .[And even if] the Christian faith may have been announced to the Indians with adequate demonstration and they have refused to receive it, yet this is not a reason which justifies making war on them and depriving them of their property. . . .[As] St. Thomas. . .says unbelievers who have never received the faith. . .are in no wise to be compelled to do so.

It is also interesting to note the manner in which Vitoria rejects the arguments put forward by Cartier and the like that they were justified in asserting the sovereignty of their monarch because of the unnatural habits—cannibalism, incest and the like—of the aborigines. In the first place he points out that war against Christians committing such acts is not permitted and in them the sin would clearly be the greater, while since they are not Christians and not under the power of the Pope, they are clearly not subject to any punishment in his name nor in that of Christ.[88] Finally, as to the suggestion that the Indians willingly accepted the protection and sovereignty of the Spanish king, he is equally adamant and a realist:[89]

> [O]n the arrival of the Spaniards we find them declaring to the aborigines how the King of Spain has sent them for their good and admonishing them to receive and accept him as lord and king; and the aborigines replied that they were content to do so. . . .[T]his title, too, is insufficient. This appears, in the first place, because fear and ignorance, which vitiate every choice, ought to be absent. But they were markedly operative in the cases of choice and acceptance under consideration, for the Indians did not know what they were doing; nay, they may not have understood what the Spaniards were seeking. Further, we find the Spaniards seeking it in armed array from an unwarlike timid crowd. Furthermore, inasmuch as the aborigines. . .had real lords and princes, the populace could not procure new lords without other reasonable cause, this being to the hurt of their former lords. Further, on the other hand, these lords themselves could not appoint a new prince without the assent of the populace. Seeing, then, that in such cases of choice and acceptance as these there are not present all the requisite elements of a valid choice, the title under review is utterly inadequate and unlawful for seizing and retaining the provinces in question."

Everything that Vitoria says here about the Spaniards and their methods of acquiring consent from the Indians is equally true of the French explorers. It might also be pointed out that while the translation here used makes reference to "aborigines" or "Indians," Vitoria like Cartier and Champlain did not use these terms, but described the native inhabitants as *barbari*.

Having more or less denied the validity of the basis normally put forward to assert the Spanish title over the Indians and their lands, Vitoria proceeds to explain how such a title could be acquired,[90] and it may well be considered that his contentions to this effect are self-seeking and hypocritical, possessing no more validity than those he rejects. On the other hand, whether one accepts the contentions he puts forward or those he rejects, the fact remains that with all his concern for the rights of the Indians he eventually agrees that their lands may be taken from them:

The first title to be named is that of natural society and fellow-ship. . .The Spaniards have a right to travel into the lands in question and to sojourn there, provided they do no harm to the natives, and the natives may not prevent them. . . .[I]f it were not lawful for the Spaniards to travel among them, this would be either by natural law or by divine law or by human law. Now, it is certainly lawful by natural and by divine law. And if there were any human law which without any cause took away rights conferred by natural and divine law, it would be inhumane and unreasonable and consequently would not have the force of law. . . .[Also,] either the Spaniards are subjects of the Indians or they are not. If they are not, then the Indians can not keep them away. If they are, then the Indians ought to treat them well. . . .The Spaniards may lawfully carry on trade among the native Indians, so long as they do no harm to their country. . . .[T]he sovereign of the Indians is bound by the law of nature to love the Spaniards. Therefore the Indians may not causelessly prevent the Spaniards from taking their profit where this can be done without injury to themselves. . . .If the Indian natives [barbari] wish to prevent the Spaniards from enjoying any of the above-named rights under the law of nations,. . .the Spaniards ought in the first place to use reason and persuasion in order to remove scandal and ought to show in all possible methods that they do not come to the hurt of the natives, but wish to sojourn as peaceful guests and to travel without doing the natives any harm, and they ought to show this not only by word, but also by reason. . . .But if, after this recourse to reason, the barbarians decline to agree and propose to use force, the Spaniards can defend themselves and do all that consists with their own safety, it being lawful to repel force by force. And not only so, but, if safety can not otherwise be had, they build fortresses and defensive works, and, if they have sustained a wrong, they may follow it up with war on the authorization of their sovereign and may avail themselves of the other rights of war. . . .[W]hen the Indians deny the Spaniards their rights under the law of nations they do them a wrong. Therefore, if it be necessary, in order to preserve their right, that they should go to war, they may lawfully do so. . . . [Despite these efforts, the Indians] may very excusably continue afraid at the sight of men strange in garb[91] and much more powerful than themselves. And therefore, if, under the influence of these fears, they unite their efforts to drive out the Spaniards or even to slay them, the Spaniards might, indeed, defend themselves but within the limits of permissible self-protection, and it would not be right for them to enforce against the natives any of the other rights of war (as, for instance, after winning the victory and obtaining safety, to slay them or despoil them of their goods or seize their cities). . . .If, after recourse to all other measures, the Spaniards are unable to obtain safety as regards the native Indians, save by seizing their cities and reducing them to subjection, they may lawfully proceed to these extremities. . . .If, after the Spaniards have used all diligence. . .to show that nothing will come from them to interfere with the peace and well-being of the aborigines, the latter nevertheless persist in their hostility and do their best to destroy the Spaniards, then they can make war on the Indians, no longer as on innocent folk, but as against foresworn enemies, and may enforce against them all the rights of war, despoiling them of their goods, reducing them to captivity, deposing their former lords and setting up new ones, yet withal with observance of proportion as regards the nature of the circumstances and of the wrongs done to them. . . .[I]t is a universal rule of the law of nations [*ius gentium*] that whatever is captured in war becomes the property of the conqueror. . . .A prince who has on hand a just war is *ipso jure* the judge of his enemies and can inflict a legal punishment on them, according to the scale of their wrongdoing. Everything said above receives confirmation from the fact that ambassadors are by the law of nations inviolable and the Spaniards are the ambassadors of Christian peoples. Therefore, the native Indians are bound to give them, at least, a friendly hearing and not to repel them. This, then, is the first title which the Spaniards might have for seizing the provinces and sovereignty of the natives, provided the seizure be without guile or fraud and they do not look for imaginary causes of war. . . .Another possible title is by way of propagation of Christianity. . . .Christians have a right to preach and declare the Gospel in barbarian lands. . . .[I]f the Spaniards have a right to travel and trade among the Indians, they can teach the truth to those willing to hear them. . .[B]ecause the natives would otherwise be outside the pale of salvation, if Christians were not allowed to go to them carrying the Gospel message. . .brotherly correction is required by the law of nature,. . .[and s]ince the Indians are all not only in sin, but outside the pale of salvation, therefore it concerns Christians to correct and direct them; nay, it seems that they are bound to do so. . . . [B]ecause they are our neighbours,. . .it concerns Christians to instruct those who are ignorant of these supremely vital matters. . . .Although this is a task committed to all, yet the Pope might entrust it to the Spaniards and forbid it to all others,. . .and not only could the Pope forbid others to preach, but also to trade there, if this would further the propagation of Christianity, for he can order temporal matters in the manner which is most helpful to spiritual matters. . . .[I]f there was to be an indiscriminate inrush of Christians from other parts to the part in question, they might easily hinder one another and develop quarrels, to the banishment of tranquility and the disturbance of the concerns of the faith and the conversion of the natives. Further, inasmuch as it was the sovereigns of Spain who were the first to patronize and pay for the navigation of the intermediate ocean, and as they then had the good fortune to discover the New World, it is just that this travel should be forbidden to others and that the Spaniards should enjoy alone the fruits of their discovery. . . .If the Indians—whether it be their lords or the populace—hinder the Spaniards from freely preaching the Gospel, the Spaniards, after first reasoning with them in order to remove scandal, may preach it despite their unwillingness and devote themselves to the conversion of the people in question, and if need be they may then accept or even make war, until they succeed in obtaining facilities and safety for preaching the Gospel. And the same pronouncement must be made in the case where they allow preaching, but hinder conversion either by killing or otherwise punishing those who have been converted to Christ or by deterring others by threats the fears. This is clear, because herein the Indians would be doing an injury to the Spaniards. . .and these would have a just cause of war. A second reason is that an obstacle would thereby be put in the way of the Indians themselves such as their princes have no right to put there. Therefore, in favour of those who are oppressed and suffer wrong, the Spaniards can make war. . . .[I]f there is no other way to carry on the work of religion, this furnishes the Spaniards with another justification for seizing the lands and territory of the natives and for setting up new lords there and putting down old lords and doing in

right of war everything which is permitted in other just wars. . . .
Suppose a large part of the Indians were converted to Christianity,
and this whether it were done lawfully or unlawfully (as by means
of threats or fear or other improper procedure), so long as they
really were Christians, the Pope might for a reasonable cause, either with or without a request from them, give them a Christian
sovereign and depose their other unbelieving rulers. . . . Another
possible title is founded either on the tyranny of those who bear
rule among the aborigines of America [the original makes no reference to America] or on the tyrannical laws which work wrong to
innocent folk there, such as that which allows the sacrifice of innocent people or the killing in other ways of uncondemned people
for cannibalistic purposes. . . . [Even] without the Pope's authority
the Spaniards can stop all such nefarious usage and ritual among
the aborigines, being entitled to rescue innocent people from an
unjust death. . . . [A]ny one may defend them from such tyrannical and oppressive acts, and it is especially the business of princes to
do so. . . . This. . . is [not] only when victims are actually being
dragged to death, but the natives can also be compelled to abstain
from such ritual. And if they refuse, it is a good ground for making
war on them and proceeding against them under the law of war,
and if such sacrilegious rites can not otherwise be stopped, for
changing their rulers and creating a new sovereignty over
them. . . . And it is immaterial that all the Indians assent to rules
and sacrifices of this kind and do not wish the Spaniards to
champion them, for herein they are not of such legal independence
as to be able to consign themselves or their children to death. . . .
There is another title. . . . Although the aborigines in question are
not wholly unintelligent, yet they are little short of that condition,
and so are unfit to found or administer a lawful State up to the
standard required by human and civil claims.[92] Accordingly they
have no proper laws nor magistrates, and are not even capable of
controlling their family affairs; they are without any literature or
arts. . .; they have no careful architecture and no artisans; and they
lack many other conveniences, yea necessaries, of human life. It
might, therefore, be maintained that in their own interests the sovereign of Spain might undertake the administration of their country, providing them with prefects and governors for their towns,
and might even give them new lords, so long as this was clearly for

their benefit. . . .[Finally,] there are already so many new converts, that it would be neither expedient nor lawful for our sovereign to wash his hands entirely of the administration of the lands in question.

Having written his account of the method whereby title may be secured over the aborigines of North America and their lands, Vitoria proceeded to discuss the nature of the law of war, "inasmuch as the seizure and occupation of those lands of the barbarians whom we style Indians can best, it seems, be defended under the law of war."[93]

It would appear that behind all the piety and expressions on behalf of the Indians, Vitoria finally accepts the claims put forward on behalf of Spain, for his arguments are as specious or as sound as any. Moreover, his comments, especially those relating to protection of the converted, prevention of cannibalism and the like, are almost identical with those put forward by Cartier and Champlain on behalf of France. Moreover, having expounded the basis on which Spain might rest its title to sovereignty over the aborigines and their lands, Vitoria proceeded to discuss the nature of the law of war, contending that insofar as the Indians are concerned neither religion, nor expansion of empire, nor glory of the prince are just causes of war[94]—a contention which runs counter to those favoured by the French explorers. Vitoria does not attempt in his *De Jure Belli* to assert or deny that war against the Indians is just, rather he assumed in the light of his earlier comments that it is; and then proceeds to explain what the prince waging a just war may or may not do, the net result appearing to affirm his earlier assertions as to the right of conquest over the Indians.

Another sixteenth century writer who was concerned with the position of the Indians, although only in passing, was Belli. Vitoria had been motivated by the wrongs committed by the Spaniards in their just wars against the Indians and he deplored the fact that they were being enslaved. Belli was of a contrary opinion:[95]

Not only in war does enslavement take place, but also apart from it. For if a person should go among a people with whom his countrymen had no ties of hospitality or friendship. . .he would be the slave of the person seizing him. With good right, therefore, the Spaniards enslaved those Indians of the West, who live far away from our world, and were unknown to the Greeks and Romans, but who were discovered in our times through perilous and bold navigation (under Spanish auspices,. . .but through the agency and toil of a man of Italy, Christopher Columbus of Genoa) with good right, I say, the Spaniards enslaved those Indians, as allowed by the law just cited. . . .(On this principle, perhaps, the afore-mentioned rulers, actuated by the Christian spirit, which they cultivate to a high degree, gave orders that if those people accepted the religion of Christ, they should live in freedom under their own laws).

Belli, thus, did not even consider it necessary for the Spaniards, or presumably other European discoverers, to attempt to make peace with the local inhabitants, nor even to have a just cause of war. In his mind, it was enough that the Indians were not allies to justify their seizure as slaves, and presumably, therefore, to be made subject to the rule of the prince who had sent out the explorer.

It is interesting to note the views of Gentili,[96] Regius Professor of Civil Law at Oxford and a Protestant. While he was no more sympa-thetic than Vitoria to the religious basis of the Spanish claims, he nevertheless agreed that a denial of the right to trade could be a ground for war, even though he questioned whether the Spanish argument to this effect was more than an ideology:

no-one doubts today that what we call the New World is joined to our own and has always been known to the remote Indi. And that is one reason why the warfare of the Spaniards in that part of the world seems to be justified, because the inhabitants prohibited other men from commerce with them; and it would be an adequate defence, if the statement were true. For commerce is in accordance with the law of nations. . . .But the Spaniards were aiming there, not at commerce, but at dominion. And they regarded it as beyond dispute that it was lawful to take possession of those lands which were not previously known to us; just as if to be known to none of us were the same thing as to be possessed by no one.

Despite this implied criticism Gentili does not question the right to claim possession of previously unknown territories, although he does

state[97] that "an unbounded thirst for power and riches. . .is not a legitimate reason for war." However, he goes on to agree with Vitoria:[98]

> I approve. . .of the opinion of those who say that the cause of the
> Spaniards is just when they make war upon the Indians, who prac-
> tised abominable lewdness even with beasts, and who ate human
> flesh, slaying men for that purpose. For such sins are contrary to
> human nature, and the same is true of other sins recognized as such
> by all except haply by brutes and brutish men. And against such
> men. . .war is made as against brutes. Thus in a state anyone
> whatever is allowed to accuse an offender against the community,
> even one who is not a member of the state, when an action is de-
> fended which is not peculiar to the state but of interest to all
> men. . . .[Further,] the Indians were not blameless in fighting for a
> king who made war unjustly.

Insofar as the issue of discovery was concerned, Gentili draws attention[99] to

> the ruling of our jurists with regard to unoccupied land. . .that
> those who take it have a right to it, since it is the property of no
> one. And even though such lands belong to the sovereign of that
> territory,. . .yet because of the law of nature which abhors a vac-
> uum, they will fall to the lot of those who take them. . . .But are
> there today no occupied lands on the earth?. . .What of Spain? It is
> the most populous country of all; yet under the rule of Spain is not
> almost all of the New World unoccupied?

In view of this, of course, not only is Gentili justifying the acquisition
by Spain of those parts of the New World occupied by Spain, but
without saying so directly he is also justifying English claims to parts
that Spain might claim, but was not effectively occupying. He also
deals with the treatment of those who have been conquered and con-
tends[100] that the conqueror acquires the whole of the conquered, and
not merely

> the things which the victor presses with his foot or holds in his
> hand. . . .[101] Therefore it is just for the vanquished to be forced to

---

adopt the government of the conquerors; or if they do not yield, it is right to crush them. . . .[And] if the victor meets with those who are alien to humanity and to all religion, these he may most justly compel to change conduct which is contrary to nature.

The discoverers solemnly record that they took over the residences, fortresses and other habitations of the Indians in accordance with the instructions given them by their princes, and Gentili comments[102]

territories, places and buildings. . .all remain in the power of the man who holds them at the time when peace is made, unless it has been otherwise provided by a treaty. For they do not return to their former owner, if the enemy are not driven out of them. . . .

It is clear, therefore, that it mattered little whether the commentator was Catholic or Protestant, the view was generally the same, namely, that the representatives of the Old World were entitled to seek establishment in the New, and if they could not achieve their purpose by peaceful means they had cause to wage a just war. If they were victorious in such a war, then they had the right to take over the property and territory of their defeated enemy. The ideological and high-sounding language which appears in the doctrine does not destroy the *raison d'état* which is constantly evident.

Writing about the same time as Gentili, Suarez[103] was confirming the views of Vitoria and other Catholic writers, and in words that again illustrate the hypocrisy of those who seek to justify their master's cause, even when they are aware that there is something artificial about the argument:

[A]s Vitoria. . .rightly observe[s], the Pope can distribute among temporal princes and kings the provinces and realms of the unbelievers; not in order that the former may take possession of these regions according to their own will, for that would be tyranny,. . . but in order that they may make provision for the sending of preachers of the Gospel to those infidels, and may protect such preachers by their power, even through the declaration of just war, if reason and a rightful cause should require it. For this purpose, then, the Pope may mark off specific boundaries for each prince, which that prince may not later transgress without committing an injustice. . . .[T]his matter, which most gravely concerns the Church, should be conducted in an orderly manner. For that is most necessary, both for preserving peace among Christian princes, and also in order that each of these princes may procure with the greater care the welfare of the people committed to his charge. . . .[O]ne ought first to try peaceful means, inviting and repeatedly urging infidel princes and states to permit the preaching of the faith in their realms, and to offer to allow security to persons who come into or dwell within their domains for the purpose of performing the task of preaching. . . .But if the unbelieving princes resist, and do not grant entrance, then. . .they may be coerced by the sending of preachers accompanied by an adequate army. In like manner, if, after the preachers have been received, the infidels should kill them or treat them wrongfully, when the victims are blameless, and for no other reason than that they have preached the Gospel, then an even better reason for just defence and, indeed, for righteous vengeance, has arisen, the latter sometimes being necessary in order that other infidel chiefs may be coerced and may fear to practise like acts of tyranny.

Suarez further maintains[104] that since the Church has a right to preach, it possesses the right to make the unbelievers listen, for since "it is permissible to employ coercion in order to prevent resistance to the preaching of the faith, if the pagans are unwilling to listen, in that very unwillingness they resist and impede the preaching of the faith; therefore,. . ." However, Suarez did not consider that it was permissible to coerce them into belief, unless they were subjects of the prince on whose behalf the coercion was being exercised. But,

if both the [pagan] king and kingdom offer simultaneous resistance [to preaching], I think that they may be forced to permit the preachers of the Gospel to live in their territories; for this tolerance is obligatory under the *ius gentium* and cannot be impeded without just cause. Moreover, that king and that people may be forced to permit these preachers to declare the word of God, without suffering violence or treachery, to those who are willing to hear; since it is probable that there will never be lacking individual persons who will hear voluntarily. For, even if we assume that the king and his kingdom are offering resistance, still, not absolutely all individuals are included under the term "kingdom," but rather, the Councils or chief men, or else the greater or greatest part of the kingdom; and always, without exception, the Church retains unimpaired the right to preach in that kingdom, and to defend the innocent (so to speak)—to defend, that is, individuals who may wish to hear the word. Accordingly, under such circumstances, there is involved no coercion to the hearing of the faith, but only a coercion to refrain from impeding the preaching of the Gospel, or placing obstacles in the way of those persons who may voluntarily choose to give ear to such preaching.

There is clearly no objective way to decide whether there are or are not persons who wish to hear the Gospel preached. Behind the dialectic and the semantics, therefore, Suarez is maintaining the right of the Church to seek the aid of the temporal power whenever it may consider this necessary and is providing the basis for that temporal power to wage a just war, the net result of which will of course be the acquisition of the pagan state's territory. In fact, he continues from the above contentions virtually to contradict all that he has already stated:[105]

[P]agans sin grievously in not accepting the faith after it has been sufficiently heard by them; therefore, on account of this sin, they may justly be punished, and through punishment coerced to accept the faith; consequently, men have power to punish the sin in question, for it pertains to the Providence of God so to order human affairs that public crimes shall not remain unpunished. . . .[Moreover,] through such coercion great good may be anticipated; since, granted perhaps that those who are coerced may be converted less sincerely or fictitiously, still those who follow,—and who will greatly outnumber the former—will believe the more easily, and many innocent children will be saved through baptism. Therefore, because of this beneficial result, the coercion in question may be allowed. For if any evil follows therefrom, that evil is not wrought, but permitted, by the Church. . . .[However,] unbelievers who are not apostates, whether subjects or not, may not be coerced to embrace the faith, even after it has been sufficiently proposed to them. . . .[I]t is essentially wrong to force unbelievers who are not subjects, to embrace the faith. . . .[C]oercion cannot occur without lawful power,. . .since otherwise all wars and all acts of violence could be called just; but the Church does not possess this lawful power with respect to such unbelievers. . . .[Further,] the Church may not exercise compulsion even upon those pagans who are temporarily subject to it, in order that they shall embrace the faith. . . .[What has been said] refers to direct coercion exerted directly to. . .the prevention of unbelief and the acceptance of the faith. . . .[But] indirect coercion is not in itself and intrinsically evil, if applied under the proper conditions. . . .[C]oercion is indirect when any right or punishment inflicted under one particular title or on account of a given offence is secondarily directed by the one exercising to the end of inducing another to exercise some act of the will; and in the case under consideration, the power to punish or to exercise compulsion on account of a just end is not lacking, while the secondary end, consisting in the conversion of another to the faith, is not evil, but. . .is in itself virtuous.

But this indirect coercion may only be applied to pagan subjects, for

even though non-subjects may not positively be afflicted with punishments and loaded with burdens, nevertheless, they may be deprived of gratuitous benefits, advantages, or favours; and such means also may well be adapted to drawing them to the faith or to a favourable inclination toward it, and may be considered as a kind of indirect coercion. . . .[As to] the examples set by the Spanish kings. . . ., [they] chiefly regard indirect coercion applied in virtue of a just title, such as was the practice of Catholic kings

to compel acceptance of the faith on the part of those temporarily subject to them, although not on non-subjects. As with his predecessors, Suarez is not unwilling to find other grounds on which just war may be waged upon pagans. Thus:[106]

in order to defend the innocent, it is allowable to use violence against the infidels in question, that they may be prevented from sacrificing infants to their gods; inasmuch as such a war is permissible in the order of charity and is, indeed, a positive duty if it can be conveniently waged. . . .[T]his course of action is licit. . .also for the purpose of freeing adults, even though the latter may consent and wish to be sacrificed to idols; because in this respect they are worse than madmen, and because, moreover, they are not lords of their own lives, so that, accordingly, any man can be restrained by another from committing suicide.

Insofar as the "justness" of war is concerned, Suarez was of opinion[107] that in the case of nonsubjects, it was essential that they should have committed some wrong to render themselves subjects, for otherwise there would be no basis for exercising jurisdiction over them by way of punishment, and among the causes of just war would be the denial, without reasonable cause, of the common rights of nations, such as the right of transit or trading. Among the principal just causes of war open to Christian princes is "the defence of the innocent," which again leads Suarez to defending the right of war in order to enable potential believers to hear and accept the Gospel.[108] In addition, once a war has taken place, the victor is entitled to take all the movable and immovable property of his enemy, so that with the success of the Christian arms the territory of the unbelieving enemy became part of the dominion of the Christian prince involved.[109]

In his *De Jure Belli ac Pacis*,[110] Grotius, often described as *the* "father" of international law, does not seek to justify seizures of new lands on the basis of spreading the Gospel or claiming a right not to be hindered in so doing, nor is he concerned with some of the pseudo-religious arguments put forward by his predecessors. He does, however, provide ample excuse for those explorers who may have attacked the local aborigines on the specious pretense that they feared attack, contending that "the first Cause of a just War, is an Injury, which tho' not done, yet threatens our Persons or our Estates."

Grotius is as much concerned as any of the other classical writers with the acquisition of title to territory, and he pays particular attention to prescription by long usage in this connection. His comments thereon are important when faced with arguments opposing a title, which arguments are newly invented and not raised until a long time after the title in contest has been asserted and generally accepted. He points out[111] that

should a Man knowingly suffer another to enjoy what is his for a considerable Time, without demanding it, it might be concluded from his Forbearance, that he designed to part with it altogether, and looked upon it no longer as his Property; unless there was any other Reason, that manifestly hindered him from making Opposition. . . .But before we can reasonably presume from a Man's Silence, that he has relinquished his Right, two Things are necessary, One is, that he should know that another possesses what belongs to him: And the other, that he should be voluntarily silent, tho' he has full Liberty to speak. . . .Amongst several other Conjectures, that serve to verify the two Conditions just mentioned, the Length of Time is of great Weight to shew that the Silence of a Proprietor is accompanied with both. . . .[B]ecause a Space of Time, which exceeds the Memory of Man, is in a moral Sense taken for Infinite, therefore a Silence for so long a Continuance will ever be sufficient for a Conjecture, unless very good Reasons be alledged to the contrary, that the Thing in Dispute is really quitted.

As to the suggestion that the acquisition of title of the lands in the New World between the fifteenth and seventeenth centuries was unjust or illegal, one should remember that

> tho' it be an allowed Maxim, that *What is originally invalid, can never be made valid by a retroactive Effect;* yet does it admit of this Exception, *unless some new Cause, capable of itself to create a Right, shall intervene.*[112]

Clearly, the long exercise of sovereignty with all the concomitant incidents of jurisdiction that go therewith constitutes the necessary *novus actus interveniens.*

Like his Catholic predecessors, when considering the justness of wars, Grotius recognised the right of a monarch to wage war against those who have broken the law of nature, though no wrong was caused to himself or his subjects, and among the causes given is the consumption of human flesh[113]—a matter which worried the Spaniards, as well as Cartier. "Of such Barbarians, and rather Beasts than Men, may be fitly said. . .that War against such is natural; and. . .the justest War is that which is undertaken against wild rapacious Beasts, and next to it is that against Men who are like Beasts."[114] Unlike his predecessors, however, Grotius[115] does not concede that there is no power to punish where jurisdiction is absent,

---

and therefore those Men are not entirely blameless, who, tho' they are too stupid to find out, or comprehend, the Arguments that serve to demonstrate these Notions [about God], do yet reject them, since these Truths lead to Virtue:. . .those who first attempt to destroy these Notions, ought, on the Account of human Society in general, which they thus, without any just Grounds, injure, to be restrained. . . .

As with Suarez, Grotius[116] rejects the argument that it is just to wage war against those unwilling to accept Christianity,

But they who punish Men, because they preach or profess Christianity, do, no Doubt of it, act against the Dictates of Reason. . . [and those] who persecute Christians, as such, do make themselves justly obnoxious to Punishment.

In the light of these extracts, it would seem that whether the religion of the writer is Catholic or Protestant, and whatever the terms in which his argument may be dressed, all are of opinion that it is just to wage war and so conquer those who reject the basic tenets of Christianity or behave in a way that Christians consider to be contrary to nature. In fact, he goes so far as to argue:[117]

Nor is the being endued with Virtues, moral or divine, or an extraordinary Capacity, a Qualification absolutely requisite for Property, unless if there be a People entirely destitute of the Use of Reason, then dispossessing them may seem defensible, as having no Right of Property. . . .The Greeks therefore were to blame, who thought the Barbarians naturally their Enemies, because they were different in their Manners, and of more shallow Apprehensions than themselves. But how far upon the Account of enormous Crimes, Crimes against Nature, or prejudicial to human Society, it is lawful to dispossess People, is a different Query.

Perhaps the sophistry with which most of the early writers approached this matter is clearest in the comment by Grotius[118] when he remarks that if there is doubt as to whether a policy is just or unjust, no action should follow in view of the doubt,

but this Advice cannot take Place, when a Man is as it were forced
to do one or the other, and yet doubts of the Lawfulness of either;
for in that Case he is to chuse the safer Side, that which he thinks to
be least unjust; for at all Times when we are under a Necessity of
chusing, then the lesser Evil puts on the Form of Good

—an argument which is reminiscent of the Machiavellian concept
that all princes are just in their actions,[119] and one providing the justification for any war to which resort might be had. This doubt to which
Grotius refers may the more easily be resolved in favour of war, in
view of the fact that he concedes[120] the right to go to war on behalf of
any persons who are afflicted, for

the last and most extensive Reason of all for assisting others [by
war] is that Relation that all Mankind stand in to each other and
this alone is sufficient.

Moreover, even if one were to deny the right of subjects to take up
arms against an oppressive ruler, "we should not yet be able to conclude from thence, that others might not do it for them."[121]

In Book III of the *De Jure Belli,* Grotius is concerned with the
waging and consequences of war and at an early point stresses a major
consequence of war, which remains relevant even though the attitude
towards war and its fruits may have changed since he wrote. At the
time he wrote, however, the law was reasonably understood and, insofar as one may be concerned with title in the middle of the seventeenth century, it is this view and not later concepts that are material:[122]

by the law of Nations, not only he that makes War for a just
Cause, but every man in a solemn War [the Carnegie translation
uses the word "public"] acquires the Property of what he takes
from the Enemy, and that without Rule or Measure; so that both
he and his Assigns are to be defended in Possession of them by all
Nations; which, as to the external Effects of it, may be called the
Right of Property. . . .But Lands are not said to be taken as soon
as they are seized on; for tho' it be true that that Part of the
Counry, which the Enemy with a strong Army has entered, is for
that Time possessed by them; yet every Possession is not sufficient

for the Effects which we are now touching of, but such a one as is durable only. . . .That Land then is reputed lost, which is so secured with Fortifications, which without being forced cannot be repossesst by the first Owner. . . .Immovable Goods are not usually taken, but by some publick Act, as by bringing in any Army, or by planting of Garrisons"

—actions which were invariably undertaken by the *conquistadores*, regardless of nationality. It is not only the territory, but also civil authority and sovereignty which accrue to the victor[123] and

as the Goods of every particular Prisoner, by the Right of War, belong to the Captors, so the Goods of the People in general belong to the Conquerors, if they please. . . .Wherefore even those incorporeal Rights, which belonged to the State, shall become the Conqueror's, as far as he pleases. . . .Yea, tho' the Conqueror leave to the Conquered *Jus Civitatis,* the form of a State, yet may he take to himself some Rights that belonged to it. For it is in his Power to limit his own Bounty as he pleases.

There is perhaps one final point made by Grotius to which we might refer, insofar as it may be alleged that the wars of conquest in the New World were unjust, although part of his comment has already been cited in a different context relating to extinctive prescription:[124]

As Things (taken in an unjust War) are to be restored to their proper Owner, so a People, or Part of them, are to be restored to their lawful Sovereigns, or even to themselves, if they were free before this unjust Conquest. . . .It has been sometimes disputed, how long a Time is allowed, before this internal Obligation to Restitution may cease?. . .If it be between Strangers each to other, it can be decided only by just Presumptions of a tacit Dereliction; of which we have spoken enough in another Place to our Purpose.

It is perhaps of interest to note that, though writing almost a century and a half after Columbus' voyage and though quoting Vitoria's *De Indis,* Grotius does not deal with the problem of the rights of the aborigines in North America nor discuss the acquisition of title to newly discovered territories. His silence is the more surprising in view of the fact that his *De Jure Belli* is dedicated to Louis XIII of France (Louis the Just) during whose reign Champlain was still opening up New France. However, the general comments Grotius makes as to the nature of a just war and its consequences are wide enough to apply to these matters.

Perhaps one of the most significant statements made in the doctrinal writing of the seventeenth century is that of Textor when he discusses the effect of state practice:[125]

Here a difficult question emerges, namely, what amount of time and usage is needed in order to beget a Law of Nations out of the usage of Kings and peoples. This same question is seen to arise about custom in civil matters, where some authorities require two years and others more, at the discretion of the judge, and where some require ten years and others a longer time still, and some leave it, as in any other undecided case to the discretion of the judge — which last-named opinion is that usually held by modern authorities. . . .But ours is a harder matter still to determine, because judges are not provided between Kings and people who acknowledge no superior. How, then, shall the doubt be resolved? My view, in brief, is that if all or most peoples, even once only, have adopted a given course of conduct, any period or interval of time is enough for the introduction of a Law of Nations in that particular; and therefore that while, absolutely, a number of acts are required proportionate to the number of peoples involved, yet relatively to individual peoples, a single act is enough. For example, if on one occasion only anything touching peace or treaties has been observed as binding, under the dictates of Reason, between the Romano-Germanic Empire and the Turkish, between the Kings of Spain and France, between British and Dutch, between Swedes and Danes, etc., nothing hinders us from declaring it to be part of the Law of Nations. These instances are, accordingly, to be combined in order to erect a Law of Nations. . . .[A]ccording to the premises, the Law of Nations is principally founded on the custom and observances of Kings and peoples. . . .

That this was indeed in accordance with the current view of the time may be seen from the treaties of the period. Article 5 of the

Treaty of Munster,[126] signed between the King of Spain, who lists among his titles "Roi des Indes Orientales et Occidentales," and the States General of the United Provinces, confirms the sovereignty over possessions already established, while Article 6 preserves the trading monopoly:

> The navigation and trade to the East and the West Indies, shall be kept up according and conformably to the grants made or to be made for that effect; for the security whereof the present treaty shall serve. . . .: And both the aforesaid Lords, the King and the States respectively, shall continue in possession of such lordships, cities, castles, towns, fortresses, countries and commerce in the East and West Indies, as also in Brazil, upon the coasts of Asia, Africa, and America respectively, as the said Lords, the King and the States respectively hold and possess after this, comprehending therein particularly the places and forts which the Portuguese have taken from the Lords and States since the year 1641, as also the forts and places which the said Lords and States shall chance to acquire and possess after this, without infraction of the present treaty. . . .
>
> And as to the West Indies, the subjects and inhabitants of the kingdoms, provinces and lands of the said Lords, the King and States respectively, shall forbear sailing to, and trading in any of the harbours, places, forts, lodgments or castles, and all others posssessed by the one or the other party. . . .

The 1670 Anglo-Spanish Treaty of Madrid[127] is similarly significant as showing what state practice regarded as law:

> . . .[I]t is agreed that the most Serene King of Great Britain, his heirs and successors, shall have, hold, keep, and enjoy for ever, with plenary right of sovereignty, dominion, possession, and propriety, all those lands, regions, islands, colonies, and places whatsoever, being or situated in the West Indies, or in any part of America, which the said King of Great Britain and his subjects do at present hold and possess; so as that in regard thereof, or upon any colour or pretence whatsoever, nothing more may or ought to be urged, nor any question or controversy be ever moved concerning the same hereafter.

The subjects and inhabitants, merchants, captains, masters of ships, mariners of the kingdoms, provinces and dominions of each confederate respectively, shall abstain and forbear to sail and trade in the ports and havens which have fortifications, castles, magazines, or warehouses, and in all other places whatsoever possessed by the other party in the West Indies; to wit, the subjects of the King of Great Britain shall not sail unto, and trade in the havens and places which the Catholic King holdeth in the said Indies; nor in like manner shall the subjects of the King of Spain sail unto, or trade in those places which are possessed there by the King of Great Britain. . . .

The present treaty shall in nothing derogate from any preeminence, right or dominion, of either confederate in the American seas, channels or waters, but they have and retain the same in as full and ample manner as may of right belong unto them; but it is always to be understood, that the liberty of navigation ought in no manner to be disturbed, where nothing is committed against the genuine sense and meaning of these articles.

The Treaty of Utrecht of 1713 between Great Britain and Spain[128] was confirmatory of the earlier treaty, while recognising British fears of French access to the Spanish Indies. It further provided:

. . .neither the Catholic King, nor any of his heirs and successors whatsoever, shall sell, yield, pawn, transfer, or by any means, or under any name, alienate from them and the crown of Spain, to the French, or to any other nations whatever, any lands, dominions or territories, or any part thereof belonging to Spain in America. On the contrary, that the Spanish dominions in the West Indies may be preserved whole and entire, the Queen of Great Britain engages that she will endeavour, and give assistance to the Spaniards, that the ancient limits of their dominions in the West Indies be restored and settled as they stood in the time of the Catholic King Charles II [of Spain], if it shall appear that they have in any manner, or under any pretence, been broken into, and lessened in any part, since the death of the aforesaid Catholic King Charles II.

These treaties make it clear that there was no doubt at that time that Spain, Great Britain and the United Provinces all recognised that

European monarchs had sovereignty over parts of the West Indies and America and could, subject to the treaties, convey or otherwise deal with such territories as they saw fit. In none does there appear any doubt of this, nor any suggestion that the local inhabitants had any rights of which account should be taken. Moreover, the treaties show a consistency of the kind that Textor has regarded as necessary to create a rule of international law, and the Anglo-French treaty signed at Utrecht in 1713[129] merely confirms this fact, and establishes the boundaries between British and French possessions in North America, ceding among others Nova Scotia, Arcadia and Newfoundland.

Pufendorf was a naturalist who sought to derive a law of nations from the precepts of natural law. He expressly controverted Vitoria's bases for the Spanish acquisition of Indian territories,[130] but even agreed that with such things as minerals in the ground which needed some overt act to acquire, the people who "occupied as a whole the home of such things, has not actually secured dominion over them, but only a right of securing dominion over them by their actual apprehension," although he argued that the sovereign of the thing which had to be used, such as the earth, to secure them would possess the right of allowing or denying such exploitation by others. However, while "this power extends even to the occupation of desert places which the supreme powers of the State may prohibit any one of their subjects from taking up[,] they do not by this restraint prevent foreigners from occupying such regions, and thus making them their own; only their own subjects are prevented. . . ."[131] Since dominion depends on occupancy, "we are said to have occupied a thing only when we actually take possession of it. . . . Therefore, it is the customary thing that occupancy of. . .land [be effected] by the feet, along with the intention of cultivating it and of establishing boundaries either exact or with some latitude."[132]

It has already been emphasised that in the sixteenth and seventeenth centuries acquisition of the lands of native inhabitants in areas previously unknown to and unoccupied by Christian princes was a recognized means of securing title. It is clear, therefore, that those who so acquired title did so in good faith and justly. In assessing whether the inhabitants could later on question such title, the views of Pufendorf on usucapion become significant:[133]

For whoever has continued the possession of a thing for the period prescribed by law, such possession having been secured in good faith, has something "added" to him which he had thus far lacked. And he to whom the law has added something can be said to have "acquired" it. . . .[T]he primary purpose of the law on usucapion is. . .to prevent states from being disturbed by uncertain and unsettled dominion. [T]he public interest is injured by those who, it may be, misuse their property, or by merely sitting at ease upon it as it were, in their ownership, allow it by their negligence to be of no service. But if a thing is appropriated by usucapion, it is at least looked after by someone, so that it is of use to the state.. . .[The purpose is] to avoid at their outset the disputes that would constantly arise, and to grant to possessors over a long period, who deserve great favour, an ultimate security in their holding. For in the first place the claim would have to be settled before a court, where the decision would be all the more difficult the longer the thing had been in the possession of others; and then the possessor would have to be ejected from his holding, and his title and good faith would be of no value to him. . . .Therefore, there is in such cases no easier way to peace, than after the period of usucapion is complete, to declare the right of the old owner extinct. . . .[I]t cannot be denied that the consent of nations, upon consideration of the peace of mankind, can assign some moral force to a period of time, in so far, at least, that upon the passage of a certain period presumptions and considerations are held to have arisen from other causes, which strengthen the right of the possessor. For although bare natural reason and the agreement of nations do not make the production of some right dependent upon the existence of some point of time, they have still been able to assign this effect to a space of time which embraces a considerable period. . . .But we do not find that the length of time within which possession in good faith takes on the strength of dominion is precisely determined either by natural reason or by the universal agreement of nations. It will have to be set with some latitude by the decision of upright men. . . .And although a man may have secured his title to a thing at a good bargain, it is still a hardship and cause for complaint, after so long a time to have a thing torn away which has, as it were, long since become an integral part of his estate.

Pufendorf points out that often the title by usucapion is an adjunct to some other ground, frequently one deriving from victory in a just war, in which case the victor is of course entitled to keep without contest what he has taken from his vanquished enemy.[134] He goes so far as to recognise the possibility of title ensuing from an unjust war as well,[135] and if an aggressor

> has ejected a monarch and put himself in his place,. . .the obligation to restore the throne does not expire until either the king [who has been displaced] and his heirs, for whom there had been acquired a right to the kingdom, are dead, or the king himself renounces his kingdom and leaves it derelict. And it is presumed that he has done the latter when he makes no attempt over a long period to recover it. . . .And if [the subjects] bear it for a moderate period as a matter of course [this too] is understood to wipe out the taint attaching to the way in which the kingdom was acquired. No attention need be paid to a few grumblers, who are not lacking in every form of state, even when the citizens have established it of their own accord.

In the case of the North American Indians it should be remembered that the European settlers displaced the Indian chiefs, who in the course of time tended to become advisers and elders of their peoples rather than monarchs with power. In the case of the chieftains in Asia or Africa, the settlers successfully claimed the right to displace those nominal rulers who failed to behave as the former considered proper, and this right was frequently exercised by the imperial ruler where, for example, Indian princes or African "monarchs" were concerned.[136]

The Views of the Positivists

In considering the law with regard to the acquisition of title from a doctrinal point of view, perhaps more important than those who refer to rules of natural law are the positivists, who were more concerned about human law and who, for the main part, were writing after the European states had established themselves on the North American continent and whose views, therefore, depend to a great extent on what they conceived the law to be in the light of state practice, without the same need that the clerics felt in justifying the assertions of the Christian kings. An example of this may be found in the writings of Bynkershoek[137] and the basis on which he decided that war may be lawful even in the absence of a declaration. He also demonstrates from state practice, that it is not necessary for a new sovereign, particularly one claiming title by war, to be in actual physical possession of all the territory he claims,[138] for it is

clear that when a part has been occupied, the whole is occupied and possessed if such is the intention of the captor. . . .Possession extends over what is occupied, and by natural law, what is occupied is brought into our possession, but even that which has not been touched all round by our hands and feet is conceived of as occupied, if that be the intention of the occupant, and the nature of the object so requires, as is the case with lands.

This point had already been made a half-century earlier by Textor,[139] who, basing himself on the *Digest,* commented generally and not merely in relation to conquest:

In obtaining possession of an estate there is no need for the party to walk over every particular bit of soil, it being enough that he should enter on some part of it with intent to possess,

and this principle received judicial recognition from Judge Huber as arbitrator in the *Island of Palmas* case[140] between The Netherlands and the United States:

Manifestations of territorial sovereignty assume. . .different forms, according to conditions of time and place. Although continuous in principle, sovereignty cannot be exercised in fact at every moment and on every point of a territory. The intermittence and discontinuity compatible with the maintenance of the right necessarily differ according as inhabited or uninhabited regions are involved, or regions enclosed within territories in which sovereignty is incontestably displayed or again regions accessible from. . .the high seas. It is true that neighbouring States may by convention fix limits to their own sovereignty, even in regions such as the interior of scarcely explored continents where such sovereignty is scarcely manifested, and in this way each may prevent the other from any penetration of its territory.

It is perhaps a truism to state that international law as classically understood is a law between states or nations. However, it is important to appreciate what is meant by these terms, and in this connection it is essential to bear in mind that the understanding has to be in accord with the views of the fifteenth to eighteenth centuries, and recent innovations based on political ideology and the new concept of self-determination are completely irrelevant. Vitoria[141] was almost alone in recognising some of the "state/nation" characteristics of the American Indians, since these "*barbari*"

are not of unsound mind, but have, according to their kind, the use of reason. This is clear, because there is a certain method in their affairs, for they have polities which are orderly arranged and they have definite marriages and magistrates, overlords, laws and workshops, and a system of exchange, all of which call for the use of reason; they also have a kind of religion. Further, they make no error in matters which are self evident to others; this is witness to their use of reason. . . . Also, it is through no fault of theirs that these aborigines have for many centuries been outside the pale of salvation, in that they have been born in sin and void of baptism and the use of reason whereby to seek out the things needful for salvation. Accordingly I for the most part attribute their seeming so unintelligent and stupid to a bad and barbarous upbringing. . . .

Most of the writers, however, would not concede this much evidence of polity and tended to deny that these "barbarians" could constitute a state and exercise the competences of civil governance. Writing in the middle of the eighteenth century Wolff,[142] who is described as a "Grotian" since he sought to combine the principles of natural law with the positivism of state practice, stated:

The perfection of a nation depends upon its fitness for accomplishing the purpose of the state, and that is the perfect form of government in a nation, if nothing is lacking in it which it needs for attaining that purpose. . . . A nation is a number of men united into a state. . . . We call a nation barbarous. . . which cares but little for intellectual virtues. . . . [S]ince barbarian nations do not develop their minds by training, in determining their actions they follow the leadership of their natural inclination and aversions. . . . That is called a cultured nation which cultivates intellectual virtues, consequently desires to perfect the intellect, and therefore develops the mind by training. And that is called a civilized nation which has civilized usages or usages which conform to the standard of reason and politeness. . . . But since barbarous nations have uncivilized usages, therefore to a barbarous nation is opposed a nation cultured and civilized. . . . Nations ought to be cultured and civilized, not barbarous. . . . Since a nation ought to be cultured. . . it ought not to follow the leadership of its natural inclinations and aversions, but rather that of reason, the law of nature imposing as it were a rule of conduct and urging, too, proper conduct. . . . Since nations ought to be cultured and civilized and not barbarous, they ought to develop the mind by that training which destroys barbarism, and without which civilized custom cannot exist.

However, the opposition which is presented of civilisation to barbarism is subject to limits:[143]

Whatever a learned and cultivated nation can contribute to make barbarous and uncultivated nations learned and more cultivated, that it ought to do. For nations ought to be learned and cultivated and not barbarous. . . . Since a learned and cultivated nation ought to do whatever it can to make a barbarous and uncultivated nation learned and more cultivated, but since, if any nation wishes to promote the perfection of another, it cannot compel it to allow that to be done; if some barbarous and uncultivated nation is unwilling to accept aid offered to it by another in removing its barbarism and rendering its manners more cultivated, it cannot be compelled to accept such aid, consequently it cannot be compelled by force to develop its mind by the training which destroys barbarism and without which cultivated manners cannot exist.

This comment appears to preserve the right of an aboriginal people to retain its independence, whatever be the attitude of another state and whatever the ideology in which the latter disguises its predatory intentions. However, having referred to the needs for perfection in government, Wolff[144] states:

> Whatever one nation is able to contribute to the preservation and perfection of another nation in that in which the other is not self-sufficient, it is bound by nature to contribute that to the other. For every nation is bound to preserve and perfect itself and its form of government. Therefore, since every nation owes to every other nation that which it owes itself,. . .one nation is bound to contribute whatever it can to the preservation and perfection of another in that in which the other is not self-sufficient.

The use of this language opens the door to any state, claiming that a "barbarous" nation lacks the wherewithal to become more civilised and therefore more perfect in government, or claiming that by denying the right of the more civilised to bring culture and civilisation to the barbarians, to contend that by refusing to accept the culture being offered the barbarous nation is in fact denying to the more civilised the right to perform its duties, and as a result providing the latter with grounds to wage a just war. In fact, such a contention would find support in the statement:[145]

> Every nation owes this duty, not only to itself but also to others, that it perfect itself and its condition. For every nation ought to contribute what it can to the perfection of another in that in which the other is not self-sufficient. Therefore, since it cannot do this, unless it perfect itself and its form of government, *it therefore ought to perfect itself also and its form of government, in order that it may be able to perform all parts of its duty toward other nations.* Therefore *it owes this duty* not only to itself, but also *to other nations, that it perfect itself and its form of government.*

If, however, one concedes that aboriginal or barbarous peoples nevertheless enjoy the rights of nationhood, one must apply to them the same considerations that Wolff introduces[146] when dealing with ordinary nations and their right to agree peacefully to submit to the overlordship or protection of a more powerful state, as Cartier and Champlain indicated was the intention of the Indians:[147]

If one nation shall not be strong enough to protect itself against the wrongs done by other nations, it can submit itself to some more powerful nation. . .Every nation is free by nature. But in respect to this right it can determine to its liking, just as shall have seemed best to it, therefore can diminish its freedom for the sake of its own advantage; this is what happens, if a nation subjects itself to another upon certain definite conditions, or grants some right to another over itself, whatever indeed that may be. But whether a nation is not powerful enough to protect itself against the wrongs done by other nations [as some Indian tribes indicated to Cartier] and whether it cannot provide for itself. . .other. . .than by subjecting itself or giving itself into tutelage to another more powerful nation, must be left to the decision of the nation itself in accordance with the principle of natural freedom. Therefore agreements entered into must be kept and *there is no question as to whether the nation has acted wisely, which has subjected itself to another for the sake of its own protection.* . . .If the nation which owes protection assumes for itself a greater right against a less powerful nation than it has by the agreement [providing for protection] and the weaker nation does not oppose it, the more powerful by the long acquiescence of the weaker at length acquires the right which it asserts, nay more, the weaker can utterly lose its supreme power and become subject to the more powerful. . . .[T]he nation which owes protection acquires at length, by long-continued acquiescence of the weaker nation, the right which it assumes for itself. . . .[On the other hand,] *if a certain nation occupies an uninhabited territory,. . . .it occupies the sovereignty over it at the same time. . .If then it occupies some uninhabited territory, to dwell in it and hold its property in it, there is no doubt but that it desires to have sovereignty over it.* But if it desires to have sovereignty for itself in that territory, it is understood not to wish to allow another to exercise in it some right belonging to sovereignty, or not to be subject to it.

Here, it would seem that Wolff is putting into legal language and theory the words which were used by the rulers in granting their commissions to the explorers going to the Indies, and subsequently embodying them into bilateral treaties.

Like his predecessors, Wolff denies the right of conversion, but since he was a Protestant writing well after the success of the

Reformation in Europe and after it had become clear that the European states were recognised sovereigns over the Indies and such areas in which they had established themselves, his comments on this subject and on the right to expel missionaries,[148] as well as his denial of the right of a prince to interfere in the affairs of another because the latter is denying basic rights of humanity to his subjects,[149] are irrelevant to the matters under consideration in this paper.

Wolff argues:[150]

> Since all lands and all things which are in a territory occupied by a nation are subject to its ownership, if there are in any territory, which a nation inhabits, desert and sterile, or uncultivated places, those belong to the nation. . .[and] no one, either foreign or native, can occupy those places and make them subject to his ownership. . . .[However,] since every nation ought to perfect its condition, desert and uncultivated places should be granted to aliens, that they may cultivate them. . . .[Moreover,] lands not subject to ownership and sovereignty or uninhabited by any nation, can be occupied and colonies established in them. . . .[and] lands that have been discovered uninhabited, or not subject to ownership and sovereignty, can be occupied by any nation. . . .But since ownership is acquired by occupation, and if a certain nation occupies an uninhabited territory, it occupies at the same time the sovereignty of it;. . .a nation has ownership and sovereignty. . .in land not subject to ownership and sovereignty, which it has occupied. But because either right is of no use, unless the. . .lands are inhabited,. . .it is necessary that colonies be established in them. . . . Since any nation is able to occupy. . .uninhabited lands, and since if any nation occupy a certain territory, all the land and the things which are in it are subject to the ownership of it, and the sovereignty in that land is occupied at the same time; the nation which first has occupied. . .uninhabited land, has ownership and sovereignty over it, and consequently the uninhabited. . .lands into which colonies are brought by the nation occupying them become an accession to the territory of that nation, however far removed they be from it, so that then it is just as if they were adjacent to it or included with the same boundaries.

Since by the middle of the eighteenth century it was clearly established that the European states had acquired colonial possessions in lands "discovered" by them which, prior to the discovery, had been inhabited only by aboriginal peoples, it may be accepted that Wolff's arguments with regard to the acquisition of sovereignty over unoccupied territories would apply with equal validity to the territories of the New World. This is unaffected by the fact that[151]

unknown lands inhabited by a nation may not be occupied by foreign nations. For since a nation which inhabits a land has occupied it, the land is subject to its ownership and also the sovereignty over it is its own property. Therefore, since no one may be deprived of his own property, it is not allowable to take from a nation the ownership and sovereignty which it has in the land that it inhabits. Therefore, since he does this who occupies land before unknown to himself but inhabited by a nation, unknown lands, inhabited by a nation may not be occupied by foreign nations. . . . *But* it is to be noted that we take the name nation with the fixed meaning which we have assigned to it, because of course it denotes a number of men who have united into a civil society, so that therefore *no nation can be conceived of without a civil sovereignty*. For groups of men dwelling together in certain limits but without civil sovereignty are not nations, except that *through carelessness of speech they may be wrongly so called*.

As, despite Vitoria's recognition of some sort of governmental arrangements among the Indians, the general view was to deny that the North American Indian tribes constituted societies politic under a civil sovereignty, it becomes clear that Wolff recognises the right of acquisition of title over such people.

Earlier writers were concerned about the nature of just war and by and large invariably found an excuse whereby each party to hostilities could plead the justness of his cause, and occasionally were prepared to argue that in certain situations each belligerent might have justice on its side. Wolff, however, maintains[152] that

war cannot be just on each side,. . . .for whatsoever reason war may be waged, the cause of only one party is just, and that of the other is unjust, even if it should happen that each of the belligerents thinks that he is favouring a just cause. [However,] the injustice of a war cannot be imputed to one who, because of ignorance or irrefutable error, thinks that he has a just cause of war when he has not. . . .

As a result, it follows that when the European powers considered they had a just cause for warlike action against the Indians and took over their lands as a consequence, Wolff provides the basis for their argument that, since they may have been in honest error as to the justness of their cause, they could not be obliged to restore what might have been taken by way of an unjust war.[153] Therefore,[154]

> when cities and territories are conquered, such sovereignty is acquired over the vanquished as exists in the people. . .and. . .the victor acquires over the vanquished in conquered cities and territories a complete and supreme sovereignty as his own peculiar property. . .[and] can change as he pleases the form which the state had before, the decision [lying] with the victor as to whether he may wish to combine the sovereignty with his own, or to keep it separate. . .

Having said this, Wolff virtually recants all that he has said before regarding unjust wars and the liability to return the fruits gained thereby, for he now recognises the difference between the law of nature and the "voluntary law of nations," whereby[155]

> so far as regards results, war is to be considered as just on either side. . . .[S]ince no nation can assume for itself the functions of a judge, and consequently cannot pronounce upon the justice of the war, although by natural law a war cannot be just on both sides, since nevertheless each of the belligerents claims that it has just cause of war, each must be allowed to follow its own opinion; consequently by the voluntary law of nations the war must be considered as just on either side, not indeed in itself, which forsooth it implies, but as regards the results of the war. . . .[S]ince by the voluntary law of nations as regards results war is to be regarded as just on either side, by the voluntary law of nations warlike occupation is the ordinary method of acquiring ownership and sovereignty over belligerents.

Although Wolff seeks to affirm the validity of natural law and to measure the behaviour of states accordingly, he is nevertheless sufficient of a positivist to be aware of the realities of state practice. While he avoids the pieties of his Catholic precursors, he is as much an apologist for state conduct as they ever were. His writings provide as much justification for the acquisition of territorial title over aboriginal lands as was the case with any naturalist or church father from 1450 until the end of the seventeenth century. Vattel is often regarded as a disciple of Wolff, and it is interesting, therefore, to note that he opens his account of the law of nations[156] with the statement that

> Nations or States are political bodies. . . .The Law of Nations is the science of the rights which exist between Nations or States, and of the obligations corresponding to these rights.

Impliedly, Vattel does not recognise aboriginal peoples as constituting "political bodies," for he states:[157]

> The cultivation of the soil. . .is. . .an obligation imposed upon man by nature. . . . .Every Nation is therefore bound by the natural law to cultivate the land which has fallen to its share. . . .Those peoples who,. . .though dwelling in fertile countries, disdain the cultivation of the soil and prefer to live by plunder, fail in their duty to themselves, injure their neighbours, and deserve to be exterminated like wild beasts of prey. There are others who, in order to avoid labour, seek to live upon their flocks and the fruits of the chase. . . .[N]ow that the human race has multiplied so greatly, it could not subsist if every people wished to live after that fashion. Those who still pursue this idle mode of life occupy more land than they would have need of under a system of honest labour,[158] and they may not complain if other more industrious Nations, too confined at home, should come and occupy part of their lands. Thus, while the conquest of the civilized Empires of Peru and Mexico was a notorious usurpation, the establishment of various colonies upon the continent of North America might, if done within just limits, have been entirely lawful. The peoples of those vast tracts of land rather roamed over them than inhabited them. . . .All men have an equal right to things which have not yet come into the possession of anyone, and these things belong to the person who first takes possession. When, therefore, a Nation finds a country uninhabited and without an owner, it may lawfully

take possession of it, and after it has given sufficient signs of its intention in this respect, it may not be deprived of it by another Nation. In this way navigators setting out upon voyages of discovery and bearing with them a commission from their sovereign, when coming across islands or other uninhabited lands, have taken possession of them in the name of their Nations; and this title has usually been respected, provided actual possession has followed shortly after. . . .[T]he Law of Nations will only recognize the *ownership* and *sovereignty* of a Nation over unoccupied lands when the Nation is in actual occupation of them, when it forms a settlement upon them, or makes actual use of them. In fact, when explorers have discovered uninhabited lands through which the explorers of other Nations had passed, leaving some sign of their having taken possession, they have no more troubled themselves over such empty forms than over the regulations of Popes, who divided a large part of the world between the crowns of Castile and Portugal.[159]

There is another celebrated question which has arisen principally in connection with the discovery of the New World. It is asked whether the Nation may lawfully occupy any part of a vast territory in which are to be found only wandering tribes whose small numbers cannot populate the whole country. We have already pointed out. . .that these tribes cannot take to themselves more land than they have need of or can inhabit and cultivate. Their uncertain occupancy of these vast regions cannot be held as a real and lawful taking of possession; and when the Nations of Europe, which are too confined at home, come upon lands which the savages have no special need of and are making no present and continuous use of, they may lawfully take possession of them and establish colonies in them. We have already said that the earth belongs to all mankind as a means of sustaining life. But if each Nation had desired from the beginning to appropriate to itself an extent of territory great enough for it to live merely by hunting, fishing and gathering wild fruits, the earth would not suffice for a tenth part of the people who now inhabit it. Hence we are not departing from the intention of nature when we restrict the savages within narrower bounds. . . .When a Nation takes possession of a distant country and establishes a colony there, that territory, though separated from the mother country, forms naturally a part of the State, as much so as its older possessions. . . .

Unlike most of his precursors, especially those not seeking expressly to justify the acquisition of title by their own prince, Vattel deals with the problem of the North American Indians and other aboriginal peoples *expressis verbis* and combines his views of natural law with an acknowledgement of actual state practice, providing the most explicit statement to uphold the legal right of the European states to enter North America and take over as colonies those "uninhabited" tracts which constituted the hunting grounds of the local people, who were not considered as having sufficient status or organization to constitute a body politic capable of forming a Nation or a State, and so equally incapable of possessing sovereignty. From the point of view of international law as it existed in the middle of the eighteenth century, the Indians of North America had never inhabited any territory to an extent sufficient to preclude newcomers regarding their lands as unoccupied and amenable to the acquisition of sovereignty. While recognising this right of access and acquisition, Vattel nevertheless rejects religious or civilising arguments that were put forward by states and their apologists to justify their actions:[160]

> [W]hile a Nation is bound to further. . .the advancement of others, it has no right to force them to accept its offer of help. . . . Those ambitious European States which attacked the American Nations [as we have seen, in his more general comments, Vattel denies that the Indian tribes constituted Nations] and subjected them to their avaricious rule, in order, as they said, to civilize them, and have them instructed in the true religion—those usurpers. . .justified themselves by a pretext equally unjust and ridiculous. It is surprising to hear. . .Grotius tell us that a sovereign can justly take up arms to punish Nations which are guilty of grievous crimes against the natural law. . . .He was led into that mistake from his attributing to every free man, and hence to every sovereign, a certain right to punish crimes in grievous violation of the laws of nature, even when those crimes do not affect his rights or his safety. But. . .the right to punish belongs to men solely because of the right to provide for their safety; hence it exists only as against those who have injured them. . . .

While this argument sounds reasonable, it must be remembered that the majority of doctrinal writing was not in accord with these views and that Grotius was regarded more highly as an exponent of the law of nations than was Vattel. Moreover, it must be remembered that Vattel was far from sympathetic to Catholicism and its claims[161] and it matters little that he rejects this basis for annexation of North America, since he justified these acts on the more basic ground of occupation of unoccupied lands, rejecting the view that the Indian tribes constituted a settled Nation; and he reiterates this when he compliments the English who "have brought their colonies in the New World to a condition where the strength of the colonies adds considerably to that of the Nation."[162] Moreover, "let us repeat again what we have said more than once, namely, that the savage tribes of North America had no right to keep to themselves the whole of that vast continent; and provided sufficient land were left to the Indians, others might, without injustice to them, settle in certain parts of a region, the whole of which the Indians were unable to occupy."[163] Since he has denied that the Indians constitute a Nation in the sense of his definition, this latter requirement is fully satisfied by the establishment of reservations or the type of guarantee of their lands that is to be found in the Royal Proclamation of 1763.[164]

Insofar as Indian claims are now based on title stemming from an alleged illegal seizure, and insofar as such claims have only been put forward in comparatively recent times, it is worth noting what Vattel, who supports usucaption and prescription as valid titles in international law, says on this matter:[165]

> In view of the peace of Nations, the safety of States, and the welfare of the human race, it is not to be allowed that the property, sovereignty, and other rights of Nations should remain uncertain, open to question, and always furnishing cause for bloody wars. Hence, as between Nations, prescription founded upon length of time must be admitted as a valid and incontestable title. If a Nation has kept silence through fear, through a sort of necessity, the loss of its right is a misfortune which it must patiently endure, since there was no avoiding it. And why should it not bear that loss as well as it would the loss of towns and provinces taken from it by an unjust conqueror and forced from its possession by a treaty of cession? However, prescription can be set up on these grounds only in a case where the possession has been long-continued and uncontested, because it is necessary that matters should be finally decided and put upon a definite and permanent basis. The argu-

ment does not hold when there is a question of possession of only a few years' duration, during which time one might be led to keep silence from prudence, without thereby being open to the accusation of having let things become uncertain, and of reviving interminable quarrels. . . . Since usucaption and prescription are so necessary to the peace and welfare of human society,. . . all Nations have consented to admit the lawful and reasonable application of them. . . . Prescription based on long tenure as well as usucaption are, therefore, supported even by the *voluntary* Law of Nations. Further still, since by virtue of that same law, Nations are regarded, in all cases open to doubt, as possessing equal rights in their mutual intercourse, prescription founded upon long and undisputed possession should hold good as between Nations, without there being the right to set up that the possession is in bad faith, unless the evidence to that effect is unmistakable; for in the absence of such evidence· every Nation must be thought to be in good faith. . . .[166]

As has been seen, Vattel is among those who deny the justness of a war in the name of religion, and he has condemned those who justified compaigns against the Indians on such specious grounds. Despite this, however, he points out[167] that in

the voluntary Law of Nations. . . the first rule. . . is that *regular war* [that is to say, actual war between States], *as regards its effects, must be accounted just on both sides*. . . . Thus the rights founded upon the state of war, the legal nature of its effects, the validity of the acquisitions made in it, do not depend, externally and in the sight of men, upon the justice of the cause, but upon the legality of the means as such, that is to say, the presence of the elements constituting a regular war.

. . . *This voluntary Law of Nations*, established from necessity and for the avoidance of greater evils, *does not confer upon him whose cause is unjust any true rights capable of justifying his conduct and appeasing his conscience, but merely makes his conduct legal in the sight of men, and exempts him from punishment*. This is sufficiently clear from the principles of which the voluntary Law of Nations is based. Consequently, the sovereign who has no just cause in authorization of his hostilities is not less unjust, or less guilty of violating the sacred

Law of Nature merely because that same natural law, in the effort not to increase the evils of human society while seeking to prevent them, requires that he be conceded the same legal rights as more justly belong to his enemy. . . .[T]he voluntary Law of Nations consists in the rules of conduct, of external law, to which the natural law obliges Nations to consent; so that we rightly presume their consent, without seeking any record of it; for even if they had not given their consent, the Law of Nature supplies it, and gives it for them. Nations are not free in this matter to consent or not; the Nation which would refuse to consent would violate the common rights of all Nations. . . .Every acquisition made in a regular war is therefore, according to the *voluntary* Law of Nations valid, independently of the justice of the cause and of the motives the victor may have in claiming the right to hold what he has taken. Accordingly, conquest has been regularly looked upon by Nations as conferring lawful title, and such title has scarcely ever been questioned. . . .

In view of this, Vattel's reasoning supports those who would argue that, even if the campaigns against the Indians were misconceived, aggressive and contrary to law, since nations have recognized the institution of war, the fruits gained thereby produce legal results, regardless of the maxim *ex injuria jus non oritur*.[168] Moreover, in the period of discovery war, even without a declaration, was regarded as perfectly legal when undertaken against non-nations in order to establish sovereignty, and the existence of rights depends upon the law that existed at the time those rights were first asserted, and not upon views or legal or political philosophies which have developed later.

One of the most important writers at the turn of the eighteenth/ nineteenth centuries was von Martens. While his work does not deal specifically with the problem under discussion, he has some comments with regard to the growth of customary international law that are relevant:[169]

. . .a custom received among the majority of the powers of Europe, particularly among the great powers. . ., is easily adopted by other powers, as far as it can apply to them; and, in general, all nations give a certain degree of attention to the customs admitted by others, although it cannot be proved that they have ever been admitted by themselves. . . .The basis of. . .new rights and obligations, is, then, the mutual *will* of the nations concerned. This will may be *declared* by words, gestures, or other marks received as the signs of thought, or by actions from which consent may be deduced: or else it may be *presumed*; for instance, what a nation has always done hitherto, we may presume it will do for the future. . . .

As has been seen, the countries of Europe which opened up the New World were reasonably consistent in their practice and there is little doubt that they believed themselves to be acting in accordance with existing law, or perhaps more correctly, to be engaged in processes which were creative of law. This appears to have been the view of Wheaton writing in the middle of the nineteenth century:[170]

The title of almost all the nations of Europe. . .to the possessions held by them in the New World. . .was originally derived from discovery, or conquest and colonization, and has since been confirmed in the same manner, by positive compact. Independently of these sources of title, *the general consent of mankind has established the principle, that, long and uninterrupted possession by one nation excludes the claim of every other.* Whether this general consent be considered as an implied contract, or as positive law, *all nations are equally bound by it;* since all are parties to it; since none can safely disregard without impugning its own title to its possessions; and since it is founded upon mutual utility, and tends to promote the general welfare of mankind.

   The Spaniards and Portuguese took the lead among the nations of Europe. . .during the fifteenth and sixteenth centuries. According to the European idea of that age, the heathen nations of the other quarters of the globe were the lawful spoil and prey of their civilized conquerors. . . . [T]he right of prior discovery was the foundation upon which the different European nations, by whom conquests and settlements were successively made on the American continent, rested their respective claims to appropriate its territory to the exclusive use of each nation. . . .[T]here was one thing in which *they all agreed,* that *of almost entirely disregarding the right of the native inhabitants of these regions. . . .It thus became a maxim of policy and of law, that the right of the native Indian was subordinate to that of the first Christian discoverer,* whose paramount claim excluded that of every other civilized nation, and gradually extinguished that of the natives. In the various wars, treaties, and negotiations, to which the conflicting pretensions of the different States of Christendom to territory on the American continents have given rise, the primitive title of the Indians has been entirely overlooked, or left to be disposed of by the States within whose limits they happened to fall, by the stipulations of the treaties between the different European powers. Their title has been almost entirely extinguished by force of arms, or by voluntary compact, as the progress of civilization gradually compelled the savage tenant of the forest to yield to the superior power and skill of his civilized invader.

At an earlier point in his work, when discussing some of the decisions of the Supreme Court of the United States concerning Indians, Wheaton looks upon the Indians as a "domestic dependent nation,"[171] but Dana as editor adds this note:[172]

It is important to note the underlying fact, that the title to all the lands occupied by the Indian tribes, beyond the limits of the thirteen original States, is in the United States. The republic acquired it by the treaties of peace with Great Britain, by cessions from France and Spain, and by relinquishments made by the several States. *The Indian tribes have only a right of occupancy. Their possession was held to be of so nomadic and uncivilized a character as to amount to no more than a kind of servitude or lien upon the land, chiefly for fishing, and hunting: the absolute title being in the republic.* Whenever the republic has bought out an Indian tribe, and induced it to remove from a section of country, the act has always been called an "extinguishment of the Indian title" upon the lands of the United States. This title of occupancy the tribes are not allowed to convey to any other than the United States. . . .

He goes on to emphasise that the courts have held that the tribes are not "foreign states" within the meaning of the Constitution, and that while they may at least within their tribal areas be outside the scope of State jurisdiction, they are nevertheless within the authority of the federal government. In fact, the relations of the Indian tribes "with the republic are *sui generis,* having been shaped and modified by time and events." They do not possess any legal status independent of their position under the law of the United States, and lack any recognition by international law which they can claim against the federal or state governments, or vis-à-vis any foreign power.

The Attitude of the United States Supreme Court

That the various writers were in fact reflecting the legal position may be seen by reference to judicial decisions, particularly those of the Supreme Court of the United States and of the Permanent Court of International Justice. Perhaps the most significant of the American decisions is that of Chief Justice Marshall in *Johnson* v. *McIntosh*:[173]

> On the discovery of this immense continent the great nations of Europe were eager to appropriate to themselves so much of it as they could respectively acquire. . . .But, as they were all in pursuit of nearly the same object, it was necessary. . .to establish a principle which all should acknowledge as the law by which the right of acquisition, which they all asserted, should be regulated as between themselves. The principle was, that discovery gave title to the Government by whose subjects or by whose authority it was made against all other European Governments, which title might be consummated by possession. The exclusion of all other Europeans necessarily gave to the nation making the discovery the sole right of acquiring the soil from the natives, and establishing settlements upon it. It was a right with which no European could interfere. It was a right which all asserted for themselves, and to the assertion of which by others all assented. . . .While the different nations of Europe respected the right of the natives as occupants, they asserted the ultimate dominion to be in themselves, and claimed and exercised as a consequence of this ultimate dominion a power to grant the soil while yet in possession of the natives. These grants have been understood by all to convey a title to the grantees, subject only to the Indian right of occupancy.

It is quite clear from the context, that the Chief Justice was using the term "occupancy" as synonymous with physical presence and not in the sense in which the term is used relevant to the acquisition of title to territory. He went on to point out that title to the land in the English-settled North American colonies had

> been granted by the Crown while in the occupation of the Indians. These grants purport to convey the soil as well as the right of dominion to the grantees. . . . The magnificent purchase of Louisiana was the purchase from France of a country almost entirely occupied by numerous tribes of Indians who are, in fact, independent. Yet, any attempt by others to intrude into that country would be considered as an aggression which would justify war. Our late acquisitions from Spain are of the same character; and the negotiations which preceded those acquisitions recognize and elucidate the principle which has been received as the foundation of all European title in America. The United States, then, have unequivocally acceded to the great and broad rule by which its civilized inhabitants now hold this country. They hold and assert in themselves the title by which it was acquired. They maintain, as all others have maintained, that discovery gave an exclusive right to extinguish the Indian title of occupancy, either by purchase or by conquest; and gave also a right to such a degree of sovereignty as the circumstances of the people would allow themselves to exercise.

Consequently, a conveyance of title derived solely from an Indian tribe in 1773 and 1775 to private persons conveyed no title.

This view of the situation was also shared by the Government of the United States:[174]

> How far the mere discovery of a territory which is either unsettled, or settled only by savages, gives a right to it, is a question which neither the law nor the usages of nations has yet definitely settled. The opinions of mankind, upon this point, have undergone very great changes with the progress of knowledge and civilization. Yet it will scarcely be denied that rights acquired by the general consent of civilized nations, even under the erroneous views of an unenlightened age, are protected against the changes of opinion resulting merely from the more liberal, or the more just, views of after times. The right of nations to countries discovered in the sixteenth century is to be determined by the law of nations as un-

derstood *at that time,* and not by the improved and more en-
lightened opinion of three centuries later.

The United States Government also adopted the traditional view
with regard to prescription and the fact that the occupant did not have
to be physically present on every inch of the territory affected:[175]

That continuity furnishes a just foundation for a claim of territory,
in connection with those of discovery and occupation, would seem
unquestionable. It is admitted by all, that neither of them is limited
by the precise spot discovered or occupied. It is evident that, in order to make either available, it must extend at least some distance
beyond that actually discovered or occupied; but how far, as an abstract question, is a matter of uncertainty. It is a subject, in each
case, to be influenced by a variety of considerations. . . . When this
continent was first discovered, Spain claimed the whole, in virtue
of the grant of the Pope; but a claim so extravagant and unreasonable was not acquiesced in by other countries, and could not be
long maintained. Other nations, especially England and France, at
an early period contested her claim. They fitted out voyages of discovery, and made settlements on the eastern coast of North America. They claimed for their settlement, usually, specific limits along
the coasts or bays on which they were founded; and, generally, a
region of corresponding width extending across the entire continent to the Pacific Ocean. Such was the character of the limits assigned by England in the charter which she granted to her former
colonies, now the United States, when there were no special reasons for varying from it. How strong she regarded her claim to the
region conveyed by these charters and extending westward of her
settlements, the war between her and France, which was termi-
nated by the treaty of Paris, 1763,[176] furnishes a striking illustration.
That great contest. . .commenced in a conflict between [En-
gland's] claims and those of France, resting, on her side, on this
very right of continuity, extending westward from her settlements
to the Pacific Ocean; and, on the part of France, on the same right,
but extending to the region drained by the Mississipi and its
waters, on the ground of settlement and exploration. Their respective claims. . .first clashed on the river Ohio, the waters of
which the colonial charters, in their westward extension covered;

but which France had been unquestionably the first to settle and explore. If the relative strength of these different claims may be tested by the result. . ., that of continuity westward must be pronounced to be the stronger of the two. England. . .had. . .the advantage of the result, and would seem to be foreclosed of contesting the principle, particularly as against us, who contributed so much to that result, and on whom that contest and her example and pretensions, from the first settlement of our country, have contributed to impress it so deeply and indelibly. . . .

The Attitude of International Tribunals

A somewhat similar approach was taken by international judicial tribunals faced with somewhat similar problems in the twentieth century. In the *Cayuga Indians* claim,[177] the Anglo-United States Arbitral Tribunal was concerned with the nature of a treaty between the Cayugas and the State of New York, and in the course of its opinion dealt with the problem of the status of the Indian "Nation":

> The obligee was the "Cayuga Nation," *an Indian tribe. Such a tribe is not a legal unit of international law. The American Indians have never been so regarded.* . . .From the time of the discovery of America the Indian tribes have been treated as under the exclusive protection of the power which by discovery or conquest or cession held the land which they occupied. . . .They have been said to be "domestic dependent nations,"[178] or "States in a certain domestic sense and for certain municipal purposes."[179] The power which had sovereignty over the land has always been held the sole judge of its relations with the tribes within its domain. The rights in this respect acquired by discovery have been held exclusive. "No other power could interpose between them."[180] So far as the Indian tribe exists as a legal unit, it is by virtue of the domestic law of the sovereign nation within whose territory the tribe occupies the land, and so far only as that law recognizes it. Before the Revolution all the lands of the Six Nations [of whom the Cayuga Nation was one] in New York had been put under the Crown as "appendant to the Colony of New York," and that colony had dealt with those tribes exclusively as under its protection. . . .New York, not the United

States, succeeded to the British Crown in this respect at the Revo-
lution. Hence the "Cayuga Nation," with which the State of New
York contracted. . ., so far as it was a legal unit, was a legal unit of
New York law. . . . The legal character and status of the New
York entity with which New York contracted was a matter of
New York law. . . . When the Cayugas divided, some going to
Canada and some remaining in New York, and when that cleavage
became permanent in consequence of the War of 1812, Great
Britain might, if it seemed desirable, treat the Canadian Cayugas as
a unit of British law or might deal with them individually as British nationals. Those Indians were permanently established on British soil and under British jurisdiction. They were and are dependent upon Great Britain or later upon Canada, as the New York
Cayugas were dependent on and wards of New York. . .[181] [T]he
Cayuga Nation has no international status. . . . [I]t existed as a
legal unit only by New York law. It was a *de facto* unit, but *de jure*
was only what Great Britain chose to recognize as to the Cayugas
who moved to Canada and what New York recognized as to the
Cayugas in New York or in their relations with New
York. . . . Legally, they could do nothing except under the guard-
ianship of some sovereign. They could not determine what should
be the nation, nor even whether there should be a nation legally.
New York continued to deal with the New York Cayugas as a
"nation." Great Britain dealt with the Canadian Cayugas as individuals. . . .

In 1933 the Permanent Court of International Justice was called
upon to decide on the sovereignty of Eastern Greenland as between
Denmark and Norway, and in so doing had occasion to examine the
status of Eskimos resident in Greenland and the extent to which they
might be able to extinguish a title established by a European power:[182]

. . . [I]t was about the year 900 A.D. that Greenland was discovered. The country was colonized about a century later. . . . [I]t
was at that time that two settlements. . . were founded towards the
southern end of the western coast. These settlements appear to
have existed as an independent State for some time, but became
tributary to the kingdom of Norway in the 13th century. These
settlements had disappeared before 1500. . . . The disappearance of

the Nordic colonies did not put an end to the King's pretension to the sovereignty over Greenland. . . .The passports delivered by the King to the leader of two expeditions. . .at the beginning of the 17th century indicate the voyage as *"ad terram nostram Grunlanium."* Some Eskimos brought back from Greenland in 1605 are described by the King as "Our subjects". . . .Similarly, foreign countries appear to have acquiesced in the claims of the King of Denmark. . . .Though at this time no colonies or settlements existed in Greenland, contact with it was not entirely lost, because the waters surrounding it. . .were regularly visited by whalers, and the maps of the period show that the existence of the general configuration of Greenland, including the East coast, were by no means unknown. . . .[The Court described the history of Danish attitudes to Greenland, including the grant of trading monopolies and the like.] [During the eighteenth century], settlements were established described as colonies, factories or stations, along the West coast. . . .Attempts to reach the East coast and effect a landing. . .led to no results. In the contention of Norway,. . .when [the documents] speak of Greenland in general, [they] mean the colonized part of the West coast. . .; Denmark, on the contrary, maintains that the expressions in question relate to Greenland in the geographical sense of the word, i.e. to the whole island of Greenland. . . .In the course of the 19th century and the early years of the 20th, the coasts of Greenland were entirely explored. . . .It is admitted by Norway that from [1822] the East coast forms part of the known portion of Greenland. . . .[By 1931] the whole East coast has been explored by Danish expeditions. . . .In 1894. . .the first Danish settlement on the East coast was established. [Norway made a number of visits between 1889 and 1929 and] built a large number of houses and cabins in the disputed territory. During the 19th century, while the Danish Government made a practice of excluding "Greenland," without qualification, from the commercial conventions it concluded and in other ways acted upon the assumption that Danish sovereignty extended to the whole of Greenland, opinions were occasionally expressed by private persons in Denmark interested in Greenland to the effect that the absence of effective occupation of the uncolonized parts exposed the territory to the risk of permanent occupation by some foreign State. . . .. [I]t was gradually made clear that, in the opinion of the Norwegian Government, the uncolonized part of the East coast of Greenland was a *terra nullius*. . .[183] and if they ceased to be *terrae nullius* they must pass under Norwegian sovereignty. . . .[and in 1930] conferred police powers on certain Norwegian nationals "for the inspection of the Norwegian hunting stations in Eastern Greenland," [and in 1931 announced its occupation of some of the territory]. . . .

The Danish claim is not founded upon any particular act of occupation but alleges. . .a title "founded on the peaceful and continuous display of State authority over the island."[184]. . .It must be borne in mind, however, that. . .it is not necessary that sovereignty over Greenland should have existed throughout the period during which the Danish Government maintains that it was in being. . . .[A] claim to sovereignty based not upon some particular act or title such as a treaty of cession but merely upon continued display of authority, involves two elements each of which must be shown to exist: the intention and will to act as sovereign, and some actual exercise or display of such authority. . . .It is impossible to read the records of the decisions in cases as to territorial sovereignty without observing that in many cases the tribunal has been satisfied with very little in the way of the actual exercise of sovereign rights, provided that the other State could not make out a superior claim. This is particularly true in the case of claims to sovereignty over areas in thinly populated or unsettled countries.

In the period when the early Nordic colonies founded. . .in the 10th century in Greenland were in existence, the modern notions as to territorial sovereignty had not come into being. It is unlikely that the chiefs or the settlers in these colonies drew any sharp distinction between territory which was and territory which was not subject to them. On the other hand, the undertaking. . .that fines should be paid to the King of Norway by the men in Greenland in respect of murders whether the dead man was a Norwegian or a Greenlander and whether killed in the settlement or as far to the North as under the Pole Star, shows that the King of Norway's jurisdiction was not restricted to the confines of the two settlements. . . .So far as it was possible to apply the modern terminology to the rights and pretensions of the kings of Norway in Greenland in the 13th and 14th centuries, the Court holds that at that date these rights amounted to sovereignty and that they were not limited to the two settlements.

It has been argued on behalf of Norway that after the disappearance of the two Nordic settlements, Norwegian sovereignty was lost and Greenland became a *terra nullius*. Conquest and voluntary abandonment are the grounds on which this view is put forward.

The word "conquest" is not an appropriate phrase, even if it is assumed that it was fighting with the Eskimos which led to the downfall of the settlements. *Conquest only operates as a cause of loss of sovereignty when there is war between two States and by reason of the defeat of one of them sovereignty over territory passes from the loser to the victorious State. The principle does not apply in a case where a settlement has been established in a distant country and its inhabitants are massacred by the aboriginal population.* . . .As regards voluntary abandonment, there is nothing to show any definite renunciation on the part of the kings of Norway or Denmark. During the first two centuries after the settlements perished, there seems to have been no intercourse with Greenland, and knowledge of it diminished; but the tradition of the King's rights lived on, and in the early part of the 17th century a revival of interest in Greenland on the part both of the King and of his people took place. That period was an era of adventure and exploration. The example set by the navigators of foreign countries was inspiring, and a desire arose in Norway and Denmark to recover the territory which had been subject to the sovereignty of the King's ancestors in the past. . . . [Everything done shows] that the King considered that in his dealings with Greenland he was dealing with a country with respect to which he had a special position superior to that of any other Power. . . .[A]s there were [then] no colonies or settlements in Greenland, the King's claims cannot have been limited to any particular places in the country.

That the King's claims amounted merely to pretension is clear, for he had no permanent contact with the country, he was exercising no authority there. The claims, however, were not disputed. No other Power was putting forward any claim to territorial sovereignty in Greenland, and in the absence of any competing claim the King's pretensions to be the sovereign of Greenland subsisted.

After the founding of. . .colonies in 1721, there is in part at least of Greenland a manifestation and exercise of sovereign rights. Consequently, both the elements necessary to establish a valid title to sovereignty—the intention and the exercise—were present, but the question arises as to how far these elements extended. . . .

The Court then found that the pretensions to sovereignty showed the intention and that there was sufficient exercise of sovereign rights thereafter to fulfil legal requirements. It held, further, that Danish sovereignty extended throughout Greenland, employing that term in the normal geographic sense, even though[185]

in many of [the] legislative and administrative acts action was only to be taken in the colonies and not in the rest of the country. The fact that most of these acts were concerned with what happened in the colonies and that the colonies were all situated on the West coast is not by itself sufficient ground for holding that the authority in virtue of which the act was taken. . .was also restricted to the colonized area. Unless it was so restricted, it affords no ground for interpreting the word "Greenland" in this restricted sense. . . .

It has also been argued on behalf of Norway that "Greenland" as used in documents of this period cannot have been intended to include the East coast because at that time the East coast was unknown. An examination however of the maps of the 17th and 18th centuries shows that the general features and configurations of the East coast of Greenland were known to the cartographers. Even if no evidence of any landings on the coast have been produced, the ships which hunted whales in the waters to the East of Greenland sighted the land at intervals and gave names to the prominent features which were observed. . . .

The conclusion to which the Court is led is that, bearing in mind the absence of any claim to sovereignty by another Power, and the Arctic and inaccessible character of the uncolonized parts of the country, the King. . .displayed. . .his authority to an extent sufficient to give his country a valid claim to sovereignty, and that his rights over Greenland were not limited to the colonized area. . . .

The Court pointed out that Denmark had entered into a number of conventions with other powers which clearly indicated the understanding that the whole of Greenland was within Danish sovereignty.

It is not difficult to extend many of the statements made by the Court in the *Eastern Greenland* case concerning the non-status of the aboriginal population, establishment of European sovereignty and its exercise, as well as the scope of that sovereignty even into unexplored and unsettled portion of the region, to the problems under discussion here in respect of sovereignty in North America.

There is one further international decision of significance, particularly as this gives a modicum of international recognition to the acts of aboriginal people, when confronted by a European trading company. It is of further interest since it dealt with issues of intertemporal law. The *Island of Palmas* case[186] arose from a dispute between the Netherlands and the United States over the sovereignty to an East Indian island. It was referred to the Permanent Court of Arbitration and Judge Huber, as sole arbitrator, stated:

> Titles of acquisition of territorial sovereignty in present-day international law are either based on an act of effective apprehension, such as occupation or conquest, or, like cession, presuppose that the ceding and the cessionary Powers or at least one of them, have the faculty of effectively disposing of the ceded territory. . . . *[P]ractice, as well as doctrine, recognizes. . .that the continuous and peaceful display of territorial sovereignty (peaceful in relation to other States) is as good as a title.* The growing insistence with which international law, ever since the middle of the 18th century, has demanded that the occupation shall be effective would be inconceivable, if effectiveness were required only for the act of acquisition and not equally for the maintenance of the right. . . .Just as before the rise of international law, boundaries of lands were necessarily determined by the fact that the power of a State was exercised within them, so too, under the reign of international law, the fact of peaceful and continuous display is still one of the most important considerations in establishing boundaries between States.
>
> Territorial sovereignty. . .involves the exclusive right to display the activities of a State. This right has as corollary a duty: the obligation to protect within the territory the rights of other States, in particular their right to integrity and inviolability in peace and in war, together with the rights which each State may claim for its nationals in foreign territory. . . .International law, the structure

of which is not based on any super-State organisation, cannot be presumed to reduce a right such as territorial sovereignty. . .to the category of an abstract right, without concrete manifestations. . . .

Manifestations of territorial sovereignty assume. . .different forms according to conditions of time and place. The intermittence and discontinuity compatible with the maintenance of the right necessarily differ according as inhabited or uninhabited regions are involved, or regions enclosed within territories in which sovereignty is incontestably displayed or again regions accessible from. . .the high seas. . . .

If. . .the question arises whether a title is valid *erga omnes,* the actual continuous and peaceful display of State functions is. . .the sound and natural criterium of territorial sovereignty. . . .

. . .International law underwent profound modifications between the end of the Middle Ages and the end of the 19th century, as regards the rights of discovery [put forward by the United States as successor to Spain] and acquisition of uninhabited regions or regions inhabited by savages or semi–civilised peoples. . . .*[A] juridical fact must be appreciated in the light of the law contemporary with it, and not of the law in force at the time when a dispute in regard to it arises or falls to be settled.* The effect of discovery by Spain is therefore to be determined by the rules of international law in force in the first half of the 16th century. . . .

As regards the question which different legal systems prevailing at successive periods is to be applied in a particular case (the so-called intertemporal law), *a distinction must be made between the creation of rights and the existence of rights.* The same principle which subjects the act creative of the right to the law in force at the time the right arises, demands that the existence of the right, in other words its continued manifestation, shall follow the conditions required by the evolution of law. International law in the 19th century, having regard to the fact that most parts of the globe were under the sovereignty of States members of the community of nations, and that territories without a master had become relatively few, took account of a tendency already existing and especially developed since the middle of the 18th century, and laid down the principle that occupation, to constitute a claim to territorial sovereignty, must be effective, that is, offer certain guarantees to other States and their nationals. . . .[D]iscovery alone, without any subsequent act, cannot at the present time suffice to prove sovereignty. . . .

If. . .the view is adopted that discovery does not create a definitive title of sovereignty, but only an "inchoate" title,[187] such a title exists. . .without external manifestation. However, according to the view that has prevailed at any rate since the 19th century, an inchoate title of discovery must be completed within a reasonable period by the effective occupation of the region claimed to be discovered. This principle must be applied in the present case, for the reasons given above in regard to the rules determining which of successive legal systems is to be applied (the so-called intertemporal law). . . .[A]n inchoate title could not prevail over the continuous and peaceful display of authority by another State; for such display may prevail over a prior, definitive title put forward by another State. . . .

. . .[I]n the exercise of territorial sovereignty there are necessarily gaps, intermittence in time and discontinuity in space. This phenomenon will be particularly noticeable in the case of colonial territories, partly uninhabited or as yet partly unsubdued. The fact that a State cannot prove display of sovereignty as regards such a portion of territory cannot forthwith be interpreted as showing that sovereignty is inexistent. Each case must be appreciated in accordance with the particular circumstances.

. . .[I]nternational arbitral jurisprudence in disputes on territorial sovereignty. . .would seem to attribute greater weight to—even isolated—acts of display of sovereignty than to continuity of territory, even if such continuity is combined with the existence of natural boundaries. . . .We *must distinguish between, on the one hand, the act of first taking possession, which can hardly extend to every portion of territory, and, on the other hand, a display of sovereignty as a continuous and prolonged manifestation which must make itself felt through the whole territory.* . . .

Insofar as Canada is concerned, the requirements of display of sovereignty, continuity of territory and natural boundaries all coincide. Moreover, there has been no allegation by any other recognised State that Canada's sovereignty in any part of what is geographically known by that name is in doubt. The sole allegation of non-possession of sovereignty has come from aboriginal peoples who, as has been indicated, have no recognised status in international law, and who are putting forward a claim that has only received validity in recent years.

Judge Huber pointed out that much of the Netherlands case depended upon a sovereignty alleged to stem from conventions made between native chieftains and the Dutch East India Company:[188]

> . . .These successive contracts are one much like another; the more recent [e.g., 1855 and 1899] are more developed and better suited to modern ideas in economic, religious and other matters, but they are all based on the conception that the prince receives his principality as a fief of the Company or the Dutch State, which is suzerain. Their eminently political nature is confirmed by the supplementary agreements. . .concerning the obligations of vassals in the event of war. The dependence of the vassal State is ensured by the important powers given to the nearest representative of the colonial Government and, in the last resort, to that Government itself[189]. . .Even the oldest contract, dated 1677, contains clauses binding the vassal of the East India Company to refuse to admit the nationals of other States. . .into his territories, and to tolerate no religion other than protestantism. . . .The authenticity of these contracts cannot be questioned. . . .
>
> If the claim to sovereignty is based on the continuous and peaceful display of State authority, the fact of such display must be shown precisely in relation to the disputed territory. It is not necessary that there should be a special administration established in the territory;. . .what is essential. . .is the continuous and peaceful display of actual power in the contested region. . . .
>
> The acts of the East India Company, in view of occupying or colonizing the regions. . .must, in international law, be entirely assimilated to acts of the Netherlands State itself. From the end of the 16th century till the 19th century, companies formed by individuals and engaged in economic pursuits (*Chartered Companies*), *were invested by the State to whom they were subject with public powers for the acquisition and administration of colonies*. . .[190] The conclusion of conventions, even of a political nature, was, by Article 35 of the Charter of 1602, within the powers of the Company. It is a question for decision in each individual case whether a contract concluded by the Company falls within the range of simple economic transactions or is of a political and public administrative nature.

As regards *contracts between a State* or a Company such as the
Dutch East India Company *and native princes or chiefs of peoples not
recognized as members of the community of nations*, they *are not, in the
international law sense, treaties or conventions capable of creating rights
and obligations such as may, in international law, arise out of treaties.*[191]
But, on the other hand, contracts of this nature are not wholly void
of indirect effects on situations governed by international law; if
they do not constitute titles in international law; they are none the
less facts of which that law must in certain circumstances take account. From the time of the discoveries, until recent times, colonial territory has very often been acquired. . .by means of contracts with the native authorities, which contracts leave the existing organisation more or less intact as regards the native population, whilst granting the colonizing Power, besides economic advantages. . ., also the exclusive direction of relations with other
Powers, and the right to exercise public authority in regard to their
own nationals and to foreigners. The form of the legal relations
created by such contracts is most generally that of suzerain and
vassal, or of the so-called colonial protectorate.[192]

In substance, it is not an agreement between equals; it is rather a
form of internal organisation of a colonial territory, on the basis of
autonomy for the natives. In order to regularise the situation as regards other States, this organisation requires to be completed by
the establishment of powers to ensure the fulfilment of the obligations imposed by international law on every State in regard to its
own territory. And thus *suzerainty over native States becomes the basis
of territorial sovereignty as towards other members of the community of nations.*

It is the sum-total of functions thus allotted either to the native
authorities or to those of the colonial Power which decide the
question whether at any certain period the conditions required for
the existence of sovereignty are fulfilled. . . .

Considering that the contracts of 1676 amd 1697. . .established
in favour of the Dutch East India Company extensive rights of
suzerainty. . .and an exclusive right of intercourse. . ., and considering further. . .characteristic acts of jurisdiction. . .in 1701
[regulating criminal justice] and 1726 [concerning nationality of
the natives] are reported, whilst no display of sovereignty by any
other Power during the same period is known, it may be admitted
that at least in the first quarter of the 18th century, and probably

also before that time, the Dutch East India Company exercised rights of suzerainty. . .and therefore *the island was at that time, in conformity with the international law of the period, under Netherlands sovereignty. . . .*

These native States were from 1677 onwards connected with the East India Company, and therefore with the Netherlands, by contracts of suzerainty, which conferred upon the suzerain such powers as would justify his considering the vassal State as a part of his territory.

Acts characteristic of State authority. . .have been established. . . .

The acts of indirect or direct display of Netherlands sovereignty. . .especially in the 18th and 19th centuries are not numerous, and there are considerable gaps in the evidence of continuous display. But apart from the consideration that the manifestations of sovereignty over a small and distant island, inhabited only by natives, cannot be expected to be frequent, it is not necessary that the display of sovereignty should go back to a very far distant period. . . .

It is not necessary that the display of sovereignty should be established as having begun at a precise epoch. . . .It is quite natural that the establishment of sovereignty may be the outcome of a slow evolution, of a progressive intensification of State control. . . .

As to the conditions of acquisition of sovereignty by way of continuous and peaceful display of State authority (so-called prescription),. . .the display has been open and public, that is to say that it was in conformity with usages as to exercise of sovereignty over colonial States. A clandestine exercise of State authority over an inhabited territory during a considerable length of time would seem to be impossible. . . .

Judge Huber pointed out that there was in international law no obligation upon a sovereign claiming by prescription to notify other states of his assumption of sovereignty. In the case of the American continent, of course, there can be no question that outside authorities are or have been, since the eighteenth century at latest, unaware of the sovereignty claimed by Canada, the United States and the independent states of South America.

It should be pointed out that the charter of the Dutch East India

Company was drawn up in the same era as those of the British East India Company and the Hudson's Bay Company, and that the legal concepts prevailing at the time were fairly general throughout Europe. It would follow that what Judge Huber had to say with regard to the Dutch East India Company as representative of the Netherlands crown, and the interpretation he has placed upon the contracts or treaties made by the Company with native princes would, broadly speaking at least, be equally valid with respect to the British Companies.[193]

In none of the cases decided by international judicial tribunals mentioned above was the principle of self-determination as it is being promoted today ever referred to. However, in two later decisions, the International Court of Justice, both in the majority judgment and in the individual opinions, made much of this new legal principle. But neither of these decisions is really relevant from our point of view. The *Namibia (South West Africa) Opinion*[194] was concerned with termination of a treaty governing a dependent territory, and the effect on sovereignty consequent thereon. In the *Western Sahara* judgement[195] what was in issue was the status of a territory after its abandonment by the colonial power, and a confrontation between two existing states, as well as the claims of the indigenous population, all of which turned on the issue whether at the time of the original colonisation the territory had in fact been *terra nullius*.

The Attitude of the Judicial Committee of the Privy Council

Perhaps it might be as well at this point to refer to one or two English imperial decisions which considered the status of treaties entered into with native princes or populations. For this purpose, we will confine ourselves to treaties which were not akin to those considered in the *Palmas* case having been made by a trading company, but will look rather at documents which appeared *prima facie* to be treaties as that term is understood in international law. *Sobhuza II* v. *Miller*[196] related to the status of the Swaziland protectorate, which

> was treated as an independent native state both by the South African Republic and by the British Government, notwithstanding a good deal of interference by both in its affairs. . . . But the South

African Republic appears, from the terms of the convention made in 1894 [between the Republic and the United Kingdom], to have become preponderant in the internal control. The relationship seems to have been recognised as being one in which Swaziland stood to the Republic as a protected dependency administered by the South African Republic. This protectorate stopped short of incorporation, but apparently it was recognised by the Convention of 1894. . .as giving the latter, without incorporation, all rights of protection, legislation, jurisdiction and administration over Swaziland and the inhabitants thereof. The natives were, however, guaranteed in their laws and customs, so far as not inconsistent with laws made pursuant to the Convention,. . .with the proviso that no law thereafter made in Swaziland was to be in conflict with the guarantees given to the Swazi people in the Convention. . . .

After the Boer War Swaziland passed under British protection and Orders in Council were issued that, contrary to the Convention, adversely affected Swazi rights. It was argued

that the Crown has no powers over Swaziland, except those which it had under the conventions and those which it acquired by the conquest of the South African Republic. The limitation in the Convention of 1894 on interference with the rights and laws and customs of the natives cannot legally interefere with the subsequent exercise of the sovereign powers of the Crown, or invalidate subsequent Orders in Council. . . .The Crown could not, excepting by statute, deprive itself of freedom to make Orders in Council, even when these were inconsistent with previous Orders.

Perhaps more to the point under consideration is the Privy Council decision in *Hoani Te Heuheu Tukino* v. *Aotea District Maori Land Board*[197] in which the Council was called upon to examine the nature of the Treaty of Waitangi,[198] of 1840, terminating the Maori Wars, and which had been signed by some 500 native chiefs, although there were relatively few from New Zealand's South Island, while a good many in North Island did not sign either:[199]

Article II of the Treaty. . .was as follows:
"Her Majesty the Queen of England confirms and guarantees to the chiefs and tribes of New Zealand. . .the full exclusive un-

disturbed possession of their lands and estates, forests, fisheries and other properties which they may collectively or individually possess, so long as it is their wish and desire to retain the same in their possession: but the chiefs of the United Tribes and the individual chiefs yield to Her Majesty the exclusive right of pre-emption over such lands as the proprietors thereof may be disposed to alienate at such prices as may be agreed upon between the respective proprietors and persons appointed by Her Majesty to treat with them in that behalf."

Under Article I there had been a complete cession of all the rights and powers of sovereignty of the chiefs. It is well settled that any rights purporting to be conferred by such a treaty of cession cannot be enforced in the courts, except in so far as they have been incorporated in the municipal law. . . .[T]he Imperial Parliament has conferred on the New Zealand legislature power to legislate with regard to the native lands, it necessarily follows that the New Zealand legislature has the same power as the Imperial Parliament had to alter and amend its legislation at any time. . . .As regards the. . .argument that the New Zealand legislature has recognized and adopted the Treaty of Waitangi as part of the municipal law of New Zealand, it is true that there have been references to the treaty in the statutes, but these appear to have invariably had reference to further legislation in relation to the native lands, and, in any event, even the statutory incorporation of the second article of the treaty in the municipal law would not deprive the legislature of its power to alter or amend such a statute by later enactments.

It is true that the Privy Council did not expressly consider whether the Treaty of Waitangi was a treaty in the international sense of the word. However, by clearly ignoring its bilateral or reciprocal character and recognizing the unilateral right of the Crown to amend or ignore it the Board clearly indicates that it did not regard it as an international instrument. While the Crown can, from the internal point of view, unilaterally amend an international treaty, and while the individual described as a beneficiary is unable to enforce such a treaty,[200] the English courts will endeavour to construe legislation as not inconsistent with the treaty or will draw attention to the fact that this was the express intention.[201] The position is perhaps most clearly stated in a statement by the United States to France in 1928:[202]

> a State complaining of the infraction of a treaty is believed to be justified in declining to admit that its rights under the agreement can be ultimately determined by a foreign local court without the consent of each party to the agreement. While it is doubtless true that French courts are bound to give effect to laws enacted by the French parliament regardless of whether such laws do in fact violate existing treaty engagements of France, it is, of course, open to this Government to hold that the legislation is in violation of existing treaty provisions and to demand that remedial action be taken to protect the violated rights of its nationals.

In the case of treaties and other agreements made with aboriginal peoples, there is no authority "to demand that remedial action be taken to protect the violated rights." From the point of view of international law the document is of purely municipal significance and the one state party to it enjoys, at least in law, whatever may be the moral view, the power to amend or interpret the document as it will.

It is clear from the doctrinal writings and the judicial practice that indigenous populations had no recognised rights when dealing with European states or their representatives, whether the latter be explorers or Companies. As a result the European states were able to acquire sovereignty over the territories inhabited by those indigenous peoples, with such sovereignty being recognized by those which had the power by international law to afford such recognition. Moreover, it is clear that the agreements made with indigenous peoples purporting to convey sovereignty in return for the protection of rights lacked any legal significance and in no way encumbered the sovereignty which the European states had acquired.

The Royal Proclamation of 1763

By the time of the Anglo-French wars French title to its settlements and their surrounding areas in North America was generally recognised. With the French defeat in 1763, the French title passed to Britain. By the Royal Proclamation of 1763[203]—the terms of which seem to have served as a model for the Treaty of Waitangi—the status of lands still occupied by Indians was regulated, at least insofar as their acquisition by non-Indian settlers was concerned. The Proclamation has been described as the Indians' Bill of Rights,[204] but this description in fact neither accords with the language nor the application and interpretation of the Proclamation. Moreover, since the Proclamation is a purely internal document issued by the Crown, it has no significance whatever in the eyes of international law, while its terminology makes it perfectly clear that it regulates the relations between Indians and private individuals, and is not concerned with any rights which the Indians might claim against the Crown itself.

The Proclamation begins by asserting the British title, "secured to our Crown by the late Definitive Treaty of Peace, concluded at Paris, the 10th Day of February last,"[205] and having established "Four distinct and separate Governments, styled and called by the names of Quebec, East Florida, West Florida and Granada," it continues

. . .And whereas it is Just and Reasonable and Essential to Our Interests and the Security of Our Colonies that the several Nations or Tribes of Indians with whom We are connected and who live under Our Protection should not be molested or disturbed in the Possession of such Parts of Our Dominions and Territories, as, not having been ceded to or purchased by Us, are reserved to them or any of them as their Hunting Grounds, We do therefore. . . declare. . .that no Governor or Commander in Chief in any of our Colonies of Quebec, East Florida or West Florida, presume upon any pretence whatsoever to grant warrants of Survey or pass any Patents for Lands beyond the bounds of their respective Governments as described in their Commissions; as also that no Governor or any Commander in Chief of any of Our other Colonies or Plantations in America do presume for the present and until Our further pleasure be known, to grant warrants of Survey or Patents for any Lands beyond the head or sources of any of the Rivers which fall into the Atlantic Ocean from the West and North West, or upon any Lands whatever, which not having been ceded to or purchased by Us as aforesaid, are reserved to the said Indians or any of them.

And We do further declare it to be Our Royal Will and Pleasure, for the present as aforesaid, to reserve under Our Sovereignty,

Protection, and Dominion, for the use of the said Indians, all the Lands and Territories not included within the Limits of Our said Three New Governments, or within the limits of the Territory granted to the Hudson's Bay Company as also all the Lands and Territories lying to the Westward of the Sources of the Rivers which fall into the Sea from the West and North West as aforesaid;

And We do hereby strictly forbid. . .all Our loving Subjects from making any Purchases or Settlements whatever, or taking Possession of any of the Lands above reserved, without Our especial leave and Licence for that Purpose first obtained.

And, We do further strictly enjoin and require all Persons whatever who have either wilfully or inadvertently seated themselves upon any Lands within the Countries above described, or upon any other Lands which, not having been ceded to or purchased by Us, are still reserved to the said Indians as aforesaid, forthwith to remove themselves from such Settlements.

And Whereas Great Frauds and Abuses have been committed in purchasing Lands of the Indians, to the Great Prejudice of Our Interests, and to the Great Dissatisfaction of the said Indians; In order, therefore, to prevent such Irregularities for the future and to the End that the Indians may be convinced of Our Justice and determined Resolution to remove all reasonable Cause of Discontent, We do. . .strictly enjoin and require, that no private Person do presume to make any Purchase from the said Indians of any Lands reserved to the said Indians, within those parts of Our Colonies where we have thought proper to allow Settlement; but that, if at any Time any of the said Indians should be inclined to dispose of the said Lands, the same shall be purchased only for Us, in Our Name, at some public Meeting or Assembly of the said Indians, to be held for that Purpose by the Governor or Commander in Chief of Our Colony respectively in which they shall lie; and in case they shall lie within the limits of any Proprietary Government, they shall be purchased only for the Use and in the name of such Proprietaries, conformable to such Directions and Instructions as We or they shall think proper to give for that Purpose; And We do. . . declare and enjoin that the Trade with the said Indians shall be free and open to all Our Subjects whatever, provided that every Person who may incline to Trade with the said Indians do take out a Licence for carrying out such Trade from the Governor or Commander in Chief of any of Our Colonies respectively where such Person shall reside, and also give Security to observe such Regulations as We shall at any Time think fit. . .to direct and appoint for the Benefit of the said Trade. . . .

And We do further expressly require all Officers whatever, as well Military as those Employed in the Management and Direction of Indian Affairs, within the Territories reserved as aforesaid for the Use of the said Indians, to seize and apprehend all Persons whatever, who standing charged with Treason, Misprisions of Treason, Murders, or other Felonies or Misdemeanours, shall fly from Justice and take Refuge in the said Territory, and to send them under a proper Guard to the Colony where the Crime was committed of which they stand accused, in order to take their Trial for the same.

It is clear from the language of the Proclamation that it refers almost exclusively to the relations between the Indians and the settlers, and attempts to protect the former from exploitation by the latter, and is primarily concerned with the prevention of sales to private persons of lands reserved for the Indians. Any such lands which the Indians may wish to sell must in the first instance be offered to the Crown. While, *prima facie*, this may imply that the Indians have a title which is good against the Crown, in the light of the overall character of the Proclamation it is clear that this is really a reference to the common law right of English citizens holding lands not to be expropriated by the Crown without proper compensation—in this case, the compensation being either sale or an act of cession which might almost be regarded, depending on the consideration flowing from the Crown, as an outright gift. It should also be noticed that the Proclamation does not purport to be immutable, for it refers to "the present and until Our further pleasure be known."

In construing the significance of the Royal Proclamation in regard to the relations between the Crown and the Indians, it must not be forgotten that the Proclamation commences by referring to "the extensive and valuable acquisitions in America, secured to Our Crown by the late Definitive Treaty of Peace, concluded at Paris." This clearly indicates that the Crown secured all rights, including those of sovereignty, previously enjoyed by France. Any rights that it conferred upon the Indians could only be non-sovereign and outside of rights already exercisable on behalf of the Crown. For reasons already indicated *"les sauvages"* had no sovereign rights of any kind in any of the territories held and governed by France. While it is true that the Capitulation of Montreal[206] provided that

> the savages or Indian allies of His Most Christian Majesty shall be maintained on the lands they inhabit, if they choose to reside there; [and] they shall not be molested on pretence whatsoever, for having carried arms and served His Most Christian Majesty. . .

this provision only created an obligation as between England and France and gave no direct right to the Indians as such. In some ways it may be argued that the Royal Proclamation was nothing more than a measure directed to giving effect to this commitment, which only related to a stabilisation of existing residential rights. If disregarded, any protest would have to come from France and could not come from the Indians themselves. Moreover, since the Indians had ceased to be French, it is questionable whether any such protest could be sustained.

The injunction that any lands reserved to the Indians, and this clearly means reserved by the Crown for Indian enjoyment and so not amenable to further private settlement, were to be offered in the first instance to the Crown merely ensured that private ownership, as that term was understood in English land law, would take second place to any desire by the Crown to extend its full ownership under that law, and, as pointed out, the method of so doing was similar to the methods used by the Crown when seeking legal ownership in this restricted sense from any other private landowner in territories governed by the Crown. In accordance with the theory of English land law, the Crown owns all the land and all that a private owner could possess was rights, even though they be in the form of an absolute freehold title in fee simple, subject to that overall "ownership." Further evidence that the lands reserved to the Indians were not regarded as "foreign" is to be found in the reference to police powers at the end of the Proclamation. At the end of the eighteenth century the modern concept of extradition in accordance with treaty had not yet developed. Nevertheless, there was no idea that a state seeking a fugitive criminal could enter the territory of the state providing hospitality in order to recover such fugitive. Everything would depend upon the goodwill of the latter state if called upon to surrender him. In the Proclamation, colonial officials are given a clear instruction that if a fugitive from justice, albeit his offence amounted to no more than a misdemeanour, sought refuge in reserved lands, the official or his representatives were to enter such lands without any consultation with the Indians, seize the fugitive and bring him to trial.

The above interpretation of the Proclamation's effect upon relations between the Crown and the Indians is similar to that adopted by the Indian Commissioners appointed by the Government of Canada in their Report of 1844,[207] drawing attention to the fact that the Proclamation

> furnished [the Indians] with a fresh guarantee for the possession of their hunting grounds and the protection of the crown. This document the Indians look upon as their charter. They have preserved a copy of it and have referred to it on several occasions in their representations to the government. Since 1763 the government, adhering to the Royal Proclamation of that year, have not considered themselves entitled to dispossess the Indians of their lands without entering into an agreement with them and rendering them some compensation. For a considerable time after the conquest of Canada the whole of the western part of the upper province, with the exception of a few military posts on the frontier and a great extent of the eastern part, was in their occupation. As the settlement of the country advanced and the land was required for new occupants or the predatory and revengeful habits of the Indians rendered their removal desirable, the British government made successive agreements with them for the surrender of portions of their lands.

There can be little doubt that this decision to abide by the terms of the Proclamation and to secure Indian surrenders by agreement was a purely policy decision based on grace. What the Crown did by agreement it could equally well have done, in the first instance by right of conquest, and latterly by executive expropriation, although this latter form of proceeding would have run counter to the common law recognition of the rights of English subjects not to be displaced without compensation. On the other hand, one must not overlook the manner in which during the period of economic expansion in England, overlapping the period of establishment of English influence in North

America, the home parliament was encroaching upon common lands by way of a series of Enclosure Acts, thus indicating that the English authorities did not regard the rights of the ordinary man as sacrosanct in any way.

Judicial decisions in both the United States and Canada have sought to interpret the effect of the European settlement and the meaning of the Proclamation. One of the earliest and most significant of such decisions is that by Chief Justice Marshall in *Johnson and Graham's Lessees* v. *McIntosh*,[208] rendered a mere sixty years after the promulgation of the Proclamation:

> . . .As. . .the title to lands. . .must be admitted to depend entirely on the law of the nation in which they lie; it will be necessary. . .to examine, not simply those principles of abstract justice, which the Creator of all things has impressed upon the mind of his creature man, and which are admitted to regulate, in a great degree, the rights of civilized nations, whose perfect independence is acknowledged; but those principles also which our own government has adopted in the particular case. . . .
>
> On the discovery of this immense continent, the great nations of Europe were eager to appropriate to themselves so much of it as they could respectively acquire. Its vast extent offered an ample field to the ambition and enterprise of all; and the character and religion of its inhabitants offered an apology for considering them as a people over whom the superior genius of Europe might claim an ascendancy. The potentates of the old world found no difficulty in convincing themselves, that they made ample compensation to the inhabitants of the new, by bestowing on them civilization and Christianity, in exchange for unlimited independence. But as they were all in pursuit of nearly the same object, it was necessary, in order to avoid conflicting settlements, and consequent war with each other, to establish a principle, which all should acknowledge as the law by which the right of acquisition, which they all asserted, should be regulated, as between themselves. This principle was, that discovery gave title to the government by whose subjects, or by whose authority, it was made, against all other European governments, which title might be consummated by possession. The exclusion of all other Europeans, necessarily gave to the nation making the discovery the sole right of acquiring the

soil from the natives, and establishing settlements upon it. It was a right with which no Europeans could interfere. It was a right which all asserted for themselves, and to the assertion of which, by others, all assented. *Those relations which were to exist between the discoverer and the natives, were to be regulated by themselves.* The rights thus acquired being exclusive, no other power could interpose between them.

In the establishment of these relations, the rights of the original inhabitants were, in no instance, entirely disregarded; but were, necessarily, to a considerable extent, impaired. They were *admitted to be the rightful occupants of the soil, with a legal as well as just claim to retain possession of it,* and to use it according to their own discretion; but *their rights to complete sovereignty, as independent nations, were necessarily diminished,* and *their power to dispose of the soil,* at their own will, to whomsoever they pleased, *was denied by the original fundamental principle, that discovery gave exclusive title to those who made it. While the different nations of Europe respected the rights of the natives as occupants, they asserted the ultimate dominion to be in themselves; and claimed and exercised, as a consequence of this ultimate dominion, a power to grant the soil, while yet in possession of the natives. These grants have been understood by all, to convey a title to the grantees, subject only to the Indian right of occupancy.*

The history of America, from the discovery to the present day, proves. . .the universal recognition of these principles. . . .France also founded her title to the vast territories she claimed in America on discovery. However conciliatory her conduct to the natives may have been, she still asserted her right of dominion over a great extent of country not actually settled by Frenchmen, and her exclusive right to acquire and dispose of the soil which remained in the occupation of Indians. Her monarch claimed all Canada and Acadie, as colonies of France at a time when the French population was very inconsiderable, and the Indians occupied almost the whole country. . . .The States of Holland also made acquisitions in America, and sustained their right on the common principle adopted by all Europe. . . .

No one of the powers of Europe gave its full assent to this principle more unequivocally than England. . . .

Thus has our whole country been granted by the crown, while

in the occupation of the Indians. These grants purport to convey the soil as well as the right of dominion to the grantees. In those governments which were denominated royal, where the right to the soil was not vested in individuals, but remained in the crown, or was vested in the colonial government, the king claimed and exercised the right of granting lands, and of dismembering the government, at his will. . . . The governments of New England, New York, New Jersey, Pennsylvania, Maryland, and a part of Carolina, were thus created. In all of them, the soil, at the time the grants were made, was occupied by the Indians. . . . *It has never been objected to. . . any [such] grant, that the title as well as possession was in the Indians when it was made, and that it passed nothing on that account.* . . .

Further proofs of the extent to which this principle has been recognised, will be found in the history of the wars, negotiations and treaties, which the different nations, claiming territory in America, have carried on, and held with each other. . . .

. . . [The 1763] treaty [between England and France] expressly cedes, and has always been understood to cede, the whole country, on the English side of the dividing line, between the two nations, although a great and valuable part of it was occupied by the Indians. . . .

By the treaty which concluded the war of our revolution, Great Britain relinquished all claim, not only to the government, but to the "propriety and territorial rights of the United States," [209]. . . By this treaty, the powers of government, and the right to soil, which had previously been in Great Britain, passed definitively to these states. We had before taken possession of them, by declaring independence; but neither the declaration of independence, nor the treaty confirming it, could give us more than that which we before possessed, or to which Great Britain was before entitled. *It has never been doubted, that either the United States, or the several states, had a clear title to all the lands within the boundary lines described in the treaty, subject only to the Indian right of occupancy, and that the exclusive power to extinguish that right, was vested in that government which might constitutionally exercise it.*

. . . [The learned Chief Justice then referred to the cessions made by the various states to the United States.] The ceded *territory was occupied by* numerous and warlike tribes of *Indians; but the exclusive right of the United States to extinguish their title,* and to grant the soil, *has never. . .been doubted.*

. . .The magnificent purchase of Louisiana, was the purchase from France of a country almost entirely occupied by numerous tribes of Indians, who are in fact independent. Yet, any attempt of others to intrude into the country, would be considered as an agression which would justify war. . . .

The United States, then have unequivocally acceded to that great and broad rule by which its civilized inhabitants now hold this country. They hold, and assert in themselves the title by which it was acquired. They maintain, as all others have maintained, that discovery gave an exclusive right to extinguish the Indian title of occupancy, whether by purchase or by conquest; and gave also a right to such a degree of sovereignty, as the circumstances of the people would allow them to exercise. The power now possessed by the government of the United States to grant lands, resided, while we were colonies, in the crown or its grantees. The validity of the title given by either has never been questioned in our courts. It has been exercised uniformly over territory in possession of the Indians. *The existence of this power must negative the existence of any right which may conflict with and control it. An absolute title to lands cannot exist, at the same time, in different persons, or in different governments.* An absolute, must be an exclusive title, or at least a title which excludes all others not compatible with it. *All our institutions recognise the absolute title of the crown, subject only to the Indian right of occupancy, and recognise the absolute title of the crown to extinguish that right. This right is incompatible with an absolute and complete title in the Indians. . . .*

. . .*Conquest gives a title which the courts of the conqueror cannot deny,* [210] *whatever the private and speculative opinions of individuals may be, respecting the original justice of the claim* which has been successfully asserted. The British government, which was then our government, and whose rights have passed to the United States, asserted a title to all the lands occupied by Indians, within the chartered limits of the British colonies. It asserted also a limited sovereignty over them, and the exclusive right of extinguishing the titles which occupancy gave to them. These claims have been maintained. . . .The title to a vast portion of the lands we now hold, originates in them. It is not for the courts of this country to question the validity of this title, or to sustain one which is incompatible with it.

. . .The title by conquest is acquired and maintained by force. The conqueror prescribes its limits. Humanity, however, acting on public opinion, has established, as a general rule, that the conquered shall not be wantonly oppressed, and that their condition shall remain as eligible as is compatible with the objects of the conquest. Most usually, they are incorporated with the victorious nation, and become subjects or citizens of the government with which they are connected. The new and old members of the society mingle with each other; the distinction between them is gradually lost, and they make one people. Where this incorporation is practicable, humanity demands, and a wise policy requires, that the rights of the conquered to property should remain unimpaired; that the new subjects should be governed as equitably as the old, and that confidence in their security should gradually banish painful sense of being separated from their ancient connections, and united by force to strangers. When the conquest is complete, and the conquered inhabitants can be blended with the conquerors, or safely governed as a distinct people, public opinion, which not even the conqueror can disregard, imposes these restraints upon him; and he cannot neglect them, without injury to his fame, and hazard to his power.

But the tribes of Indians inhabiting this country were fierce savages. . . .To leave them in possession of their country, was to leave the country a wilderness; to govern them as a distinct people was impossible. . . .The Europeans were under the necessity of either abandoning the country, and relinquishing their pompous claims to it, or of enforcing those claims by the sword, and by the adoption of principles adapted to the condition of a people with whom it was impossible to mix, and who could not be governed as a distinct society, or of remaining in their neighbourhood, and exposing themselves. . .to the perpetual hazard of being massacred. . . .[A]s the white population advanced, that of the Indians necessarily receded. . . .The soil, to which the crown originally claimed title, being no longer occupied by its ancient inhabitants, was parcelled out according to the will of the sovereign power, and taken possession of by persons who claimed immediately from the crown, or mediately, through its grantees or deputies. That law which regulates. . .the relations between the conqueror and the conquered, was incapable of application to a people under such circumstances. The resort to some new and different rule, better adapted to the actual state of things, was unavoidable. . . .However extravagant the pretension of converting the discovery of an inhabited country into conquest may appear; if the principle has been asserted in the first instance, and afterwards sustained; if a country has been acquired and held under it; if the property of the great mass of the community originates in it, it becomes the law of the land, and cannot be questioned. So, too, with respect to the concomitant principle, that *the Indian inhabitants are to be considered merely as occupants, to be protected, indeed, while in peace, in the possession of their lands, but to be deemed incapable of transferring the absolute title to others.* However, this restriction may be opposed to natural right, and to the usages of civilized nations, yet, *if it be indispensable to that system under which the country has been settled, and be adapted to the actual condition of the two people, it may perhaps be supported by reason, and cannot be rejected by courts of justice.* . . .

[By] the proclamation issued by the king of Great Britain in *1763,. . .*the crown reserved under its own dominion and protection, for the use of the Indians, "all the lands and territories lying to the westward of the sources of the rivers which fall into the sea from the west and north-west," and strictly forbade all British subjects from making any purchases or settlements whatever, oᴛ taking possession of the reserved lands. . . .

According to the theory of the British constitution, all vacant lands are vested in the crown, as representing the nation; and the exclusive power to grant them is admitted to reside in the crown, as a branch of the royal prerogative. . . .[T]his principle was as fully recognised in America as in the islands of Great Britain. All the lands we hold were originally granted by the crown; and the establishment of a regal government has never been considered as impairing its right to grant lands within the chartered limits of [a] colony. . . .*So far as respected the authority of the crown, no distinction was taken between vacant lands and lands occupied by the Indians. The title, subject only to the right of occupancy by the Indians, was admitted to be in the king, as was his right to grant that title.* The lands, then, to which this proclamation referred, were lands which the king had a right to grant, or to reserve for the Indians. . . .

It has never been contended that the Indian title amounted to nothing. Their right of possession has never been questioned. The claim of government extends to the complete ultimate title, charged with this right of possession, and to the exclusive power of acquiring that right. . . .

Less than ten years later, in *Worcester* v. *State of Georgia,*[211] Chief Justice Marshall was again concerned with the question of Indian rights and the nature of the Royal Proclamation. Having reiterated his views on the nature and significance of discovery, particularly in regard to North America, the Chief Justice stated:

The principle [of discovery]. . .was an exclusive principle which shut out the right of competition among those who had agreed to it; not one which could annul the previous rights of those who had not agreed to it. It regulated the right given by discovery among the European discoverers; but could not affect the rights of those already in possession, either as aboriginal occupants or as occupants by virtue of a discovery made before the memory of man. It gave the exclusive right to purchase, but did not found that right on a denial of the right of the possessor to sell.

The relation between the Europeans and the natives was determined in each case by the particular government which asserted and could maintain this pre-emptive privilege in the particular place. The United States succeeded to all the claims of Great Britain, both territorial and political; but no attempt. . .has been made to enlarge them. So far as they existed merely in theory, or were in their nature only exclusive of the claims of other European nations, they still retain their original character, and remain dormant. So far as they have been practically exerted, they exist in fact, are understood by both parties, are asserted by the one, and admitted by the other.

Soon after Great Britain determined on planting colonies in America, the king granted charters to companies of his subjects who associated for the purpose of carrying the views of the crown into effect, and of enriching themselves. The first of these charters was made before possession was taken of any part of the country. They purport, generally, to convey the soil, from the Atlantic to the South Sea. This soil was occupied by numerous and warlike

nations, equally willing and able to defend their possessions. . . .
They were well understood to convey the title which, according to
the common law of European sovereigns respecting America, they
might rightfully convey and no more. This was the exclusive right
of purchasing such lands as the natives were willing to sell. The
crown could not be understood to grant what the crown did not
affect to claim; nor was it so understood.

The power of making war is conferred by these charters on the
colonies, but defensive war alone seems to have been contem-
plated. . . .

This power to repel invasion, and, upon just cause, to invade
and destroy the natives, authorizes offensive as well as defensive
war, but only "on just cause". The very terms imply the existence
of a country to be invaded, and of an enemy who has given just
cause of war. . . .

. . .[T]hese grants asserted a title against Europeans only, and
were considered as blank paper so far as the rights of the natives
were concerned. The power of war is given only for defence, not
for conquest.

The charters contain passages showing one of their objects to be
the civilization of the Indians, and their conversion, to Christianity
—objects to be accomplished by conciliatory conduct and good
example; not by extermination.

. . .Fierce and warlike in their character, [the Indians] might be
formidable enemies, or effective friends. Instead of rousing their
resentments, by asserting claims to their lands, or to dominion
over their persons, their alliance was sought by flattering profes-
sions, and purchased by rich presents. . . .Not well acquainted
with the meaning of words, nor supposing it to be material
whether they were called the subjects, or the children of their father in Europe; lavish in profession of duty and affection, in return
for the rich presents they received; so long as their actual independence was untouched, and their right to self-government acknowledged, they were willing to profess dependence on the power
which furnished supplies of which they were in absolute need, and
restrained dangerous intruders from entering their country; and
this was probably the sense in which the term was understood by
them.

Certain it is, that our history furnishes no example, from the settlement of our country, of any attempt on the part of the crown to interfere with the internal affairs of the Indians, farther than to keep out the agents of foreign powers, who, as traders or otherwise, might seduce them into foreign alliances. The king purchased their lands when they were willing to sell, at a price they were willing to take; but never coerced a surrender of them. He also purchased their alliance and dependence by subsidies; but never intruded into the interior of their affairs, or interfered with their self-government, so far as respected themselves only. . . .

The proclamation issued by the King of Great Britain, in 1763,. . .forbids the governors of any of the colonies to grant warrants of survey, or pass patents upon any lands whatever, which, not having been ceded to, or purchased by, us (the king), as aforesaid, are reserved to the said Indians, or any of them. . . .

Such was the policy of Great Britain towards the Indian nations inhabiting the territory from which she excluded all other Europeans; such her claims, and such her practical exposition of the charters she had granted; she considered them as nations capable of maintaining the relations of peace and war; of governing themselves, under her protection; and she made treaties with them,[212] the obligation of which she acknowledged. . . .

As to Chief Justice Marshall's reference to the power of war as being for defence only, and not for conquest, it should be remembered that, as the classicists pointed out, over a period of time even what had been wrongly established could eventually constitute a good title, especially in the absence of any strong opposition, which accords with the maxim *quieta non movere*. Moreover, in his references to Indian desires to preserve their "independence," it is clear that the Chief Justice has in mind matters of internal concern and organisation only,[213] and is in no way using the term in the sense in which it is employed in international law.

The leading Canadian case on the meaning of the Royal Proclamation of 1763 and the rights of the Indians thereunder is *St. Catherine's Milling & Lumber Co. v. The Queen.*[214] The shortest judgment in the Supreme Court is perhaps that of the Chief Justice. In Sir William Ritchie's view[215]

all ungranted lands in the province of Ontario belong to the crown as part of the public domain subject to the *Indian right of occupancy* in cases in which the same has not been lawfully extinguished absolutely to the Crown, and as a consequence to the province of Ontario. I think *the crown owns the soil of all the unpatented lands, the Indians possessing only the right of occupancy, and the crown possessing the legal title subject to that occupancy, with the absolute exclusive right to extinguish the Indian title either by conquest or by purchase.*

In his support, he cited *Story on the Constitution*:[216]

It is to be deemed a right exclusively belonging to the Government in its sovereign capacity to extinguish the Indian title and to perfect its own dominion over the soil and dispose of it according to its own good pleasure. . . .The crown has the right to grant the soil while yet in possession of the Indians, subject, however, to the right of occupancy.

Ritchie C.J. went on to point out that lands

within the Province of Ontario. . .are necessarily, territorially, a part of Ontario, and the ungranted portion of such *lands not specifically reserved for the Indians, though unsurrendered and therefore subject to the Indian title, forms part of the public domain of Ontario,* and they are consequently public lands belonging to Ontario. . .and. . .the Province of Ontario has a clear title to all the unpatented lands within its boundaries as part of the Provincial public property, subject only to the right of Indian occupancy, and *absolute when the Indian right of occupancy is extinguished.*

He goes on to point out that

when the Dominion Government, in 1873[217] extinguished the Indian claim of title, its effect was. . .simply to relieve the legal ownership of the land belonging to the Province from the burden, incumbrance, or however it may be designated, of the Indian title. . . .

From the point of view of construing the nature of Indian rights and the meaning of the Proclamation it is not important to assess the relative weight of concurring from dissenting judgments, or to enquire whether a particular judge was in the majority or not. It is therefore sufficient to examine the judgment from these points of view in the order in which the members or the Supreme Court delivered their opinions. The fullest judgment was that delivered by Strong J., who stated:[218]

. . .The word "trusts" would not be an appropriate expression to apply to the relation between the crown and the Indians respecting the unceded lands of the latter.[219] . . .[S]uch relationship is. . .rather one analogous to the feudal relationship of lord and tenant, or, in some aspects, to that one, so familiar in Roman law, where the right of property is dismembered and divided between the proprietor and a usufructuary. . .

In the Commentaries of Chancellor Kent[220] and in some decisions of the Supreme Court of the United States we have very full and clear accounts of the policy [followed by the Crown in dealings with the Indians in respect of their lands]. It may be summarily stated as consisting in the *recognition by the crown of a usufructuary title in the Indians to all unsurrendered lands.* This title. . .was one which. . .sufficed to protect the Indians in the absolute use and enjoyment of their lands, whilst at the same time they were incapacitated from making any valid alienation otherwise than to the crown itself, in whom the ultimate title was, in accordance with the English law of real property, considered as vested. . . .[I]n the United States a traditional policy, derived from colonial times, relative to the Indians and their lands has ripened into well established rules of law, and the result is that the lands in the possession of the Indians are, until surrendered, treated as their *rightful though inalienable property, so far as possession and enjoyment are concerned;* in other words, that the *dominium utile is recognized as belonging to or reserved for the Indians, though the dominium directum is considered to be in the United States.* Then, if this is so, as regards Indian lands in the United States, which have been reserved to the Indians by the constant observance of a particular rule of policy acknowledged by the United States courts to have been originally enforced by the crown of Great Britain, how is it possible to suppose that the law can, or rather could have been, at the date of confederation, in a state any less favourable to the Indians whose lands were situated within the

dominion of the British crown, the original author of this bene-
ficent doctrine so carefully adhered to in the United States from the
days of the colonial governments?. . .

. . .[T]he exclusive right of legislating respecting Indian affairs is
attributed by [the British North America Act,[221] s. 91 (24)] to the
Parliament of Canada. This must include the right to control the
exercise by the Indians of the power of making treaties of surrender, and since. . .it is only by means of treaties of surrender that
the Indian title can be properly surrendered or extinguished, Parliament must necessarily have the power, as incident to the general
management of the Indians, of so legislating as to restrain or regulate the making of treaties of surrender which might be deemed
improvident dispositions of Indian lands. . . .

Such a control over the power to make "treaties" is hardly consistent with the claim that the Indians remained in sovereign control
over their lands, nor is it consistent with what international law regards as a treaty[222] and treaty-making competence. Strong J. continued

. . .[A]t the date of confederation the Indians, by the constant
usage and practice of the crown, were considered to possess a certain proprietary interest in the unsurrendered lands which they occupied as hunting grounds; that this usage had either ripened into a
rule of the common law as applicable to the American Colonies, or
such a rule had been derived from the law of nations and had in this
way been imported into the Colonial law as applied to the Indian
Nations; that *such property of the Indians was usufructuary only* and
could not be alienated, except by surrender to the *crown as the ultimate owner of the soil.* . . .

. . .[The *Proclamation of 1763*] had the force of a statute and was
in the strictest sense a legislative act,. . .remained in force at
the date of confederation. . .[and] gives legislative expression
and force to. . .the right of the Indians to enjoy by virtue of a
recognized title, their lands not surrendered or ceded to the
crown; it prohibits all interference with such lands by private persons by way of purchase or settlement, and limits the right of
purchasing or obtaining cessions of Indian lands to the king exclusively. . . .

Henry J. delivered an unwritten judgment and dealt with the effect of the purported conveyance by the Indians which was under consideration in the case:[223]

. . .[A]fter the conquest of this country all wild lands, including those held by nomadic tribes of Indians, were the property of the crown and were transferred to those who applied for them only by the crown. It was never asserted that any title to them could be given by the Indians. In 1763, after the conquest, the crown issued a proclamation by which all persons were prohibited from trading with the Indians in regard to purchase of lands, and it was declared that all such transactions should be void. The Indians were not permitted to transfer any of their rights as to the land to any individual, and no such transfers were valid unless made by the crown. . . .I suppose nobody will assert that if a private individual entered upon any of the lands at any time the Indians could legally object, as the law does not permit them by any legal means to recover possession of the land, or recover damages for any trespass committed thereon. I mention this to show that *the Indians were never regarded as having a title*. . . .

Now, suppose an individual had purchased from the Indians a part of the territory the crown would have the right to ignore the transfer. The Indians might have no further claim, but the extinguishment of the Indian right would enure to the benefit of the crown. If the Indian claim had been extinguished by private persons it would, without doubt, have operated in favour of the crown. . . .

. . .The Indians were not in possession of any particular portion of the land: for years and years they might never be on certain portions of it; they could not be said to have yielded possession [by the alleged conveyance], for that they cannot be assumed to have had, but virtually only relinquished their claim to the lands as hunting grounds. . .

In these words Henry J. makes it very clear that, in his view of the law, the Proclamation was an act of regal bounty intended to protect the Indians in the quiet enjoyment of the lands which they then held as hunting grounds. Any legal title, he thought, belonged solely to the crown, so that if there were a purported conveyance in breach of the Proclamation, such conveyance was not merely void preserving the Indians involved in their possession as if no conveyance had taken place, but extinguished all Indian rights in the land which became part of the patrimony of the crown as unburdened territory. As he saw it, therefore, not only did the Indians not have the legal title to the land, but whatever title they possessed to enjoy the land was conditional on their making no attempt to convey the title.

Taschereau J. expressly accepted the reasoning in the *Johnson* Case, and applied it to the situation in French Canada:[224]

. . .The King was vested with the ownership of all the ungranted lands in the colony as part of the royal domain, and a royal grant conveyed the full estate and entitled the grantee to possession. The contention, that the royal grants and charters merely asserted a title in the grantees against Europeans or white men, but that they were nothing but blank papers so far as the rights of the natives were concerned, was certainly not then thought of, either in France or in Canada. [The learned judge then referred to the grants from 1578, and *not] in any grant of land whatever during the 225 years of the French domination, can be found even an allusion to, or a mention of the Indian title.*

. . .The King granted lands, seigniories, territories, with the understanding that if any of these lands, seigniories, or territories proved to be occupied by aborigines, on the grantees rested the onus to get rid of them, either by chasing them away by force, or by a more conciliatory policy, as they would think proper. In many instances, no doubt, the grantees, or the King himself, deemed it cheaper or wiser to buy them than to fight them, but that was never construed as a recognition of their right to any legal title whatsoever. The fee and the legal possession were in the King or his grantees.

Now, when by the treaty of 1763, France ceded to Great Britain all her rights of sovereignty, property and possession over Canada and its islands, lands, places and coasts,. . .it is unquestionable that the full title to the territory ceded became vested in the new sovereign, and that he thereafter owned it in allodium[225] as part of the crown domain, in as full and ample a manner as the King of France had previously owned it. . . .To exclude from the full operation of the cession by France all the lands then occupied by the Indians, would be to declare that not an inch of land passed to the King of England, as, at that time, the whole of the unpatented lands of Canada were in their possession in as full and ample a manner as the 57,000 square miles of the territory in dispute can be said to be in possession of the 26,000 Indians who roam over it.

Now, when did the Sovereign of Great Britain ever divest himself of the ownership of these lands to vest it in the Indians? When did the title pass from the Sovereign to the Indians?. . .The appellants. . .contend that such was the effect of the royal proclamation. . . .

Now, as I read these clauses, they. . .far from supporting the appellants' case, are entirely adverse to them. . . .It is to crown lands, to lands owned by the crown but occupied by the Indians, that the proclamation refers. The words *"for the present". . .are equivalent to a reservation by the king of his right, thereafter or at any time, to grant these lands when he would think it proper to do so.* He reserves for the present for the use of the Indians all the lands in Canada outside the limits of the Province of Quebec as then constituted. Is that, in law, granting to these Indians a full title to the soil, a title to these lands? Did the sovereign thereby divest himself of the ownership of this territory? I cannot adopt that conclusion, *nor can I see anything in that proclamation that gives the Indians forever the right in law to the possession of any lands as against the crown. Their occupancy under that document has been one by sufferance alone.* Their possession has been, in law, the possession of the crown. At any time before confederation the crown could have granted these lands, or any of them, by letters patent, and the grant would have transferred to the grantee the *plenum et utile dominium,* with the right to maintain trespass, without entry, against the Indians. A grant of land by the crown is tantamount to conveyance with livery of seisin. *This proclamation of 1763 has not,* consequently,. . .*created a legal Indian title. . . .*

It was further argued for the appellants that the principles which have always guided the crown since the cession in its dealings with the Indians amount to a recognition of their title to a beneficiary interest in the soil. There is. . .no foundation for this contention. For obvious political reasons, and motives of humanity and benevolence, it has, no doubt, been the general policy of the crown, as it had been at the times of the French authorities, to respect the claims of the Indians. But this, though it undoubtedly gives them a title to the favourable consideration of the Government, does not give them any title in law, any title that a court of justice can recognize as against the crown. . . .

The necessary deduction from such a doctrine [put forward by the appellants] would be, that all progress of civilization and development in this country is and always has been at the mercy of the Indian race. Some of the writers cited by the appellants, influenced by sentimental and philanthropic considerations do not hesitate to go so far. But legal and constitutional principles are in direct antagonism with their theories. The Indians must in the future, every one concedes it, be treated with the same consideration for their just claims and demands that they have received in the past, but, as in the past, *it will not be because of any legal obligation* to do so, *but as a sacred political obligation, in the execution of which the state must be free from judicial control.* . . .

Taschereau J. clearly recognised that Great Britain succeeded to all the rights of France, and, since he denied that France had recognised any aboriginal rights in the land, he pointed out that, regardless of the English land law principle that the crown owns the land, there could be no recognition of aboriginal rights by Great Britain. He conceded that, in practice, the crown might in fact have recognised certain Indian rights in the land, but there was nothing more than a moral acknowledgement of such rights, and certainly nothing that could be construed as legal recognition thereof.

Gwynne J., who described the Proclamation as "the Indian Bill of Rights,"[226] was the member of the Supreme Court who went furthest in recognising an Indian right in the lands, going so far as to hold that the English and the French attitudes towards the Indians differed:[227]

. . .It may be admitted that the Kings of France recognized no title in the Indians in any part of the territory in the possession of the Kings of France, whose mode of dealing with the Indians was to make, *ex gratia,* crown grants of land for their conversion, instruction, and subsistence, but the fact that the Kings of France so dealt with the Indians presented no obstacle to the Sovereign of Great Britain, upon acquiring the French title, placing the Indians upon a more just and equitable footing, and recognizing their having a certain title, estate and interest in the lands so acquired by the Crown of Great Britain; and in point of fact this proclamation, ever since its issue, has been faithfully observed in its integrity. . . in all. . .the British possessions in North America. . . .

Gwynne J. referred to a number of grants, patents and treaties with the Indians, pointing out that in some of the latter the Indians expressly reserved some of their rights or certain tracts of land and that these reservations were recognised by the Crown.

After the most explicit recognition by the crown of the Indian title for upwards of a century in the most solemn manner—by treaties entered into between the crown and the Indian nations in council assembled according to their national custom, and by deeds of cession to the crown and of purchase by the crown, prepared by officers of the crown for execution by the Indians—it cannot, in my opinion, admit of a doubt that at the time of the passing of the British North America Act Indians in Upper Canada were acknowledged by the crown to have, and that they had, an estate, title and interest in all lands in that part of the Province of Canada formerly constituting Upper Canada for the cession of which to the crown no agreement had been made with the nations or tribes occupying the same as their hunting grounds, or claiming title thereto, which estate, title and interest could be divested or extinguished in no other manner than by cession made in the most solemn manner to the crown. . . .It is the lands *not ceded to or purchased by* the crown which are spoken of in the proclamation of 1763 as the *lands reserved to* the Indians for their hunting grounds. . . .

When the Indians in the deeds or treaties by way of cession of land to the crown reserved from out of the lands given in the instruments of cession. . .certain particularly described portions of the lands so generally described, for the special uses, occupation or residence of particular bands, the parts so reserved did not come under the operation of the deed or treaty of cession, but were reserved and excepted out of it and so continued to be just as they were before, lands not ceded to, or purchased by, the crown and therefore remained still within the designation of "Lands reserved for the Indians," or "Indian Reserves.". . .

. . .[T]he Indians had an estate, title, and interest in the tract as their hunting ground, declared and acknowledged in the most solemn manner by all the sovereigns of Great Britain since the Proclamation of 1763, which precluded the Provincial Government from interfering therewith in any manner, and which title, estate, and interest could only be divested and extinguished by a cession made in solemn manner by the Indians to Her Majesty. . . .

If Gwynne J. was right in arguing that the King of Great Britain was able to and did place the Indians in a better legal position than had been the case under his predecessors, he must of course have recognised that what the King so gave or did, he could equally, by proper process of law, take away or undo. Moreover, his contention regarding the rights of Indians under the Proclamation are still only relevant as between the Indians and the settlers, for the crown has reserved a superior right to forbid any transfer from the Indians to such persons. The limit of the Indian control over their "estate, title or interest" is, in fact, recognised by Gwynne J. when he concedes this restriction on their freedom to alienate and acknowledges that conveyance may only be made to the Crown.

When the issue reached the Judicial Committee of the Privy Council, that body agreed with the majority of the Supreme Court that under the Proclamation the Indians had no more than a usufructuary right in their lands, thus rejecting the view taken by Gwynne J. Delivering the opinion, Lord Watson stated:[228]

. . .The territory in question has been in Indian occupation from the date of the proclamation until 1873 [the date of the North West Angle Treaty]. During that interval. . .the policy of [the] administrations has been all along the same in this respect, that the Indian inhabitants have been precluded from entering into any transaction with a subject for the sale or transfer of their interest in the land, and have only been permitted to surrender their rights to the Crown by a formal contract. . . .[T]here has been no change since the year 1763 in the character of the interest which its Indian inhabitants had in the lands surrendered by the treaty. *Their possession, such as it was, can only be ascribed to the general provisions made by the royal proclamation in favour of all Indian tribes then living under the sovereignty and protection of the British Crown.* . . .[T]he terms of the instrument. . . .shew that *the tenure of the Indians was a personal and usufructuary right, dependent upon the goodwill of the Sovereign.* The lands reserved are expressly stated to be "parts of our dominions and territories;" and it is declared to be the will and pleasure of the sovereign that, "for the present," they shall be reserved for the use of the Indians, as their hunting grounds, under his protection and dominion. . . . *[T]here has been all along vested in the Crown a substantial and paramount estate, underlying the Indian title, which became a plenum estate, whenever that title was surrendered or otherwise extinguished.* . . .

The Privy Council declined to consider the exact nature of the interest actually held by the Indians in the land, considering it sufficient to point out that their right was purely that of a usufructuary, with the absolute title vested in the Crown.

All that remains to point out in so far as the attitude of Canadian judicial decisions to the Royal Proclamation is the judgment in *R.* v. *White and Bob*[229] in which Norris J.A. reviewed Marshall C.J.'s decision in *Johnson* v. *McIntosh,* and found it "entirely consistent with the opinion of the Privy Council in *St. Catherine's*" case, and concluded that the Proclamation was "declaratory and confirmatory" of Indian rights, and "was made on the basis of a claim to dominion and its protective provisions became applicable in fact to Indians as their lands came under the de facto dominion of representatives of the British Crown." Since these two decisions were to the effect that the Crown held the absolute title, while the Indians enjoyed no more than a usufructuary right, it becomes clear that as recently as 1965 the Canadian judicial approach to the question of Indian rights under the Proclamation, whatever idealistic or moral language in which the view was expressed, acknowledged that Indian rights under the Proclamation certainly did not amount to rights of sovereignty, and were dependent upon the attitude adopted towards them by the crown. This point was reiterated by Gould J. in *Calder* v. *Att. Gen., British Columbia*[230] when he pointed out that the view of the United States Supreme Court in *Tee-Hit-Ton Indians* v. *U.S.*[231] that the power of Congress is supreme and can extinguish Indian title "is equally applicable in English law in the form of the supreme power of the crown." The fact that the Indians have at present no rights against the English Crown under the Proclamation or the "treaties" has recently been confirmed by the English Court of Appeal, holding that any rights thereunder are held against Canada, and are subject to interpretation by the Canadian courts.[232]

> [T]he obligations under the proclamation and the Treaties are obligations of the Crown in respect of Canada. . .[F]or the Indian peoples to bring an action. . .to enforce these obligations. . .is in the courts of Canada. . . .[A]lthough the relevant agreements with the Indian peoples are known as "treaties", they are not treaties in the sense of international law. They were not treaties between sovereign states. . .[T]he cession of land by the Indians, in exchange for which the Crown granted certain rights and privileges, was to the government of the Dominion of Canada for Her Majesty the Queen. Next, when the Crown agreed to lay aside reserves for the Indians, they were to be administered and dealt with for them by Her Majesty's Government of the Dominion of Canada. . . .[A]ny treaty or other obligations still owed by the Crown to the Indian peoples of Canada are owed by the crown in the right of the Dominion of Canada. . . .If such obligations still exist. . .their extent is. . .a matter for the courts of Canada.

There is no need to consider here any later judicial decisions or comment relating to Indian land claims since, to a great extent, they stem from the newly developed concept of aboriginal rights[233] now embodied in the Charter of Rights and Freedoms.[234] However, there is as yet no clear definition of what is meant by "aboriginal rights," and it is debatable whether the courts, or the federal or provincial governments would accept any argument to the effect that such rights entail dissolution of the rights of the crown or Canadian sovereignty over the whole of the territory of Canada, including any land to which aboriginal title might be acknowledged as existing.

Conclusion

It is of course true that the decisions of both the United States and the Canadian courts were delivered in the light of their own understanding of the law and of crown prerogatives. However, these views reflect the ideas of the legal systems that were prevailing at the time they were rendered and are in direct descent from those held when the North American continent was "discovered" and settled by Europeans. The international law concerning title to territory was evolved by the European countries and has been accepted by all countries in the world, including those which were formerly held under colonial rule and title to which was acquired in much the same way as was the case in North America. Evidence of this is to be found in the manner in which the countries of South America and the members of the Organization of African Unity hold firmly to the boundaries that were established by their former colonial rulers, on the basis of European views of international law. Analysis of the practice of the explorers, of the rulers who commissioned them, of the treaties made between those rulers, of the administrations appointed by those rulers, both in their everyday practices and in the so-called treaties signed with the Indians; as well as the decisions of the courts called upon to deal with Indian rights, especially as alleged to exist under the Proclamation of 1763 and by way of conquest either of the Indians or the former French sovereign, all confirm that whatever title the Indians were acknowledged as having in the land, they certainly did not and do not possess anything similar to sovereignty. Their title is solely that which is acknowledged as remaining with them by the Crown; it amounts to no more than a right to live on and enjoy the use of such lands as have not been granted to settlers or taken into the complete exercise of jurisdiction by the Crown; and this Indian title is subject to the overriding sovereign rights of the Crown as ultimate owner who may, subject to such legal procedures as may be required by the local law, extinguish whatever title remains to the Indians.

Insofar as international law is concerned, there can be no doubt that the title to the land belonged, in the first instance, to the country of those who first discovered and settled thereon. Subsequently, the title thereto passed to the state which defeated the first sovereign in battle or acquired the territory from the latter by treaty. Insofar as settlement itself was concerned, international law has never required that every inch of the land claimed needs to be occupied, in the sense of someone being actually present thereon. It was sufficient that the ruler claiming sovereignty was able to prevent any other ruler from contesting his title. Moreover, international law did not recognise the aboriginal inhabitants of such newly discovered territories as having any legal rights that were good as against those who "discovered" and settled in their territories. From the point of view of international law, such inhabitants became the subjects of the ruler exercising sovereignty over the territory. As such, they enjoyed no rights that international law would recognise, nor was international law concerned with the rights which they might enjoy or which they might claim under the national law of their ruler. In addition, although international law is a developing process, subject to change, particularly in the light of developing ideas as to the rights of man and of peoples, it has never been conceded by international law, or for that matter by national law, that newly developed legal concepts are retroactive so as to destroy rights which had been established, however improperly *ab initio*, before such new ideas became current and acceptable. In order to ascertain whether or not a legal title to land exists, it is well established by both doctrine and practice that this issue must be tested in accordance with the law as it existed at the time that the title was alleged to have accrued, and not in accordance with the law as it is alleged to exist at the time when the title is challenged. This is especially so when the title in question has existed over a lengthy period of time for the law looks to stability and order, even though this may not always accord with current views of morality or the legal principles that may have evolved, particularly when these principles are still controversial and of such recent enunciation that it may well be questioned whether they in fact exist. Even when it may be possible to argue that international law in, for example, the sphere of individual and group rights, has by way of treaty come to accept certain rights which were not known at the time of the discoveries, these rights cannot be put forward to destroy rights which are well-established and recognised. While the right of an individual to some protection against his own state may have evolved and may operate to protect every individual within that state; and while group rights may equally have hardened to an extent that no group may be discriminated against within the state; this is not to say that the rights thus introduced are of so intrinsic a character that they may be regarded as overriding rights of states which are clearly recognised by international law. The fact that such group rights may constitute the basis for upholding a plea for self-determination[235] as against an alien ruler, this only applies, to the extent that it applies at all, in a case where the alien ruler represents a minority denying rights to a local majority.[236] It is not even possible to argue that recognition of the political or other rights of the minority are sufficient to give that minority even the rights of local self-government, beyond those that the national government is prepared to concede. To go further would be to threaten the security and integrity of the state, which would be contrary to principles of customary international law as well as specific provisions of the Charter of the United Nations.

Abbreviations

A.C.	Appeal Cases (Great Britain) 1891–
All E.R.	All England Reports (Great Britain) 1935–
App. Cas.	Appeal Cases (Great Britain) 1875–90
Brit. Y.B. Int'l Law	British Yearbook of International Law
C.T.S.	Consolidated Treaty Series
D.L.R.	Dominion Law Reports (Canada) 1912–
I.L.M.	International Legal Materials, 1962–
I.C.J. Rep.	International Court of Justice Reports 1947–
Int'l Arb.	Moore's International Arbitrations, 1898
P.C.I.J.	Permanent Court of International Justice
Pet.	Peters' United States Supreme Court Reports 1828–42
R.S.C.	Revised Statutes of Canada
S.C.R.	Supreme Court Reports (Canada) 1876–
St. Tr.	State Trials (Great Britain) 1163–1820
U.N. Rep. Int'l Arb. Awards	United Nations, Reports of International Arbitral Awards, 1948–
U.S.	United States Supreme Court Reports, 1875–
W.W.R.	Western Weekly Reports (Canada)
Wall.	Wallace's United States Supreme Court Reports 1865–76
Wheat.	Wheaton's United States Supreme Court Reports 1816–27

Notes

1. See, e.g., *Island of Palmas Case* (1928) 2 U.N. Int'l Arb. Awards, p. 831, at p. 845: "As regards the question which of different legal systems prevailing at successive periods is to be applied in a particular case (the so-called inter-temporal law), a distinction must be made between the creation of rights and the existence of rights. The same principle which subjects the act crea-tive of a right to the law in force at the time the right arises, demands that the existence of the right, in other words, its continued manifestation, shall follow the conditions required by the evolution of law." See, also, Ad-visory Opinion of International Court of Justice on *Western Sahara* 1975 I.C.J.Rep. 12, at pp. 27, 38.
2. F.G. Davenport, *European Treaties Bearing on the History of the United States and Its Dependencies,* 4 vols. (Washington: Carnegie Endowment for Inter-national Peace, 1917), p. 75; Latin text, p. 72 (a number of earlier and later Bulls to the same general effect are reproduced in this volume).
3. Ibid., p. 93, confirmed by Treaty of Madrid, 1495, ibid., p. 104.
4. Ibid., p. 110.
5. The Bull *Romanus Pontifex,* 8 January 1455, ibid., p. 20.
6. P. Fauchille, *Traité de Droit International Public,* Vol. I, Part II (Paris: Librai-rie Arthur Rousseau, 1925), p. 687; for Queen Elizabeth's attitude, see her letter to the Spanish Ambassador, Mendoza, note 20 below.
7. Spotorno, *Memorials of Columbus* (1823), p. lvi.
8. C. Columbus, *Four Voyages to the New World,* tr. and ed. R.H. Major (Lon-don: Hakluyt Society Publications, 1847; New York: Corinth reprint, 1961), pp. 142-43 (Third Voyage); p. 22 (Second Voyage); p. 12 (First Voy-age); pp. 195, 201 (Fourth Voyage).
9. Biblioteca de Autores Españoles, *Obras de Fernández de Navarrette,* Vol. 2 (1955): III *Colección de los Viajes y Descubrimientos,* 60, no. X (the English translation is from J. Goebel, *The Struggle for the Falkland Islands* (New Haven: Yale University Press, 1927), p. 91, who cites a different edition of Navarrette).
10. *The Voyages of Jacques Cartier,* tr. H.P. Biggar (Ottawa: Publications of Public Archives of Canada, no. 11 1924), pp. 64-66, 225. It should be noted that the translation uses the term "Indian" which nowhere appears in the original French manuscript.
11. Ibid., pp. 85, 89.
12. Ibid., pp. 251, 249 respectively.
13. *The Works of Samuel de Champlain,* ed. H.P. Biggar, Vol. 2 (Toronto: Champlain Society Publications, 1925), pp. 272, 297.
14. Ibid., Vol. 4, p. 157. For an analysis of the meaning of the word "savage" see O.P. Dickason, *The Myth of the Savage and the Beginnings of French Colo-nialism in the Americas,* especially ch. III (Ph.D. thesis, University of Ot-tawa, 1977).
15. E.g., *Works of Samuel de Champlain,* note 12 above, Vol. 4, pp. 108, 165.

16. E.g., ibid., pp. 51 *et seqq.*

17. 18 December 1497, J.H. Williamson, *The Voyages of the Cabots* (London: 1929), p. 30. (Italian original in H.P. Biggar, *Precursors of Cartier 1497-1534,* (Ottawa: Publications of the Archives of Canada no. 5, 1911), p. 17.

18. Pasqualigo letter, 23 August 1497, Williamson, *The Voyages of the Cabots,* p. 29.

19. Samuel Purchas, *Hakluytus Posthumus or Purchas His Pilgrimes,* Vol. 2 (1905), p. 129 (c. A.S. Keller and Others, *Creation of Rights of Sovereignty Through Symbolic Acts 1400-1800* (New York: AMS Press, 1967), p. 57).

20. William Camden, *Annales Rerum Anglicae,* Vol. 2 (1717), pp. 359-60.

21. See note 6.

22. W.S.W. Vaux, ed., *The World Encompassed by Sir Francis Drake* (London: Hakluyt Society Publications, 1854), p. 75.

23. Ibid., p. 82.

24. Richard Hakluyt, *The Principal Navigations, Voyages, Traffiques and Discoveries of the English Nation,* Vol. 3 (Glasgow: James MacLehose, 1903), p. 32.

25. Ibid., Vol. 7, p. 326.

26. Ibid., Vol. 8, pp. 53-54.

27. C.C.A. Gosch, ed., *Danish Arctic Exploration 1605-1620* (London: Hakluyt Society Publications, 1894), p. 10.

28. See *Eastern Greenland* case, P.C.I.J., 1933, M.O. Hudson, *World Court Reports,* Vol. 3 (Washington: Carnegie Endowment for International Peace, 1938), p. 151, 155.

29. B.F. French, ed. *Historical Collections of Louisiana and Florida* (New York: 1869), p. 167.

30. F. Parkman, *La Salle and the Discovery of the Great West,* Vol. 1 (Boston: 1897), p. 53.

31. Quoted, S.P. Hildreth, *Pioneer History* (Cincinnatti: 1849), p. 24.

32. 1697, 1713, 1748 F.L. Israel, *Major Peace Treaties of Modern History, 1648-1967,* Vol. 1 (New York: 1967, pp. 145, 223, 269, resp.).

33. W. Coxe, *Account of the Russian Discoveries between Asia and America* (London: 1804), pp. 1-2.

34. Ibid., pp. 33-36.

35. Keller, *Creation of Rights of Sovereignty,* p. 144.

36. Coxe, *Account of the Russian Discoveries,* pp. 302-3, 330-39.

37. E.g., *Works of Samuel de Champlain,* Vol. 1, pp. 272, 295; Vol. 2, p. 196; etc., and see text to note 13.

38. M. Lescarbot, *History of New France,* tr. and ann. W.L. Grant (Champlain Society Publication of 1618 edition), Vol. 1 (Toronto: 1907), p. 17.

39. O.P. Dickason, *The Myth of the Savage,* p. 215.

40. Francisco López de Gómara, *Histoire generalle des Indes occidentales et Terres neuves qui jusques à present ont esté descouvevte,* tr. M. Fumée (Paris: Michel Sonnius, 1569), p. 233 (c. ibid.)

41. L. Hanke, "Pope Paul III and the American Indians," *Harvard Theological Review* 30 (1937), pp. 65, 72.

42. D. Alden, "Black Robes Versus White Settlers," in H. Peckham and C. Gibson, eds., *Attitudes of Colonial Powers Toward the American Indian* (Salt Lake City: University of Utah Press, 1969), p. 30.

43. C. Horton, "The Relations Between the Indians and the Whites in Colonial Virginia," (M.A. thesis, University of Chicago, 1921), p. 20 (c. Dickason, *The Myth of the Savage*, p. 224).

44. 20 May 1493, *Obras de Fernandez de Navarrette*, Vol. 2, p. 284.

45. 5 March 1496, R. Hakluyt, *Voyages Touching the Discovery of America* (1582) (London: Hakluyt Society Publications, 1850), pp. 21-22 [italics added]. (See also Biggar, *Precursors of Cartier*, p. 9.)

46. 18 December 1497, Biggar, *Precursors of Cartier*, p. 19.

47. 12 May 1500, ibid., p. 35 [italics added].

48. 19 March 1501, ibid., pp. 50 *et seqq.* [italics added].

49. In the patent of 9 December 1502 to Hugh Elyot and others, the formula is different in that the patentees may "in no wise occupy themselves with nor enter the lands, countries, regions or provinces of heathens or infidels first discovered by the subjects of our very dear brother and cousin the King of Portugal, or by the subjects of any other princes soever, our friends and confederates, and in possession of which these same princes now find themselves" (ibid., p. 82).

50. See, e.g., *Calvin's Case* (1608) 2 St. Tr. 559, and in modern times *Joyce* v. *Director of Public Prosecutions* [1946] A.C. 347.

51. Duties payable by those claiming to exercise the elective franchise within certain cities and boroughs, before becoming entitled to vote.

52. Biggar, *Precursors of Cartier*, p. 114.

53. 27 March, ibid., pp. 148, 151-52.

54. See text to notes 9-12 and "The True and Last Discouerie of Florida," made by Capt. Jean Ribault in 1562. Hakluyt, *The Principal Navigations*, p. 91, at 103, 113.

55. 17 October 1540, H.P. Biggar, ed., *A Collection of Documents Relating to Jacques Cartier and the Sieur de Roberval*, (Ottawa: Public Archives of Canada, no. 14, 1930), p. 128.

56. 11-13 November 1540, ibid., p. 140.

57. Treaty of Nice.

58. 15 January 1540, *Collection de Manuscrits relatifs à la Nouvelle-France*, Vol. 1 (Québec: Archives de Québec, 1883), pp. 30, 32-33.

59. W.L. Grant, *Voyages of Samuel de Champlain 1604-1618* (1907), p. 122 [italics added].

60. *Works of Samuel de Champlain*, Vol. 3, pp. 251-52, 258-60 [italics in original].

61. Ibid., Vol. 2, pp. 326-27, 329.

62. Ibid., p. 339.

63. 15 October 1612, ibid., Vol. 4, pp. 209-14 [italics added].
64. See, e.g., ibid., Vol. 1, pp. 295-96.
65. Ibid., Vol. 4, pp. 9-11.
66. Reference to this grant is to be found, ibid., Vol. 1, p. 279.
67. W.I. Morse, ed., *Pierre Du Gua, Sieur de Monts. Records: Colonial and "Saintongeois."* (London: Bernard Quarich, 1939), p. 4.
68. *Works of Samuel de Champlain*, Vol. 3.
69. Ibid., p. 236.
70. Ibid., Vol. 2, pp. 218-20.
71. Davenport, *European Treaties*, p. 203; the background is summarised at pp. 199-201. See also Anglo-Dutch treaty, Westminster, 1598, ibid., p. 241.
72. Ibid., p. 217.
73. Ibid., p. 220, note 9, letter of Spanish plenipotentiary at Cateau-Cambrésis to King Philip, 13 May 1559. See also extract from c. 1565 letter in Spanish by member of Council of the Indies, same note at p. 221.
74. Ibid., p. 20.
75. Ibid., p. 75; see note 2.
76. See Spanish letter cited at note 73.
77. Davenport, *European Treaties*, p. 225.
78. Ibid., p. 247, note 4.
79. Ibid.
80. See note 41 above; and Brion, *Bartholomé De Las Casas: Père des Indiens* (1927).
81. Francisco de Vitoria, *De Indis Noviter Inventis* (1532), English translation of 1696 text by J.P. Bate (Washington: Carnegie Classics, 1934). Quotations are cited from the Carnegie Classics 1917 edition of Vitoria's *De Indis et de Jure Belli Relectiones*.
82. Ibid., sect. II, 4-7 (pp. 136-37).
83. Ibid., sect. I, 1 (p. 116).
84. Ibid., sect. I, 19, 24 (pp. 125, 128).
85. Ibid., sect. II, 7 (p. 139).
86. Ibid., sect. II, 8, 11 (pp. 141, 143).
87. Ibid., sect. II, 13-15 (pp. 144-45).
88. Ibid., sect. II, 16 (p. 147).
89. Ibid., (p. 148).
90. Ibid., sect. III (151-62).
91. For contemporary comment, see D. Erasmus, *Dulce bellum inexpertis*, 1515, *sub-nom Bellum*, (Eng. tr. (Barre, Mass: Imprint Society, 1972), p. 17); see, also, L.C. Green, *Essays on the Modern Law of War* (Dobbs Ferry, N.Y.: Transnational, 1985), p. 155.
92. See comments of International Court of Justice in *Western Sahara* case, note 1, pp. 41-42.
93. Vitoria, *De Jure Belli Hispanorum in Barbaros,* opening sentence (p. 165).
94. Ibid., paragraphs 10-12 (p. 170); see also Balthazar Ayala, *De Jure et Officiis Bellicis et Disciplina Militari* (1582), tr. John Pawley Bate, Lib. I, Cap. II, ss. 28, 29 (Washington: Carnegie Classics, 1912), pp. 20-21.

95. Pierino Belli, *De Re Militari et Bello Tractatus* (1563), part II, ch. XII, 5; tr. Herbert C. Nutting (Washington: Carnegie Classics, 1936), p. 85.

96. Alberico Gentili, *De Jure Belli* (1612), bk. I, ch. XIX; tr. John C. Rolfe (Washington: Carnegie Classics, 1933), p. 89.

97. Ibid., ch. VII (p. 34).

98. Ibid., ch. XXV (p, 122, 126).

99. Ibid., ch. XVII (pp. 80–81).

100. Bk. II, ch. V, X, XI (pp. 307, 338, 341).

101. See text to notes 139, 140.

102. Ibid., ch. XVII (pp. 381).

103. Francisco Suárez, *De Triplici Virtute Theologica* (1621), disp. XVIII, s. II; *(Selections From Three Works,* tr. G.L. Williams and Others (Washington: Carnegie Classics, 1944), pp. 746–47, 748–49.

104. Ibid., pp. 756.

105. Ibid., s. III (pp. 757–58, 760, 763–66).

106. Ibid., s. IV (p. 770); see also, text to note 90.

107. Suárez, *De Triplici Virtute,* disp. XIII, s. IV (pp. 816–17).

108. Ibid., s. V (pp. 826–27).

109. Ibid., s. VII (pp. 841, 850)

110. Hugo Grotius, *De Jure Belli ac Pacis* (1625), bk. I, ch. I, s. II; English translation (London: 1738), p. 131; tr. Francis W. Kelsey (Washington: Carnegie Classics, 1925) p. 172.

111. Ibid., bk. II, ch. IV, ss. V–VII (pp. 176–77; 222–24).

112. Ibid., s. XI (pp. 181; 227), citing *Digest,* Lib. L. Tit. XVII [italics in original].

113. Ibid., ch. XX, s. XL (pp. 437; 505); see also Richard Zouche, *Juris et Judicii Fecialis* (1650), Part II, s. VII; tr. J.L. Brierly (Washington: Carnegie Classics, 1911), p. 116.

114. Grotius, *De Jure Belli,* bk. II, ch. XX, s. XL (pp. 438; 506).

115. Ibid., s. XLIV, XLVI (pp. 440, 444, 445; 508, 513, 514).

116. Ibid., s. XLVIII, XLIX (pp. 447, 448–49; 516, 517–18).

117. Ibid., ch. XXII, s. X (pp. 478; 550).

118. Ibid., ch. XXIII, s. II (pp. 484; 558).

119. *Il Principe,* 1532, ch. 18.

120. Grotius, *De Jure Belli,* bk. II, ch. XXV, s. VII (pp. 505; 584); see also Zouche, *Juris et Judicii Fecialis,* part II, s. VII.

121. Ibid.

122. Grotius, *De Jure Belli,* bk. III, ch. VI, ss. I, IV, XI (pp. 580, 583, 587; 664, 667, 672).

123. Ibid., ch. VIII, ss. I, IV (pp. 608–9, 610–11; 697, 699–700).

124. Ibid., ch. XVI, ss. IV, V (pp. 697; 781–82).

125. Johann Wolfgang Textor, *Synopsis Juris Gentium* (1680), ch. I; tr. John Pawley Bate (Washington: Carnegie Classics, 1916), pp. 6–7.

126. 1 *Consolidated Treaty Series,* p. 68.

127. 11 *Consolidated Treaty Series,* 395, arts. VII, VIII, XV.

128. 28 Ibid., 325, art. VIII.

129. 27 Ibid., 477, art XIII.

130. Samuel Pufendorf, *De Jure Naturae et Gentium* (1688), ch. III; tr. C.H. and W.A. Oldfather (Washington: Carnegie Classics 1934), pp. 364-65.

131. Ibid. See also Zouche, *Juris et Judicii Fecialis,* part II, s. V (p. 110): "If any part of the territory of another people is deserted, it may be occupied by strangers; since what is not cultivated is not deemed to be occupied by others."

132. Pufendorf, *De Jure Naturae et Gentium,* bk. IV, ch. VI (p. 577).

133. Ibid., ch. XII (pp. 646, 651-52, 655-56); see also Grotius, note 112 above.

134. Ibid., bk. VIII, ch. VI (p. 1310).

135. Ibid., bk. VI, ch. VII (pp. 1086-87).

136. The wishes of the Indian princes or of the rulers of African protectorates counted for little when the Crown granted independence.

137. Cornelius van Bynkershoek, *Quaestionum Juris Publici* (1737), bk. I, ch. II; tr. Tanney Frank (Washington: Carnegie Classics, 1930), p. 25.

138. Ibid., ch. VI (pp. 44-45).

139. Textor, *Synopsis Juris Gentium,* ch. VIII, c. Dig. 42, 2, 1, 1 (p. 66); see also Pufendorf, *De Jure Naturae et Gentium,* bk. IV, ch. IX (p. 609).

140. (1928) 2 U.N. Rep. Int'l. Arb. Awards, 831, 840. See also Indiv. Op. of Judge Basdevant in *Minquiers and Ecrehos* case I.C.J. Rep. 1953, 47, 48, *re* places "which are uninhabited and most of which are uninhabitable."

141. F. de Vitoria, *De Indis,* s. I, 23 (pp. 127-28), see, also, *Western Sahara* opinion, note 1, pp. 41-42.

142. Christian Wolff, *Jus Gentium Methodo Scientifico* (1764), ch. I, ss. 29, 35, 52-55; tr. Joseph H. Drake (Washington: Carnegie Classics, 1934), pp. 20-21, 24, 43-46.

143. Ibid., ch. II, ss. 168-69 (p. 89).

144. Ibid., s. 166 (p. 88).

145. Ibid., s. 180 (p. 94) [italics added].

146. Ibid., ch. I, ss. 80, 84, 85 (pp. 47, 49, 50) [italics added].

147. See, e.g., note 13 above.

148. Ibid., ch. II, ss. 259-62 (pp. 133-35); see also ch. III, s. 297 (p. 150), and Emer de Vattel, *Le Droit des Gens ou Principes de la Loi Naturelle* (1758) bk. II, ch. IV, s. 60; tr. Charles G. Fenwick (Washington: Carnegie Classics, 1916), p. 133.

149. Wolff, *Jus Gentium Methodo Scientifico,* s. 258 (p. 132).

150. Ibid., ch. III, ss, 275-76, 279, 291-92 (pp. 140-41, 152, 147-48).

151. Ibid., s. 309 (pp. 156-57) [italics added].

152. Ibid., ch. VI, ss. 633-35 (pp. 324-25).

153. Ibid., ch. VII, ss. 787-88 (pp. 406-8).

154. Ibid., ss. 869-70, 873 (pp. 446-47, 448).

155. Ibid., ss. 888, 892 (pp. 454-55, 456-57).

156. Vattel, *Le Droit des Gens ou Principes de la Loi Naturelle* (1758), Intro., ss. 1, 3 (see n. 148).

157. Ibid., bk. I, ch. VIII, s. 81; ch. XVIII, ss. 207-10 (pp. 37-38; 84-86).

158. This touches upon the disputes between Canada's Indians and those who oppose their unrestricted 'treaty' right to hunt.
159. See, e.g., notes 6 and 20 above.
160. Vattel, *Le Droit des Gens,* bk. II, ch. I, s. 7 (pp. 115-16).
161. Ibid., ch. IV, s. 61 (pp. 133-34).
162. Ibid., ch. VII, s. 87 (p. 140).
163. Ibid., s. 97 (p. 143).
164. R.S.C. 1970, app. II, no. 1.
165. Vattel, *Le Droit des Gens,* ch. IX, s. 149-50 (p. 159).
166. See, for contention that 'good faith' is a fundamental principle of international law, G. Schwarzenberger, "The Fundamental Principles of International Law," *Hague Recueil* 87 (1955), pp. 290-326.
167. Vattel, bk. III, ch. XII, ss. 190, 192; ch. XIII, s. 195 (pp. 305-6, 307) [italics in original].
168. See Schwarzenberger, "Fundamental Principles," pp. 209-10.
169. G.F. von Martens, *A Compendium of the Law of Nations,* tr. Wm. Cobbett (London: Cobbett and Morgan, 1802), pp. 4, 47-48 [italics in original].
170. Henry Wheaton, *Elements of International Law,* R.H. Dana edition (Boston: Little, Brown, 1866), ss. 165-66 [italics added].
171. Ibid., s. 38.
172. Ibid., note 24 [italics added].
173. (1828) 8 Wheat. 543, 572-73, 579, 587.
174. Secretary of State Upshur to Everett, U.S. Minister to England, 9 October 1843, Mss. Instr. G.B., c.F. Wharton, *International Law Digest,* Vol. 1 (Washington: Government Printing House 1886), p. 5 [italics in original]. See, also, note 1.
175. Secretary of State Calhoun to Pakenham, British Minister, 3 September 1844, Mss. Notes G.B., ibid., pp. 6-7; see also, notes 101, 139, 140.
176. Israel, *Major Peace Treaties,* vol. 1, p. 305.
177. (1926) 6 U.N., Rep. Int'l. Arb. Awards, 173, 176-77, 179.
178. *Cherokee Nation* v. *Georgia* (1831) 5 Pet. 1, 17.
179. *Holden* v. *Joy* (1872) 17 Wall. 211, 242.
180. *Johnson* v. *McIntosh,* (1828) 8 Wheat. 543, 578.
181. See L.C. Green, "North America's Indians and the Trusteeship Concept," *Anglo-American Law Review* 4 (1975), p. 137.
182. *Legal Status of Eastern Greenland* (1933) P.C.I.J. (3 Hudson, *World Court Reports,* pp. 151, 154, 155, 156, 157, 158, 159, 161, 164, 165, 166, 170-72.) [Italics added.]
183. Land belonging to no one and, therefore, open to the sovereignty of any state occupying it.
184. *Island of Palmas* case (1928); 2 U.N., Rep. Int'l. Arb. Awards, 831.
185. *Eastern Greenland,* (Hudson, pp. 173-75).
186. (1928) 2 U.N., Rep. Int'l. Arb. Awards, 831, 839, 840, 845-46, 855 [italics added].
187. An inchoate title is one which is incomplete or partial, needing something further to make it legally final.

188. *Palmas Case,* pp. 856, 857, 858-59, 863-64, 867, 868.

189. This should be compared with the similar agreements made by the British East India Co. with Indian princes and Malayan sultans, see, e.g., *Salaman v. Sec. of State in Council for India* [1906] 1 K.B. 613; see, also, *Mighell v. Sultan of Johore* [1894] 1 Q.B. 149.

190. For judicial comment on the dual role of the East India Co. as merchants and a sovereign power, see *Gibson v. East India Co.* (1839) 5 Bingh. N.C. 273; *Ex-Rajah of Coorg v. East India Co.* (1860) 29 Beav. 300, 308-9. For a judgment concerning the activities of the British South Africa Co., see *In re Southern Rhodesia* [1919] A.C. 211.

191. For analysis of Canada's Indian treaties, see L.C. Green, "Legal Significance of Treaties affecting Canada's Indians," *Anglo-American Law Review* 1 (1972), p. 119.

192. See e.g., the cases reported in *British International Law Cases,* vol. 1, pp. 543-634.

193. See notes 189-92.

194. I.C.J. Rep. 1971 16.

195. I.C.J. Rep. 1975 4.

196. [1926] A.C. 518, 522, 528.

197. [1941] A.C. 308, 324, 327.

198. 89 Parry, *Consolidated Treaty Series,* p. 473.

199. See Sir Kenneth Roberts-Wray, *Commonwealth and Colonial Law* (London: Stevens, 1966), p. 102.

200. See, e.g., *Civilian War Claimants Association Ltd. v. The King* [1932] A.C. 14.

201. See, e.g. D.H.N. Johnson on *Parke, Davis & Co. v. Comptroller-General of Patents* [1954] A.C. 321, in 31 Brit. Y.B. Int'l Law (London: Oxford University Press, 1954) p. 467.

202. Assistant Secretary of State Castle to French Ambassador, 21 April 1928, Department of State file 851.502/25, c. 5, G.H. Hackworth, *Digest of International Law* (Washington: Government Printing House, 1962), pp. 167-68.

203. R.S.C. 1970, Appendices, p. 123, at 127.

204. See, e.g., *R. v. Kogogolak* [1959] 28 W.W.R. 376, 378 (*per* Sissons, J.)

205. 42 Parry, *Consolidated Treaty Series,* p. 279.

206. 1760, Art. 40, c. in *St. Catherine's Milling & Lumber Co. v. The Queen* (1887) 13 S.C.R. 577, 585.

207. 22 January 1844, c. ibid., 633.

208. (1828) 8 Wheat. 543, 572-74, 575, 576, 579-80, 581, 583, 586, 587-92, 594, 595-96, 603; 21 U.S. 240, 253-54, 256, 257-58, 259, 260-61, 262, 266 [italics added].

209. Paris, 1763 (Israel, *Major Peace Treaties,* vol. 1, p. 345), Art. I.

210. See, also, *Ex-Rajah of Coorg v. East India Co.,* note 190.

211. (1832) 6 Peters 515, 543-49; (31 U.S. 405, 426-30).

212. For an analysis of the legal character of these treaties, see Green, note 191.

213. See e.g., 6 Peters at 552-56 (31 U.S. 433-36).
214. (1887) 13 S.C.R. 577; Privy Council (1889) 14 App. Cas. 46.
215. At 599-601 [italics added].
216. 4th ed., S. 687.
217. North West Angle Treaty No. 3.
218. At 604, 608, 612-13, 614-16, 626 [italics added].
219. See L.C. Green, "Trusteeship and Canada's Indians," *Dalhousie Law Journal* *3* (1976), p. 104.
220. 12th ed., Vol. 3, pp. 349 *et seqq.*
221. Now the Constitution Acts, 1967-1982.
222. See Vienna Convention on the Law of Treaties, 1969, 8 I.L.M. p. 679, Art. 2, 1(a): ". . .'treaty' means an international agreement concluded between States in written form and governed by international law. . . ."
223. At 639, 640-41 [italics added].
224. At 644-49 [italics added].
225. Land held absolutely in one's own right, and not of any lord or superior to whom any duty is due in respect thereof.
226. At 652 and 674 [italics in original].
227. At 651-52, 663-65, 764-75.
228. 14 App. Cas. 46, 54-55 [italics added].
229. (1965) 50 D.L.R. (2d) 613, 636, 644 (affd. 52 D.L.R. [2d] 481).
230. (1969) 71 W.W.R. 81, 95 (affd. 74 W.W.R. 481).
231. (1955) 348 U.S. 272.
232. *R. v. Sec. of State for Foreign and Commonwealth Affairs: Exp. Indian Assn. of Alberta* [1982] 2 All E.R. 118, *per* Ld. Denning M.R. 129; Kerr, L.J. 131; May L.J. 160-62.
233. See, e.g., M. Asch, *Home and Native Land* (Toronto: Methuen, 1984).
234. Art. 35(i): "The existing aboriginal and treaty rights of the aboriginal peoples of Canada are hereby recognized and affirmed."
235. Speaking at the conference of La Francophonie, Quebec, 2 September 1987, Mr. Clark, Secretary for External Affairs, stated that in the view of Canada "self-determination" implied independent statehood.
236. See, e.g., International Covenant on the Rights of Indigenous Peoples, (adopted in principle by the Third General Assembly of the World Councel of Indigenous Peoples [an unofficial body lacking any legal status], May 1981,) Arts. 1-4, 1981, Asch, *Home and Native Land,* p. 133; U.N. Declaration on the Granting of Independence to Colonial Countries and Peoples, 1960, Gen. Ass. Res. 1540 (XV).

concepts of sovereignty at the time of first contacts

Etablissement des François à la
Nouvelle France.

Establecimiento de los Franceses
en la nueva Francia

OLIVE P. DICKASON

Detail from Clouet's *Carte d'Amerique,* 1782. Reprinted with permission from the Public Archives Canada, National Map Collection, NMC 11879.

Legitimacy of Power

The Ecclesiastical Aspect[1]

The spectacular expansion in the fifteenth and sixteenth centuries of Europe's geographical knowledge of the world, and of the world's relationship to the universe,[2] was crucial to the development of notions of political authority that would lead to the emergence of international law. Central to the process was the evolution of the concept of sovereignty, which took on unforeseen dimensions with the discovery of the New World.[3] As Europe wrestled with the issues involved in applying its political and social concepts to territories and peoples the existence of whom it had only recently learned, certain points became clear. For one, while there was no agreement about the extent to which Christians held priority over non-Christians in temporal as well as spiritual affairs of state, nevertheless a consensus developed, on secular and humanistic grounds, that New World peoples did not possess full sovereignty, either in the persons of their princes or in regard to their territory. Although European colonizing powers were committed in principle to the rule of law and the universal right of access to that law, in practice none ever seriously doubted its right to assert unilaterally its dominion over the lands and persons of Amerindians. In the words of Henry Wheaton (1785-1848), American jurist and diplomat, it became "a maxim of policy and of law, that the right of the native Indians was subordinate to that of the first Christian discoverer, whose paramount claim excluded that of every other civilized nation, and gradually extinguished that of the natives."[4] This challenged and even contradicted concepts in legal thinking that had been evolving since the twelfth century.

The issue of political authority had been engaging the attention of European canonists (experts in church law) at least since the twelfth century and civilists or jurists (experts in civil law) since the thirteenth. In terms of the personalized political thinking of the day, the problem involved the ideal of universalism that had once been expressed by the Roman Empire and symbolized by the emperor, versus the regionalism of emerging territorial states headed by a local king. In ecclesiastical terms, it concerned the powers of the pope as head of the universal church,[5] *vis-à-vis* the temporal powers of the emperor and national monarchs. When the kings had confined their activities to their own or related peoples, the question of sovereignty did not have to be seriously considered. But when Western Europeans began to contest control of the Holy Land with the Saracens, problems that had not been satisfactorily resolved, or perhaps not seriously considered, took on new importance.

Rights of Non-Christians

The question first arose in an ecclesiastical context. Did non-Christians—all those who were *extra ecclesiam* (outside the church)—possess natural rights to property? Did their rulers exercise legitimate authority? In short, did unbelievers possess *dominium* (lawful possession of property and political power)?[6] Were Christians justified—indeed, did they have a duty—to wage continual war against infidels (a term at that time usually applied to Saracens, which included Turks and Moors)? Was war legitimate as a means for conversion? The irony of these concerns lies in the fact that most Europeans, far from challenging the legitimacy of the non-Christian Roman Empire, upheld it as a model, particularly as it was during the time of Augustus during whose reign (63 B.C. - 14 A.D.) Christ was born and died.[7] In the midst of these debates came the dawning awareness that in Asia and Africa there were nations scarcely known to Europeans, only a few of whose inhabitants were Christian; then came the realization that in the ocean between Europe and Asia there existed lands totally unknown to Europeans, whose inhabitants had not only never heard the Christian gospel but had never even heard of it. What was the status of these peoples, and what were their rights? Specifically, were Europeans justified in claiming the "rights of discovery" over their lands and in waging wars of conquest against them? Surprising as it may seem in the light of what actually happened in the New World, the weight of canonical opinion, both before and after

Columbus's voyages, upheld the rights of non-Christians to property and to their own governments; further, that wars could only be waged against them for a just cause.[8] Wars for conversion were futile, even when militarily successful, as instead of winning hearts they encouraged passive resistance. Some canonists, citing Paul's admonition that Christians should "be at peace with all men"[9] went so far as to deny that any war could be considered "just," as war by its very nature injured the innocent as well as the guilty.

In the course of the Middle Ages, Western Europeans, although fragmented politically since the collapse of the Roman Empire, maintained (and even vigorously developed) a widespread network of trade routes, stretching into Russia, the Middle East and the Orient, which necessitated the active formulation of mercantile and maritime law.[10] This was abetted by technological advances such as the introduction of the horse collar and subsequently the heavy, wheeled, mortarboard plough, which by improving the productivity of agriculture indirectly contributed to the expansion of trade.[11] In the midst of these developments, Europeans continued to cling to the ideal of a universal community as it had been expressed by the Roman hegemony. Although they never realized this ideal as such, they did create a new form of it through the medium of one of its imperial legacies, Christianity, which Constantine (emperor, 306-337) had recognized within the Roman Empire in 313, and which had succeeded in eliminating serious competition with the closing of the schools in Athens in 529. Christianity's vision of corporate and indivisible unity was expressed by the term *ecclesia*, which defined the relationship between man and the cosmos as the worldly kingdom of God headed by the pope. It reflected the tenet that Christ had united in himself the previously fragmented powers of the world.[12] By the thirteenth century the symbol of the cross was recognized (if still not always accepted) in the remotest corners of Europe, and the papacy was in unchallenged control of spiritual affairs and expanding into temporal realms as well.[13] But the success of a common religion was not repeated in the political sphere, and what remained of Roman imperial cohesion became severely battered as east vied with west, and both suffered pressures from the north. Byzantium and the Frankish kingdom each claimed direct descent from Rome, and the pope claimed to be the inheritor of St. Peter, who as the chosen successor of Christ was the sole channel for the authority of the omnipotent

God. According to the latter theory, the emperor could receive his share of this authority only from the pope in the latter's capacity as guardian of the "two swords," symbolizing temporal and spiritual powers.[14] This was not a position that was accepted by Europe's reigning princes, most of whom maintained that monarchical authority was independent of the church, on the grounds that God delegated power directly to both pope and temporal ruler, each in his own proper sphere.[15] The power struggle which ensued was not between the secular and the ecclesiastic so much as it was between two versions of theocracy, as both parties were firmly within the church; the lay princes were not concerned with the destruction of papal authority, but rather with its limitation.[16] In this, they were generally supported by the jurists, who as a group upheld the equality and independence of secular power.[17] But it was the work of the most renowned theologian of them all, St. Thomas Aquinas (1225?-1274), on the recently recovered Aristotelian texts, showing how the thought of St. Augustine (Aurelius Augustinus, Bishop of Hippo, 350-430) could be combined with that of Aristotle (384-322 B.C.) within the framework of Scriptures, that showed the way for Christians to assimilate pagan concepts in politics as well as philosophy. (In later medieval philosophical disputes, Aristotle's authority approached that of the Bible. He was commonly referred to simply as The Philosopher.) St. Thomas, in working out a new relationship between the spiritual and the temporal, did not resolve all its latent ambiguities which would become evident in practical affairs, and so his work was used by both sides in support of their positions. He has been called the first Whig.[18]

Law and Theology Separate

The growing interest in the content of Roman law as well as in Roman forms of the exercise of power provided still another focus for the study of the source of power and the right of princes to rule.[19] The Camaldolite canonist Gratian (Graziano, d.c.1158) is generally credited with initiating the study of church law as distinct from theology with his *Concordia canonum discordantium* (1140), known as the *Decretum*. Gratian set himself the task not only of assembling all known canon law, but also of resolving its many contradictions by means of the dialectical method. Diverse as the law could be, especially when based upon customary practice, it was presumed to have an underlying rational cohesion which made it possible to consider such an enterprise. As Gratian saw it, "human law consists of that which is rational."[20] Although his work never received the official sanction of the papacy, and did not even achieve its basic purpose, still it laid the foundations for medieval jurisprudence. As such, it has been called "the most successful textbook ever written."[21] Gratian was not so much interested in problems connected with infidels as he was with those surrounding excommunication; it would not be until the early thirteenth century that attention would begin to turn toward non-Christians to any significant degree. Within Christendom, the first concern was with Christians who had broken the rules, particularly if the violators were in authoritative positions. Excommunication was a powerful weapon in a world where the church was in effect the state and where baptism was the rite of admission into society. A ruler who had been excommunicated no longer possessed the substance of power, even though he went through the motions of its exercise, because, in the words of Gratian, *potestas nulla est extra ecclesiam* (there is no legitimate authority outside the church). Two generations of canonists later, *potestas*, with its ecclesiastical connotations, had been replaced by *imperium*, with its connotations of secular power backed by force, and the phrase had become *extra ecclesiam non est imperium* (there is no political authority outside the church). This reflected the church's increasing control over secular affairs. An extreme advocate of papal authority, the Welshman Alanus Anglicanus (fl. 13th century), whose posts included that of law professor at Bologna, contended that since all power came from God, Christ had necessarily passed on its two manifestations, the temporal and the spiritual "swords," to Peter and to his successors as heads of the church.[22] As the church formed one body, Christ could have only one vicar on earth, which meant that the papacy was the office through which these powers were exercised or delegated. No one anywhere was excepted, as all legitimate authority, imperial or otherwise, derived from the church: *nullum imperium extra ecclesiam*. Alanus qualified this, however, by positing that *dominium* depended upon a state of grace, a position that not only hearked back to the heresy of Donatism in the fourth century, but which anticipated the teaching of John Wyclif (c. 1330-1384).

Considerable controversy was aroused by an example that Gratian used to illustrate papal action in the temporal sphere. It concerned the sanction provided by Zacharias (pope, 741-752) which allowed Charles Martel's son Pepin (reign, 741-768) to depose Childeric and accede to the throne of the Franks. Such a papal move would draw the approval of Dominican Guido Vernani (d. 1348?), lecturer at Bologna, who saw the pope of necessity acting for the whole of society, epitomizing as he did the oneness of *universitas fidelium*.[23] Whether upholding this position or opposing it, protagonists developed a wide array of ingenious and subtle arguments. Decretist Uguccio (Huguccio) da Pisa (d. 1210), of the generation preceding Alanus, counted the future Innocent III among his students, and would exercise a strong influence over Jean de Paris and William of Ockham. A leader in developing canon law as a discipline separate from theology, Uguccio held that the king's power came ultimately from the people, a fact which the papal coronation did no more than consecrate. He suggested that the pope's right to grant title to the emperor stemmed from the breakdown of Roman government rather than from a grant of divine power as such;[24] after all, emperors had preceded popes in Rome. Separating spiritual from temporal powers was God's means of promoting humility and curbing pride of office.[25] But in the final analysis, Uguccio could not deny the superiority of the spiritual over the temporal: the pope had the right to judge the emperor, which the emperor could never claim over the pope. Whatever the particular line of reasoning, from the time of the Visigoths the ruler legitimized his position by receiving his crown from a spiritual authority, as Pepin did from St. Boniface ("Apostle of the Germans," c. 680-755) in 752, and Charlemagne from Leo III (pope, 795-816) in 800, when the king received the additional title of Emperor of the West.

This concern with legitimacy of power became particularly intense during the pontificate of Innocent III (pope, 1198-1216), when the papacy was at its most powerful. A competent administrator, Innocent favored the doctrine that the inclusion of all in one meant the supremacy of one over all: unity entailed monarchy, more specifically, papal monarchy.[26] Recognizing, however, that actual power lay with the secular monarchies (down to mid-eleventh century, emperors had been choosing popes), he did more than anyone, with the exception of St. Bernard of Clairvaux, to develop the concept of the papacy as mediator between the spiritual and the temporal, as well as between rulers.[27] It was during this period that the political aspect of legitimacy of power came to dominate over the ecclesiastical. Innocent maintained that in the matter of papal and imperial jurisdictions, the division of the Roman Empire into two halves had in itself limited imperial power. In *Venerabilem*[28] he used *imperium* to mean an office which conferred title, but neither power nor territory, reserving for the pope the right to countermand the choice of princes for the holders of such offices. Decretalists, on the other hand, tended to see *imperium* as an office within the church, but with a larger significance than that granted by Innocent. The canonist Tancredi (d. about 1236), professor at Bologna whose gloss on *Venerabilem, de electione* became the standard, held that the pope could take over the jurisdiction of any ruler seriously suspected of wrongdoing.[29] According to Tancredi, *extra ecclesiam non hic est imperium* (outside the church, there is no political authority in this world).[30] Some canonists modified this by holding that the lay ruler became a true monarch through divine right, the *sacrum imperium*,[31] and could lose this *imperium* only by becoming a heretic or a schismatic; others, while not so certain about this, thought that excommunication of a ruler freed his subjects from the obligation of obedience.

Legitimacy Outside the Church

From there it was but a short step to enlarge the question of legitimacy of power by including non-Christians, a move which began in 1234, when Gregory IX (pope, 1227-1241) mentioned the issue in his *Decretales*, without, however, expanding on it. Non-Christian populations in Europe (principally Jews and Moslems) provided the first focus for attention. Innocent III had questioned the propriety of the exercise of power by non-Christians over Christians, but had not denied its legitimacy. The responsible use of power was independent of religious belief, and any delegate who abused this power laid himself open to the possibility of discipline:

> Indeed, an official of this kind may be denied intercourse with Christians in commercial and other matters until that which was

robbed from Christians by the official shall be turned to the use of
the poor. . .and let him lay down the office with shame, which he
irreverently assumed. This also applies to pagans.[32]

The wisest course, however, would be to avoid placing non-
Christians in positions of authority over Christians. This modified
earlier prohibitions against the naming of pagan judges in Christian
communities. Further changes occurred as a result of problems raised
by the Crusades. The starting point was another letter of Innocent III,
Quod super his,[33] which was commented on by Innocent IV (pope,
1243-1254), who as Sinibaldo dei Fieschi had been a noted canonist
widely regarded as "the light of the law. . .who knew the laws better
than anyone else."[34] Innocent IV extended the points at issue to include the right of Christians to retake the Holy Land; a right which he
carefully circumscribed by stating that only the pope could authorize
an attack on a non-Christian prince. At the same time, he defended
the right of non-Christians to exercise power; his formulation became the standard for this position, just as that of Hostiensis became
the classic for the opposing view.[35]

In the meantime, Mongol incursions, beginning in 1222 on the
southeastern borders of Russia, took Europe by surprise, dramatically highlighting the issue from an unexpected quarter. Islam, as
worried as Christendom at this turn of events, in 1238 proposed an
alliance against these "common enemies of civilization," but Europeans could not bring themselves to accept such a compromise. Their
attitude was that infidel "dogs" should be allowed to destroy one another, which would leave the field clear for Christians to establish
"one fold and one shepherd." At one point it looked as though that
might actually happen, when in 1258 the Mongols took Baghdad, destroyed the Abbasid Khalifate, and proceeded to march against
Syria.[36] But instead of mutual destruction, Mongols were getting the
upper hand, as their mobile armies had already shown signs of doing
in Europe. Innocent had quickly decided that the wiser course would
be to explore the possibility of peace, so he had sent a mission in 1245
to the Tartar khan, in what became the first of several such initiatives
on the part of Christian Europe.[37] The Mongols reciprocated with
missions of their own, and with proposals for an alliance against Islam for the retaking of Jerusalem. They had taken the precaution
placing these embassies in the charge of Nestorian Christians; in

1287, one of these leaders attended mass in St. Peter's in the presence of the pope.[38] Despite the Mongols' demonstrated tolerance toward Christianity, Europeans were slow to react, and the opportunity was lost.

On the Christian right to take the Holy Land, Innocent IV argued that the Roman jurisdiction over the area had been inherited by the emperor, one of whose titles was King of Jerusalem, and that he had been unjustly deprived of it by the Moslems. Therefore the Christians had not only a right but a duty to reconquer the area for its rightful ruler, as long as this was done with proper authorization. Innocent used similar arguments to justify the re-taking of Spain from the Moslems.[39] There was another side to this picture: did the fact that Europe had once been pagan mean that non-Christians had a right to retake it? No, said Innocent, because Europe's conversion had been voluntary.[40] If the Holy Land and Spain had been voluntarily converted to Islam, then Christians would not automatically have the right to retake them, either.

On the question of the legitimacy of secular power outside of the church, Innocent IV held that all rational creatures, Christian or non-Christian, had the right under natural law to own property and to exercise political authority in their own lands:

. . .possessions and jurisdictions can lawfully exist. . .among pagans, for these things were made not only for the faithful but for every rational creature. . .it is not permitted to the Pope, or to the faithful, to take away either their lordships or jurisdictions from the pagans, for as much as they possess [them] without sin. . .[41]

In other words, the right to own property or to exercise political power depended neither upon being Christian or in a state of grace, as long as these rights were exercised in conformity with natural law. However, since the authority of the pope extended to all men, he did have the right to intervene on behalf of Christian subjects who were being abused by a non-Christian ruler:

. . .also against other pagans, who now hold land in which Christian princes have had jurisdiction, the Pope may justly make a rule, and decree that they must not unjustly molest Christians who fall under their jurisdiction, what is more, he may exempt those

[Christians] altogether from their jurisdiction and lordship. . . .If they should illtreat Christians, he can sentence them to be deprived of their jurisdiction and lordship. However, it must be an important cause which would come to that, for the Pope should support them [the heathen rulers] as much as he can, provided there should not be danger to Christians, nor a grave scandal brought about.[42]

If the non-Christian ruler presented a threat to his Christian subject's religion, then Innocent IV was unequivocal that the pope could depose him from office, on the grounds of misuse of power. If possible, this should be done by persuasion (including monetary inducements) rather than by force, as the legitimacy of the ruler's office was not at issue.[43] In such a case, the right of a people to select their ruler would be superseded by the responsibility of the pope to provide for their spiritual welfare. Thus Innocent IV, even as he defended the infidel's right to exercise authority, was firm in his position that all earthly human power, without exception, was of divine origin, and redounded ultimately to the pope.

The Christian Sword

Although Innocent IV's arguments established a strong case on theoretical grounds, in the practical arena the laurels went to the opposite view, *extra ecclesiam non est imperium*. Apart from the principles that were considered to be involved, non-Christians governing Christians was an emotional issue. Scriptural support against such a situation was discerned in St. Paul's stand against Christians appearing before non-Christian judges.[44] It was popularly believed that since the dominion of infidels could never be just, it was always permissible to wage war against them.[45] This was the extreme version of the position of Henrico de Segusio, cardinal of Ostia (d. 1271, generally known as Hostiensis), a leading member of the Sacred College, and a student of Innocent IV.[46] Although on many points he was in accord with "dominus meus," as he referred to Innocent, he took issue with him on the recognition of non-Christian right to exercise power over Christians, or, for that matter, to their exercise of any kind of authority at all: "infidels, neither recognizing nor obeying the power and authority of the Roman Church, are not worthy to have kingdoms, government, jurisdiction nor dominion."[47] Non-Christian rulers could not possess dominion *de iure*:

> It seems to me that with the coming of Christ every office and all governmental authority and all lordship and jurisdiction was taken from every infidel lawfully and with just cause and granted to the faithful through Him who has the supreme power and who cannot err.[48]

Such reasoning was reminiscent of the Donatist argument, dating back to the fourth century, that a priest could not exercise sacramental power while in a state of sin. It had been condemned as heretical, but had never quite died, and was finding new life as Hostiensis extended it to political and social spheres. Even in those spheres, outside the church as they were, Hostiensis still saw lordship as a divine gift that must necessarily be based in justice, which could only be found through the grace of God. It followed that those who lacked such grace, such as sinners and the unbaptized, could not qualify for *dominium*. In practice, Hostiensis qualified his position, and allowed that non-Christian rulers could possess dominion *de facto*:

> . . .we steadily assert that by right infidels should be subject to the faithful, and not the reverse. . . .we allow however that infidels who recognize the lordship of the church are to be tolerated by the church; wherefore they are not to be forced into the faith. . . .Such people also may have possessions and Christian dependents and even jurisdiction by the toleration of the church.[49]

Toleration was possible only if heathen rulers did not abuse their Christian subjects, and then just to the extent necessary to avoid persecution: "But also, if they illtreat Christians, [the pope] can sentence them to be deprived of the jurisdiction and lordship which they have over them."[50] Patience was advised, as "where Christians live under the jurisdiction of infidels whom they are not able to resist, then they must possess themselves with patience, and in practice recognize the infidels' jurisdiction."[51]

Hostiensis firmly placed both of the "two swords" within the church, as it was God's channel for all power, spiritual and temporal. In the tradition of Alanus Anglicanus, he contended that the pope possessed "plenitude of power" which the cardinal described as the "supreme and surpassing superiority and power and authority (which) has been granted to him without reservation in all matters. . . ."[52] A vigorous expression of this position was the bull of Boniface VIII (pope, 1294-1303), *Unam sanctam* (1302), which stated further that the "spiritual power excels any earthly one in dignity and nobility."[53] Equally convinced was the Augustinian theologian, Egidio Colonna (Aegidius Romanus Colonna, also known as Giles of Rome, 1247-1316). In his *De Ecclesiastica Potestate* (1302), he maintained that "all lordship, whether of things or persons, whether giving use or power, can only exist with justice under the Church and through the Church." Moreover, "all infidels are deprived of every kind of possession and lordship and power."[54]

The Papacy and Infidels' Rights

Not all advocates of papal overlordship used that argument to downplay the rights of infidels. An Augustinian who was an uncompromising papalist, Augustino Trionfo d'Ancona (Augustinus Triumphus, c. 1270/73-1328), master of theology at Paris and later active at the court of Naples, held that since infidel rulers did not hold their titles from the pope, they could not be deprived of them without just cause.[55] An influential voice that agreed with Hostiensis at one point, but which later supported Innocent IV, was that of Oldrado da Ponte (d. 1335) doctor of both canon and civil law who taught at Padua and Bologna and saw papal service at Avignon:

> Thirdly, for the same reason, by which we would not rob peaceful Jews, pagans, and Saracens of their goods, for the same reason we should not deprive them of their dwellings even outside their native land. . . . And what they possess, they possess by the law of nations, whether it be objects, or places, or jurisdictions, and that justly, according to custom which is common to all. . .as Innocent clearly holds. . . . And their sins were the cause of the expulsion of the Amorites, Canaanites, and Jebusites from their lands by the children of Israel—especially idolatry, which is against the law of nature, which proclaims there is one God. . . .But the Jews and the Saracens are not idolaters, but unbelievers in other ways, nei-

ther are such persons public enemies of reigning Christian princes, therefore they should not be expelled.[56]

Although expelling non-Christians without just cause "violates the precepts of charity," with sufficient reason a Christian prince would not only be justified in moving against non-Christians, he could do so without papal approval. In favoring such independence of action, Oldrado not only parted company once more from Innocent IV, but also from Hostiensis.[57] Because non-Christians were wild folk who habitually contravened natural law, they needed to be led with a firm hand to the true faith and peaceful ways.

A path similar to Oldrado's was followed by Giovanni Andreae (1270-1348), an eminent lay-academic at Bologna, who also began by upholding the position that Christ's coming had transferred all power, including the secular, to the Christian faithful who made up the church. In his later days, however, he wrote in support of Innocent IV:

> I have seen certain formal writings concluding for seven reasons that the prince should not expel peaceful infidels from his territories without legitimate cause. . . .I have other sheep which are not of this fold, that of the church. . . .Therefore the successor of Peter must sustain and defend them, and not attack them or permit them to be harmed. . . .Again, the heavens belong to the lord of heaven, but the earth he gave to the sons of men, therefore what the law of human society has granted is not to be denied to them.[58]

The late Middle Ages saw two canonists, both princes of the church, concurring with Innocent IV in their commentaries on *Quod super his*. Francesco Cardinal Zabarella (1360-1417), a Thomist and ecclesiastical diplomat prominent in the Council of Constance, was, if anything, even firmer than Innocent in favor of non-Christian rights:

> These things having been laid down with respect to the aforesaid question, which are to be conscientiously taken note of, Innocent says that lordships, possessions, and jurisdictions can lawfully without sin exist among the heathen. For these things were not only made for the heathen but for any rational creature. . .[59]

Such matters were in the realm of natural law, which did indeed apply to all men without regard to faith, agreed Panormitanus. That was the name by which Niccolò de' Tudeschi (1386-1445), Benedictine abbot and archbishop of Palermo, was known. Panormitanus, who became as distinguished as his teacher Zabarella, taught at Siena, Parma, and Bologna:

> Innocent has dealt at large and very carefully with this very subject and in the first place he concludes that heathen lawfully hold dominions and principalities and other goods since God subjected the world to rational creatures and did not distinguish among men; afterward the law of nations came in, and it had the same provision.[60]

These views drew the approval of Bolognese lawyer Domingo de Sancto Geminiano (d. before 1436), who like Zabarella was a pupil of Antonio de Butrio (1338-1408), the Bolognese decretalist,

> As Innocent observes. . .these persons could not occupy the said places, since the heathen who do not wage war against the faithful ought not to be expelled from their lands, since they may possess them lawfully, since by divine law before their occupation it was permitted to anyone to occupy land. . . .From which Innocent concludes that it is not allowed to the faithful, not even the Pope, to take away from the heathen without just cause their possessions, lordships or jurisdictions which they hold, since they may justly possess them.[61]

Infidels could enjoy this right as long as they maintained the peace and did not fight Christians.[62] But once they turned hostile, it was the pope's responsibility—indeed, duty—to take measures to protect the faithful. Giovanni da Legnano (d. 1383), professor of civil and canon law at Bologna, agreed with Innocent that the Crusades were a legitimate expression of papal authority in response to the unjust aggressions of Islam in the Holy Land; then nudged the argument over to the Hostiensian position by adding that Christians could fight the infidels anyway, as unbelievers.[63] Since there could be only one lord of the world, and since the spiritual was superior to the material, the authority for waging wars against the infidel rested with the pope. This opinion held considerable weight at the time, as the city of Bologna was contesting papal power during the decade 1350-1360.

Perhaps the most spirited attempt to realize the implications of Innocent IV's position was that of Paulus Vladimiri (Paweł Włodkowic z Brudzewa, c. 1370-c. 1435) rector of the University of Cracow, who was sent by Poland to the Council of Constance in 1414 to take up the cudgels in the century-old battle against the Teutonic Knights, an order founded in 1198 to wage war against infidels in defense of Christianity. Polish authorities had turned to the university for help in its campaign to prove that the Order had long since lost sight of its original purpose, and had become enmeshed in pursuing its own aggrandizement even at the expense of Christian peoples. This had happened when the Order had begun to acquire Polish territories in 1308; it had taken Poland a century before it had been able to curtail the process in 1410, and finally stop it with the second Peace of Toruń in 1466.

This was not the first time the Order was being challenged; notable among earlier critics had been the English Franciscan Roger Bacon (1210/1215-1292) who had charged that the Teutonic Knights "hinder greatly the conversion of unbelievers, owing to the wars that they are always stirring up and because they wish to have complete sway."[64] Vladimiri brought his prestige as an established scholar[65] and diplomat into the fray. He argued that neither the propagation of the faith nor the papal plenitude of power provided sufficient justification for waging war against the infidel and depriving him of his dominion.[66] He held that infidels within their own domains were subject only to natural law and not to Christian positive law, whether canon or civil; and that wars could not be waged justly against them by reason of their unwillingness to accept Christianity.[67] Since the Order had waged such wars, it had unjustly deprived infidels of their legal rights, and should be compelled by the Council to make restitution.[68]

Vladimiri's position not only opposed the accepted medieval practice of expanding Christianity by the sword as well as by the word, but also flew in the face of the fact that the papacy had tacitly supported the Order for two centuries. An unspoken point of contention concerned who had the right to authorize war against pagans, the pope or the king, a problem that had been indirectly solved in the case of Lithuania in 1385-86, when it had officially converted to Catholicism, and had also entered into a dynastic union with Poland. Vladimiri was thus able to skirt the issue, and to concentrate on the evidence of history to prove that the Order had not only behaved very badly, but had used the faith to disguise its self-interest when it had done so. In the end, he rejected warfare altogether as an instrument for the extension of Christianity, as even so-called "just" wars spread misfortune and destruction.[69] On this point also, Vladimiri was following in the footsteps of Bacon, who had argued against wars as a means of evangelization before Clement IV (pope, 1265-1268) on the grounds that their real aim was domination. Bacon had held that such wars frustrated rather than promoted the work of conversion, which could better be achieved by preaching.[70] Vladimiri carried the argument further: he urged the Council to reject as "wicked and against reason" the doctrine denying unbelievers their rights under natural law; and sought to have those rights, as taught by St. Thomas Aquinas, enshrined in positive law binding upon all Christians.[71]

Although Vladimiri did not win a clear-cut decision, his systematization and marshalling of his arguments on juridical and historical as well as theological grounds foreshadowed international law, just as the issues he addressed foreshadowed those which were to arise with the discovery of the Americas. More than a century later, Bartolomé de Las Casas would use similar techniques in his impassioned attempt to halt the course of the Spanish conquest of the New World. The issue of Poland and the Teutonic Knights pointed to a shift that was occurring in relations between Christians and non-Christians. The papacy, from being the focus, and often the initiator of diplomatic moves between the two camps, increasingly found itself in the role of mediator, as St. Bernard had advocated.

Dominium continued to be debated without much change in terms until well into the sixteenth century. For example, according to the eminent Spanish canonist Diego Covarruvias y Leyva (Didacus, 1512-1577), professor at the University of Salamanca and adviser at the Council of Trent,

> in this matter the conclusion which we think more true would be that war cannot be declared justly against the heathen simply because they are heathen even by the authority of the Emperor or the Pope. . .for unbelief does not deprive the heathen of their dominion, which they have by natural law. . .therefore, heathen, by rea-

son of their unbelief and lack of desire to accept the faith of Christ, in no way lose their dominion over things or territories which they hold and have come to possess by human law; whence it must be that for this cause war cannot be justly declared against them by Christians even in public authority; which conclusion Innocent and the Cardinal [Francesco Zabarella] think appears to be true in [their comments on] the aforesaid chapter, *Quod super his. . .*[72]

It is clear from all this that despite overwhelming canonical support for a universal Christian society with the pope as its soul breathing life into its body, and as its head providing a sense of direction, there was also an influential undercurrent of continuing recognition that universality did not necessarily mean uniformity. Although the debate was almost entirely in theological terms, a substantial body of canonists supported the view that legitimate authority did exist in societies other than Christian, and that their princes were entitled to rule. Today, some maintain that Innocent's authority outweighed that of Hostiensis during the later Middle Ages and early Renaissance.[73] Then, as now, the rich variety of views provided plenty of material for argument. Scholars working in the material today can point to the tradition of liberalism among early canonists, culminating with the decretals of Innocent IV; they can also point to another tradition, exemplified by Hostiensis, upholding the ideal of a uniform, theocratic society which tolerated non-Christians only to the extent necessary to avoid persecution or other dangers. It was the less tolerant of the two traditions which came to prevail in practice: the accepted rule of action was that Christians had a duty to convert the heathen, and if persuasion did not succeed, then force should be used.[74] Europe's discovery of the New World would provide a new arena in which these issues would continue to be fought out. In the meantime, the legal traditions of the Roman Empire, never entirely forgotten, had begun to gather force, and together with the rediscovery of the thought of the classical world, particularly that of Aristotle, would lend new dimensions as well as new directions to the debate.

Legitimacy of Power

The Secular Aspect and the Rise
of International Law

Historians, in their search for the "father" of international law, usually accord the laurel to one of the leading jurists of the Age of Discovery or of the period immediately following. A favorite is Hugo Grotius (Huigh de Groot, 1583-1645), jurist and statesman whose *De jure belli ac pacis*, translating natural law into contemporary terms, was published in 1625; others would accord the honor to his mentor, Alberico Gentili (1552-1608), Regius Professor of Civil Law at Oxford University; many more are inclined to award it to Dominican Francisco de Vitoria (1480?-1552), Primary Professor of Sacred Theology at the University of Salamanca, whose lectures "De Indis" and "De jure belli Hispanorum in barbaros" were first delivered in the 1530s, and published after his death under various titles, beginning in 1557. Today, they are known as *De Indis et de jure belli relectiones*. An examination of the thought of these men, however, reveals that they were all arguing within established legal traditions that were already several centuries old by Vitoria's time. Recently, attention has been turning to the much earlier figure of Innocent IV, whose commentary on Innocent III's *Quod super his* is gaining recognition as being of pivotal importance.[1] The problem of the source of authority took on a new aspect as more attention began to be focused on human law and its relationship to natural and divine law.

Until the Age of Discovery, the line between theology and law was not clearly drawn; jurisprudence was conceived after the Roman model as "the knowledge of things divine and human," an art rather than a science, but sharing with it the assumption of an ordered universe that was also moral.[2] Since all law was seen as emanating from justice, "the art of goodness and fairness" (*Digest* I.1.1), jurists drew parallels between the functions of lawyers (*sacerdotes Iustitiae*) and those of priests (*sacerdotes Ecclesiae*); in the words of the Roman juris-consult Domitius Ulpianus (Ulpian, d. 223), "we jurists worship Justice."[3] Issues could slip from one realm to the other, as did the question of the legitimacy of power outside the church, or of its exercise without express ecclesiastical approval; it had begun as an ecclesiastical problem, but had acquired secular and political overtones during the second half of the twelfth century. The process had been enormously encouraged during the thirteenth century by the rediscovery of Aristotle's manuscripts through the medium of Arab scholars, reinforcing the growing importance of civil (Roman) law. Although it was clearly recognized that Roman law had originated in pre-Christian times, and so was largely the work of pagans,[4] it became interwoven, and sometimes even fused, with canon law, so that mastery of both fields became necessary for effective legal scholarship. According to Ullmann, medieval canon law was both more realistic and more resilient than the civil law of the period; it was most influential during the fourteenth and fifteenth centuries.[5] Even as civil law gained in authority, the tendency to quote Scripture remained, pointing to the still unchallenged supremacy of the spiritual over the temporal, despite the growing independence of the latter.[6] The codes developed by the later Middle Ages have been called "supranational" rather than international, concerned as they were with the relationship of individuals to institutions, and exacting as they did obedience throughout Christendom.[7] Innocent IV, in his attempt to work out a peaceful *modus vivendi* between Christians and non-Christians, made a major contribution to the basic formulations needed for what would become the law governing relationships between states rather than between rulers. [8]

The ancestry of international law as expressed in the phrase *jus gentium* has been traced back to Rome in 242 B.C., when the office of a special magistrate was created to take care of legal matters relating to foreigners, since the *jus civile* applied only to Roman citizens.[9] Not at first an international law, it became associated with the earlier Greek philosophical concept of natural law, which Cicero (126-43 B.C.) pithily defined as *non scripta sed nata lex* ("law is not written, but born"). The concept of a set of guiding principles residing in nature and common to all living things entered the medieval canonists' lexicon via Roman law: "Nature teaches natural law to all animals. . . natural law is nature, it is God because God is the nature of nature and teaches all animals."[10] *Jus gentium*, however, arose from human will; in modern terms, it is the consensus of the international community.[11]

Fusing Classical and Christian Thought

St. Thomas Aquinas, pondering Aristotle's thought, and the teachings of the Church Fathers, concluded that natural law (*jus naturale*), discernible by human reason, was an aspect of eternal law (*jus aeternum*), which was beyond human comprehension.[12] In his phrasing, it was the "participation of the rational creature, by his intellect and reason, in the eternal law."[13] He agreed with the Greek concept of natural law as a criterion of right conduct, a principle of reasonableness that pre-existed states and was promulgated in each man through his nature (*lex naturalis*). Consequently, the rights of man predated states.[14] All mankind shared in natural law, and all types of states came within its orbit; whatever contradicted its principles was not binding on any one.[15] In the later Middle Ages, its greatest expression was considered to have been the Roman Empire.[16] St. Thomas, in accord with Aristotle that the natural objective of a state was the material well being of its citizens, sought to correlate this with the Christian ideal of absolute justice (divine law, revealed in Scripture), a system higher than that of either natural law or man-made (positive) law, but supplementing them. Thus was preserved and carried forward the cherished medieval concept of the unity of mankind. Although he saw the temporal power as being separate from the spiritual power, and he even accepted the autonomy of the state in temporal matters, St. Thomas did not put it on an equal footing with the spiritual authority of the church.[17] The resultant ambiguity in his work was shared with theologians generally; even the Angelic Doctor had not been able to avoid it.

In synthesizing Greek and Christian thought, and incorporating elements of Roman jurisprudence, St. Thomas provided ammunition for each of two principal views of human society: that it was a unified whole receiving its right to governance directly from God; and that it was a collection of diverse entities each receiving its right indirectly from God through the people. The first of these supported the theory of papal supremacy, which would prevail over the conciliarist movement during the later Middle Ages. The second had found long since a congenial atmosphere at the University of Paris, where St. Thomas himself had taught, and where this school of thought would continue to be developed. Even as St. Thomas elaborated this aspect of his thinking, an older civilist was looking back to the ideal of the universal empire as he interpreted Justinian's laws.

Francisco Accursio of Bologna (c. 1185-c. 1263), eminent glossator, turned to Roman law for his commentaries on Justinian's *Corpus Iuris Civilis* (Body of Civil Law, comprising the Codex, Digest (Pandects), Institutes, and Novels);[18] his work was for centuries a standard authority for European law schools. According to Accursio, natural law gave rise to sovereignty via *jus gentium* and thus logically preceded it. Accursio, in common with the prevailing opinion of his fellow glossators and commentators, saw *jus gentium* in its narrow sense, which emphasized national distinctions. As such, it was not a good thing. [19] The rise of national monarchical sovereignties had been instrumental in the destruction of the unity which had once been realized by the Roman Empire. On the positive side, these national sovereigns represented their people, through whom they received their authority by means of *lex regia*, a constitutional device borrowed from Roman law by which citizens conferred (some say "transferred" or even "surrendered") power to the ruler.[20] This implied pre-existing rules (natural law) which were binding on the prince as well as on his subjects. Commenting on the text, *quod principi placuit, legis habet vigorem* (what has pleased the Prince has the force of law), Accursio observed that "not every statement of the Prince is law."[21] At the time, sovereignty was conceived of as residing in the person of the ruler: *rex superiorem non recognoscens est princeps in regno suo* (the king, not recognizing a superior power, is first in his own kingdom); the king is *majestas*.[22] Even though the ruler had no superior to restrain him, he was also subject to the law, but through internal rather than external discipline.[23] Prelate and jurist Henry Bracton (c. 1210-1268) in his basic compilation of English common law (*De legibus et consuetudinibus Angliae*), observed that not only was the king under the law, he could not change it unilaterally.[24] It was a principle that would be severely challenged with the rise of monarchical absolutism during the seventeenth and eighteenth centuries. This polarization was exemplified by Louis XIV of France's great minister, Jean-Baptiste Colbert (1619-1683), for whom "all the legislative power of this kingdom resides in the person of the sovereign."[25] Such a comment would have raised eyebrows, to say the least, during the thirteenth and fourteenth centuries. The contrast is evident when Colbert's approach is compared with that of Lorenzo Ispano (fl. twelfth/thirteenth centuries), canonist at the University of Bologna: "The people through election make an emperor but not the empire [*imperium*], just as the cardinals promote someone to a jurisdiction [the papacy] that is given by God."[26]

Gap Widens Between Church, State

This idea was a starting point for a student of St. Thomas's, Jean de Paris (c. 1240/41-1306; his family name was Quidort). Like his master a Dominican, Jean picked up on his theme of the separation of church and state, and developed it with the help of some ideas borrowed from Uguccio and Lorenzo Ispano. Teaching at the University of Paris, he became involved in controversy to the point of being charged with heresy, which in that theocratic age was equivalent to high treason. This was hardly surprising, as his naturalistic conception of society led to a system of thought far removed from the hierocratic concept of life.[27] In his view, man being by nature a political or civil animal meant that it is natural for him to live in a community in the form of a state or kingdom under the direction of one person concerned with the general good. Such a communal life is based on natural law and the law of nations, even though the "temporal, like the spiritual, derives immediately from God. . . imperial authority is from God alone. . . . The pope does not have his sword from the emperor any more than the emperor has his sword from the pope. . . ."[28] This power was conveyed by popular consent: a "king exists by the will of the people."[29] The same rule applied to prelates, Jean wrote, as their power did not come "through the mediation of the pope, but immediately from God and from the people choosing and consenting"; the principle of *lex regia* applied to the ecclesiastical realm just as it did to the secular.[30] Despite their common source of legitimate power, the temporal and the spiritual were separate realms. The state was primarily concerned with the material and human needs of its citizens; the church, being above nature, was concerned with spiritual ends: "Wherefore Christ is said through faith to reign over hearts and not over possessions."[31] Jean, by limiting *ecclesia* to being no more than a unity of faith, was restricting the cherished medieval concept of universality to the spiritual domain, where in his view it properly belonged. He did not believe that universality was practical, or even possible, in the complexities and diversities of the secular world; what was good at one level was not necessarily so at another. In his eyes, the society of man was fundamentally human, but not necessarily Christian.[32]

Dante Alighieri (1265-1321) was, if anything, even more positive on the point of the separation of church and state, and bitterly castigated popes, such as Boniface VIII, for interfering in the affairs of temporal rulers. In *De monarchia* (first published in 1559, but probably written 1310-1313), he held that the church was a supernatural conception that took its form from the kingdom of Christ, and so was not of this world. Human society, on the other hand, arose out of natural law and includes all mankind, non-Christian as well as Christian.[33] The Roman Empire was used by Dante as an example of state organization outside of Christianity which had been justly established with divine approval.[34] He favored secular monarchy as the most effective form of government, and particularly "the perfect monarchy of the immortal Augustus," who despite the fact he was pagan, had reigned during the only period of universal peace known by the world.[35] It was during Augustus's reign that Christ chose to become man—in fact, a Roman citizen.[36] The Christian variation of this would be for the head of state to be both emperor and pope, and completely identified with the community, so that he was the state.[37] Dante's espousal of the monarchical form of government was in tune with the popular sentiment of his day, but it aroused opposition as well. Guido Vernani vigorously attacked it in favor of purely papal monarchy.[38] Alonso de la Vera Cruz (1507-1584) also objected, not so much to Dante's support of monarchy as such, but to his exaggeration of the role of the Roman Empire; as he pointed out, "the Romans never extended their sway so that they could be said to possess universal dominion."[39] Monarchy would remain the ideal for a long time; the Spanish jurist, Jesuit Francisco Suárez (1548-1617), considered by many to be the last of the great scholastics, would share it.[40]

The source of monarchical power continued to be a troubled point. Was the state a natural development of the aboriginal family, or did it emerge as a rational, creative act of the will uniting the community?[41] The jurist Cino (Cynus) de Pistoia (1270-1337), who besides teaching (he counted Oldrado da Ponte among his pupils), served as an assessor for Henry VII (Holy Roman Emperor, 1312-1313), and was a close friend of Dante and Petrarch, compared imperial and national legal systems in order to determine jurisprudential positions. He also demonstrated the importance of judicial precedence in interpreting common law. In attempting to correlate the two recognized sources for monarchical power, God and the people, Cino held that the empire and institution of the emperor was divine, but the emperor himself had his roots in the people: *Imperium a Deo, sed imperatur a populo.*[42] God (*natura naturans*) was the source of justice, but it was the emperor (*natura naturata*) who enacted the law.[43]

Perhaps the most famous of the advocates of power arising from the people was Marsilio (Marsilius) of Padua (1270-1342), rector of the University of Paris, who developed its theoretical basis.[44] Going much farther than Jean de Paris, he separated church and state to the point where they had nothing in common: in his book, *Defensor Pacis* (1324), "Nature and supernature became two completely separate realms, and a proposition that was false in one could be perfectly true in the other."[45] Marsilio did this by declaring that God as the author of nature was an article of faith, and hence outside of political science; within its own realm, the state was supreme.[46] He saw the power of the state as arising solely from the people, whether they were Christian or not; sovereignty in temporal affairs rested in them, just as in spiritual matters it rested in the church; if a cleric transgressed civil laws, he would be subject to civil justice. Using the Roman concept of *civis*, he who is autonomous and independent, he saw the citizen as lawmaker with the power of instituting any kind of government he preferred, rather than as *subditus*, the subject passively accepting laws from his ruler, who was the living law (*lex animata*). His definition of "citizen" was that of Aristotle, which excluded slaves, foreigners, women and children; also, Marsilio gave more weight to those who were important than to the rank and file. Even so, he freed natural law from divine sources, and human society from the necessity of a Christian purpose. But Christianity should be allowed to flourish, as it was practical for a society to have only one faith, if only for political reasons. In his words, the state was "living nature," an expression of the will of its citizenry.[47] Not surprisingly, the papacy condemned a number of passages in *Defensor Pacis*, and declared Marsilio a heretic.

The comparative legal approach of Cino was to be the medium through which Marsilio's ideas would be developed by Bartolo de Sassoferrato (1314-1357), "immortal master" of Perugia, pupil of Cino and of Oldrado da Ponte, among others, who has been called the greatest of the medieval civil lawyers. Bartolo's work, more than that of any other jurist, paved the way for the Renaissance.[48] He provided the legal framework for Marsilio's political theory, by combining the necessary ingredients from Roman law: the concepts of the citizen, of customary law, and of *lex regia*. Unwritten customary law, created by means of the tacit consent of the citizen, became written (statutory or positive) law by means of his explicit consent. Bartolo placed sovereignty in the people by conceiving of them as prince (*civitas sibi princeps*). The practical means for realizing this was through the popular assembly electing the council, the legislative body which represented the citizens, and which received its power directly from them: *Concilium repraesentat mentum populi.*[49] This of course was diametrically opposed to those who held that the ruler received his power either directly from God, or indirectly through the pope, but in either case without the intervention of the people. The populist line of thought was to be carried on by Alberico Gentili in Oxford, following his exile from Perugia, and by the Spanish Jesuit philosopher Juan de Mariana (1536-1623). The problem of reconciling the needs of the community with the wishes of the king, when the two were in conflict, led some medieval thinkers to posit the right of revolution and tyrannicide.[50]

Monarchs Assert Sovereignty

As these theoretical debates on the nature of political authority progressed, they provided national monarchs with a rationale for contesting the universality of papal and imperial powers. Edward I of England (reign, 1272-1307), and especially Philippe IV of France (reign, 1285-1314), both asserted sovereign rights against the canonist pope Boniface VIII; eventually, the monarchs prevailed.[51] But their victory was *de facto* only; even though the emperor had lost much of his power,[52] it took another confrontation a few years later before European monarchs won independence *de jure*. In 1313, Emperor Henry VII found Robert of Naples (reign, 1309-1343) guilty of *lèse majesté*, and summoned him to appear before an imperial tribunal in Pisa. Since Robert's kingdom was technically a fief of the papacy, the monarch ignored the summons and appealed instead to Clement V (pope, 1305-1314), whose interests lay with the French and so found in his favor. Clement's decree *Pastoralis cura* (1313), provided the first official endorsement of the doctrine that the king was sovereign in his own territories.[53] Henry VII's initiative was the last attempt to assert the overlordship of the emperor, which, however, continued to exist in theory.[54] Clement's decree limited more than imperial authority: in acknowledging the sovereignty of the king it had also restricted the power of the pope, reversing as it did the position of such canonists as Tancredi who had held that there was no legitimate authority outside of the church.[55] Medieval barriers to the development of international, as distinct from supranational, law were weakening.[56] The way was being paved for the actions of monarchs during the Age of Discovery, who on their own authority would claim sovereignty over non-Christian lands, only asking for papal authorization to evangelize in order to justify the deed after it had been done. To that extent, at least, the monarchs had succeeded in replacing the popes as God's agents.

A qualification to the tenet that "a king is emperor within his realm" was added by Baldo degli Ubaldi (1327-1400), a disciple of Bartolo, and one of the rising corps of lay academics teaching at the universities; the future Gregory XI was one of his pupils. Following in the footsteps of his master, Baldo's grasp of law was wide, including its canon, civil and feudal aspects. In his thought, the shift in power from Roman emperor to king was legitimate when it was seen as a transfer: "The commonweal has its majesty after the example of the Roman people, provided that it be free and have the right to create a king."[57] As Baldo saw it, such transfers did not affect the overlordship of the emperor; indeed, from the imperial perspective, they could be seen simply as an unwillingness on the part of the emperor to impose his will.[58]

Universality Loses Ground

Whatever the proposed subtleties for the division of power between church and the state, the net effect was the same: it undercut universality, in both its spiritual and temporal aspects.[59] The unity of the natural and the supernatural, faith and reason, the corporate group and the individual, which the great scholastics had sought to achieve, was being fractured and separated from spiritual values, presaging the Reformation of the sixteenth century. No single principle was safe: even such a popular one as the sovereignty of the king quickly realized its limits when a monarch sought to expand his jurisdiction over other territories. In that case, it could be argued that according to natural law, it was not the will of the ruler, but that of the people whose territory was at issue, which should decide the matter.[60]

The Franciscan William of Ockham (1299-1349) was a leading exponent of this development. Unlike St. Thomas, Ockham did not accept Aristotle's argument that natural law was verifiable by reason; instead, he held that universal ideas and general concepts were names only, whose truth could not be demonstrated. Universal propositions having no reality in a world of tangible things, universality itself was a delusion which clearly could not influence practical goals and decisions. Neither could it serve as the basis for a moral order.[61] If natural law operated at all, it could be only through a command from God or from a human authority. Since all societies were subject to natural law, religion could not be used as a criterion for their legitimacy. Pagan societies, too, could be founded on right, an opinion which Ockham shared with Jean de Paris, Marsilio, and Dante.[62] Politics was emerging as a social science rather than as a branch of theology.[63]

The Christian ideal of one world under Christ with the pope acting as his vicar had depended upon the bonding power of faith to overcome ethnic, linguistic or biological differences. It was Europe's prime social force for a thousand years, coming closest to realizing its ideal during the first part of the thirteenth century. But by the end of the century, the decline in authority of the papal judiciary was already evident, as the papal court was being called upon to decide fewer and fewer of the "great questions" confronting society.[64] The moment of crisis came later, with the decree *Sacrosancta* (1415) of the Council of Constance (1414-1417) asserting the Council's superiority over the pope; a decree which has been called "the most revolutionary official document in the history of the world."[65] It was the culminating moment for the conciliarists; however, the condemnation of *Sacrosancta* by Pius II (pope, 1458-1464) was the *coup de grâce* which led to the failure of the conciliar movement, despite its strong continuation in France as well as in Scotland.[66] Its defeat paved the way for the subsequent rise of absolutism; an ironic development, in view of the horror that absolutism had almost universally inspired among earlier jurists. Covarruvias was reflecting an ancient legal tradition when he wrote that "we are constrained to abhor and flee from any suggestion of absolute power."[67]

For all such sentiment, Renaissance thinkers had been unable to resolve a contradiction in their idea of man: the dominant overlord versus the link in the cosmos. It was a problem that had been compounded by the realization that earth was not the centre of the universe. Neither had they succeeded in stilling the intellectual ferment which had been triggered by the absorption of Aristotelian concepts; the form that ferment took under the influence of such thinkers as Marsilio and William of Ockham would point the way to the future. Not even the pope could dispense with natural law, and popular consent in some form, if only that of acceptance, was recognized as a fundamental requirement for functional government, whether ecclesiastic or secular. Man was by nature political, which meant that only in and through the State could he achieve his full potentialities.[68]

The old dream of global society as a unified, organic whole made up of interacting diverse elements, based on harmony rather than uniformity, was expressed by Nikolaus von Kues (Nicholas of Cusa, 1401-1464), in *De Concordantia Catholica* (1514).[69] Although he expressly rejected the position of Marsilio, Nikolaus, a canonist who was later to become a cardinal, still reflected something of the Paduan's position when he maintained that community consent or consensus was the medium through which divine will expressed itself.[70] Leaders were "those who are vigorous in reason, are naturally lords and rulers of others, but not through coercive law or judgment rendered against the unwilling."[71] Thus, in both ecclesiastical and secular spheres, even though authority was of divine origin, *quod omnes tangit ab omnibus approbetur*, what touches all is to be approved by all; he illustrated this with the popular belief that Christ, in confirming Peter as head of the church, only did so after the Apostles had chosen him for leader. The maxim, which in Roman law had been a simple principle of procedure, had been expanded into a principle of general consent, a process that had occurred two centuries before Nikolaus. In his words,

> Therefore since all are by nature free, then every rulership whether based on written law or on living law through a prince. . .can only come from the agreement and consent of the subjects.[72]

The principle was seen as being particularly apt in matters of faith, as Christ was only interested in willing behavior. On the basis of renewal, consensus and concord, Nikolaus laid out a comprehensive program for the reform of church and empire.[73] But his moderate proposals were not realized; instead, reaction overtook moderation and positions polarized, developments which were to lead to the Reformation and eventually to the French Revolution.

Nikolaus had sought to rescue the universalist dream by advocating the concept of a Christian empire made up of sovereign kingdoms, over which the emperor would preside as a sort of referee seeing that justice was maintained. It was an early version of federalism with emperor/pope as head.[74] It was a notion that would be translated into rationalist terms by Calvinist Johannes Althusius (1557-1638), law professor at Herborn, and syndic of the town of Emden, in his *Politica methodice digesta*, first published in 1603. He saw sovereignty, the "supreme right of universal jurisdiction," as being inherent in a people as a corporate whole, basing his position on *Digest* III.4.7.1, "The ruler is greater than individuals but not greater than the whole people." The sovereign collectivity could contain more or less autonomous units, each deriving its authority from common consent working its way to the top through the various administrative levels. The doctrine of consent, he wrote, really meant that "what touches all should be acted on by all." The power of the commonwealth overrode that of the king, whom it could depose; it also overrode that of the ecclesiastical realm, although the ruler would be bound by a decision of a general church council.

Thus, by the time Europe was establishing its hegemony in the Americas, church and state had effectively separated. Although national monarchs saw their power as deriving ultimately from God, they claimed sovereignty on the basis of natural law as expressed through the will of the people. From that same basis also arose human (or statutory) law and the law of nations. As the church lost its power to control national sovereignties, the *jus gentium* of Roman times began to take on the aspects of international law. In the meantime, however, when European monarchs were first presented with the dazzling prospects of the New World, they were limited only by their own strength, resources, and sense of divinely-ordained mission; the church was losing its power to control more quickly than international law was gaining it.

Crossing the Atlantic

If there was no international body of law in place to govern the situation that arose with Spain's discovery of the Americas, as some have claimed,[1] there was an evolving practice. The Spanish Crown's move to obtain Rome's sanction for its claims to the new discoveries in return for Spain's promise to evangelize, was based on precedent that dated back to the Age of the Crusades, although by the end of the thirteenth century lay leaders were taking matters into their own hands. This is illustrated by the action of the Sicilian admiral Ruggiero di Lauria (c. 1245-1305), when he conquered two islands off Tunis, and offered them to Boniface VIII on condition that they be granted back to him as a papal fief. The pope accepted on the grounds that the infidels who had threatened the security of Christendom would be brought into the fold, as Ruggiero promised to do. In this way, both spiritual and temporal goals were served; provision was made for the conversion of the infidel, and the ruler's claims were recognized. It was a practical accommodation aimed at the realization of universality, which the papacy saw as being threatened by an Islam that was cordoning Christianity off from the rest of the world.[2] The price was recognition of independent princely temporal powers, as Clement V would acknowledge in the case of Robert of Naples. Where once the popes had preached the Crusades to which the princes had rallied in support, the process had become one of papal recognition of the independent aggressions of Christian princes, while rescuing whatever measure of control they could under the circumstances. Even as early as the beginning of the fourteenth century, it was clear that the initiative for spreading Christianity was being assumed by the temporal monarchs; by the beginning of the next century, Poland's success in her long contest with the Teutonic Knights marked the final phase of this shift of power. As Ruggiero demonstrated, princes could now act first and bargain with the pope afterward; papal grants assumed more of the character of acquiescence to *faits accomplis*. The practice was not always followed, however, and donations sometimes preceded colonial action, as when the Canaries were awarded to Castile in 1344, and Portugal obtained a grant to non-Christian lands on the West Coast of Africa in 1455 from Nicholas V (pope, 1447-1455).[3] On the other hand, Spain did not go to Rome before commissioning the 1492 voyage of Columbus (Cristoforo Colombo, 1451-1506), which has led one authority to claim that the papal bulls of the following year were not grants at all but simply a recognition of the claims of the Christian monarchs.[4] Such situations did present popes with a dilemma. As King Duarte of Portugal (reign, 1433-1438) implied during his negotiations with Eugenius IV (pope, 1431-1447) over the Canaries, refusal on the part of the popes to sanction such enterprises and to transform them into evangelizing missions would simply open the way for unscrupulous persons such as pirates and slave traders to attack and occupy the lands of the infidels without any regulation at all, flouting the authority of God and the pope.[5]

Discovering the Canaries

Spain's acquisition of the Canaries, easily her most important overseas possession until the discovery of the Americas, in many ways foreshadowed what would happen in the New World. Once known to classical antiquity but long since forgotten, the islands had come once more within the purview of Europeans when a Genoese expedition stumbled across them while trying to reach India by circumnavigating Africa toward the end of the thirteenth century. A more precise date that is widely accepted for this rediscovery is 1312, when the Genoese Lancellotto Malocelli visited Lanzarote, one of the archipelago's islands. Of the islands' native inhabitants, reported to speak seven mutually unintelligible languages, one group attracted particular attention. This was the Guanches who, as would be the case later with Amerindians, were observed to be nearly wild men who inhabit the forest, [who] are not united by a common religion, nor are they bound by the chains of law, they are lacking in normal social intercourse, living in the country like animals. They have no contact with each other by sea, no writing, no kind of metal or money. They have no houses and no clothing except for coverlets of palm leaves or goat skins which are worn as an outer garment by the most honored men. They run barefoot quickly through the rough, rocky and steep mountainous regions, hiding. . .in caves hidden in the ground.[6]

This description is similar to that which would be made of Amerindians,[7] with two principal exceptions: the reference to maritime expertise, which the Guanches apparently lacked but which coastal Amerindians possessed to a high degree; and cannibalism, not reported in the Canaries, but quickly evident in the Indies. As also with Amerindians, Europeans presumed that conversion of the Canarians would be a simple matter, because the Guanches, like New World peoples, were reported as "having no law, belonging to no religion, worshiping only the sun and the moon."[8] When Luis de la Cerda (fl. fourteenth century), grand admiral of France and a member of Castile's royal house, successfully applied to be granted the Canaries as a papal fief from Clement VI (pope, 1342-1352), he did so on the grounds of his desire to convert the native Guanches to Christianity; Clement not only acceded' to his request, but named Luis "Prince of the Fortunate Isles," as the Canaries were known, at least partly in recognition of the fact that Luis's family had long been active in evangelization. Although the islands did not possess the gold and wealth in natural resources that would become such a factor in the Americas, Europeans quickly appreciated their strategic position for operations against Moslem Africa. Rivalries between France, Spain, and Portugal complicated the conquest of the islands, which was eventually effected by Spain with unexpected difficulty (1478-1493), after Portugal had recognized its right to do so in the Treaty of Alcaçovas, 1479. In return Spain had agreed to recognize Portuguese claims along the African coast as well as in the Azores, Madeira, and the Cape Verde Islands.

Spaniards had by now established the pattern of behavior that they would follow when they would encounter Amerindians. When not fighting the Canarians or expropriating their lands, they killed them off with overwork and bad treatment. But there was an important difference. The war against the Canarians had been elevated to the level of a crusade by Benedict XIII (pope in Avignon, 1394-1423) with his bull *Apostolatus officium* (1403), something which never happened to Amerindians. Benedict's action legitimated Spain's conquest of the islanders, despite the fact that they had neither refused entry to missionaries nor initiated hostilities. Benedict was reflecting the Christian stereotype of non-Christians who, like Ishmael, the wanderer and "wild ass of a man," were naturally against their fellow men, and needed the bridle of Christianity in order to become civilized.[9] The provisions of Benedict's bull were later repeated by Nicholas V; but despite that classification, or perhaps because of it, the missionary church was charged with the natives' protection. It was a responsibility which was taken seriously enough that at one point it was used to obtain a papal ban against further Spanish expansion on the islands. But the king successfully asserted himself, and after 1465 complaints about the treatment of the natives were dealt with by the Spanish court rather than by Rome.[10] This gave rise to the anomalous situation of the royal court protecting the natives at the same time as it was conquering them by such means as the use of Spain's infamous dogs of war, animals so fierce that one dog was reputed to be the equal of ten men. Amerindians were later to experience the accuracy of that assertion.[11] No dedicated figure of the stature of Las Casas arose to stir the conscience of the court, and by 1515 the aborigines of Gran Canaria were well on their way to extinction. The Guanches disappeared as a people, just as the Tainos and Arawaks were destined to do from Hispaniola, in what would become a series of exterminations of peoples in the New World.

Swan Song of Papal Grants

The most celebrated of the papal grants were those of Alexander VI (pope, 1492-1503), dividing the American hemisphere between Spain and Portugal, and involving a previously undreamed of expanse of territories. It was the grand swan song of this type of papal politics, which in any event was already in decline and would no longer be practised after the middle of the sixteenth century.[12] Alexander, a native of Valencia and a member of the Spanish branch of the Borgia family, issued two bulls called *Inter caetera*, the first one dated 3 May 1493, and the second dated for the following day, 4 May, but actually issued 28 June and predated. The first of these authorized the rulers of Spain to bring under their sway "countries and islands" discovered by Columbus, along with "their residents and inhabitants, and to bring them to the Catholic faith."[13] The second *Inter caetera* added to the terms of the first by drawing a line of demarcation "from the Arctic pole, namely to the north, to the Antarctic pole, namely to the south. . .the said line to be distant one hundred leagues towards the west and south of any of the islands commonly known as the Azores and Cape Verde," assigning to Spain the exclusive right to evangelize and trade in all lands to the west of that line not already under the control of a Christian prince.[14] Another bull, *Eximiae devotionis*, was also dated 3 May, but apparently did not become effective until July. It confirmed and made more explicit the grant of the new-found lands which had been conceded already in the first *Inter caetera*.[15] The fourth and final bull issued by Alexander that year relating to the New World was *Dudum siquidem*, dated 26 September. It further extended and confirmed Spain's grant, giving her the right to exclude subjects of other crowns from those lands west of the line, and revoking earlier papal grants to Portugal that appeared to be in conflict with Spanish claims arising out of her discoveries. Neither bulls nor treaties, of course, could bind third parties, so that apart from the moral support they provided in the terms of international relations, it remained incumbent upon each of the nations involved to make good its own claims. At this juncture there does not seem to have been any question of consulting the Amerindians, or even of ascertaining their rights.

The basis on which Spain could assert these claims was laid out in the second *Inter caetera*:

> With this proviso, however that none of the islands and mainlands, found and to be found, discovered and to be discovered, beyond that said line towards the west and south, be in the actual possession of any Christian King or prince up to the birthday of our Lord Jesus Christ just past from which the present year one thousand four hundred and ninety three begins. And we make, appoint, and depute you and your said heirs and successors lords of them with

full and free power, authority, and jurisdiction of every kind; with this proviso, however, that by this our gift, grant, and assignment no right acquired by any Christian prince, who may be in actual possession of said islands and mainlands prior to the said birthday of our Lord Jesus Christ, is hereby to be understood to be withdrawn or taken away.[16]

The exact import of that wording was controversial at the time and has been much argued about ever since. Perhaps the single most important question it raised was whether or not Alexander VI was authorizing war against Amerindians, at least implicitly. Las Casas, of course, denied any such intention, while Sepúlveda claimed that he did. Another interpretation has it that the pope was asserting the right to spread Christianity rather than denying the right of non-Christians to *dominium*.[17] At the time of the bulls, every Spaniard was said to have believed that the pope had granted Spain outright possession of her discoveries, a view that was reinforced when it was realized that these territories had been previously unknown to Europeans.[18]

If such a papal grant had become a mere formality by this time, why had Fernando (reign, 1474-1516) and Isabel (reign, 1474-1504) bothered to obtain it, even if precedent sanctioned such a course of action?[19] There was an important legal point at issue, and the wily Fernando was lengthening the odds as much as he could against challenges to Spain's claim. All the best legal authorities agreed that rights of discovery could only be invoked in the case of unoccupied territory, as set out in Justinian's *Institutes* (2.1.12); but on Guanahani, Columbus had planted Spain's flag and gone through the prescribed ritual of possession before a group of wondering Tainos. Not only that, he had no hesitation in naming the island San Salvador although he already knew that Amerindians called it Guanahani.[20] Since the newly discovered land was irrefutably occupied—Columbus referred to its inhabitants as "numberless"; later a French missionary would observe it was "all filled with people, like an anthill with ants. . . .it seems that God put a bottomless pit in those lands where there is the greatest quantity of all types of humans"[21]—the alternative for Spain was to obtain the right to evangelize. It was with imperial interests in mind that Fernando and Isabel sought papal sanction to take whatever measures would be necessary to evangelize the non-Christian inhabitants of this new world.

Background Considerations

At the same time, it strengthened Spain's position to acknowledge papal authority in spiritual matters. In this way pope and monarch recognized each other as supreme in their separate domains while at the same time upholding their own positions.[22] Such mutual support was particularly important at this time when the pope was facing increasing challenge from monarchs seeking to control the church within their borders.[23] Even Spain, that most Catholic of countries, never allowed the pope to exercise direct authority in her overseas domains, either at the time of discovery or later. When Paul III (pope, 1534-1539) attempted to do so in 1537 with his bull *Sublimis deus sic dilexit* in defence of the rights of Amerindians, an attempt that was repeated by Urban VIII (pope, 1623-1644) in 1639, Spanish authorities simply took care to see that the bulls were not allowed to go into effect in their colonies.

The fact that during most of the sixteenth century, Spanish clergy and missionaries acted as protectors of Amerindians, and were at one period officially designated to do so, did not alter that situation.[24] So, even as Spain sought to use papal authority to strengthen her position, and officially based her New World claims on the the 1493 bulls, particularly the second *Inter caetera*,[25] she was careful to do this in conjunction with measures that were clearly within the temporal sphere: by invoking the rights of discovery, by negotiating demarcation lines with Portugal, such as those agreed upon in the Treaties of Tordesillas (1494) and Saragossa (1529), and by the use of force. The expediency with which these measures were used is illustrated by Spain's disregard of the Treaty of Saragossa in 1542-1543, when she occupied the Philippines over the protests of Portugal. In the end Portugal had to resign herself to the Spanish action, but the dispute was not formally resolved until 1750.

Despite the wording of the bulls, Spain's right to appropriate and move into already occupied lands was not above legal challenge, as became quickly evident in the reactions of other monarchs, such as those of France and England. The problem resided in natural law: if the law applied to all men, then what about Amerindians? Did they not have the right to administer their own lands under their own laws? As earlier with the Guanches, the answer was found in the lifestyle of Amerindians. Going naked as "their mothers bore them"[26] and not being organized into social, political or religious institutions as far as Europeans could see, they were judged to be living more like animals than human beings. It was an opinion that was strongly reinforced when Columbus encountered cannibal Caribs. Since such a lifestyle and customs were not thought to indicate rationality, Amerindians were classed as "savages," not yet fully human but capable of becoming so, living in a state of nature "sans roy, sans loy, sans foy," according to the sixteenth-century catch-phrase that especially annoyed Las Casas because it was so ubiquitous.[27] In the minds of Europeans, it placed Amerindians outside of natural law since they did not fit into any of its categories, being somewhere between beasts and humans. Reports that they lived in harmony in their communities under the guidance of councils of elders, who also advised on external affairs, including wars, did not countervail the prevailing stereotype. Later, Charles Secondat, Baron de Montesquieu (1689-1755), would attempt to do so when he attributed the widespread lack of a developed civil code among Amerindians to their communal use of land: "The division of land is what principally increased the civil code. Amongst nations where they have not made this division, there are very few civil laws."[28] On the other end of the spectrum, Loys Le Roy (c. 1510-1577), professor of Greek at the Collège Royal and political philosopher, was of the opinion that even the most civilized of monarchies should have as few laws as possible consistent with good administration, as there was nothing more pernicious than "a multitude of superfluous laws."[29] Even if the essentially political nature of humans meant that they could only perfect themselves as members of an organized state, it was still possible to go too far and to overwhelm the individual by allowing the state to become an end in itself. On the whole, however, state organization, even too much, was seen as preferable to not enough, because *civitas* was an even more perfect image of God than was man.[30]

The Trappings of Authority

In the European view, the adoption of clothing symbolized the development of law, authority and power: the lavishly dressed prince epitomized civility, the naked Amerindian, the state of nature.[31] This was the reason Columbus was taken aback when he was visited by an eighty-year-old cacique "who seemed respectable enough though he wore no clothes," and who furthermore displayed "sound judgment" despite his nudity.[32] Such observations were not enough to convince Europeans that peoples who habitually went naked, even on the most solemn occasions, were likely to possess social order or government, or were even capable of them. Spanish colonial governors were instructed to gather these people into towns under the tutelage of responsible persons who would see to it that they wore clothes "como personas razonables," and that they curbed their habit of frequent bathing because of the harm it was reported to do.[33]

As if their nudity, along with their cannibalism, were not enough, many of these people were polygynists, which to Europeans was just another indication that they were outside natural law. Life in "the manner of beasts in the woods" had an even more serious implication: it meant that New World peoples had no religion at all, and so could not even be classed as infidels. On the positive side, it led Europeans to believe that they would be easy to convert, since they had no religion to unlearn.

Old World infidels, whose right to *dominium* and *imperium* Europeans had been debating for so long, were socially and politically organized within hierarchical institutions which, even if based on non-Christian principles, were conceded to possess authority, despite arguments about its legitimacy. Coming to terms with such authority involved theological and political considerations, but could be worked out apart from actual conquest. Besides, the civilizations of Arabic and Turkish Islam and of European Slavs shared some experiences with western Europeans; for one thing, they had all, to a greater or lesser degree, been exposed to Romano-Hellenic imperialism. That meant a certain commonality that could facilitate attempts at intercourse. The Mongols, untouched by such influences, presented greater challenges, but still diplomatic relations had been engaged; when Christian missionaries were sent to them, it was with the permission of the khans. The fact that the Mongols—"Tartars" as they were usually referred to by Europeans—were the most successful warriors of their time, having been prevented from conquering Europe only because of divisions among themselves, may also have had something to do with Europe's conciliatory approach. Conciliation was inspired more by expediency than by respect for their civilization, however; Mongols were considered to be barbarous by nature, and not likely to want to live in peace, in contrast to Christians, who had become domesticated.[34]

Such reservations apart, the essential humanity of Old World unbelievers was not seriously questioned, as it was with Guanches and Amerindians. The latter suffered from a double jeopardy on top of their infidelity: besides possessing savage natures, they were also in their cultural infancy.[35] Those two factors combined to convince Europeans that Amerindians could not possess the same rights as those whose natures had been refined by Christianity, and who had attained the maturity of civility. While that was not a view that attracted unanimous support among leading canonists or theologians—for one, Alonso de la Vera Cruz, professor of theology at the University of Mexico during the decade following its founding in 1551, flatly rejected it—it became entrenched in popular belief. It was also quickly noted that Amerindians, unlike Tartars, were conciliatory, and lacked "iron of whatever kind, as well as arms, for these are unknown to them; nor are they fitted for weapons, not because of any bodily deformity, for they are well built, but in that they are timid and fearful."[36] The implications had been immediately apparent to Columbus: "with fifty men they can all be subjugated and made to do whatever is required of them."[37]

The conquests of Mexico and Peru would later confirm first impressions that Amerindians by nature were "half-way between man and beast, as they have neither developed nor learned the arts of peace and war as have the people of the other three parts of the habitable world." How otherwise could so few Spaniards have conquered armies of "numberless" barbarians?[38] In the days of first contact, such observations became particularly pertinent when Amerindians were seen wearing gold and pearls, and were soon found to possess silver, but did not value them in the same way that Europeans did; for one obvious example, neither Mexica nor Maya used precious metals for currency, preferring cacao beans for the purpose.[39] As Columbus stated in his report on his fourth voyage, the "lands of this part of the world, which are now under your Highnesses' sway, are richer and more extensive than those of any other Christian power. . . ."[40] The prospect of those riches acted as a powerful catalyst as Europeans immediately began to manoeuvre to find legal and moral justification for taking control of the New World.

Into a Strange World

E urope's centuries-old debate on the rights of man was given a
new focus when she realized that across the Atlantic the Americas lay between her and Asia. But a subtle change occurred in the
tone of the discussion: the old concern about man in relation to the
divine, the part in relation to the whole, which had been so pronounced in the Middle Ages, receded in importance as the extent of
the material rewards to be gained from the exploitation of New
World resources came to be appreciated more fully. The old ideals
were not entirely lost—as witness the vigorous debates on the rights
of Amerindians and the justness of their conquest that took place during the first half of the sixteenth century in Spain—but as national
states shook free from church control, the politics of imperial expansion gained the field. During the second half of the century, the principles in front rank of importance were those of freedom of the seas,
and rights of discovery and trade, rather than those of universal justice and the unity of mankind.[1]

It was the Spaniards, with their traditional concern for the rights of
man within the framework of the law, who hammered out the theoretical case for Amerindian rights. When Spanish actions in the New
World did not measure up to the high ideals that had been elaborated
in scholastic thinking, Spanish denunciations created the public
scandal out of which the Black Legend was born.[2] Although the
Dominican Bartolomé de Las Casas[3] was to become the personifica-
tion of this campaign, his was not the only, or even the first, voice to
be heard. The question of the Spanish right to colonize in the New
World, and the way in which it could be done legally, was already
under official consideration in Spain when the issue came to a head
dramatically in Hispaniola in 1511. Missionaries sent out to evangel-

ize Amerindians had become increasingly dismayed at the disregard of the colonists for the rights of Amerindians, particularly after Isabel's death in 1504. Isabel had considered those rights seriously enough to have been upset by Columbus's action treating Amerindians as chattels when he brought some to Spain for distribution to friends and officials. Her efforts to protect her new subjects were soon tempered, however, when she learned of the existence of such "unnatural" customs as cannibalism on the West Indian Islands. One of her last acts was to authorize the enslavement of Caribs, the first New World cannibals to be encountered by Europeans. This was extended the following year to all Amerindians found to eat humans. Despite sporadic subsequent attempts to protect their liberty, the way was opened for indiscriminate wars of conquest and enslavement of Amerindians.[4]

How could evangelization be carried out under such conditions? Particularly disturbed were a group of Dominicans who had come out the year previously under Fray Pedro de Córdoba (1460-1525). Selecting Antonio de Montesinos (1486?-c. 1530) as their principal spokesman because of his oratorical skills, and carefully choosing the occasion for maximum effect, they lashed out at *repartimiento* (in practice, a system of forced labor). According to historian Antonio de Herrera y Tordesillas (1559-1625), *repartimiento* had begun unofficially under Columbus's brother, Bartolomeo (c. 1437-1518), who ordered that conquered Amerindians pay part of their tribute to the crown in the form of work in such projects as the royal mines and public construction, and for the balance work for conquistadors to whom they were commended.

It was a form of the Spanish *señorio* designed to compensate the conquistadores for their services in acquiring these new territories for the crown. The system had been formalized by Nicolás de Ovando (c. 1460-1518), who assumed office as governor of Hispaniola in 1502, and was reaffirmed in 1509, when Christopher Columbus's son, Diego (c. 1478-1526), replaced Ovando.[5] Since Isabel had expressly proclaimed that Amerindians were free and were to be paid for their labor, in theory they were tributaries of the crown, with the conquistadores acting as collectors.[6] In fact, however, a quasi-feudal lordship was forming, with all its implications of counter authority to the crown.[7] By the time that Montesinos raised his cry, the crown had already abandoned its efforts at suppressing *repartimiento* and was seeking rather to control it.[8] Denouncing this "cruel and horrible servitude" to which Amerindians were being reduced, Montesinos demanded by what right war had been waged "against these people, who dwelt quietly and peacefully in their own land?"[9] As the Dominicans saw the situation, the settlers had placed themselves in a state of mortal sin by invading and taking over Amerindian lands without just cause, and unless they repented and made restitution, could no more be saved than infidel Moors or Turks. When the colonists demanded that Montesinos either retract or leave the island with his fellow Dominicans, another denunciatory sermon followed. The settlers, successfully rallying Franciscan missionaries to their cause, sent one of them to the royal court to argue that the Amerindians could only be converted if they were personally subjected to Spanish control. They were naturally so indolent that without personal servitude they would not work for their new overlords.[10] The friar emissary, after a crisis of conscience, joined forces instead with Montesinos, who had also gone to Spain to plead his cause. Diego Colón's partisan report of the affair influenced the court to regard the sermons as an attack on the royal administration; it ordered Montesinos and his fellow friars to be silenced, which was supported by the superior of the Dominicans in Spain. But the issues of the rights of Amerindians and the legality of their conquest were not to be so summarily disposed of. Even as the friars were disciplined, the first Laws of Burgos were passed in 1512, inaugurating a long series of measures that sought to balance interests of empire with rights of Amerindians. Recognizing, if not fully approving, *repartimiento*, the laws attempted to regulate it in favor of Amerindians. They did not succeed; despite a great deal of high-sounding rhetoric, and a mass of legislation, the Spanish government never came fully to grips with the matter of Amerindian rights.

Defining Humanity

The situation that had so aroused Montesinos and his fellow Dominicans had developed as a result of the opinion generally accepted in Europe that New World peoples, although human in form, were not fully fledged human beings. The consequences of that view had been formulated by a Scots Dominican who had no direct interest either in Spain or in the New World. His comments, published the year before Montesinos' sermon, were concerned with matters of principle rather than with the realities of colonization. John Major (1469-1550), leading scholastic theologian in Paris who had taught Vitoria, was a conciliarist who held that the body faithful of the church, properly represented in a general council, was superior to the Supreme Pontiff.[11] But he also held that the pope had been acting within his jurisdiction when he had authorized Spain to evangelize Amerindians, and supported Spanish New World colonization as a means of achieving that end. Major did this, despite upholding the right of non-Christian societies to political dominion, because of reports that Amerindians lived according to nature, like animals.[12] In their case, Major thought that Aristotle's doctrine of natural servitude "that some men are by nature free and others servile," would apply; the consequence, of course, was that Amerindians did not qualify for *dominium*.[13] According to Parry, Major was the first to use this dictum of Aristotle's in connection with New World peoples.[14]

The importance of that classification is almost impossible to overestimate, as it became the theoretical mainspring not only for *repartimiento* and slavery, but also for the colonial movement itself. That it crystallized so quickly in relation to Amerindians, and on a point of theoretical principle rather than through the direct experience of actual contact, points to the difficulties Europeans immediately experienced in fitting the strange civilities of the Americas within their concept of world order. Its importance was realized by Las Casas, who at Valladolid would go to considerable lengths to refute it.[15] Vera Cruz, on the scene in Mexico City, taught that simple observation revealed the falsity of the doctrine: far from being inferior, some Amerindians were "outstanding" and "most eminent."[16]

Part of the difficulty arose from the ambiguity of the term "natural servitude": depending upon the context, it could simply denote servility, such as that imposed upon servants and war captives, or it could mean the slavery that was considered to be the natural lot of those who did not have the mental capacity to become fully developed human beings, such as barbarians who indulged in inhuman practices. In the first case the condition was not necessarily permanent, as those to whom it applied were seen as human, and thus capable of learning reason. Major appears to have used the term in the sense of servility rather than of slavery.[17] In that sense, the doctrine of natural servitude would attract powerful support, such as that of Franciscan Juan (Cabedo) de Quevedo, (d. 1519), first Bishop of Darién (today's Panama), who in 1519 unsuccessfully upheld Major's line of thought against Las Casas before Charles V (Holy Roman Emperor, 1519-1556; as king of Spain, 1516-1556, he was Carlos I).[18]

The charges of the Dominicans in Hispaniola pressured the Spanish court into speeding up the drafting of laws to regularize the situation in the Indies. Among the learned men assembled at Burgos to consider Spain's legal position in this regard was Dominican Matías de Paz (1468/70-1519), professor of theology at the University of Salamanca, who had been added to the original group through the influence of Las Casas, apparently because of his measured support for human rights.[19] Matías's treatise, "De dominio regum Hispaniae super Indos" ("Concerning the Rule of the King of Spain over the Indies"), finished in 1512, is one of the earliest full treatments of the legal and ethical aspects of the conquest that have survived.[20] Matías, approaching the issue in the terms by which it had been argued in Europe since the thirteenth century, held that Christian princes could wage war against infidels, but only to spread the faith;[21] if the infidels agreed to hear the Christian message, their lands could not with justice be invaded or permanently taken over against their will. In accepting the presence of missionaries, they would be accepting also the dominion of a Christian prince, who, however, did not have the right to enslave them.[22] The appointment of such a prince must be authorized by the pope, and the people were not to be oppressed, but could be required to provide certain services and to pay taxes and levies as did citizens in all states, including Spain. By implication Matías attacked enforced servitude, a position he would later make explicit; he also held that Amerindians should be allowed to have houses and property of their own.[23] If oppression occurred, then restitution should be made. Las Casas was to point out a principal weakness implicit in the idea of restitution: to whom could it be made, in view of the rapidity with which the oppressed Amerindians were dying off?[24]

Juan López de Palacios Rubios (1450-1524), a member of the Council of Castile and a leading jurist, was the author of the other surviving treatise, "De las Islas del mar Océano" ("Of the Ocean Isle"). Although he acknowledged the rights of non-Christians more clearly than Matías, he joined with him in arguing along lines that were closer to Hostiensis than to Innocent IV, as Las Casas did not fail to observe.[25] Natural law applied to Amerindians as to any of God's creatures, and the fact that they were infidels, did not in itself prevail over the fact that they were rational beings, and had the right to property and control over their own affairs. But Palacios Rubios did not see those rights as being absolute; they were only valid with the consent of the church, once that institution was aware of the Amerindians' existence.[26] Even then, they could be lost in war justly waged against them. Despite his firm conviction that Amerindians could not be forced, any more than anyone else, to become Christians, Palacios Rubios considered that their refusal to recognize the superior authority of the Christian Church, or to listen to its missionaries, was cause for a just war. In this, he was attuned to the mood of his day; without denying Amerindian right to *dominium*, he asserted the grounds on which Christians could override that right.[27]

Apparently Palacios Rubios saw himself as acting in the interests of Amerindians when he agreed to put into legal form the procedures deemed necessary to require them to submit peacefully to Spain and to accept her missionaries, in accordance with the 1493 bulls. This document—*requerimiento*, "requirement"—was to be read to Amerindians before undertaking military action against them. Ridiculed as it has been, it was a serious attempt on the part of the Spanish crown to observe its legal obligations, especially in view of its concern to have its wars of conquest labelled "just," and recognized as such by other European monarchs. Certainly Palacios Rubios saw it in that light; when asked about it, he held that it would protect the legal rights of all concerned, if the proper forms were observed. It was not a conviction that was widely shared, and Las Casas had little difficulty in demolishing the document's theoretical basis.[28] Written in 1513, its first recorded use was in Darién in 1514; in 1526, its use was reinforced with additional requirements, such as the presence of two ecclesiastics to ensure that the proper forms were being followed, a measure which Las Casas supported.[29]

An amplified and sterner version concluding with the threat of war *a fuego y a sangre* if the natives did not fall into line with Spanish plans was used in Mexico in the 1540s.[30] What may have been the last use of *requerimiento* was in Chile during the 1550s. It was finally superseded by other legislation in 1573 during the reign of Felipe II (1556-1598).[31] The new regulations strengthened the civil arm in colonial administration, and gave the *coup-de-grâce* to the church's role in Amerindian affairs, which had been declining during the previous half-century; bishops were no longer officially the protectors of New World peoples.[32] At the same time it sought to soften the effects of colonization: discoveries were no longer to be called conquests, Spaniards were to avoid displaying greed for the possessions of Amerindians, who in no way were to be harmed "for all we seek is their welfare and their conversion."[33]

New Laws for New Needs

In spite of all this soul-searching, the best that the court had been able to accomplish in its Laws of Burgos, was a continuation of its regulation of *repartimiento*, later identified with *encomienda*, rather than its abolition.[34] The system had not been invented in response to New World needs, although it was adapted to meet its specific conditions; it had been long in use in Spain, and was introduced to the Canaries at the same time as to the New World. At first *repartimiento* accorded with the practice of Amerindians themselves, at least insofar as it concerned the payment of tribute; but the Spaniards soon increased their demands beyond established local norms by such measures as sending Amerindians to work in mines.[35] These demands even exceeded the provisions allowed for under Spanish law, as Augustinian Alonso de la Vera Cruz pointed out with careful detail.[36] Finally put on a full juridical basis in 1563, *repartimiento* took different forms in various parts of Spanish America, and also had varying lengths of life. As a means of providing agricultural labor, it was already nonfunctional in central Mexico by mid-sixteenth century, although it was not abolished there until early in the seventeenth century; in Brazil, attempts to suppress slavery led to a variation of *repartimiento* during the closing decades of the seventeenth century; and in the Andes, in the silver mines of Potosí, where enforced labor was known as *mita*, it continued until the end of the colonial period.[37] Even abolition in the colonies did not always take immediate effect; in the Yucatan, for instance, private *encomiendas* continued for a year, until 1786.

Repartimiento's long and varied life illustrates the tenacity of the belief in natural servitude, particularly as it proved to be so useful in economic terms. The thirty-five ordinances that made up the Laws of Burgos assumed the right of Spaniards to regulate Amerindian life to conform to their notions of Christian civility, and also, incidentally, to provide a labor force for the Spanish exploitation of New World resources. Regulating conditions of work in the mines was a principal preoccupation of the laws.[38]

Spain's concern about the legality of her position in the New World was genuine enough, but it was within the context of European imperial politics.[39] Perhaps even more seriously, Spanish legislators at first assumed the same conditions and values for the Indies as existed in Europe; the process of adapting Spanish law to New World realities took time to work out.[40] Still, in theory, the mutual rights and obligations of *jus gentium*, binding upon all nations, applied in the New World "in the same way as the pre-political Law of Nature had been binding upon individuals when they were living in a state of nature."[41] Or, as Vitoria saw it, Europe's emerging law of nations was being established through a "consensus of the greater part of the whole world," even when based on human rather than natural law.[42] Universal application of those rights and obligations presumed a universally similar perception of what they were. That this might not always be the case in practice had occurred to St. Thomas:

> the law of nature, in its first principles, is the same among all men. . . . But in its particular details, which are, as it were, conclusions from the general principles. . . it may fail in validity on account of some particular obstacles. . . [or]. . . it may fail of being known.[43]

Later, St. Thomas went a step further, and said that under certain circumstances natural law itself could change. This flexibility did not alter its essential character, but allowed for the implementation of human law. For example, neither private property nor slavery were imposed by natural law.[44] On the other hand, neither did it allow for such a fundamentally different view as that of the Maya, who far from seeing law arising out of justice, considered it to be an expression of the inevitable order of the universe: in the language of the Yucatec Maya, prophecy—"the word"—had the secondary meaning of "law."[45]

Vitoria did not directly address the possibility of exceptions or variations, but observed that principles which had been generally accepted had the force of law "even though the rest of mankind objected thereto."[46] In effect this meant that the European view of natural law was applied to Amerindians whether they agreed or not. For example, Spaniards (along with Europeans generally) condemned the Amerindian custom of individual human sacrifice, conducted according to established rules, but accepted indiscriminate mass slaughter in battle, without any notion of ritual.[47] Even as Europeans insisted on their version of natural law in principle, they disagreed among themselves as to its application in practice, as each of the colonizing nations claimed the sovereign right to enact and enforce its own human (or statutory) law.

At this early date, before it was aware of the existence of either the Mexica hegemony or the Inca empire, Spain may not have considered the possibility of Amerindians possessing sovereignty, but it did recognize that quite apart from their position under natural law, they had rights by the very fact that it was claiming some of them as subjects. Accordingly, spurred by a colonization project worked out by Las Casas for settling Spaniards and Amerindians in planned towns (which, incidentally, did not succeed), Spain began enquiries and experiments to ascertain which Amerindians qualified for liberty (that is, to live like Spaniards), and which should be enslaved. The first of these enquiries, that of the Hieronymite friars sent to Hispaniola for the purpose in 1517, contributed information about colonial attitudes and practices toward Amerindians, which twenty years later would aid Las Casas and a group of concerned bishops and officials who had gone to Rome to lobby for papal intervention on behalf of Amerindians. They convinced the pope to issue the bull, *Sublimis deus*.[48] The immediate result of the Hieronymite enquiry, however, was to recommend against liberty for Amerindians, except for one individual. A subsequent enquiry led to the establishment of model villages, in which selected Amerindians were to be supervised in their new life in the Spanish manner.[49] Their failure seriously weakened arguments against reducing Amerindians to enforced service, as well as those in favor of allowing them even limited personal proprietary rights.

By the time Vitoria was preparing the first of his lectures on Amerindian rights at the University of Salamanca in 1532, Spain had conquered the Mexica and was in the process of conquering the Inca in Peru.[50] These peoples were politically organized in ways that Europeans understood, and they displayed the hallmarks of civility in that they wore clothes, traded, and built cities. But some aspects of their systems were so strange, and others so unacceptable, that Europeans wondered if it really had been Amerindians who had built the cities that aroused the admiration of the conquistadors.[51] Their conquest was justified on the grounds of violations of natural law, the most frequently cited being human sacrifice and cannibalism, tyranny and idolatry. Widespread sodomy was also cited (Oviedo and Gómara being the principal sources), but this was flatly denied by Las Casas, who said that although he was among the earliest Spaniards to arrive in the New World, he had rarely found it; Vera Cruz, from his years as missionary and then as professor at the University of Mexico, remarked that Amerindians were not "so depraved morally, nor did they indulge in vice so commonly as some hold."[52] Polygyny, although frequently practiced in the Americas and viewed by Europeans as against natural law, was not singled out as a justification for war. Rather, it was seen simply as another manifestation of the perversity of pagans. In the words of Jesuit José de Acosta (1540-1600), whose stay in the New World (1571-1587) was passed almost entirely in Peru and Mexico, "amongst the Barbarians all is contrary, for that their government is tyrannous, using their subjects like beasts, and seeking to be reverenced like gods."[53] According to Vitoria, it followed that Spain not only had a right, but a duty, to seize "the provinces and the sovereignty of the natives";[54] in his words, "it is immaterial that all the Indians assent to rules and sacrifices of this kind and do not wish the Spaniards to champion them, for herein they are not of such legal independence as to be able to consign themselves or their children to death."[55]

Other grounds would be the prevention of Spaniards from preaching the gospel; an attempt on the part of Amerindian princes to force Christian converts to return to idolatry; or resistance to the "natural right" of Spaniards to travel to Amerindian lands, to be received on friendly terms, to sojourn and trade there.[56] Spaniards, for their part, had the responsibility of acting for the good of the aboriginals, and not just for their own benefit.[57] Amerindians could prevent the use of force altogether if they voluntarily came under the sway of Spaniards, either by alliance or friendship.[58] It will be noted that all the citations supporting the Spanish position come from Vitoria's third lecture, which may have been given in 1539, or shortly thereafter. In his earlier lectures, he had been concerned about upholding Amerindian rights; in his later lecture, while still maintaining that Amerindians "were in peaceful possession of their goods, both publicly and privately. . .[and] they must. . .not be disturbed in their possessions unless cause is shown," he goes on to consider the circumstances that would justify interfering with Amerindian title, even to the point of apparently arguing against himself.[59] Las Casas reported that the emperor had taken exception to the influential professor's exposition of Amerindian rights;[60] Vitoria, wishing "to moderate what seemed to the Emperor's party to have been rather harshly put," qualified his original position.[61] He did this with some ambivalence, not quite certain about reports of Amerindians' lack of intelligence, particularly as he never went to America and does not appear to have had any direct contact with Amerindians, he still thought it likely that they were "little short of that condition," in which case their governance should be entrusted to those better equipped intellectually than they.[62] This transformation of Amerindians "from nature's slaves to nature's children" (the expression is Pagden's) would later provide a popular argument for colonization.

Where Vitoria reconsidered, at least to a certain point, others were less compromising. One of his pupils, Bartolomé de Carranza (1503–1576), archbishop of Toledo, lecturing on the Indies, held that Alexander VI's bestowal on Spain of the right to evangelize in the New World meant, in effect, that the Spanish king was tutor to the Amerindians. Once the tutoring was completed, the natives should be restored to their former liberty.[63] Vitoria's position on the "natural right" of foreigners to trade in Amerindian lands was also faulted by one of his pupils, in this case Diego de Covarrubias, who doubted that such a "right" would be compatible with sovereignty.[64] Las Casas joined in disagreeing with Vitoria on this, citing Baldo degli Ubaldi among other authorities to support his stand that Amerindians would be within their rights to refuse such permission if they did not wish to have traders among them. This position would be echoed by such jurists as Samuel Pufendorf in the seventeenth century.[65]

Still, it would be difficult to overestimate the influence Vitoria's arguments, which, if anything, gained in force after the Reformation. Such eminent jurists as Alberico Gentili and Hugo Grotius led the way. Gentili agreed with those who say that the cause of the Spaniards is just when they make war upon the Indians, who practiced abominable lewdness even with beasts, and who ate human flesh, slaying men for that purpose. For such sins are contrary to human nature. . . .And against such men. . .war is made as against brutes.[66]

Grotius would also concur that breaking the laws of nature, such as eating human flesh, justified war: "the most just war is against savage beasts, the next against men who are like beasts."[67] Grotius was writing about barbarians in general, and not Amerindians in particular. Both Grotius and Gentili agreed with Vitoria that wars against non-believers "simply because they do not share the faith" were unjust. Grotius extended this to include those unwilling to accept Christianity as well as heretics; however, those who were impious to their own gods merited punishment. Gentili added that unbelievers should be dealt with patiently, and neither constrained nor exterminated, as punishing "a guilty person whom you have no right to punish is equivalent to chastizing an innocent person."[68]

Amerindians True Lords

In the meantime, it was a student of Vitoria's who had been a missionary in the New World who pointed out the illogic of perceiving Amerindians as beasts bereft of reason who should be punished for their crimes against nature. Vera Cruz, who became a professor of theology at the newly opened University of Mexico, launched his teaching career with a series of lectures on Amerindian rights. Eventually entitled "Relectio de dominio infidelium et iusto bello," they were given between 1553 and 1556. Vera Cruz observed that if it were true that Amerindians were irrational, as was commonly believed, "it would follow that they could not sin, and so all their vices, their licentiousness, their drunkenness, their promiscuity, incest, sodomy and all the rest could not any more be imputed to them than to brute animals."[69] If they were to be held responsible for their sins (which Vera Cruz approved), then they must be judged capable of dominion. The theologian also disagreed with Vitoria that such sins were grounds for deprivation of *dominium*.

As a defender of Amerindian rights, Vera Cruz was one of a large body of religious figures in the New World working for the same cause, but whose learned, legalistic approach lacked the drama that Las Casas so skilfully employed, and so attracted much less attention. The arguments of the Augustinian and the Dominican had similar starting points: that Amerindians had been true lords of their lands since time immemorial, and that Europeans had unjustly deprived them of their *dominium*. Neither pope nor monarch had any right under natural law to make grants of Amerindian lands without the express consent of the peoples whose territories were involved.

But where Las Casas maintained his campaign in the terms of those first principles, never finding any vindication whatsoever for the Spanish presence in the New World, Vera Cruz carefully examined selected cases (excessive tribute, *repartimiento*, *dominium*, just war, among others), where he found that indeed Amerindian rights had been violated, and restitution desperately needed to be done. But once he established that Amerindians had as much claim to the protection of natural law as had Spaniards, he then proceeded to find in favor of Spanish rule in the Americas; in this, he went even further than his teacher, Vitoria, had done. Even if the conquest could not be justified—and he did not think that it could—the fact remained that Christianity had been introduced to the natives "who embraced it enthusiastically." Since "it was morally certain that, left to themselves and under their former kings and chieftains, they would not be able to persevere in the faith but would fall away and apostatize; it would follow. . .that such lords might justly be deposed and deprived of their dominion, regardless how legitimate it might otherwise be. . . .Accordingly, the Catholic king now governs them lawfully."[70] If it could be proven beyond doubt that there would be no danger of apostasy, then Amerindians could legitimately retain their own rulers. As Vitoria had also done, Vera Cruz maintained that tyranny, human sacrifice, and cannibalism justified removal of native rulers and their reduction to servitude. Those were not compromises that Las Casas ever made. Las Casas was indebted to the early Vitoria; it was the later Vitoria whose concepts and ideas Vera Cruz developed in such depth and detail.

Vera Cruz did not have Las Casas's flair for publicity; in the eyes of colonial officials, his support of Spanish rule was not sufficient to counterweigh his defence of Amerindian rights. They blocked the publication of those particular lectures, although he had no difficulty in getting others into print. It would be the twentieth century before Vera Cruz's analysis of Spanish colonialism would appear in an authoritative edition.[71]

The fact that the first lectures by the professor of theology at the newly-established University of Mexico were searching examinations of Amerindian rights *vis-à-vis* the Spaniards is another of the many indications that Europe's expansion into the Americas did not accord with proclaimed principles. Both Vera Cruz and Vitoria recognized, and even acted upon, the need to defend Amerindian rights. But when those rights conflicted with the Christian mission to teach and evangelize the world, a role for which they felt Spain to be uniquely well qualified, there was no question that it would be Amerindian rights which would be sacrificed to what was perceived as the superior order. An example of the type of reasoning that resulted is illustrated by Baltasar Ayala, the Antwerp-born jurisconsult who held a military financial post under Felipe II of Spain. He began by claiming that just wars were enjoined by the law of nations, and permitted both by canon and divine law.[72] Agreeing that it was "not a function of the church to punish unbelievers who have received the Christian faith," he also held that neither was it a function of infidels to hinder the spread of the Gospel, and since such an action on their part was "a wrong to Christians, who are entitled to preach the Gospel the world over," it would justify an attack against them.[73] Pierino Belli of Alba (1502–1575), military adviser to both the Duke of Savoy and Felipe II, did not need even that much of an excuse for attacking and enslaving Amerindians; for him it was sufficient that they were remote, out of touch with the rest of the world, and "unknown to Greeks and Romans." But he agreed with Carranza that if they accepted Christianity, they should be allowed to live in freedom under their own laws.[74]

Such justifications for European intervention in the New World fitted the mood of the times, and consequently became very influential as colonizers endlessly resorted to them to support their projects. France and England would not only make effective use of them, but would be ingenious in elaborating them to fit their own particular colonial activities. In the meantime, a voice was raised in defence of human rights that caught the attention of the highest power in Spain. The soul-searching that resulted did not deflect the course of empire, but restated basic principles effectively enough that they are still being heard today. More than that: they are fuelling aboriginal rights movements around the world. Las Casas's vision of a just society is, if anything, more powerful than ever.

Is All Mankind One?

E mperor Charles V on 14 September 1519 announced that "By
donation of the Holy Apostolic See and other just and legitimate
titles we are lord of the West Indies, the islands and mainlands of the
Ocean Sea already discovered and to be discovered."[1] It was a claim
that was already being challenged by France and England, among
other nations. But the most effective challenge of all came not from
foreigners, but from Spaniards, and from one in particular: Fray
Bartolomé de Las Casas (1484-1566), on his father's side scion of a
family reputed to have *converso* antecedents.[2] Taking up his position
solidly within the medieval juridical tradition that had been so elo-
quently championed by Innocent IV and Paulus Vladimiri, Las Casas
defended the rights of Amerindians on the grounds that legitimate
power did exist outside the church.[3] In his letter of 20 January 1531 to
the Council of the Indies, he fired the opening salvo in what has been
called the political phase of his long involvement. Like Montesinos
before him, he urged those in authority (in this case, members of the
Council) to look to their souls, which he feared were in mortal
danger because of official tolerance of what Spaniards were doing to
Amerindians.[4] He told them that the right of Amerindians to exercise
dominium was enshrined in both natural and canon law, and was also
supported by Old World historical precedent. The strength of the
arguments of Las Casas lay not only in their firm basis in the legal
theory, but also in his skilful use of history and theology.[5] Paulus
Vladimiri had earlier used similar debating techniques; but where the
Polish scholar had been embroiled in a specific situation in the Old
World, Las Casas was deeply involved with a generalized problem in
the New.[6] Both advocates had the advantage of arguing from first-
hand knowledge.

Las Casas, during fifty years of labors on behalf of Amerindians, never deviated from his view that none of the wars the Spaniards had waged against them had been just. This position was all the more remarkable in that Las Casas had started his New World career accepting the validity of Spanish actions, to the extent of being an *encomendero*, and accepting the enslavement of blacks; in fact, he did not get around to denouncing black slavery until late in life. The frankness of Las Casas on this subject encouraged doubts on the part of later scholars as to the integrity of his conversion, which had been a gradual process beginning with his renunciation of his *encomienda* in 1514. A study of his record, however, reveals that once he took up the cudgels on behalf of Amerindians, he was not only consistent in his arguments, he gained conviction as he went along. In his last memorial to Charles V and his council shortly before his death, Las Casas was still maintaining that Spain had unjustly usurped the kingdoms and lordships of the Indies which by right of possession since time immemorial had belonged to the Amerindians, that *encomiendas* were iniquitous and tyrannical, placing those who supported or benefited from them in a state of mortal sin, that by far the greatest part of the riches Spain had obtained from the New World had been stolen; and the only way that Spain could absolve itself from the evils of its actions in the Americas was to make restitution. He insisted on this to the end, although fully cognizant of the practical difficulty, not to say impossiblity, of working out such a policy.[7] Furthermore, concluded Las Casas, Amerindians would have justice on their side if they rose up against the Spaniards and eliminated them from the face of the earth.[8] This was not the only, or even the first, time Las Casas had made such a statement. In 1543, for example, he collaborated in a joint letter to the emperor which set out to prove that Amerindians could with justice make war on the Spaniards and kill them.[9] Just before his death, he sent a similar letter to Pius V (pope, 1566-1572), the only time he defied his king by appealing directly to Rome on what was essentially a temporal matter.[10]

Self-defence, of course, was universally conceded to be the right of all under natural law; but even so, those were strong words. Throughout his very active career as *procurador de los indios*, as Francisco Cardinal Ximénes Cisneros (1436-1517)[11] dubbed him in 1516, Las Casas consistently had access to Spain's seats of power; not only was he never silenced either by the crown or by the church, even in his most vociferous criticisms of Spanish behavior toward Amerindians, but he never had any difficulty getting his voluminous writings published.[12] The fact that he had been able to catch and hold the attention of his king throughout his struggle testifies to his power of persuasion, backed as it was by his grasp of legal principles which was outstanding even in a nation which at that time led Europe in jurisprudence. After the death of Las Casas, the mood of the Spanish administration changed, as Felipe II's concern about the growing power of colonists, and their unremitting hostility toward the defender of the Amerindians, shifted the emphasis away from human rights; eventually, in 1659, Las Casas's *Brevissima Relación* was banned in Aragon, and later in all of Spain.[13]

The situation was quite otherwise for Juan Ginés de Sepúlveda (1490-1573), the learned lay jurist and royal historiographer who opposed Las Casas. He did not get royal approval for the publication of *Democrates Secundus*, his defence of Spanish wars of conquest in the New World; when he succeeded in getting an abridged version published in 1550, it was in Rome. Copies which filtered into Spain were confiscated and burned.[14] A good argument can be made that up until the resignation of Charles V and his retreat into a monastery, Las Casas, the fighting monk, was in an oblique way a spokesman for the royal conscience; he appeared to have had as little difficulty in getting *cédulas* passed in favor of his projects as he did in getting his works published.[15] From the days of Isabel, the crown had accepted Amerindians as a special obligation. Spain's poor record in fulfilling that obligation dramatically illustrates both the ambivalence and limitations of royal power, particularly when operating at a distance through the intermediary of officials caught between conflicting forces.[16] Nevertheless, although some might find it hard to conceive, without the intervention of Las Casas and a host of others who shared his convictions, Amerindians would have been even worse off than they were.

Confrontation at Valladolid

By far the most famous of the many confrontations Las Casas faced during a contentious career was the one against Sepúlveda, in Valladolid, 1550-1551. Charles V ordered a moratorium on New World conquests, and the hearings were convened to determine as far as they could whether the atrocities reported to him were true, and to recommend a suitable plan by which such evils might be avoided, so that the Indians might be returned to their former freedom, and by which, at the same time, that New World, once it had been calmed by advantageous laws and careful instructions, might be governed in the future.[17]

Although Sepúlveda presented his arguments in three hours, in contrast to Las Casas who needed five days, the case stretched on for almost a year; neither the record of the proceedings nor, with one exception, the opinions of the judges have been found. In the end, no formal decision was handed down. Each side claimed victory, and the conquests continued, although more carefully regulated than before.[18]

Since Sepúlveda stood for those policies which Las Casas spent most of his life fighting, his position is worth briefly examining here. An Aristotelian humanist who, never having gone to the New World, knew nothing of the civilizations of Amerindians—as Las Casas pointedly observed, "God deprived Doctor Sepúlveda of knowledge of all this"[19]—the imperial chronicler developed his arguments from those of Hostiensis. He had four main points, beginning with the character of Amerindians.[20] Basing his position on the testimony of administrators who had worked in the Americas, such as that of Spain's official historian Oviedo (1478-1557), Sepúlveda assumed that Amerindians were unlettered barbarians, vicious and unruly, whose learning capacity was limited to the mechanical arts, who were incapable of governing themselves and therefore in need of being controlled by others more learned and cultured than they.[21] From this it can be deduced, on the authority of St. Augustine and Aristotle, that according to natural law, Amerindians were obliged to obey those who were superior in virtue and intelligence to themselves; refusal on their part to do so would justify war. Secondly, since according to Innocent IV pagans who violate natural law may be punished by Christians, Amerindians must accept Spanish domination because of their idolatry and human sacrifice. As Sepúlveda pointed out, Hostiensis, Giovanni Andreae, and Panormitanus all agreed with Innocent that the pope's power to enforce natural law extended to those outside the church.[22] Thirdly, the Amerindian practice of sacrificing innocent persons (especially children) in their demonic rituals should be stopped. Protecting the innocent from injury was an obligation under natural law, which in this case could only be done by subjugation. Sepúlveda's fourth and last argument was that his proposed measures were necessary for the spreading of the Christian faith. Christ acknowledged that sometimes force was necessary, as the parable of the banquet illustrates (Luke 14.23), and the Emperor Constantine had condoned its use. Sepúlveda, admitting that divine law forbade baptizing the unwilling, still thought that coercion could be helpful in getting them into the correct frame of mind. Because Las Casas's responses to these points, contained in the *Apologia* he read at Valladolid, are also to be found scattered through throughout his voluminous writings, they will be dealt with in the general context of his life-long struggle, rather than in the particular situation of the confrontation itself.[23]

Las Casas held that the only justification for Spain's presence in the New World at all came from the papal bulls of 1493, which had been drawn up specifically for the purpose of bringing Amerindians into the fold of Christianity. Since the pope had no coercive powers himself, he could not grant such powers to anyone else.[24] He was not the lord of the world, but the steward of God, and his jurisdiction was voluntary and spiritual; despite the wording of the bulls, all that Alexander VI had been empowered to give the Spanish king was *ius ad rem* (acting title); this could only be converted into *ius in re* (full title) through the willing consent of the Amerindians.[25] If the *dominium* of infidels was legitimate in the Old World, as a substantial body of canonists agreed, then, Las Casas reasoned, it must also be legitimate in the New, despite differences in the two situations.[26] He went so far as to argue that the Hostiensian position was heretical. In the Old World, the wars against the Saracens and Moors had been justified on the grounds that those peoples had usurped Christian territories; consequently Christians could legitimately retake those countries and depose offending rulers, as St. Thomas Aquinas and Innocent IV had argued. What was more, Islam, in some cases at least, had had ample opportunity to hear the Christian message, but had rejected it, sometimes with violence toward converts. But in the recently discovered New World, where the gospel had never been heard before, no such arguments could be made.[27] Besides, the first Amerindians encountered by Europeans had been notably peaceful. In this, as in other situations that would develop later, the Old World paradigm (with the exception of the Canaries) was turned upside down: Christians were the invaders, not the reverse, and the violence of Amerindians (as had been that of the Canarians) was the reaction of self-defence. Taking issue with Innocent IV on this point, Las Casas tirelessly denied that the church under any circumstances had authority over non-Christians living within their own jurisdictions, and marshalled a number of authorities in support of his position. In particular, he cited Zabarella:

> The power of the pope concerns the Christian people only and not other sects, so that in no way is it his business to judge those who are outside [the faith].[28]

Unwillingness to listen to the message of the missionaries did not justify papal interference in non-Christian polities.[29] Neither, without a cause recognized by all as just, which was not the case, could European rulers legitimately deprive Amerindians of their lands, or legitimately make a single slave. Las Casas rejected out of hand attempts to compare Christian conquests in the New World with those of ancient Rome in the Old; the actions of a non-Christian state, before the advent of Christianity, did not provide a valid basis for comparison, even though natural law had preceded and applied to both.[30] The Spanish monarchs recognized the logic of that position; sweeping as their claims could become, they knew that in the eyes of their countrymen, the most that they could claim would be precedence over positive statutory law. And even that was not universally agreed upon.[31]

Natural Law Applies to All

The points at issue were both wider and deeper than the matter of unacceptable practices; they concerned the fundamental ways of life of Amerindians. Did a hunting and gathering subsistence necessarily imply living like animals, as Major had accepted? Or were Amerindians in their cultural infancy, as Montaigne accepted? If they were culturally at the ABCs, did that mean that they were themselves like children, not yet capable of exercising adult human rights? Did the Aristotelian doctrine of the superior ruling the inferior, in effect creating two classes of human beings, apply in this case? Las Casas thought not; he argued that since natural law applied to all mankind, all mankind shared the same rights, and none could be excluded on any grounds whatsoever. Indeed, if the object of Christianity was to unite mankind, then it was unthinkable that there should be such a division. As for Aristotle's dictum concerning superiority/inferiority among humans, and the right of those in the former group to reduce members of the latter to servitude, it should be remembered that The Philosopher was not a Christian, and that Christ sought souls, not property.[32] Liberty was not only a fundamental right in natural law, it was a basic requirement for evangelization: the individual must come willingly to God. As Las Casas saw it, Spain could only realize the evangelical mission entrusted it by the pope through peaceful persuasion, not by force or enslavement. Such a procedure offered no guarantees of success, as infidels were not obliged to accept Christianity. Las Casas trusted the power of rational Christian argument to convince them of the errors of their beliefs.[33] He rejected Sepúlveda's claim that Alexander VI had exhorted Fernando and Isabel to subject Amerindians by means of war. Each of the debaters cited the bull *Inter caetera* to prove his point.[34] Incidentally, insofar as spiritual ends required, Las Casas fully accepted the pope's authority in secular matters, including those of the infidel.

Las Casas's vision that all mankind is one, strongly linked as it was with that of the early church, was also planted in the situation of his day. He did not argue solely from legal principles, but from personal acquaintance with the people on whose behalf he was acting. As he declared on more than one occasion, he had been among the earliest Spaniards to go to the New World, and what he had learned about Amerindians had not been from books, but from what he had actually seen and experienced.[35] He was in the New World off and on from 1502 until his fourth and final return to Spain in 1547, and in his travels in America became familiar with the civilizations of the Mayans and the Mexicans, as well as with simpler lifestyles. That said, however, it must be admitted that the record hints at his knowledge of Amerindians being wide-ranging rather than profound; for one thing, there is no suggestion that he ever learned an Amerindian language.[36] Still, he had a lively enough appreciation of Amerindian life to see no reason to equate hunting and gathering with animality or lack of human qualities:

> Some few have not yet reached the perfection of an ordered government, as was the case with all peoples of the world in the beginning, but this does not mean that they lack the necessary reason to be easily brought to an orderly, domestic, and political life.[37]

Las Casas identified several levels of barbarism, of which only one was barbarous in the full sense of the term. "Barbarians of this kind (or better, wild men) are rarely found in any part of the world and are few in number when compared with the rest of mankind." Nowhere was there a whole race of men that could be fitted into that category, or which did not have the ability to govern itself.[38] He repeatedly emphasized the point:

> From the fact that the Indians are barbarians it does not necessarily follow that they are incapable of government and have to be ruled by others, except to be taught about the Catholic faith and to be admitted to the Holy Sacraments. They are not ignorant, inhuman or bestial. Rather, long before they had heard the word Spaniard, they had properly organized states, wisely ordered by excellent laws, religion, custom. They cultivated friendship and, bound together in common fellowship, lived in populous cities in which they wisely administered the affairs of both peace and war justly and equitably, truly governed by laws that in many points surpass ours. . . .[39]

Besides, Las Casas added with not a little touch of irony, had not the Romans used the "civilizing" argument to justify their conquest of the barbarian Spaniards? Did the tyranny of the Romans toward the Spaniards justify the tyranny of the Spaniards toward the Amerindians?[40]

In one of his later works, *Apologética Historia*, begun as part of his *Historia* but which he had expanded separately as the history grew in bulk, he observed that Amerindians

> Not only have shown themselves to be very wise peoples and pos-

sessed of lively and marked understanding, prudently governing and providing for their nations (as much as they can be nations, without faith or in knowledge of the true God) and making them prosper in justice; but they have equalled many diverse nations of the world, past and present, that have been praised for their governance, politics and customs, and exceed by no small measure the wisest of all these, such as the Greeks and Romans, in adherence to the rules of natural reason.[41]

Amerindians, far from being inferior, had demonstrated a cultural capacity that was second to none. Vera Cruz was also among those who regretted that the Spaniards had destroyed native political institutions rather than leaving them intact and working through them, which would have been to the advantage of all.[42]

Sacrifice a Form of Worship

As for those whose customs included human sacrifice, Las Casas upheld the position of the church that the oppressed and innocent must be protected, while at the same time pointing out that human sacrifice once had been widespread even among European peoples, including Spaniards.[43] Sacrifice is the highest form of worship, and is an obligation under natural law that is due to God alone. But natural law does not prescribe the way in which this obligation is to be carried out; rather, that is left to human law, which once passed, is to be obeyed. Since "nothing in nature is greater or more valuable than the life of man or man himself," it was not surprising that "unbelievers who have neither grace nor instruction" should sacrifice the "supremely precious thing," that is, human beings, particularly when the welfare of the state was at stake. Human sacrifice, far from being forbidden by natural reason, was prompted by it. All things, even men, are owed to God, Las Casas argued, as God himself had made clear when he had commanded Abraham to sacrifice his only son, although he had not required the act to be carried out.[44]

There was no offence against natural law, Las Casas claimed, so horrible as to justify wholesale conquest and enslavement of entire peoples. He flatly denied that either human sacrifice or the eating of human flesh justified waging war on any kingdom.[45] Punishment in such a case was a prerogative of God; and, as Suárez would later observe, God was capable of avenging himself. Moreover, "it would not have been well for the human race had men received this power from God, for the greatest disorder would have resulted therefrom." Concerning the protection of the innocent, Suárez remarked that "if the reasoning in question were valid, it would always be permissible to declare such a war on the ground of protecting innocent little children."[46]

What was more, Las Casas added, the church did not have the authority to punish the sins of infidels committed within the borders of their own territory.[47] As far as human (positive) law was concerned, within their own borders Amerindians were their own masters and subject only to their own laws:

> No pagan can be punished by the Church, and much less by Christian rulers, for a superstition, no matter how abominable, or a crime, no matter how serious, as long as he commits it precisely within the borders of the territory of his own masters and his own unbelief.[48]

Las Casas, in parting company from Innocent IV, was reaffirming even more strongly than Innocent had done the sovereignty of non-Christians (in this case, Amerindians) within their own national borders. Before condemning the actions of others, he added, Spaniards should look to their own. They sacrificed "to their well beloved and adored Goddess of Greed more victims in one year than the Indians in one hundred years." It was a sentiment that would later reverberate in Montaigne.[49] To Sepúlveda's argument that armed intervention would prevent crimes against nature, the response was that justice was not served through the slaughter and suffering of many for the sake of the preservation of a few.[50] "Therefore," Las Casas warned, "let those who, under the pretext of spreading the faith, invade, steal, and keep the possessions of others by force of arms—let them fear God, who punishes perverse endeavors."[51]

The obligation of the church to teach the gospel to all nations did not imply that Christians were allowed to force unbelievers to hear the gospel. Quite the opposite, Las Casas argued: "Divine Providence instituted only one and unique method of teaching the true religion throughout the world and throughout time, which is through willing persuasion by means of gentle reasoning."[52] He contended that the "wedding banquet" parable in the fourteenth chapter of Luke, in which the lord bids the servant to "compel them to come in, that my house may be filled," refers not to external coercion, but to the interior compulsion of the voice of God. Resorting to the authority of St. John Chrysostom ("The Golden Mouth," 334-407) in support of his interpretation, Las Casas added that in another sense, the passage referred to heretics, not pagans. Turning this time to St. Augustine, he held that restraining those who refused to persevere in the faith they had accepted was an entirely different matter from forcing those who had not only never heard the gospel, but did not even know there was one. This argument found Vera Cruz taking the opposing side; he thought the parable meant what it said literally, and that there were occasions when choice should not be allowed.[53] In Las Casas's view, unless Christianity was spread gently and with charity, it would defeat its own purpose. Warfare implanted hatred rather than the meek and gentle spirit of Christ.[54] As he pointedly asked, "What advantage is there in destroying idols if the Indians, after being treated in this way, keep them and adore them secretly in their hearts?" Christians would serve their purpose much more effectively if they first sought to "break the idols" in the hearts of pagans.[55] Although Las Casas does not appear to have known about them, his arguments mirrored those of Roger Bacon in the thirteenth century to the pope, and those of Paulus Vladimiri early in the fifteenth century to the Council of Constance.[56]

New Laws a Hollow Victory

The persistent campaigning of Las Casas and his fellow Dominicans, and the pervasive authority of Vitoria, were major influences in the passage of the New Laws in 1542.[57] Amerindians were no longer to be enslaved for any cause whatsoever, and those who were being unjustly held were to be put at liberty. Existing *encomiendas* were to be severely restricted, and no more were to be granted; when present holders died, their Amerindians were to revert to the crown. No more Amerindians were to be captured in expeditions, and the amount of tribute exacted was to be controlled by the governor. Even the Council of the Indies was subjected to an inspection, and was temporarily suspended during the process. It was at this time, 1544, that Las Casas was consecrated bishop of Chiapas, a position he held until the debate with Sepúlveda in Vallodolid, 1550, although he was in the colony for only two of those years, 1545-1546.

The high hopes of Las Casas and his associates were doomed to be dashed, as their success in getting the new legislation passed proved to be a hollow victory. They had overestimated the power of the law to engage the compliance of the *encomenderos*. Quite the contrary, the reaction of the settlers was so violent, and so sustained, leading to open rebellion and the deaths of a viceroy in Peru and of a bishop in Nicaragua, that by 1546 the most controversial of the measures restricting *encomiendas* had been modified or revoked.[58] Against this tide, Las Casas won what could have been an important victory in a decree of 1549, prohibiting new conquests. But it, too, proved to be short-lived, and was revoked in 1556. In the midst of these disappointments, the crown quietly continued its efforts to curb *encomiendas*, so that in Mexico by 1642 it had succeeded in bringing all but 140 under the control of the king. In Andean Venezuela after 1718, they reverted to the crown as they fell vacant.[59] The motives for this, however, had less to do with Amerindian rights than with the crown's desire to curb the powers of the *encomenderos*, who demonstrably had become able to challenge the royal court itself. Las Casas's success during his lifetime in winning the ear of Charles V had been at least partly due to the fact that the court saw the defence of Amerindian rights as a means of controlling the *encomenderos*, whose power was based on the denial of those rights. It was a fortuitous conjunction of goals that did not endure long after the death of the friar, when long-simmering antilascasian sentiment erupted into the fore. Predictably, it led to a worsening of the lot of Amerindians; even the comparative moderation of such men as Vera Cruz was seen as too much in favor of aborigines.[60]

The crown had relatively more success with the abolition of Amerindian slavery, although it was forced to continue the judicial practice of condemning natives convicted of criminal offences to enforced service. But it refused to allow this for life.[61] Also, it was unable to stop the taking of Amerindians as slaves in frontier wars, which continued until well into the eighteenth century. The great debate at Valladolid had aired the issues, but had not resolved the practical problems involved. The justice of waging war against

Amerindians continued to be debated, with lessening conviction, until some new development, usually on a frontier, would reactivate the issue. An illustration of what could happen is provided by the discovery of silver deposits in the land of Mexico's Chichimecs in mid-sixteenth century. When the Chichimecs resisted the consequent invasion of their territories, Spanish colonials raised the cry of the necessity of war *a fuego y a sangre*. An exhaustive investigation into the justifiability of such an action by the Third Mexican Provincial Council (1585) led to bitter exchanges between the colonists, who saw no sound reason whatsoever for Amerindian resistance to Spanish expansion, and the bishops, who pointed out that the Amerindian behavior could be seen as self-defence. Although the Council finally decided that war by fire and blood could not be justified under the circumstances, hostilities and enslavement of prisoners continued.[62] The 1542 laws represent the last major attempt on the part of the crown to modify seriously the colonial system which by now was thoroughly established in its American colonies. The doctrine of consent had been given a new and restricted meaning: "what touches all is to be approved by all" had come to mean "what touches all who are heard is to be approved by all who are heard." In the clamor, Amerindians were not being heard, not only in Spain, but in Europe generally. The Council of Trent, for instance, did not include representatives of New World bishops; Amerindian affairs were not on the agenda.

Speaking Out

Not that Amerindians had nothing to say when they got the chance. If they became Christian, some Mexicans wondered, would the Spaniards then be obliged to leave their country? Some Spanish authorities endorsed the principle that Christianization should be accompanied by the restoration of self-government.[63] In 1552, certain Amerindians from Texcoco presented the town council with a petition claiming ownership of a large part of Mexico.[64] In 1566, the year of his death, Las Casas served as a witness in a suit brought by Amerindians of Cobán against their *encomendero*.[65] Others petitioned the king for relief from burdens, such as the tithe and tribute.[66] Despite the battles that had been waged on the question of the universality of human rights, such attempts at speaking out did not stand much chance of success, even though in New Spain Amerindians had access to the courts. The prospects of immediate advantage were much too powerful for long term altruism to achieve anything more than amelioration, and in minor aspects at that, of the Amerindians' lot. The law that prevailed was not the natural law that Las Casas upheld so vigorously, but one that was rooted in the politics of power.

Las Casas's battle for human rights was based on principles that far from being new, were solidly established even in his day. St. Thomas had laid them out clearly, and Las Casas was a faithful disciple. What was new was the application of those principles to strange and unforeseen situations. From one point of view, Las Casas could be classed as a reactionary in his insistent reaffirmation of old ideals that were appearing to be anachronistic in the light of new worlds and new opportunities. But from another point of view, he can be classed as a progressive with a vision of the future as he asserted the relativity of human affairs. Rather than being judged by the standards of a global ideal, peoples should be assessed within the framework, and from the point of view, of their own cultures. As Todorov has pointed out, this was a position in human affairs that would be paralleled for the physical world by another Dominican, Giordano Bruno (1548-1600), working on the basis of the ideas of Copernicus. The ideas of Las Casas were tolerated, but those of Bruno were not, and the latter was publicly burned by the Inquisition as a result.[67] The reason lay at least partly in the fact that Bruno denied the Christian hierarchy which placed the spiritual over the material, a point to which Las Casas never pushed his arguments. Columbus's voyages not only enlarged Europe's perception of the world, they accelerated forces that would change the Old World as profoundly as the arrival of Europeans would change the New World.

Routes of Challenge

Trade and Land

As was readily foreseeable, the papal bulls of 1493 did not sit well with other European rulers whose initial discontent ballooned into outrage when the extent of the grants was realized. As the Spanish ambassador to France reported in 1540, the French monarch had stated flatly that the pope did not have the power "to distribute lands among kings, and that the Kings of France, and other Christians, were not summoned when the partition took place." The ambassador plaintively admitted to his monarch, "I have not been able to settle anything but that his subjects shall not go to your lands or ports."[1] The following year, the French king informed the Portuguese ambassador that "he intended to proceed with conquests and voyages, which were his right as well as that of other princes of Christendom, and intended to preserve friendship and good understanding with certain princes of the Indies."[2] Such bluster notwithstanding, the bulls had placed the powerful weapons of tradition and official sanction in the hands of Spain and Portugal, and those nations were prepared to use them to whatever extent and by whatever means necessary to defend their positions. This was particularly serious in the case of Spain, already well on her way to becoming the superpower of sixteenth-century Europe. Of the two nations which were most inclined to take up the challenge—France and England—France was initially in the better position for such an enterprise. Since a head-on confrontation placed too much at risk, including chances of success, the French crown cast around for other means of realizing its goals.

The first way that presented itself developed out of France's burgeoning textile industry, for which red dye, very rare in Europe, was much in demand.[3] Quickly taking advantage of the new source of the dye presented by the brazilwood that flourished along Brazil's Atlantic coast, the French moved to form alliances with the Tupinambá-Guaraní, in whose lands the best stands were found. Since this was territory that was indisputably within the Portuguese zone of influence according to the papal bulls, the French did not waste any time in making territorial claims that would have been controversial at best. Instead, invoking the right for all nations to participate in this new trade as well as the freedom of the seas for right of access,[4] French merchants, with tacit royal encouragement and support, concentrated on developing the Tupinambá-Guaraní as partners for the cutting and preparation of the dyewood for shipping to Europe. Since the Tupi were the original inhabitants, or at least were there when the Europeans arrived, they had a right to be consulted, and to have their wishes taken into account. The legal basis for this was expressed in the Roman legal maxim that had long since become established in canon law, *quod omnes tangit, ab omnibus approbetur* (that which touches all is to be approved by all).[5] Wondering loudly if the doctrine did not apply to Amerindians as well as to Europeans and other peoples of the world, the French set about cultivating alliances with Amerindians in those areas where they wished to establish themselves. They reinforced this approach by bringing delegations of native Brazilians to France to be presented at court where they formally requested French protection for their lands and people, and asked for missionaries to instruct them in Christianity. Baptismal spectaculars were staged at court for some of these visitors, with the greatest nobles standing in as godparents. A favorite public pageant of the period, the royal civic entry, came to include Amerindians (usually Brazilians) in the procession of captives who made their submission to the king.[6]

Such public proclamations of France's claimed right to evangelize and colonize in the New World were more successful in marshalling the French people's support for their crown's projects than in convincing colonial rivals. When the Portuguese succeeded in making a spectacular capture of a richly laden French trading vessel, the *Pélerine*, in 1532, the French claimed restitution not only on the grounds of freedom of the seas and freedom of trade, but also on the grounds that Europeans had no jurisdiction over Brazilian natives.[7] The Portuguese were able to destroy eventual French attempts at colonizing in Brazil, and finally, to curtail French trading activities along its coasts. But it took them more than a century to do so.

Fifteen years before their first attempt to settle in Brazil (1555-1560), the French had made a similar effort in Canada on the St. Lawrence (1541-1543). They had done this because in that northern region European territorial claims were poorly defined, and therefore open to dispute. The French, initially cautious, saw their opportunity in the fact that it was not clear at first on which side of the dividing line Canada lay. The Portuguese, already active in the cod fisheries of the Grand Banks, inclined toward the view that at least the eastern portion of the land was theirs, and in the second decade of the sixteenth century sought to back up this position by establishing a colony somewhere on the North Atlantic Coast (generally believed to have been on Cape Breton Island, but no supporting archaeological evidence has been found). It was not much longer lived than the first French attempts would later be on the St. Lawrence and in Brazil, but for different reasons: the Portuguese were not really interested in colonizing so far north when they already had more than enough colonial projects in other parts of the world. While they attached considerable importance to the exploitation of the fisheries, they could continue that activity without the encumbrance of colonization.[8] Spaniards were inclined to share this approach in regard to their own claims, but with some reservation, as in addition to the cod fisheries, Spanish Basques were developing a profitable oil industry from the whale run in the Strait of Belle Isle and the walrus rookeries in the Gulf of St. Lawrence. Then as now, oil was important for Europe's energy needs, and the North Atlantic Coast was proving to be a major source. Further complicating the scene, the activities of French Breton fishermen were acknowledged by cartographers, who regularly included "Tierra de los bretones," "C. del breton," or variations thereof in their maps of the region. In effect, the Bretons were considered to have been the discoverers of those coasts, despite the voyage of Giovanni Caboto under the English flag in 1497.

Challenging the Demarcation

The uncertainties of the situation were such that in 1524 France was emboldened to challenge the papal demarcation directly by sending

Giovanni da Verrazzano (c. 1485-1528) to explore the North Atlantic Coast, an enterprise that had the sanction of the king, but which was supported and perhaps initiated by Lyons mercantile interests. Ostensibly the explorer was looking for a passage to the Orient, but he was instructed also "to go in search of new lands for this most serene crown of France."[9] Although the northwestern route to the Orient proved to be as elusive for Verrazzano as for others, his accomplishment in ascertaining that Acadia in the north was connected by 2400 kilometres (1500 miles) of continuous coast to Florida in the south has been ranked in importance with Cabral's discovery of Brazil twenty-four years earlier. Verrazzano established beyond doubt that North America was a continent distinct from Asia.[10] Unfortunately his instructions for this voyage are lost; so is his official report to François I (reign, 1515-1547). The principal evidence known to have survived consists of several copies of a letter draft that appears to have formed part of that report. On this fragmentary basis it has been argued that since the letter "mentions neither acts of taking possession nor territorial claims," Verrazzano did not have such a purpose in view, despite observations to the contrary by such a well-known colonizer as René Goulaine de Laudonnière (d.c. 1572) and the Jesuit missionary Pierre Biard (1567/68-1622).[11] Two of the most widely-known French cosmographers of the sixteenth century, François de Belleforest (1530-83) and André Thevet (1516/17?-1592), both categorically claimed that the lands from (and including) Florida to the north had been discovered and taken possession of by the French in the name of their king.[12] The argument against French imperial intentions also ignores the fact that the explorer reported his discoveries in proprietary terms: "all the land we found was called Francesca after our Francis."[13] He then proceeded to name specific places with an eye to gratifying the king: an island after his mother, a region after a royal duchy, a bay after the king's sister, and so on. Other important French personnages were similarly honored; Verrazzano was not only claiming territory for France, he was seeking high-placed support for another voyage to those coasts. The argument against this interpretation also ignores reported official interest in the commercial prospects raised by the voyage, spurred by citizens eager to capitalize on them: "And we hope that S.M. will entrust him [Verrazzano] again with half a dozen good vessels and that he will return to the voyage."[14] In this he was successful, and four ships were repaired and equipped for what appears to have been conceived as a colonial enterprise. It was reported that he intended

> to persuade the Most Christian King to send to those regions a good number of people, to live in certain places of the foresaid coast, which have a temperate climate, a very fertile soil with very beautiful rivers and harbors suitable for any fleet; the inhabitants of which places would be the source of many good effects, among others that of bringing those rough and ignorant people to the divine worship and to our most holy faith and of showing them how to cultivate the land, by means of transporting some animals from our Europe to those most spacious fields.[15]

But European politics interfered. François, realizing that his planned invasion of Italy in his war with the Holy Roman Empire's Charles V would involve him on sea as well as on land, included Verrazzano's ships among those he requisitioned. Thus was the proposed colonization voyage aborted.[16] François's capture at Pavia in 1525, and the year he spent as prisoner of the Spanish, meant that he was too involved at home to follow up on Verrazzano's work. The explorer's untimely death in the Lesser Antilles in 1528 provided the *coup de grâce*, at least for the time being.[17]

Despite François's failure to capitalize on Verrazzano's achievements, other European powers apparently were disposed to recognize that they gave France a valid claim to the North Atlantic Coast. This is evidenced by the speed with which cartographers adopted the explorer's nomenclature. Verrazzano's original map has not survived; what is presumed to be a copy, by his brother Girolamo, is dated 1529. But two years earlier, in 1527, Vesconte de Maggiolo (fl. 1504-1549) already had availed himself of Verrazzano materials for his beautifully executed world planisphere. His is the first map that has come down to us to label the coast north of Florida "Francesca."[18] Also worthy of special note is the Robertus de Bailly globe of 1530, which closely follows the cartography of Girolamo.[19] An anonymous Portuguese map, dated c. 1550, shows six fleur-de-lys flags along the coast from Florida to Labrador, indicating some sort of recognition of a French claim to the territory, all the more remarkable because of Portugal's own claims.[20] Giacomo de Gastaldi (d. 1568) used Verrazzano's place names in his 1548 map, apparently the prototype for his much better-known chart which illustrated Giovanni Ramusio's *Navigationi et Viaggi* III, in 1556. Gastaldi labelled the northeastern region "La Nuova Francia," a name that had first been used by Girolamo da Verrazzano under the form "Nova Gallia," but in conjunction with Yucatan. [21] That France had established a generally recognized claim is evident enough; it is equally evident that François I was unable to take immediate advantage of it. There appears to have been some French trading voyages in the Chesapeake Bay area, and perhaps along adjacent coasts, but that is all. The fact that by 1524 it had become perfectly clear that at least Florida and its adjacent coasts were on the Spanish side of the line may have contributed to France's caution in making immediate claims. [22] Later, it would have no hesitation about using Verrazzano's voyage as the basis for its assertions of title to New France. [23]

Ambiguous Claims

Still, the voyage clearly established the feasibility for France of acquiring an overseas empire, which fitted in nicely with François' dream of national aggrandizement. It gave him room to manoeuvre, at least toward the north, where colonial land claims were particularly vague in geographical terms. His explorers could set up crosses, a favorite means by which Europeans claimed territories they considered to be uninhabited, but could always say that they were simply navigation markers should there be objections. [24] No evidence has survived that Verrazzano did so, but Jacques Cartier followed this practice in 1534, and again in 1535-36. That Spain was concerned about France's activities is evidenced by the fact that she kept a watch on them, without, however, making any overt moves to interfere. [25] Cartier is reported to have used the navigational marker explanation when a native headman, presumed to be Donnacona of Stadacona (a Laurentian Iroquois village on the site of Quebec City), objected to the cross he had erected. [26] Even at that early date, Amerindians had a clear perception of the implications of such actions on the part of Europeans.

France's circumspection in this regard was motivated by concern about the reactions of her European rivals, rather than by commitment to the rights of Amerindians as such. In selecting Canada as the site for her first colonization project in the Americas, she relied upon discovery claims she had established officially during the Cartier voyages and unofficially through the activities of Breton fishermen, as well as upon Iberian disinterest in the north, and the fact that both Spain and Portugal were fully occupied with more immediately attractive colonization projects elsewhere. Even so, France was careful to so arrange matters that as far as Spain was concerned,

> Cartier has gone to make discoveries in parts not belonging to us nor the most Serene King of Portugal; saying that to uninhabited lands, although discovered, anyone may go.[27]

In this particular case, the French had not found it useful to classify the aboriginal peoples as inhabitants, as they had done in Brazil. Neither did they invoke the doctrine of *quod omnes tangit* as they were doing with the Brazilian natives in face of the aggressive stance of the Portuguese. Instead, they resorted to the legal fiction of *terra nullius*, of uninhabited lands; the precedent for such a position had been established by the Portuguese when they claimed rights of "discovery" along the well-populated African coast toward the end of the fifteenth century.[28] It was founded on the argument that the aborigines, living a wandering life without settled abode, "like beasts in the woods," were not inhabitants according to European law, as they ranged rather than inhabiting the land. The commission of Admiral Philippe de Chabot (1480-1543) to Cartier for his second voyage makes no mention of aboriginal inhabitants at all, but simply instructs him to complete the discovery of territories "beyond New-found-land" that he had begun on his first voyage.[29] If these lands were uninhabited, then neither Spain nor any other power could legally prevent France from claiming the rights of discovery, and following up with settlement, despite the papal division.

Once such a claim was made, the next step was to secure it by establishing a colony. Since there were people in the region, (it was consistently reported as being well populated), that fact had to be dealt with in one way or another. Accordingly, when France moved in 1541 to establish a settlement on the St. Lawrence in lands "uninhabited or not possessed or controlled by a Christian prince," its commission to Jean-François de la Rocque de Roberval (c. 1500–1560), after affirming a general intention to spread Christianity, turned belligerent in tone, and authorized him

> to go and come into the said strange countries, to land and enter into them and put them in our hand, as much by way of amity or friendly agreements, if that may be done, as by force of arms, strong hand, and all other hostile means, to assail towns, castles, forts, and habitations, and to construct and build or have constructed and built others in said countries, and to place inhabitants therein, to create, constitute, establish, dismiss and displace captains, justices, and generally all other officers that shall seem good to him, in our name, and whatever shall seem to be necessary to him for the maintenance, conquest, and protection of the said countries, and to attract the peoples of them to the knowledge and love of God and to settle and to hold these in our obedience. . .[30]

This was not the language Admiral Gaspard II de Coligny (1519–1572) would use later when commissioning his colonial attempts, first in Portuguese Brazil, and then almost immediately in Spanish Florida (1562–1565). In both of those cases, the presence of colonial rivals ensured that officially, at least, the French would cultivate alliances with the Amerindians. In Brazil, this meant developing and extending the trading alliances they already had firmly in place with the Tupinambá; in Florida, it meant establishing new alliances, although this was not entirely successful as the French became infected with gold fever, lost sight of their original purpose, and consequently ran afoul of local politics. On the St. Lawrence, where colonial rivalry was less immediately evident, there was also less attention paid to maintaining good relations with the Amerindians, in spite of an early awareness of prospects for a lucrative fur trade. As in the case of Florida, visions of gold blinded the colonists to other realities, in this case their unfamiliarity with northern conditions, particularly the climate. The failure of the St. Lawrence colony in 1543, however, did not dampen hopes for a happier outcome in the future. This was indicated by an inscription on the Descelliers world map of 1550: "As it is not possible to trade with the people of this country because of their aloofness and the intemperance of the land and small profits, they [the French] had returned to France and hoped to come back when it pleased the King."[31] That the king had every intention of pursuing the matter was soon evident: in 1550 Henri II (reign, 1547-1559) commissioned Geographer Guillaume Le Testu (c. 1509-1572) to map the New World, particularly those areas where France was trading, or perceived promising commercial prospects, such as Brazil and Canada. In his *Cosmographie universelle selon les navigateurs tant anciens que modernes. . .* (Le Havre, 1555), dedicated to the admiral of France, Le Testu illustrated Canada with the French lilies fluttering over it.[32] Interestingly enough, the Portuguese mapmaker, Antonio Pereira, in 1545 had also shown the fleur-de-lys flying in Canada, indicating French settlements (probably fishing stations).[33]

Variant circumstances in Brazil and Canada had led the French to use different methods in each country to challenge the Alexandrine bulls. In the first case, they had concentrated on trading alliances with the natives rather than on territorial claims, a technique which brought substantial commercial benefits but which did not result in permanent colonies. In Canada, the French claimed the rights of discovery before sending out colonists to make their presence a *fait accompli*, and at first did not include the aborigines in their plans. The colony's failure quickly revealed such a course of action to have been an error: along with the need to learn how to survive in a rigorous climate, the burgeoning demands of the fur trade, and escalating colonial rivalry with the English, this provided convincing evidence that a system of Amerindian alliances, already proven useful in Brazil, would be effective here also. But alliances did not involve recognition of aboriginal rights in principle, and once the French succeeded in establishing a colony at Quebec in 1608, they were were soon making grants of land to colonists without any prior consultation with the aborigines. The argument has been advanced that the St. Lawrence valley had been abandoned. This was true as far as established villages were concerned; but it was being used as a hunting territory. The French themselves recognized that their procedure was not only beyond the pale of natural law, but even of *jus gentium*, as Paris lawyer Marc Lescarbot (c. 1570-1642), who was in Acadia 1606-1607, observed:

> The earth pertaining, then, by divine right to the children of God, here is no question of applying the law and policy of Nations, by which it would not be permissible to claim the territory of another.

This being so, we must possess it and preserve its natural inhabitants, and plant therein with determination the name of Jesus
Christ and of France.[34]

Since the law of nations was deemed not to apply, it was a short step
to assume rights in the New World that did not exist in the Old,
where in law rulers could not arbitrarily appropriate lands without
the consent of the individuals or communities involved.[35] The French
did this according to the seigneurial system, which in Europe had
reached its fullest development in France during the Middle Ages, but
they did not extend it to the persons of Amerindians as both the
Spanish and Portuguese had done. What this reflects is the difference
in economies between the French and the Spanish/Portuguese colonies: the latter were based on agriculture (including sugar plantations) and mining, both labor intensive; the French, once successfully
established on the St. Lawrence, concentrated on trade in furs, the
production of which was long a monopoly of Amerindians. The alliances that were essential for such an enterprise involved a *de facto* recognition of Amerindian rights, just as they had done in Brazil. Evidence abounds in colonial records that the Amerindian allies, whether
in Brazil or in Canada, regarded themselves as free and sovereign
partners of the French. The French, for their part, had little hesitation
about interpreting their actions one way in the colonies and quite differently in Europe, a procedure which can hardly be described as
unique to them.[36] Like their colonial rivals, they never wavered from
their view that Amerindians as "hommes sauvages" were living
metaphors for anti-social forces which it was their duty to reduce to
order through evangelization—*humaniser*, as it was usually expressed.
The rights they recognized for Amerindians were those of the individual, not of the community or nation.

Ambiguous Diplomacy

An illustration of this diplomatic double-think concerns an episode
well-known in the history of New France, when French officer
Simon-François Daumont de Saint-Lusson (d. 1677), acting under
orders "to take possession, in his place and in his Majesty's name, of
the territories lying between the East and the West, from Montreal as

far as the South Sea, covering the utmost extent and range possible,"
in 1671 convoked a gathering at Sault Sainte-Marie. The French officer had received his orders from Jean Talon, intendant of New
France 1665-1668 and 1670-1672, who for his part had been instructed "to cause the name and the sovereignty of our invincible
Monarch to be acknowledged by even the least known and the most
remote Nations." Calling together officials, missionaries and representatives of fourteen Amerindian nations at the local Jesuit mission,
Saint-Lusson formally took possession of "the land of the Ottawa."
A cross was erected, and a post to which the arms of France were affixed, while the crowd cheered "Long live the King" and a sod of
earth was raised three times. There were speeches on the part of
French and Amerindians; the Ottawa themselves came late, but
agreed with what had been done, swearing allegiance to the French
king in their turn.[37] In the evening, a great bonfire was lit. The French,
asking for permission to trade and for free passage, also asked "that
the fires of the Ojibway and the French be made one, and everlast-
ing." They undertook to always see that the people who had entered
the pact were protected.[38]

By this ceremony, the French considered that they had acquired
suzerainty over this vast region, and the natives considered they had
won a valuable new ally. Such a *double-entendre* was characteristic of
possession ceremonies in the presence of aboriginals with whom the
colonial power wished to remain on good terms.[39] It should also be
noted that the aborigines were far from being oblivious to European
interest in their land, but at that point they neither knew the capacities
of French power nor possessed the means to prevent colonial expansion. The Iroquois, for instance, were not happy when the French under Governor-General Louis de Buade de Frontenac et de Palluau
(1622-1698) established Fort Cataraqui on their territory in today's
southern Ontario in 1673, but they were unable to prevent it. At
Sault Sainte-Marie, the Amerindians could have been lulled into a
false sense of security because they so heavily outnumbered the
French, and were separated from them by such great distances.

But imperial rivalries could make strange bedfellows, and so
France, which considered itself the most civilized of nations, made alliances with Amerindians it considered savage, in order to invoke the
principle of consent, and so legitimize its New World claims. Later,
during colonial wars with Britain, the French would disclaim respon-

sibility for the actions of Amerindians fighting in their cause on the grounds that they were independent allies, and so not under their control. That approach opened the way for the later claim that this was a form of recognition, and as such could be used to support the position that Amerindians had been acknowledged as sovereign during early encounters with Europeans, at least by implication.[40] That this was far from what the absolute monarchs of France had in mind at the time became only too clear once they were successful in establishing colonies in Amerindian lands; at that point, there was no question in the mind of French officialdom but that the laws of France applied to the natives as well as to the settlers. For instance, in the Treaty of Utrecht in 1713, France ceded large portions of her North American colonies, including Acadia, to Britain. Despite the fact the natives of Acadia had fought consistently and effectively in the French cause, their lands were given up without their consent or even their knowledge; in fact, the only Amerindians mentioned in the treaty were the Five Nations, and that because they were being claimed as subjects by the British. It had apparently never occurred to French officialdom to consult with their own allies. Aboriginal rights never were the subject of debate in France that they were in Spain; however, in the final analysis, as far as the natives were concerned in the terms of international law, there was little to distinguish the French approach from the Spanish in the matter of Amerindian sovereignty.

Jus Gentium Takes on
New Meanings

France was far from being alone in her challenges to Spanish and Portuguese claims in the New World; in fact, the immediate reaction of those European powers in a position to act was to move as quickly as possible to take advantage of the new opportunities that glittered on the horizon of the Atlantic. At first, little, if any, thought was given to the rights of the people of those beckoning lands; Isabel of Castile was an exception, and her concern was for Amerindians as Spanish subjects. Europeans, seeing themselves as the "children of God," did not question the priority of their rights over those whom they regarded as human in shape but little else. Religion had ceased to be central to the issue of sovereignty, which by this time was being argued in humanist terms; but humanism was not more favorable to Amerindians than theology had been. Instead, it reinforced the perception of Amerindians as "savages" living outside of society, a perception which influenced Europeans into sweeping aside concerns about legitimacy of authority, and sovereign and individual rights as far as natives of the New World were concerned, except perhaps tangentially as a means of belaboring colonial rivals. Those rivalries transformed the search for legitimacy of power into a jockeying for recognition on the part of the European family of nations. In practice, this meant acceptance of colonial claims in regard to territory and right to trade.

Columbus had set the example when he had claimed the rights of discovery over inhabited lands, going through symbolic acts that in his eyes, as well as those of Europe, established the validity of his claim.[1] England's Henry VII lost no time in following suit when he issued letters patent for exploring and colonizing ventures, such as the one to the Venetian Giovanni Caboto (John Cabot, c. 1450-1498) and his sons in 1496. Not referring at all to the duty of spreading

Christianity, Henry was concerned instead with granting the power "to acquire and keep the riches, fruits and profits" of the lands he hoped would be discovered and brought under his sway.[2] His commission had the tone of a letter of marque; in other words, of licensed piracy, as he instructed his explorers

> to seek out, discover and finde whatsoever isles, countries, regions, or provinces of the heathen and infidels whatsoever they be. . .to set up our banners and ensignes in every village, towne, castle, isle, or maine land of them newly founde. And that the aforesaid John and his sonnes. . .may subdue, occupy, and possesse all such townes, cities, castles, and isles. . .getting unto us the rule, title, and iurisdiction of the same villages, townes and castles, and firme lands so found.[3]

Other monarchs behaved similarly, even those who been accorded the papal mission to go forth and evangelize. Manoel of Portugal (reign, 1495-1521) in 1499 issued letters patent to João Fernandes (fl. 1486-1505) granting him the "governorship of any island or islands, inhabited or uninhabited, which he may discover and find anew" on the Portuguese side of the line.[4] The following year he made a similar grant to Gaspar Corte-Real (c. 1450/55-1501) to go and find islands and to establish himself there "with full power and authority without appeal or redress from him or from his heirs and successors."[5] The wording of Roberval's commission was almost exactly repeated when later colonizers were instructed to "take and conquer the said barbarians" should the natives oppose friendly French overtures to establish in their lands.[6] Juana of Castile, concerned about Spain's suzerainty on its side of the papal dividing line, in 1511 assigned Juan de Agramonte to go to Newfoundland and there establish himself with "high justice and civil jurisdiction." Should it be necessary, he was to inform officials "of all the cities and towns and places of these kingdoms and dominions," about his authorization, so they could respect it.[7]

Symbols of Possession

How was a claim to newly "discovered" territory to be established? The usual method was to leave some sign, such as a cross with the national coat of arms affixed, an appropriately engraved lead plaque, a jar containing national coins, or perhaps a cairn enclosing a message to inform later arrivals of what had occurred. Procedures tended to vary with the circumstances, and were not above challenge: thus France contested Portugal's claims in Brazil, then raised the cross of possession herself in Canada; Sir Francis Drake (c. 1540-1596) nailed a silver coin to a post as a statement of claim to New Albion (as he called the North American west coast) for England during his 1577-1580 voyage, which did not prevent Elizabeth I (reign, 1558-1603) from challenging similar procedures on the part of Spain. She told a Spanish ambassador that possession could not be claimed "only on the ground that the Spaniards have touched here and there, have erected shelters, have given names to a river or a promontory: acts which cannot confer property."[8] The obvious corollary to this was that claims to rights of discovery needed to be followed by settlement in order to be recognized as valid. In the words of Elizabeth, "without possession, prescription is of no avail."[9] This would be England's thrust in 1583 when she sought to establish a foothold in North America, with Sir Humphrey Gilbert (c. 1537-1583) acting as the spearhead.[10]

Furthermore, Elizabeth added, the Law of Nations, besides sanctioning such possession, also prescribed that territorial claims ought not

> to hinder other princes from carrying on commerce in these regions. . .nor yet from freely navigating the vast ocean since the use of the sea and air is common to all men; further that no right of the ocean can inure to any people or individual since neither nature nor any reason of public use permits occupation of the ocean.[11]

Elizabeth, in taking this line of argument, was taking issue with a point made by Vitoria, who had postulated exclusive trade as one of the rights of discovery, which could be supported by the use of arms if necessary.[12]

By the time of Elizabeth, monarchs with colonial ambitions were routinely claiming the "natural right" to trade in their commissions for overseas enterprises. Gentili, for one, wondered about the limits of these claimed rights, such as those of free access. How far could traders legitimately penetrate a foreign realm on their own initiative, without permission? He thought that it would be within the bounds of natural law for a country to allow trade on its borders but to restrict access to its interior.[13] Gentili, of course, was thinking of a nation that was organized into a state. Regions inhabited by prestate societies did not have the administrative apparatus to control the entry of aggressive European trading missions. For example, by the end of the sixteenth century, France was openly granting trading monopolies for the region of the Gulf of St. Lawrence, which other European powers by this time recognized as French territory.[14] The English and the Dutch behaved similarly. As the creation of monopolies indicates, once trading relationships were established in such regions, they became exclusive to the European powers concerned, and earlier arguments about the right under natural law of open access to trade were no longer heard. The "natural right" to trade had been transformed into an instrument for territorial possession.

This had happened as a consequence of the early realization that visual apprehension or primacy of exploration in themselves were not enough, as Thomas Gage (1603?-1656), an ex-Dominican at one time in the service of Spain, pointedly observed:

And to bring in the title of first discovery, to me it seems as little reason that the sailing of a Spanish ship upon the coast of India should entitle the King of Spain to that country, as the sailing of an Indian or an English upon the coast of Spain should entitle either the Indians or the English unto the dominion thereof. No question but the just right or title to those countries appertains to the natives themselves, who, if they should willingly and freely invite the English to their protection, what title soever they have in them no doubt but they may legally transfer it or communicate it to others. And to say that the inhuman butchery which the Indians did formerly commit in sacrificing so many reasonable creatures to their wicked idols was a sufficient warrant for the Spaniards to divest them of their country, the same argument may by much better reason be enforced against the Spaniards themselves, who have sacrificed so many millions of Indians to the idol of their barbarous cruelty, that many populous islands and large territories upon the main continent are thereby at this day utterly uninhabited, as Bartholomeo de las Casas, the Spanish Bishop of Oaxaca [sic] in New Spain, hath by his writings in print sufficiently testified. But to end all disputes of this nature; since that God hath given the earth to the sons of men to inhabit, and that there are so many vast countries in those parts not yet inhabited either by Spaniard or Indian, why should my countrymen the English be debarred from making use of that which God from all beginning, no question, did ordain for the benefit of mankind?[15]

Gage's comment about Amerindians voluntarily transferring title to their lands mirrored Vitoria's earlier proposition, to the effect that Amerindians, "aware alike of the prudent administration and humanity of the Spaniards" could, if they wished, freely accept the King of Spain as their sovereign. Vitoria extended this to Amerindians involved in a just war, who could "summon the Spaniards to help and share the rewards of victory with them," observing that this had been a favorite technique of the Romans for expanding their empire.[16] It was an idea that colonizers found appealing, as it would have marshalled the moral force of the doctrine of consent on their behalf.

What Amerindians Thought

As was to be expected, such wishful thinking did not often work out in practice. When Amerindians welcomed the newcomers, it was not as overlords, but as visitors and potential allies. Perhaps the best-known example of this was when the Tlaxcalans joined Cortés against the Mexica; less well-known was the alliance of the Micmac of the Canadian Atlantic seaboard with the French against the British. In both of these cases, the natives found the Europeans more willing to accept help in their wars than to acknowledge the sovereignty of their allies, and Tlaxcalans as well as Micmac found themselves classed as subjects. That had not been a role that either of them had envisioned for themselves; as with Amerindians generally, they were as devoted to their independence as Europeans. Spanish historian Gómara seems to have been aware of this, despite his hero-worship of Cortés, when he reported the conquistador's first successful attack against a native stronghold. The invaders began by proclaiming a long list of the benefits that would accrue to the Amerindians if they would welcome the Spaniards into their town and houses. The people of Potonchán were frankly incredulous, replying that "they had no desire for advice from people whom they did not know," and as for welcoming them into their homes, they did not like the looks of the Spaniards.[17] Later in the Yucatan, the Maya recorded that "they did not wish to join the foreigners; they did not desire Christianity."[18]

Implicit in all this was the acknowledgement in principle that Amerindians had rights to their lands, however those rights were to be defined. This was recognized very early by Martín Fernández de Enciso (fl. 1450-1495), lawyer, geographer, and navigator, whose *Summa de geografia* (published 1519) may have been the first substantial book on America to appear in Spanish. He reported that a group of Amerindians, upon being informed of the papal donation, laughed and wondered that the pope would be so liberal with what was not his. They also thought that the Spanish king must be poor because he was asking for the lands of others.[19] The story received wide circulation when it was repeated by Gómara in his *Historia*, and reached an even wider public when his work was translated into French, going through six editions before 1609.[20] The French made much of it, but more from anti-Spanish sentiment than from concern for Amerindian rights.

There are other similar stories in early accounts. Herrera tells of the natives of Tabasco, who when called upon to submit to the Spaniards, replied that they already "had a Lord of their own, and did not know why they who were just come should offer to impose another Lord upon them."[21] Similarly, when a chief (possibly Donnacona) objected to the cross Cartier had set up without permission in Gaspé Harbor in 1534, pointing "to the land all around about, as if he wished to say that all this region belonged to him," the French captain "held up an axe to him, pretending we would barter it for his furskin. . . .we explained to them by signs. . .that we would soon come back and bring them iron wares and other goods. . . .[The Amerindians] made signs to us that they would not pull down the cross, delivering at the same time several harangues which we did not understand."[22] The English, too, observed such behavior, as reported in 1624 by the Virginia Assembly:

> We never perceaved that the natives of the Countrey did voluntarily yeeld themselves subjects to our gracious Sovraigne, nether that they took any pride in that title, nor paide at any tyme any contributione of corne for sustenation of the Colony, nor could we at

any tyme keepe them in such good respect of correspondency as we became mutually helpful each to the other but contrarily what at any [time] was done proceeded from feare and not love, and their corne procured by trade or the sworde.[23]

Amerindian sensitivity about their sovereignty had little influence on colonizers, who continued to claim any territories they were the first Europeans to visit, regardless of the presence of natives. Juan de Grijalva (d. 1527) did that in 1518 when he came upon the well-populated and built-up island of Cozumel off the Yucatan coast. Explaining his presence to the local Mayans as a trading expedition, he unhesitatingly affixed the Spanish coat of arms to a tower and proclaimed the suzerainty of the Spanish king, which in his eyes was pure formality as he considered that all New World peoples were already Spain's vassals as a consequence of the papal grant. Grijalva's action was something of an embarassment to the Spanish court, which did its best to play down the incident, basing its claim to the Yucatan on the subsequent conquest.[24]

Nature of Habitation

The fundamental issue of what constituted rights of "discovery" continued to raise problems, as the Spaniards with their concern for legalities were only too well aware. We have already seen that Vitoria, in the second of his lectures on Amerindians during the 1530s, incurred imperial displeasure when he pointed out that legally, Europeans could only claim territorial rights over lands which were not occupied.[25] He based his position on the principle laid down in Justinian's *Institutes* (2.1.12), "natural reason admits the title of the first occupant to that which previously had no owner." It was a position that later would draw the support of Grotius, among others.[26]

How, then, was occupation to be defined? Since apart from the Mexicans, Mayans, and Peruvians, and perhaps semi-sedentary agricultural groups, Amerindians were migratory, having "no particular property or parcell of that country, but only a general residence," the English turned to the theory that they were not truly occupying the land, as the Portuguese had done earlier in Africa and the French in Canada:

although the Lord hath given the earth to the children of men. . .is the greater part of it possessed & wrongfully usurped by wild beasts, and unreasonable creatures, or by brutish savages, which by reason of their godless ignorance, & blasphemous Idolatrie, are worse than those beasts which are of the most wilde and savage nature. . . .[They] have no interest in it [the land] because they participate rather of the nature of beasts than men.[27]

The divine, Samuel Purchas (1577-1626), who inherited Richard Hakluyt's monumental project of publishing voyage accounts, was voicing the general sentiment of his countrymen when he wrote that since it was a duty to make the earth productive, those lands that were not being cultivated could be taken without injustice to anyone, "especially where the people is wild, and holdeth no settled possession in any parts." He added that "Virginia hath roome enough for her own [Amerindians] (were their numbers an hundred times as many) and for others also. . .[who] seeke habitations there in vacant places, with perhaps better right than the first, which. . .I can scarsly call Inhabitants."[28] He was adding to an idea that had already been expressed by Sir Thomas More (1478-1535) in his *Utopia* when he had written that the most just cause for war was "when any people holdeth a piece of ground void and vacant for no good and profitable use, keeping others from the use and possession of it which notwithstanding by the law of nature ought thereof to be nourished and relieved."[29] Such an argument, in Vera Cruz's view, needed to be severely qualified: simply because a community has an abundance "it is not to be deprived of the ownership of its lands, unless it be for some other reason that has to do with the common good so that he who abounds is to give to the needy."[30]

Type of use as a criterion for rights of occupation was a development of the Age of Discovery; one looks in vain in medieval jurisprudence for such an approach. In earlier formulations, original acquisition was equated with occupation, and there were no qualifiers as to mode of life or usage. A professor of jurisprudence at Heidelberg, Johann Wolfgang Textor (1638-1701), although writing in the seventeenth century, was basing himself on the *Institutes* and did not distinguish between occupation and ownership when he wrote that

Occupation takes now one name and now another, according as the objects of it differ. In the case of wild land-animals, it is called hunting or capture by hunting; in the case of fish and water-animals, fishing. . .in the case of inanimate things. . .it is called finding.[31]

The term "occupation" applied to locality as well as to the things being hunted and fished. Hunting and fishing were occupations by which original entitlement was acquired. Unoccupied lands were considered public property, a classification which could, under certain circumstances, include uncultivated lands. But there was a problem: how to distinguish between lands that were unclaimed and therefore open to the first taker, and those that were merely unoccupied, but were still public property? As Gentili put it, even vacant lands

> belong to the sovereign of that territory. . .yet because of that law of nature which abhors a vacuum, they will fall to the lot of those who take them. So be it, but let the sovereign retain jurisdiction over them.[32]

Grotius agreed: "uncultivated land ought not to be considered occupied except in respect to sovereignty, which remains unimpaired in favour of the original people."[33] In other words, establishing proprietary right on a first come first served basis did not necessarily disturb sovereign right, as such possession could be valid only with the consent of the original inhabitants.

This was not the principle which operated in face of the rich prospects of the New World; instead, a way was found around it by classifying land occupied by migratory and semi-sedentary peoples as *terra nullius* or, perhaps more precisely, *vacuum domicilium*, in the phrasing of Massachusetts Governor John Winthrop (1587/88-1649). In effect, those phrases meant that proprietary rights could only exist within the framework of law enacted by an organized state; the land of prestate people without such law was therefore legally vacant. Such arguments, long used to vindicate rights of discovery, had soon been extended to claim that territorial possession could not effectively exist without positive law.[34] It is a position that ignores habitation from "time immemorial," or at least regards it as irrelevant to an organized state. According to Jennings, up until the first known deed of sale in 1633 recording an English land purchase, "New Englanders did not recognize the legitimacy of land ownership by Indians to the extent of negotiating for its conveyance."[35] The English had begun to change their minds after the Dutch, in 1623, had started to purchase Amerindian lands. Even Winthrop changed his views, and in 1642 purchased 1,260 acres along the Concord River.[36] Roger Williams (1603?-1683), founder of the colony of Rhode Island, had advocated such a course of action, which admitted Amerindian proprietary rights at least to the extent that such rights were provided for in English Common Law, without, however, acknowledging Amerindian sovereignty. Williams made himself very unpopular in Massachusetts when he denied that the royal charter gave valid title to land, a position which Las Casas and Vera Cruz would have applauded.

Colonizing Rhetoric

Colonial rhetoric became ingenious and imaginative. Would not Amerindians benefit if the English brought them their version of the Christian message in return for the right to settle in their territory? Sir George Peckham (d. 1608), the merchant adventurer who was associated with Sir Humphrey in the latter's attempt to establish a colony in Newfoundland, while supporting such an exchange, realized a hidden danger: "trade and traffike (be it never so profitable) ought not to bee preferred before the planting of the Christian fayth."[37] Such concern was diluted, however, by the counter argument that since Amerindians did not manage their lands properly, it was perfectly justifiable for Europeans to obtain them in exchange for the "full recompense" of teaching the Christian message.[38] Not only would they be realizing God's will through improving the land, they would be giving more than full value in return. If Amerindians proved refractory, then it might be necessary to use force; even among the clergy, there were those who saw little hope for evangelization unless the shamans had "their throats cut."[39] Peckham's warning notwithstanding, missionary zeal soon took second place to colonial expansion; in Virginia, this led to the exasperated natives, led by Opechancanough (d. 1646), attempting, with considerable bloodshed, to drive out the English in 1622.[40] The episode was more successful in substituting a colonial campaign for the "extirpating of the Salvages" in place of evangelization than it was in deterring colonization. In any event, the idea of using Christian teaching as a justification for taking Amerindian land had not met with universal support. Purchas, for one, expressed reservations:

> It was barbarous Latine to turn fides into feodum. . .to dispossess Barbarians of their Inheritance, and by their want of Faith to increase our fees of Inheritance. . .Christ came not to destroy the Law but to fulfill it. . .[41]

Purchas remained faithful to this principle even after the Virginia uprising. In a passage worthy of Las Casas, he wrote that it was not "lawfull for Christians to usurpe the goods and lands of Heathens; for they are villains not to us; but to our and their Lord." Purchas did not, however, allow his ethical convictions to overwhelm his appreciation of the colony's commercial promise, and maintained that the English should continue to exercise their natural right of "cohabitation and commerce" with Amerindians. Because trade was a right, it had always been considered legal to back it up by the use of force (a position that had been espoused by Vitoria), particularly if the power to do so was available, as the younger Richard Hakluyt (1552?-1616) had bluntly put it,

> "If we finde the countrey populous, and desirous to expel us, and iniuriously to offend us, that seeke but iust and lawfull trafficke, then by reason that we are lords of navigation, and they are not so, we [can]. . .in the end bring them all in subiection and to civilitie."[42]

Under the circumstances, the English would be showing restraint by using trade to put Amerindians into debt, and then take lands in payment.[43] Since their attacks on the English were a violation of natural law, they had forfeited their rights. According to Purchas:

> I follow the hand of God, which have given England so many rights in Virginia, right naturall, right nationall, right by first discovery, by accepted trade, by possession surrendered voluntarily, continued constantly, right by gift, by birth, by bargaine and sale,

by cession, by forfeiture in that late damnable trechery and massacre. . . .Gods bounty before, his justice now hath given us Virginia.[44]

It would have been difficult, if not impossible, for Purchas or any
other Englishman to see the Amerindian action as having been
defensive, and thus as an exercise of right under natural law.[45] Purchas's attempt at equitable judgment did not last long, and he was
soon referring to Amerindians as "so bad a people, having little of
Humanitie but shape, ignorant of Civilitie, of Arts, of Religion; more
brutish than the beasts they hunt." A pamphleteer wrote to his
patron, the year of the massacre, that Amerindians were "naturally
borne slaves. . . .There is a naturall kind of right in you, that are bred
noble, learned, wise and virtuous, to direct them aright, to governe
and to command them."[46] A text that was cited in the wave of condemnation of the Amerindians' actions was taken from Gentili. The
Oxford jurist, considering personal responsibility in wars, found that
Amerindians were no more blameless than anyone else "in fighting
for their king when the latter made war unjustly."[47]

Attempts at Accord

The uprising did have the effect of getting the English to pay more attention to obtaining the assent, or at least quiescence, of Amerindians
to their settlement plans, as well as to the ostensible legality of their
procedures for the acquisition of land. The process had already begun
in 1620 by means of a peace treaty, when the Plymouth colony's first
governor, John Carver, (c. 1576-1621) negotiated an agreement with
Massasoit (1580/90?-1661), head chief of the Wampanoags. Although
the original text has been lost, contemporary accounts report that
Massasoit promised not to harm the English and to punish those of
his people who did; and each side agreed to help the other if "unjustly" attacked.[48] The French had long been negotiating alliances
with aboriginals, in Brazil as well as in North America, but according
to the custom of the Amerindians, rather than in the written European form. As the French reasoned, this was the best means of obtaining an operational agreement that the Amerindians could understand and respect; besides, if European forms were followed, there

was the risk of recognition of Amerindian sovereignty, at least by inference. In the English way of doing things, a treaty had to have the royal seal in order to possess international significance. In any event, in view of their stand that America was *terra nullius*, it is not clear what status the English accorded these treaties at any level from a legal standpoint.[49]

The fine points of justifying the taking over of Amerindian lands continued to bedevil Europeans. Samuel Pufendorf (1632–1694), professor at Heidelberg and later at Lund, Sweden, held that physical appropriation was necessary to transform the rights of discovery into the rights of property. He was careful to add, however, that this was not a right under natural law, but by agreement among men:

> men in the beginning lived on things open to all; and that only after pacts introduced property in the shape of houses and of stores collected for future uses, did property in the form of fields gradually come to be recognized.[50]

Textor, drawing on the authority of Justinian's *Digest*, added that

> In obtaining possession of an estate there is no need for the party to walk over every particular bit of the soil, it being enough that he should enter on some one part of it with intent to possess. . .[51]

These were not the concerns of Emer de Vattel (1714–1767), the Swiss diplomat whose *Le Droit des Gens* (1758) attained a success rivalling that of the work of Grotius. It was he who wrote that nations were bound by natural law to cultivate the land, and those who "roamed" rather than inhabiting their territories, thereby taking up more land than was their due, could be lawfully restricted within narrower territorial limits.[52] Vattel also formulated the inverse of that position:

> But it is questioned whether a Nation can thus appropriate, by the mere act of taking possession, lands which it does not really occupy, and which are more extensive than it can inhabit or cultivate. It is not difficult to decide that such a claim would be absolutely contrary to the natural law, and would conflict with the designs of nature, which destines the earth for the needs of all mankind, and

only confers upon individual Nations the right to appropriate territory so far as they can make use of it, and not merely to hold it against others who may wish to profit by it. Hence the Law of Nations will only recognize the *ownership* and *sovereignty* of a Nation over unoccupied lands when the Nation is in actual occupation of them, when it forms a settlement upon them, or makes actual use of them. In fact, when explorers have discovered uninhabited lands through which the explorers of other Nations had passed, leaving some sign of their having taken possession, they have no more troubled themselves over such empty forms than over the regulations of Popes, who divided a large part of the world between the crowns of Castile and Portugal.[53]

It should be noted that Vattel was not questioning national sovereignty, but rather the legality of indiscriminate acquisitions of territory for which there was no particular requirement at the moment. He did not distinguish between the land needs of hunting and gathering migratory peoples and those who were agriculturally-based, perhaps because of the prevalent belief that nomadism was wasteful of land resources, and in any event, God wanted the land to be farmed. Vattel countered his vagueness on that point by explicitly acknowledging that "Every Nation which governs itself, under whatever form, and which does not depend on any other Nation, is a *sovereign State*. Its rights are, in the natural order, the same as those of every other State."[54]

By the time Vattel wrote those words, colonial hegemony over Amerindians had proceeded too far to be affected by such reaffirmations of the natural law principle of the right to self-government.

Conclusion

The Changing Face of Sovereignty

International law as it evolved in Europe began to emerge as the Law of Nations (*jus gentium*) during the Age of Discovery as a result of the shift of power from the supranational church to national monarchies.[1] It can be seen as a movement to capture in secular terms an ideal that had proved to be elusive in the spiritual realm; the unity of mankind was not lost as a goal, but its realization came to be sought on an international rather than supranational scale. Before the appearance of Christianity, classical Rome had achieved remarkable success in a secular context, through the medium of her technology, and the imposition of her political and social institutions. Once Rome lost her grip, her type of imperial dominance eventually proved to be unworkable in the welter of *res publicae* that took over the European scene. But the conviction remained that unity was not only achievable, it was necessary for the self-realization of mankind. Of the voluminous writings produced by medieval theologians, canonists, and jurists in pursuit of this goal, two illustrate especially well the belief in an all-embracing rationality that ordered the world into a comprehensive whole: *Concordia canonum discordantium* (1140), usually referred to as the *Decretum*, compiled by the canonist Gratian; and *Summa Theologiae* (written 1265-1273), by the theologian St. Thomas Aquinas, which ranked next only to the Bible in authority. These works, each in its own period, provided basic formulations that guided medieval thinkers in their search for answers that could be translated into workable legal systems.

A comprehensive system posed a central issue, that of power. As Gratian observed, "Knowledge is not enough, there must also be power."[2] Consequently, a great deal of time and effort was spent wrestling with questions clustering around authority, rights to governance, and property; in a word, *dominium*. In the Middle Ages these issues were defined in an ecclesiastical context, beginning with problems within Christianity, such as the rights of heretics to exercise authority (which concerned Gratian), then moved on to external concerns, such as relationships with non-Christians, and definitions of mutual rights, which St. Thomas included in his sweeping analyses. Two principal lines of thought concerning non-Christians and *dominium* emerged during the thirteenth century. Innocent IV, following St. Thomas, upheld the rights of non-Christians to property and the exercise of authority, while Hostiensis maintained that Christ had assumed all powers with his coming, which meant that those who did not acknowledge him automatically lost their rights. Thus stated, the positions of the two schools appear contradictory, and they were usually so presented by their followers; however, both Innocent and Hostiensis qualified their stands, so that in effect the actual difference between them, while vital, was not one of absolute contradiction. Innocent held that non-Christian, or secular, power was legitimate *de iure*, although secondary to that of Christians, while Hostiensis held that such power could only be tolerated *de facto* under certain circumstances. Slight as that distinction may appear, it was of fundamental importance to the Law of Nations. Innocent's position implied the possibility of unity through diversity, never easy to work out in practice. A just war could not be waged against a people simply because they did not share the faith. The majority of canonists agreed with Innocent on this in principle; however, it was the Hostiensian position that fuelled the ideological motor of Europe's expansion, perhaps because in the field of action it lent itself more readily to simplification of issues and rationalization of the growth of empires. It also related well to the doctrine, never fully suppressed even though declared heretical, which held that a state of grace was necessary for the legitimate exercise of *dominium*. As non-Christians, besides lacking baptismal regeneration, were also by definition sinners, they could not possibly be in the state of grace required to own property or govern with justice. Vera Cruz pointed to a logical consequence of this position. If it were true that unbelievers held dominion unjustly, "then not only the king or emperor but even any individual Christian would have been authorized to appropriate their possessions."[3] Sir Edward Coke (1552-1634), at the time England's enormously influential Chief Justice of the Common Pleas, enunciated still another consequence in connection with Calvin's case (1608):

> if a Christian King should conquer a kingdom of an infidel, and bring them under his subjection, then *ipso facto* the laws of the infidel are abrogated for that they be not only against Christianity, but against the law of God and nature. . .and in that case, until certain laws be established amongst them, the King by himself, and such Judges as he shall appoint, shall judge them and their causes according to natural equity, in such as kings in ancient times did with their kingdoms.[4]

In spite of such opinions, protests against the wars of conquest were surprisingly frequent, and usually made under the banner of human rights. Typical was the observation of Fray Alonso de Espinosa in 1594: "It is an acknowledged fact, both as regards divine and human right, that the wars waged by the Spaniards against the natives of these islands [the Canaries], as well as against the Indians in the western regions, were unjust and without any reason to support them."[5]

Another aspect of the problem of *dominium* during this period was the relationship between spiritual and temporal powers. The primacy of the spiritual was generally acknowledged, at least as far as ecclesiastical affairs were concerned; but in the temporal realm there were competing claims, particularly on the part of feudal lords and regional princes who, besides seeking to limit the powers of the pope (which had reached their peak at the end of the twelfth and in the early thirteenth centuries), were also challenging each other, not to mention the overriding pretensions of the Holy Roman Emperor. By the time of the discovery of the Americas, national rulers were gaining the upper hand over pope and emperor in the superior echelons of power, and over feudal lords in the inferior. The manoeuvring that this struggle of hierarchies involved was illustrated in the action of Fernando and Isabel when they asked the pope to approve their already claimed "rights of discovery," and to clarify their position *vis-à-vis* the competing claims of Portugal. Alexander VI had no choice but to acquiesce, and to divide the right to evangelize in unknown parts of the world between Spain and Portugal. Even so, the two powers did not hesitate the following year to conclude a separate treaty relocating the papal dividing line without consulting Rome, although again the pope was asked to approve the result.

Such actions were in line with the development of the concept of national sovereignty. At first sovereignty was conceived in personal terms: the monarch knew no superior authority: *rex superiorem non recognoscens est princeps in regno suo.*[6] With national monarchs controlling the politics of expansion, each with his particular interests in view, concerns about the overriding importance of justice arising out of natural law gave way in practice to the expediencies of colonization as justified in human law (*jus gentium*). Individualism took over in international law, as it also did on a different scale in industrial and social relations. The immutable principles of justice and the common good were constantly reaffirmed, but the continually shifting politics of specific situations demanded a flexibility in legislation that tended to place short-term considerations ahead of long-term goals. As Bartolo had observed two centuries before the Age of Discovery, "Certain it is that the morality of our governing law varies as custom changes through time." [7] A twentieth century version of that same idea says "Law may be stable, but it cannot be still."[8] In practice, the monarchs were controlled, when they were controlled at all, by agreements worked out with each other on an ad hoc basis. These agreements were frequently more honored in the breach than in the observance; in the final analysis, it was power that ruled the day, and it was usually in the service of one special interest or another. Le Roy was not alone in considering that it was according to natural order for the stronger to dominate the weaker.[9]

The growing body of national legislation and the attendant juridical opinions of every shade and hue made it steadily easier to judicially vindicate a wide variety of actions, even contradictory ones. Principles that had seemed moderate enough in an Old World setting took on different aspects in the New. An outstanding example of this is Aristotle's doctrine of natural servitude, of the hierarchy of superior and inferior, and of the right of the superior to rule the inferior, and to be served by them. The conjunction of circumstances and events during the Age of Discovery, particularly the increasing emphasis on commercialism and exploitation, gave this tenet a pivotal importance. Today it is difficult to conceive the extent of the influence exercised during the high Middle Ages and early Renaissance by

Aristotle, "The Philosopher."[10] Even toward the end of the seventeenth century, he was being cited as a final authority. The right—indeed, the duty—of the superior to rule the inferior combined with the Hostiensian doctrine to become the rationale for colonial expansion, while the doctrine of natural servitude was used to vindicate the exploitation of native labor and the mushrooming slave trade.[11]

Even within their established spheres of influence, national states experienced difficulties in working out their laws and in enforcing them. When those nations expanded overseas, their problems compounded as distances complicated communication and the exercise of authority. Spain illustrates these difficulties particularly well, although they were experienced by all the colonizing powers in similar situations. Spain, a leader in scholastic thought, which such men as Vitoria and Suárez translated into legal terms, conscientiously tried to realize the principles of social justice in its imperial administration. It failed, despite a bewildering array of well-intentioned laws backed up with impressive displays of official authority. The case of the feudal institution of *repartimiento-encomienda* is only one example among many others of what happened. The Spanish monarchs, having recently succeeded in curbing the power of feudal lords that this system had nourished within their European territories, had no desire to see it reappear in their overseas possessions. Yet it quickly did so in Hispaniola, although in a variant form, and when efforts were made to curb it, the colonists simply invoked the famous formula, *Obedezco pero no cumplo* ("I obey but do not fulfil (execute)"). Official tolerance of such behavior up to a certain point allowed for a considerable amount of decentralization in practice in what was theoretically a highly centralized system.[12] In the view of the conquistadors and other settlers, *encomienda* was a customary practice to which they had every right; they did not consider it an infringement of the rights of Amerindians since the latter were outside of natural law and its restraints. Spain, the nation where the law was so respected that even the king was not considered to be above it, found that it could not enforce measures that were resented, and resisted, by the colonists. In the end, it resorted to controlling *encomienda* rather than trying to abolish it. Of all the colonizing powers, Spain experienced the widest gap between idealistic royal intentions—Charles V did regard himself as the temporal head of Christendom, whether or not this was generally acknowledged[13]—and actual events in the colonies. Impelled by commercial advantage, those events were being acted out at a high cost in human terms, giving pause to the more thoughtful. Montaigne put it aptly, with the experiences of the Indies, Mexico and Peru in mind:

> Who ever set the utility of commerce and trading at such a price? So many cities razed, so many nations exterminated, so many millions of people put to the sword, and the richest and most beautiful part of the world turned upside down, for the traffic in pearls and pepper![14]

In this rapidly evolving scene, Amerindians had lost out on several counts. Their rights under natural law were not being effectively translated into human (positive) law by any of the colonizing powers, despite partial attempts to do so. In fact, it could not have happened, as colonization by definition was based on a denial of those rights. Not being Christian, Amerindians were open to colonial crusades under the banner of evangelism. It came to be generally believed that becoming Christian automatically implied the acceptance of Christian governance: the Bible in exchange for Amerindian lands and *dominium*. On the secular side, prestate New World peoples (particularly those who wore few or no clothes) were subjected to colonial administrations on the grounds that they were in their cultural infancy, and thus unqualified to govern themselves; those who had developed their own state structures were subjected to wars of conquest on the grounds that their customs violated natural law. In either case Amerindians were classed as savages, not fully developed as human beings (indeed, according to some writers, not yet fully in possession of reason). Not only were they considered to be beyond the pale of natural law, but also that of *jus gentium*. "We are christianized, while they treat us like animals," the Maya lamented.[15] To those who protested that Amerindians had been governing themselves to their own satisfaction before Europeans arrived, the answer was that they could not have been doing so very effectively, or the newcomers would not have been able to form alliances with their native enemies and overwhelm them as they did. On the other hand, as Amerindians came under colonial control, they were often able to retain their own social forms to a large extent.[16]

In pragmatic terms, Europe's ascendancy in the Americas had

much less to do with the viability of Amerindian governments than with its own technological and political development. Iron was more practical than stone and bone, despite the high degree of sophistication to which Amerindians had developed their technology.[17] European animal husbandry, particularly the use of the horse, provided a capacity for heavy transport far exceeding that available to Amerindians. So important was this animal to the conquest that the death penalty was not deemed too severe for infractions of the ban on sale of horses to Amerindians. By way of contrast, Amerindian excellence in plant husbandry did not furnish compensating advantages. Finally, European state organization made for strategic advantages that Amerindian prestate societies could not match, despite consistently impressive military achievements. Those Amerindian societies that were organized into states, and which could consequently marshal armies that frequently outnumbered those that Europeans sent over, were outclassed on the technological levels just mentioned. Lescarbot perceived the reality when he wrote that "Indian tribes were defenceless in the presence of those who have ruined them, and did not resist as did those peoples of whom the Holy Scripture makes mention."[18]

The question of technological development illustrates the profound importance of basic philosophical and ideological orientation. Amerindians easily matched Europeans in ingenuity and expertise, as was evident in certain types of metal work that developed on the northwestern coast of South America, Panama, Costa Rica and Oaxaca; silverwork on display at the market at Tenochtitlan impressed Spaniards as surpassing anything they had ever seen.[19] In a seminal report on those techniques, Lechtman points out that where in the Old World metallurgy was associated with the practical uses of warfare, transportation and agriculture, in the New the association was with the symbolism of religious beliefs, political power and social status.[20] In the Amerindian cosmogony, gold and silver were paramount colors, representing as they did the sun and the moon. The concern of Amerindian metal workers was to produce ceremonial objects as contexts for these colors, which communicated important information when the items were used in rituals and on public occasions. Europeans, on the other hand, focused on mundane rather than ideologically oriented uses for their metallurgy, such as improving tools and weaponry. Consequently they had the practical equipment necessary for the establishment of their hegemony, in the New World as elsewhere.[21] In another sphere, also, this wide difference in ideological approach became critical when Europeans and Amerindians met. Amerindians wondered if their strange visitors were sons of the Sun, and attempted to influence them with lavish gifts; Motecuhzoma II (reign, 1502-1520) and Atahuallpa (reign, c. 1528-1533) looked to the gods for guidance on how to proceed in this unprecedented situation. According to the hearsay account reported by William Bradford (governor of Plymouth Plantation, off and on, 1621-1656), Massasoit's decision to make contact with the English had been preceded by an assembly of shamans: "before they came to the English to make friendship, they gott all the *Powachs* of the country, for 3 days togeather in a horid and divellish maner, to curse & execrate them with their cunjurations, which assembly & service they held in a dark & dismale swampe."[22] That description of a native council is a good indicator of the prevalent reaction of Europeans: not only did they class Amerindians as savages, but also in association with the devil. Conquistadors, of whom Hernán Cortés (1485-1547) is an outstanding example, studied them and launched projects to learn their languages as well as their political and social differences in order to divide and conquer them.[23] This negative approach intensified with time, as in the case of the Puritans.[24] The fact that the conquests could not be justified in terms of natural or divine law proved to be no deterrent as colonizing monarchs, loudly announcing their sovereignty, claimed the prerogative of authorizing expeditions under their own rules. In this each and every one was solidly backed by the majority of his people. Law had come a long way from the days when it had been considered a branch of ethics.

For every law or recognized practice claimed on the part of a colonizing nation seeking to legitimate its position, there was a challenge or counterclaim solidly based in legal precedent. The battle was fought on two levels: the primary one concerned with the rights of man and the need to see that justice was done; and the secondary one concerned with immediate national goals. To medieval thinkers, the primary goal meant divine sanction was mandatory "to have any right to frame laws for each other and for the world."[25] As they saw it, this was evident in natural law, since justice was the source of authority and could not be mandated away by human law.[26] Under the law of nations, on the other hand, things "are only good or bad in so far as the law makes them so."[27] Where manmade law (positive, or statutory) is insufficient or does not apply, then natural law takes over. It was in recognizing the distinction as well as the interplay of these two levels that Las Casas was so effective; among the many who opposed colonization in principle (including Montaigne), the Dominican was the most successful in exposing the basic issues. That he was unable to stop the march of empire does not impugn the validity of his stand; his arguments upholding the unity of mankind have not only withstood the test of time, they are being revived today by aboriginal peoples who are once more claiming their right to sovereignty and self-determination. Continuous use and possession of land "from time immemorial" as a basis for title dates back to Roman times, when jurists considered it to be a self-evident rule of natural law. It was recognized in Justinian's code, and continued under feudalism in common law.[28] But it interfered with the politics of expansion, and so was circumvented during the Age of Discovery. The view is still being argued that quite apart from the rights and wrongs of the situation, "the fundamental principle that the Indians had no right by virtue of their ancient possession either of the soil or of sovereignty has never been abandoned, either expressly or by implication."[29] Even the advocates of that position, however, have acknowledged that Amerindians, as well as aboriginal peoples in general, are entitled to enough land for subsistence, in accordance with the principle of natural law that the earth was intended to provide for all mankind. Seen in the light of these considerations, the American colonial conquests are in the highest possible degree a living past.[30]

Notes

I   LEGITIMACY OF POWER: THE ECCLESIASTICAL ASPECT

1. The research and writing of this paper was made possible by a grant from the Social Sciences and Humanities Research Council of Canada; much of the work was done at the Newberry Library, Chicago, whose staff was co-operative and helpful well beyond the call of duty. Translations of Latin texts, unless otherwise indicated, were done by Dr. Nicholas Wickenden, University of Alberta, who has been most generous with his advice and criticisms. A preliminary essay using some of this material has appeared under the title "Old World Laws, New World Peoples and Concepts of Sovereignty" in *Essays on the History of North American Discovery and Exploration* (Arlington: The University of Texas at Arlington, 1988).

2. Astronomer Mikolaj Kopernik (Nicolas Copernicus, 1473-1543) established that earth was not the centre of the cosmos. This was of fundamental importance to medieval thought, which saw the universe as an articulated whole, and emphasized the priority of the whole over the part. In the Christian orthodoxy of the time, the earth was central to the universe and man was central to earth. See Otto Gierke, *Political Theories of the Middle Age*, tr. Frederic William Maitland (Cambridge: Cambridge University Press, 1900; reprinted, Boston: Beacon Press, 1958), p. 7-8.

3. Jean Bodin's *Six livres de la Republique* (1576), which appeared in English as *The six bookes of a commonweale* in 1606, is generally credited with being the first full-scale work devoted to the subject of sovereignty. However, it drew on a considerable body of thought that had grown around the topic during the preceding centuries. *Majestas* was the usual Latin word for sovereignty.

4. Henry Wheaton, *Elements of International Law* (1866), (Washington: Carnegie Institution, 1936), pt. II, s. 166, p. 203. The dictum that territories occupied by migratory hunting tribes are legally *terra nullius* is central to the work by Arthur S. Keller, Oliver J. Lissitzyn and Frederick J. Mann, *Creation of Rights of Sovereignty through Symbolic Acts* (New York: Columbia University Press, 1938; AMS reprint, 1967).

5. Christianity had predominated in Europe since the days of Charlemagne (reign, 768-814), and was still expanding.

6. Shades of meaning and aspects of *dominium* are discussed by Francis Oakley in *The Political Thought of Pierre d'Ailly* (New Haven: Yale University Press, 1964), pp. 66-92.

7. See, for example, Dante's *De monarchia*.

8. Kenneth J. Pennington, Jr., "Bartolomé de Las Casas and the Tradition of Medieval Law," *Church History* XXXIX no. 2 (1970), p. 160. The best overview of the origins of European diplomatic and political concepts that came into play in the Americas during the Age of Discovery is that of James Muldoon, *Popes, Lawyers, and Infidels* (Philadelphia: University of Pennsylvania Press, 1979); also recommended is the synthesis of Silvio Zavala, *La Filosofía Política en la Conquista de América* (Mexico: Fondo de Cultura

Económica, 1947). (In English, *The Political Philosophy of the Conquest of America*, tr. Teener Hall (Mexico: Editorial Cultura, 1953), which is the edition cited here.) See also Robert Benson, "Medieval Canonistic Origins of the Debate of the Lawfulness of the Spanish Conquest" *First Images of America: The Impact of the New World on the Old*, ed. Fredi Chiappelli, 2 vols. (Los Angeles: University of California, 1976), Vol. I, pp. 327-34. A basic work on European political thought is by R.W. and A.J. Carlyle, *A History of Mediaeval Political Theory in the West*, 6 vols. (Edinburgh and London: Blackwood, 1903-1936). Very useful overviews are provided by the series *Histoire du droit et des institutions de l'église en Occident* under the general editorship of Gabriel Le Bras. Volume VII, *L'Age classique 1140-1378*, by Gabriel Le Bras, was published in Paris, Sirey, 1965.

9. Romans 12.18.

10. Arthur Nussbaum, *A Concise History of the Law of Nations* (New York: Macmillan, 1954), pp. 27-35.

11. Archibald R. Lewis, *The Northern Seas* (Princeton, N.J.: Princeton University Press, 1958), pp. 165-66.

12. James Muldoon, "A Canonistic Contribution to the Formation of International Law," *The Jurist* XXVIII (1968), p. 271.

13. Denys Hay, *Europe: The Emergence of an Idea* (New York: Harper and Row, 1966), p. 20.

14. The "two swords" theory in this form was introduced by the Cistercian St. Bernard of Clairvaux (1090-1153), but the idea of two co-ordinate powers was ancient, having been expressed in various forms at least as far back as Gelasius I (pope, 492-496). There was a difference of opinion as to whether the pope was the guardian of both swords, or whether the lay ruler received his directly from God. There were also shifts in meanings of phrases as they were used for different purposes, greatly complicating the understanding of the texts. See Brian Tierney, "The Continuity of Papal Political Theory in the Thirteenth Century," *Medieval Studies* XXVII (1965), p. 227; and Muldoon, *Popes, Lawyers*, pp. 14-15. In its later form the theory was said to derive from Luke 22.38: when the disciples displayed two swords to Christ, he replied, "Enough." (Walter Ullmann, *A History of Political Thought: The Middle Ages* (Harmondsworth: Penguin, 1965), pp. 137-38). The popular formulation of the idea of the pope as the "Vicar of Christ" acquiring his title through Peter who alone had "the power of the keys" dates from Leo I (440-461). (Arthur P. Monahan, *John of Paris on Royal and Papal Power* (New York and London: Columbia University Press, 1974), xiii). However, it did not officially appear in the collections of canon law until the decretals of Innocent III. Alfons M. Stickler has analysed the allegory of the two swords in minute detail in a series of articles, which are commented on by Brian Tierney in "Some Recent Works on the Political Theories of the Medieval Canonists," *Traditio* X (1954), pp. 610-12.

15. This version had been advocated by Alcuin (c. 732-804), the English scholar who had been adviser to Charlemagne, and was taken up by Henry IV (king

of Germany from 1056, Holy Roman Emperor 1084-1106) in 1076. (Ullmann, *Political Thought*, pp. 110, 137-38.) It should be noted that at this time Castile was a theocratic monarchy. Its great collection of Visigothic law, *Forum judicum* (Fuero Juzgo), considered to be well in advánce of its time in some ways, was the work of the bishops who controlled the judicial system. (Ernest Nys, "Les publicistes espagnols du XVIe siècle et les droits des indiens," *Revue de droit international et de législation comparée*, XXI (1889), pp. 534, 536; Juan Sempere y Guarinos, *Considérations sur les causes de la grandeur et de la décadence de la monarchie espagnole*, 2 vols. (Paris: Renaud, 1826), Vol. I, pp. 6-7; Vol. II, pp. 212-14.)

16. F.H. Hinsley, *Sovereignty* (London: C.A.Watts, 1966), pp. 58-59; Michael Wilks, *The Problem of Sovereignty in the Later Middle Ages* (Cambridge: Cambridge University Press, 1963), p. 70; Cecil N.S. Woolf, *Bartolus of Sassoferrato* (Cambridge: Cambridge University Press, 1913), pp. 70-73.

17. Gierke, *Political Theories*, pp. 118-19, n. 38.

18. John Neville Figgis, *The Political Aspects of St. Augustine's 'City of God'* (Gloucester, Mass.: Peter Smith, 1963: First edition, New York: Longmans Green, 1921), p. 94.

19. The following discussion owes much to James Muldoon, "Extra Ecclesiam non est imperium: The Canonists and the Legitimacy of Secular Power," *Studia Gratiana* IX (1966), pp. 559-60. See also the introduction by Ernest Nys in Francisco de Vitoria's *De Indis et de Jure Belli Relectiones*, ed. James B. Scott (Washington: Carnegie Institution, 1917), pp. 9-100.

20. "Lex humana est quicquid rationis consistit." (Cited by Bartolomé de Las Casas, *De Thesaurus de Peru*, tr. and ed. Angel Losada under the title *Los Tesoros del Peru* (Madrid: Consejo Superior de Investigaciones Cientificas, 1958), p. 74.)

21. Walter Ullmann, *Law and Politics in the Middle Ages* (Ithaca and New York: Cornell University Press, 1975), p. 165; Joseph Balon, "La 'ratio,' fondement et justification du droit avant Gratien," *Studia Gratiana* IX (1966), pp. 11-26; Stephan Kuttner, *Gratian and the Schools of Law 1140-1234* (London: Variorum, 1983). Although the *Decretum* had been frequently reproduced in manuscript copies for three centuries, the fortuitous development of the printing press encouraged even more its circulation and use. The *Decretum* was first printed in Strasbourg in 1471. Commentators on canon law came to be known as decretists, as the *Decretum* was the standard text used for the purpose; those commenting on the decrees (decretals) of the popes, were called decretalists.

22. On the evidence of his commentaries, Alanus had begun by upholding the separation of spiritual and temporal powers, but by 1202 had espoused the theocratic position. See Alfons M. Stickler, "Alanus Anglicanus als Verteidiger des monarchischen Papsttums," *Salesianum* 21 (Turin: 1959), pp. 346-406.

23. Wilks, *Problem of Sovereignty*, p. 32. Vernani took issue with Dante's espousal of secular monarchies, claiming that mankind needed no power other than

that of the pope for the conduct of life: "non esset necesaria in hominibus potestas alia." (*De reprobatione Monarchiae*, ch. 1, p. 130. Cited by Wilks, *Problem of Sovereignty*, 32.) For Dante's argument in favor of secular monarchies, see *infra*, ch. 2, 166.

24. Muldoon, "Extra Ecclesiam," pp. 559-60; see also Sergio Mochi Onory, *Fonti Canonistiche dell' Idea Moderna dello Stato* (Milan: 1951), pp. 143-77. Uguccio published his *Summa* on the *Decretum* about 1188-90.

25. Brian Tierney, "Some Recent Works," p. 598.

26. Wilks, *Problem of Sovereignty*, pp. 38-39.

27. Ibid., p. 164.

28. This was a letter by Innocent III which was incorporated into the decretal *De electione & electi potestate*. (Gregory IX, *Decretales* (1559), I.6.34: pp. 154-58.)

29. "Iste est ergo unus casus in quo iudex ecclesiasticus potest se immiscere saeculari iuristicioni, scl. . .cum iudex saecularis est suspectus et recusatur." Cited by Wilks, *Problem of Sovereignty*, p. 513, n. 3.

30. Muldoon, "Extra Ecclesiam," pp. 562-63.

31. Wilks, *Problem of Sovereignty*, p. 75.

32. "Officiali vero huiusmodi tamdiu Christianorum communio in commerciis & aliis denegetur, donec in usus pauperum Christianorum secundum providentiam diocesani episcopi convertatur quicquid fuerit a Christianis adeptus occasione officii sic suscepti: & officium cum pudore dimittat, quod irreverenter assumpsit. Hoc idem extendimus ad Paganos." (Gregory IX, *Decretales* V.6.16: p. 1515, De Iudaeis Sarracenis & eorum servis.)

33. Gregory IX, *Decretales* III.34.8: pp. 1176-77, De voto & voti redemptione.

34. This was the opinion of a contemporary, Antonio Roselli, as cited by Muldoon, *Popes, Lawyers*, p. 126.

35. See, for example, Vincente Beltrán de Heredia, "Un precursor del Maestro Vitoria, el P. Matías de Paz, O.P., y su tratado 'De Dominio Regnum Hispaniae super Indos,'" *La ciencia Tomista* (1929), pp. 13-14; and Silvio Zavala's introduction to *De las islas del mar Océano por Juan López de Palacios Rubios* (Mexico: Fondo de Cultura Económica, 1954), pp. LXXI-LXXV. Also, Carlyle and Carlyle, *Medieval Political Theory*, Vol. V, pp. 323-24.

36. Christopher Dawson, *Mission to Asia* (Toronto: University of Toronto Press, 1980) pp. vii-xxxv; Tadeusz Wyrwa, *La pensée politique à l'époque de l'humanisme et de la renaissance* (Paris: Librairie Polonaise, 1978), pp. 38-41.

37. Innocent's letters to the "Emperor of the Tartars" are reproduced in Dawson, *Mission to Asia*, pp. 73-76.

38. R.W. Southern, *Western Views of Islam in the Middle Ages* (Cambridge, Mass.: Harvard University Press, 1962), p. 65.

39. These examples were to be used by Paulus Vladimiri when he argued Poland's case against the Teutonic Knights at the Council of Constance (1414-1417). (Stanislaus F. Belch, *Paulus Vladimiri and his Doctrine concerning International Law and Politics*, 2 vols. (The Hague: Mouton, 1965), Vol. I, p. 464. See also *infra*, 157.)

40. Muldoon, *Popes, Lawyers*, p. 12.

41. The text in full reads: ". . .possessiones et iurisdictiones licite sine peccato possunt esse apud infideles haec. enim. non tamen pro fidelibus. sed pro omni rationabili creatura facta sunt, ut est pradictum. ipse enim solem suum oriri facit super bonos. et malos. ipse etiam volatilia pascit, Matthei c. 5. circa fin. et 6. et propter hoc dicimus, non licet Papae, vel fidelibus, auferre sua, sive dominia, sive iurisdictiones infidelibus, quia sine peccato possident. . ." (Innocent IV, *Commentaria super libros quinque decretalium* (Turin: 1581), ad 3.34.8, fol. 176va-vb. In Muldoon, "Extra Ecclesiam," pp. 573-74, n. 45.)

42. ". . .sed et contra alios infideles, qui nunc tenent terram, in qua iurisdictionem habuerunt Christiani Principes, potest Papa iuste facere praeceptum, et constitutionem, quod non molestent Christianos iniuste, qui subsunt eorum iurisdictioni, immo quod plus est, potest eos eximere a iurisdictione eorum, et dominio in totum. . .si male tractarent Christianos, posset eos privare per sententiam iurisdictione, et dominio, quod super eos habent. tamen magna causa debet esse, quod ad hoc veniat, debet. enim. Papa eos quantum potest sustinere, dummodo periculum non sit Christianis, nec grave scandalum generetur." (Ibid., fol. 177ra. In Muldoon, "Extra Ecclesiam," p. 574, n. 47.)

43. A letter sometimes attributed to Innocent IV, *Eger cui levia*, takes a contrary position and denies the legitimacy of power outside of the church. The attribution of this letter is doubtful. (Muldoon, "Extra Ecclesiam," pp. 575-78. See also Benson, "Medieval Canonistic Origins," p. 333 n. 12.) However, it should be noted that the subtleties of medieval argument left plenty of room for unresolved contradictions, which has greatly complicated the task of sorting out the thinking of the period. See Wilks, *Problem of Sovereignty*, p. ix. Theologian Pierre Abélard (1079?-1142) used these contradictions to develop the dialectical method of encouraging his students to think for themselves, and so incurred official wrath. (Brian Tierney and Sidney Painter, *Western Europe in the Middle Ages, 300-1475* (New York: Knopf, 1983), pp. 306-7.)

44. I Cor. 6.1-8. This is a weak argument when one considers Paul's express recognition of the jurisdiction of Caesar (Acts 25.10-11); and implicitly that of infidel princes in general when he urged obedience to those in authority without mention of the religious factor (Romans 13.1-7, a passage which has been called pivotal to Christian political thought), as did Peter (I Peter 2.13-14, 18). See also Belch, *Paulus Vladimiri*, Vol. I, p. 404.

45. J.N. Figgis, *Political Thought from Gerson to Grotius: 1414-1625* (New York: Harper, 1960), p. 21.

46. Hostiensis's *Summa decretalium*, culminating the glosses and commentaries of the previous century, is considered to have laid the basis for the development of the *jus commune*. It was known as *Summa aurea* ("Golden Summation") because it was so much admired.

47. ". . .infideles, qui nec potestatem Ecclesiae Romanae nec dominium recognoscunt nec ei obediunt, indignos regno, principatu, jurisdictione, et omni

dominio. . . ." (*Super III Decretalium* (1581), 128vb, no. 27, in Belch, *Paulus Vladimiri*, Vol. I, p. 393.)

48. "Mihi tamen videtur quod in adventu Christi omnis honor et omnis princi-patus et omne dominium et iurisditio de iure et ex causa iusta, et per illum qui suppremam manum habet nec errare potest omni infideli subtracta fuerit ad fideles translata." (Hostiensis, *Lectura quinque Decretalium*, 2 vols. (Paris: 1512), 3.34.8., fol. 124v, in Muldoon, *Popes, Lawyers*, p. 16.) See also *Summa aurea*, bk. III, tit. 34.

49. ". . .unde constanter asserimus quod de iure infideles debent subici fidelibus. non econtra. . . .Concedimus tamen quod infideles qui dominium ecclesie recognoscunt sunt ab ecclesia tolerandi: quia nec ad fidem precise cogendi sunt. . . .Tales etiam possunt habere possessiones et colonos christianos; et etiam iurisdictionem ex tolerantia ecclesie." (Hostiensis, *Lectura*, ad 3.34.8. fol. 124va, in Muldoon, "Extra Ecclesiam," p. 578, n. 58.) Brian Tierney an-alyzes Hostiensis's thought on the role of popes in maintaining the faith in *Church Law and Constitutional Thought in the Middle Ages* (London: Variorum Reprints, 1977), ch. 10, 368-372. See also Wilks, *Problem of Sovereignty*, p. 166.

50. ". . .Immo et si male tractent christianos potest eos, privare per sententiam iurisdictione et dominio quo super eos habent." (Hostiensis, *Lectura*, ad 3.34.8. fol. 124va, in Muldoon, "Extra Ecclesiam," p. 579, n. 59.)

51. "Sed ubi Christiani sub dominio infidelium habitant quibus nec resistere pos-sunt: necesse est quod patientiam habeant: et de facto ipsorum dominium recognoscant." (Ibid., p. 579, n. 60).

52. J.A. Watt, "Hostiensis on *Per venerabilem*: the role of the College of Car-dinals," in Brian Tierney and Peter Linehan, eds., *Authority and Power* (Cam-bridge: Cambridge University Press, 1980), p. 104. There is some debate whether Hostiensis considered this plenitude of power to reside in the pope personally, or in the pope with the cardinals. (Ibid., pp. 106-13.)

53. Tierney and Painter, *Western Europe in the Middle Ages*, p. 481. Stickler ob-served that the idea of papal plenitude of power received its "legislative fixa-tion" with Boniface's bull. ("Concerning the Political Theories of Medieval Canonists," *Traditio* VII (1949-1951), p. 450.)

54. Aubrey Gwynn, *The English Austin Friars in the Time of Wyclif* (London: Ox-ford University Press, 1940), pt. II, ch. 4 at p. 60.

55. Figgis, *Gerson to Grotius*, p. 21. Augustino Trionfo and Egidio Colonna were colleagues.

56. "Tertio eadem ratione, qua non debemus Iudaeos, et paganos, et Sarracenos pacificos rebus suis spoliare, eadem ratione nec eorum habitaculis et ex terra nativa privare. . .Et quod possident, iure gentis possident, sive res, sive loca, sive iurisdictiones et sic iuste, et iustitia fori, non poli. . .Sicut hoc clare tenet Innocentius. . .Item causa expulsionis Ammorraeorum, Cananaeorum, et Iebusaeorum ab eorum terris per filios Israel peccata eorum fuerunt, maxime idololatria, quae est contra legem naturae, que clamat unum Deum. . .Sed Iudaei et Sarraceni non sunt idololatriae, sed alias infideles, neque tales

publici hostes principum regentium Christianorum, ergo non debent expelli."(Oldrado da Ponte, *Consilia*, (Romae: 1576), consilium 264: pp. 152v-153. Cited by Pennington from a different edition in "Bartolomé de Las Casas," p. 153, n. 16. See also Belch, *Paulus Vladimiri*, pp. 394, 405. Earlier, in his consilium 72, Oldrado had maintained that only Christian *dominium* could be *de iure* and that all others were in effect trespassers. For Oldrado's role in the formulation of the papal decree *Pastoralis cura* in 1313, see *infra*, ch. 2, p. 169 and n. 53. The following discussion in general follows Pennington.

57. Muldoon, *Popes, Lawyers*, pp. 20-21.

58. "Vidi quaedam solennia scripta septem rationibus concludentia, quod princeps pacificos infideles de suis terris absque legitima causa non debet expellere. . . .Alias oves habeo, quae non sunt ex hoc ovili scilicet ecclesiae. . . .Successor ergo Petri habet illas pascere et defendere, ergo non impugnare, vel laedi permittere. . . .Item coelum coeli domino, terram autem dedit filiis hominum, ergo negandum eis non est, quod ius humanae societatis concedit." (Johannes Andreae, *Additiones* to Guilielmus Durantis [the Elder], *Speculum iuris*, 3 vols. (Venice: 1585), Vol. III, p. 488, in Pennington, "Bartolomé de Las Casas," p. 153, n. 18.) Giovanni died a victim of the Black Death.

59. "His premissis que sunt memoriter notanda quoad premissam questionem, dicit Innocentius quod dominia, possessiones et iuristictiones licite sine peccato possunt esse apud infideles. Hec enim non tantum pro infidelibus sed pro qualibet rationibili creatura facta sunt. . ." (Zabarella, *In librum primum (-quintum) decretalium*, 5 vols. in 3, (Lyons: 1557-1558), Vol. III, fol. 181r, in Pennington, "Bartolomé de Las Casas," p. 153, n. 19.) Zabarella's debt to Jean de Paris has been frequently noted.

60. "Innocentius multum exquisite tractat hic istam materiam et primo concludit quod infideles licite tenent dominia et principatus et alia bona quia deus subiecit orbem rationabili creature nec inter homines distinxit postea supervenit ius gentium et habuit locum illud." (Panormitanus, *Commentaria, seu lecturae in quinque libros decretalium*, 8 vols. (Lugduni, 1531-1555), Vol. VI, fol. 177v. Cited by Pennington, "Bartolomé de Las Casas," 153, n. 19.)

61. "Ut notat Innocentius. . .isti non potuissent occupare dicta loca, quia infideles, qui non expugnant fideles, non debent expelli de terris suis, cum licite possideant, cum de iure divino ante occupationem permissum fuit occupare terram cuilibet. . . .Ex quibus concludit Innocentius quo non licet fidelibus nec etiam Papae sine causa iusta auferre infidelibus possessiones, dominia, vel iurisdictiones, quas tenent, cum iuste possideant." (Dominicus de Sancto Geminiano, *Consilia*, (Venetiis, 1581), consilium 96, fol. 80v. Cited by Pennington, "Bartolomé de Las Casas," p. 154, n. 21.)

62. ". . .hoc autem loquitur de infidelibus quiete manentibus et non impugnantibus Chrisitianos." (Dominicus, *Consilia*, fol. 81v; in Pennington, "Bartolomé de Las Casas," 154, n. 25.)

63. Giovanni da Legnano, *Tractatus De Bello, De Represaliis et De Duello*, tr. James Leslie Brierly (Washington: Carnegie Institution, 1917), pp. 231-32.

64. ". . .fratres de Domo Teutonica multum perturbant conversionem infidelium propter guerras quas semper movent, et propter quod [vo]lunt omnino dominari." (*The "Opus Majus" of Roger Bacon*, 3 vols., ed. and intro., John Henry Bridges (Oxford: Clarendon Press, 1897-1900: reprint, Frankfurt/Main, Minerva G.m.b.H., 1964), Vol. III, p. 121.)

65. He was a student of Pietro d'Ancarano (1330?-1416), lay canonist who taught at the University of Bologna at the same time as Zabarella and Antonio de Butrio. Closely associated with Baldo degli Ubaldi, Pietro opposed Hostiensis.

66. Frederick H. Russell, "Paulus Vladimiri's Attack on the Just War: A Case Study of Legal Polemics," in Tierney and Linehan, eds., *Authority and Power*, p. 243; Muldoon, "Contribution of Medieval Canon Lawyers," p. 484.

67. Belch, *Paulus Vladimiri*, Vol. I, pp. 428-30, 460-63. This argument would later be supported by Hugo Grotius, *The Law of War and Peace (De Jure Belli ac Pacis, 1625)*, tr. Francis W. Kelsey (Washington: Carnegie Institution, 1911, Bobbs-Merrill reprint, 1925), bk. 2, ch. 20, s. XVIII, s. LI, pp. 516-21. In the opinion of Grotius, neither could wars be waged justly against anyone because of error in interpreting divine law.

68. Russell, "Paulus Vladimiri's Attack," 244. My thanks to Dr. John-Paul Himka, University of Alberta, for his assistance with Polish history.

69. Ibid., 253. See also Nussbaum, *Law of Nations*, p. 38. St. Thomas Aquinas held that three conditions were necessary for a war to be just: legal authority, just cause, and right intention. The lack of any one of these could render a war unjust. (*Summa Theologiae* IIa IIae, q. 40, art. 1.) In this he was following the thought of St. Augustine. (J.A. Fernández-Santamaria, *The State, War and Peace. Spanish Political Thought in the Renaissance 1516-1559* (Cambridge: Cambridge University Press, 1977) p. 126ff. See also Silvio Zavala, "The Doctrine of Just War" in Lewis Hanke, ed., *History of Latin American Civilization: The Colonial Experience* (Boston: Little Brown, 1967), pp. 126-35.) In 1680, almost three centuries after Vladimiri's arguments at Constance, Spain drew up the *Recopilación de las Leyes de Indias*, in which it was declared "that war cannot and must not be waged against the Indians of any province in order that they may receive the Holy Catholic Faith or give us obedience, or for any other cause whatsoever." (*Recopilación de las Leyes de Indias*, Law 9, bk. III, ch. 4. In Zavala, *Philosophy of the Conquest*, p. 36.)

70. *"Opus Majus,"* Vol. III, pp. 121-22. See also Southern, *Western Views*, p. 57.

71. Belch, *Paulus Vladimiri*, Vol. I, p. 412.

72. "Sed nihilominus sit hac in re conclusio, quam veriorem esse censemus, bellum adversus infideles ex eo solum quod infideles sint, etiam authoritate Imperatoris, vel Papae iuste indici non potest. . .nam infidelitas non privat infideles dominio, quod habent iure humano. . .ergo, infideles ex eo quod infideles sunt, nec volunt Christi fidem suscipere, minime amittunt dominium rerum, nec provinciarum, quas obtinent, iureque humano habuerunt: quo sit ut ex hac causa bellum adversus eos a Christianis etiam authoritate publica indici iuste non valeat: quam conclusionem in specie veram esse censent In-

nocentius & Cardinalis [Francesco Zabarella] in dict. cap. Quod super his. . . ." (Didaci Covarruvias a Leyva, *Opera omnia* (Frankfurt: 1592), Vol. I, pp. 547-48.) Even such a confirmed papalist as Baltasar Ayala (1543-1612) agreed unreservedly, observing that "their infidel character does not divest them of those rights of ownership which they have under the law universal [*jus gentium*], and which are given not to the faithful alone but to every reasonable creature." (*Three Books on the Law of War and on the Duties Connected with War and on Military Discipline* (*De jure et officiis bellicis et disciplina militari libri III*, 1582), tr. John Pawley Bate (Washington: Carnegie Institution, 1912), bk. I, ch. 2, s. 28, p. 20.)

73. See, for example, Honorio Muñoz, *Vitoria and the Conquest of America*, (Manila: University of Santo Tomas Press, 1938), pp. 96-97. This work was first published in 1935.

74. Belch, *Paulus Vladimiri*, Vol. I, p. 21.

2 LEGITIMACY OF POWER: THE SECULAR ASPECTS
AND THE RISE OF INTERNATIONAL LAW

1. Venancio D. Caro, "Las controversias de Indias y las ideas teoló-jurídicas medievales que las preparan y explican," *Anuario de la Asociación Francisco de Vitoria* VIII (1947-1948), pp. 13-53; Garrett Mattingly, *Renaissance Diplomacy* (Boston: Pub House, 1955); Benson, "Medieval Canonistic Origins," pp. 327-34; Muldoon, "Canonistic Contribution," p. 265; idem, "Contribution of Medieval Canon Lawyers," pp. 483-97. One of the better short studies on the rise of international law remains that of Ernest Nys, *Les origines du droit international* (Brussels and Paris: 1894).

2. Ernst H. Kantorowicz, *The King's Two Bodies* (Princeton: Princeton University Press, 1957), p. 139.

3. Ibid, pp. 120, 123, 139. See also Walter Ullmann, "Baldus's Conception of Law," *Law Quarterly Review* LVIII, no. 231 (1942), pp. 387-88.

4. The canonist Bartolo di Sassoferrato, for one, called attention to this. (Woolf, *Bartolus*, pp. 47-48.) In the first upsurge of new ideas, the civilists were Italian, while the canonists were of many nations. Sergio Mochi Onory traces these developments in *Fonti Canonistiche*.

5. Ullmann, *Law and Politics in the Middle Ages*, pp. 164-165. Recent developments in canon law are traced out by Bernard F. Deutsch in "Ancient Roman Law and Modern Canon Law," *The Jurist* XXVII (1967), pp. 297-309; ibid., XXVIII (1968), pp. 23-27, 149-62. See also Hinsley, *Sovereignty*, pp. 73-76.

6. Kantorowicz, *Two Bodies*, p. 117. Gierke put it another way: "The work of development was done by Legists and Decretists on the ground provided by the texts of Roman and Canon Law, and partly by Divines and Philosophers on the ground of Patristic and Classical Philosophy." (*Political Theories*, p. 75.)

7. Nussbaum, *Law of Nations*, p. 17; Muldoon, "Contribution of Medieval Canon Lawyers," pp. 484-86.

8. A different concept of international law is postulated by the Academy of Sciences of the USSR, Institute of State and Law, in a book entitled *International Law* (Moscow: Foreign Languages Publishing House, 1962). It holds that each stage of human society, whether or not state organization has been achieved, has an international law, and that its origins must be looked for in China, Egypt, and India. The first known treaty was signed in 1278 B.C. between the Egyptian Rameses II and the Hittite Khattushilish III. (Ibid., p. 28).

9. Nussbaum, *Law of Nations*, p. 13. Nussbaum traces out shifts in the use of the phrase *jus gentium* and the evolution of its meaning, ibid., pp. 14-15. See also Gierke, *Political Theories*, pp. 74-76. According to Nys, Isidore of Seville (560?-636), who as archbishop of Seville headed the church in Spain from about 600 to 636, in his *Etymologiae* used the phrase *jus gentium* in the same sense as does international law today. (Vitoria, *De Indis*, p. 62; see also pp. 56-57.)

10. "Ius naturale est quod natura omnia animalia docuit. . .ius naturale est quod natura, id est deus, quia deus est natura naturans et docuit omnia animalia." (*Odofredus super Digesto Veteri* (Paris: 1604), ad 1.1.1.3 (no foliation). Cited by Tierney, *Church Law and Constitutional Thought*, ch. 7, p. 318.) Odofredus (d. 1265), was expanding a comment by his teacher Accursio, who in his turn had used Ulpian's definition of natural law. See *Digest* I.1.3, and *Institutes* I.2.1. Grotius would later exclude animals. (*Law of War and Peace*, bk. I, ch. I, s. XI, pp. 41-42.) In the nineteenth century it would be defined as "the law imposed on mankind by common human nature, that is, by reason in response to human needs and instincts." (Otto Gierke, *Natural Law and the Theory of Society 1500 to 1800*, tr. Ernest Barker (Boston: Beacon Press, 1957), p. xxxvi. First published in English in 1934 by Cambridge University Press in two volumes.) See also appendix 1, Ernest Troeltsch's essay, "The Ideas of Natural Law and Humanity in World Politics," ibid., pp. 201-22.

11. James Brown Scott, *The Spanish Conception of International Law and of Sanctions*, (Washington: Carnegie Endowment for International Peace, 1934), p. 80.

12. St. Thomas Aquinas, *Summa Theologiae* Ia IIae, q. 93, art. 2. The concept of natural law has been traced back to the Stoics and was transmitted to medieval Europe via the *Corpus Iuris Civilis* of Justinian I (Emperor of Byzantium, 527-565), as well as through the Church Fathers and Aristotle. Gratian identified its precepts with those of Scripture. (*Decretum*, dist. 1. In Ewart Lewis, "Natural Law and Expediency in Medieval Political Theory," *Ethics* 50 (1940), p. 145.)

13. ". . .quia rationalis creatura participat eam intellectualiter & rationaliter, ideo participatio legis aeternae" (*Summa Theologiae* Ia IIae, q. 91, art. 2.).

14. F.S. Ruddy, "Origin and Development of the Concept of International Law," *The Columbia Journal of Transnational Law* VII, no. 2 (1969), pp. 235-38; Bernice Hamilton, *Political Thought in Sixteenth Century Spain* (Oxford: Clarendon Press, 1963), p. 5; and Nussbaum, *Law of Nations*, p. 38. The

principle of reasonableness was later defined by Baldo degli Ubaldi as "quod lex consistit in substantia rationis, et ratio ipsa naturalis et substantia rationis est communis omnibus mundi hominibus" (rationality is the substance of law, which both by its nature and its substance is common to all mankind). (Cited by Las Casas, *Los Tesoros*, p. 74.)

15. Aquinas, *Summa Theologiae* Ia IIae, q. 94, art. 1-6; Gierke, *Political Theories*, p. 174. St. Thomas cited St. Augustine: "There is no law unless it be just." ("Non videtur esse lex quae iusta non fuerit: unde inquantum habet iusticia, intantum habet de virtute legis."(*Summa Theologiae* Ia IIae, q. 95, art. 2.)

16. This was a theme of Dante's *De monarchia*. See *infra*, ch. 1, p. 166.

17. Ruddy, "Origin and Development," p. 239.

18. The term "glossator" is applied to twelfth and thirteenth century jurists who restored and interpreted Justinian's law books, which had been compiled during the sixth century. (Woolf, *Bartolus*, p. 4.) The period of the classical glossators is usually considered to have lasted from Gratian's *Decretum* (1140) to Giovanni Andreae (d. 1348), but some extend it to the Council of Trent (1545-1563, off and on). (Stickler, "Concerning the Political Theories," p. 453.) It has been said that as their commentaries and interpretations accumulated, the glossators came to be read rather than the Justinian compilation, so that they ended up by exercising greater influence than the law books themselves. Accursio's work alone compiled 96,260 glosses. The fourteenth centenary of the promulgation of Justinian's work was marked in 1934 by the International Juridical Congress of the *Pontificum Institutum Utriusque Iuris* in Rome. The occasion included the seventh centenary of Gregory IX's *Decretales*.

19. Accursio went so far as to write that *jus gentium* was no more than a collection of statutes, i.e., man-made laws. See Ernest Nys's introduction to Vitoria, *De Indis*, pp. 56-57; and Walter Ullmann, *The Papacy and Political Ideas in the Middle Ages* (London: Variorum Reprints, 1976), Vol. VI, pp. 694-95.

20. Kantorowicz, *Two Bodies*, p. 298. The jurisconsult, Azzone dei Porci (Azo, d.c. 1230) was one of those who held that the people conceded power. (*Summa Azonis* (Venice: Angeli Raphaelis, 1581), 1070.55-59.) Ayala interpreted *lex regia* very differently, considering it to be a divine ordinance by which "all sovereignty and power has been conferred on the prince as against the people." (*De jure et officiis bellici*, bk. I, ch. 2, s. 25-26, p. 18.) See also Walter Ullmann, *The Growth of Papal Government in the Middle Ages* (London: Methuen, 1955), pp. 354-58.

21. Tierney, *Church Law and Constitutional Thought*, ch. 3, pp. 392-97. A closely related concept is found in the *Digest*, to the effect that a decision of the emperor has the force of law (I.2.12 and I.4.1).

22. The maxim has been traced back to the eleventh century. See Francesco Calasso, *I Glossatori e la teoria della Sovranità*, (Milan: 1951).

23. Tierney, *Church Law and Constitutional Thought*, ch. 3, pp. 392-93.

24. Ullmann, *Law and Politics*, p. 220.

25. J. Gilissen, *Les sources du droit en Europe occidentale (XIIe-XXe siècle)*, (Brussels: Presses Universitaires de Bruxelles, 1978), p. 49.

26. Cited by Tierney, *Religion, law, and the growth of constitutional thought 1150-1650* (Cambridge: Cambridge University Press, 1982), p. 41. See also Onory, *Fonti Canonistiche*, pp. 285-88.

27. Wilks, *Problem of Sovereignty*, p. 88.

28. Monahan, *John of Paris*, pp. 8-9, 41. Jean wrote *De Potesate Papali et Regia* in 1302/1303, at the time of France's confrontation with Boniface VIII.

29. Ibid., pp. 43, 99.

30. Jean carried this line of reasoning to the point of maintaining that a general council, consisting of the cardinals acting on behalf of the whole church, could depose a pope who proved himself unworthy. (Ibid., pp. 43-44.) Thus he was the first major political philosopher to argue corporation law. (Tierney, *Religion, law*, p. 91.)

31. Monahan, *John of Paris*, p. 36; Ruddy, "Origin and Development," pp. 239-40; Ullmann, *Political Thought*, pp. 200-204.

32. Wilks, *Problem of Sovereignty*, pp. 92, 105.

33. Dante, *Monarchy and Three Political Letters*, tr. Donald Nicholl and Colin Hardie (London: Weidenfeld and Nicolson, 1954), III.14, pp. 88-89; III.15, pp. 89-91. On the resemblance between Dante's *De monarchia* and the earlier *De ortu, progressu et fine Romani imperii*, by Engelbert, Abbot of Admont (c. 1250-1331), see Woolf, *Bartolus*, p. 303; and Ewart Lewis, *Medieval Political Ideas*, 2 vols., (London: Routledge & Kegan Paul, 1954), Vol. II, pp. 444-48; p. 485. Engelbert, who did not share the ideas of Jean de Paris, had been moved to write his work because of the erosion of power being suffered by the Holy Roman Empire as its component kingdoms became increasingly self-assertive. Kantorowicz holds that Dante's dependence on other writings only serves to underscore the novelty of his approach. (*Two Bodies*, pp. 452-53.)

34. Dante, *Monarchy*, II. 11-12, pp. 55-59. According to William of Ockham, the Roman Empire had been legitimate because it had been acquired with the consent of the majority of those subjected to it (Wilks, *Problem of Sovereignty*, p. 106, n. 5). St. Augustine also upheld the Roman conquest of the world as justified. (*De Civitas Dei* V. 15, 16.)

35. Dante, *Monarchy*, 11, p. 18; I.16, p. 26.

36. Dante, *Monarchy*, I.XVI; Kantorowicz, *Two Bodies*, pp. 465-66.

37. Wilks, *Problem of Sovereignty*, pp. 117, 158.

38. *Supra*, ch. 1, n. 23.

39. . . .non deventum est ad hoc ut Romani habuerunt universale dominium. (Ernest J. Burrus, tr. and ed., *The Writings of Alonso de la Vera Cruz*, 5 vols., (Rome: Jesuit Historical Institute, 1968-1972), II.VII.388, p. 243.)

40. *A Treatise on Laws and God the Lawgiver (De Legibus, ac Deo Legislatore*, 1612), in *Selections from Three Works*, tr. Gwladys L. Williams et al., 2 vols. (Washington: Carnegie Institution, 1944), II, bk. III, ch. 4, s. 1, p. 383.

41. To these, Egidio Colonna added a third possibility: that the state had origi-

nated in an act of violence, such as conquest. (*De regimine principum libri III* 1498), Vol. I, bk. III, ch. 6.

42. Ullmann, *Law and Politics*, p. 108; Kantorowicz, *Two Bodies*, p. 103 n. 49.

43. "Authore differunt: quia Iustitiae author est Deus, ut hic not. qui est natura naturans. Iuris author est homo, ut Imperator, qui est natura naturata." (*Cyni Pistorensis. . .in Digesti Veteris libros commentaria* (Frankfurt, 1578), fol. 3rb. In Tierney, *Church Law and Constitutional Thought*, ch. 7, p. 319.) Cino also endorsed Justinian's definition of the king as living law: *princeps non est homo, sed est lex animata in terra.* Aristotle's version was of the king as living justice.

44. The potentialities of Roman law in defense of secular power had first been realized by Pietro Crasso (fl. eleventh century), one of the Ravenna masters, who had espoused the cause of Emperor Henry IV against Gregory VII (pope, 1073-1085). Pietro had envisioned the king as "tutor of the peace," appointed by divine dispensation so as not to be impeded by anyone, including the pope. The king must be obeyed by everyone. (Ullmann, *Growth of Papal Government*, pp. 382-83.)

45. Wilks, *Problem of Sovereignty*, p. 97, paraphrasing Marsilio: "Dicunt enim ea esse vera secundum philosophiam sed non secundum fidem catholicam" ("They say this is true in philosophy but not in the Catholic faith"). See also Ullmann, *Political Thought*, p. 206; and Alan Gewirth, *Marsilius of Padua The Defender of the Peace* (New York: Columbia University Press, 1951), pp. 70-71.

46. Ullmann, *Law and Politics*, pp. 282-83. According to C.W. Previté-Orton, ed., *The Defensor Pacis of Marsilius of Padua* (Cambridge: Cambridge University Press, 1928), p. ix, Marsilio shared his authorship with Giovanni di Jandun (d. 1328).

47. Ruddy, "Origin and Development," p. 240. Ruddy holds that Machiavelli (1469-1527) carried Marsilio's ideas to their logical extreme in *The Prince* (1513), in which he did away with the supreme authority of law without replacing it with anything. (Ibid., p. 243.)

48. Ullmann, *Political Thought*, pp. 214-19; J.N. Figgis, "Bartolus and the development of European political ideas," *Transactions of the Royal Historical Society* (1905), pp. 156-68. Bartolo was not yet twenty years old when he obtained his doctor's degree in 1334. (Woolf, *Bartolus*, p. 2.) Las Casas frequently cited him.

49. Ullmann, *Law and Politics*, p. 110. While Bartolo held that sovereignty lay with the people for ordinary city-states (*civitas*), for those that extended their territories and became more powerful, he thought that monarchy was best, and he upheld the overlordship of the emperor. (Woolf, *Bartolus*, pp. 153-61, 175-82.)

50. Lewis, *Medieval Political Ideas*, Vol. I, p. 275; Gierke, *Natural Law*, p. 70.

51. James Westfall Thompson and Edgar Nathaniel Johnson, *An Introduction to Medieval Europe 300-1500* (New York: Norton, 1937), pp. 848, 957-59.

52. In the words of Bartolo, "Major pars mundi non obedit principi" (the major

part of the world does not obey the prince). In Walter Ullmann, "The Development of the Medieval Idea of Sovereignty," *English Historical Review*, CCL (1949), p. 6.

53. Ullmann, "Medieval Idea of Sovereignty," pp. 1-33. See also Wilks, *Problem of Sovereignty*, pp. 421-32; and Arnold Van Gennep, *Traité comparatif des nationalités*, (Paris: Payot, 1922), ch. II, pp. 32-47. Oldrado da Ponte had been one of Clement's advisers.

54. The kings of France had traditionally considered themselves independent of the emperor, a position that had been acknowledged by Innocent III in *Per Venerabilem*. (Ullmann, "Medieval Idea of Sovereignty," pp. 7-17.) Innocent's letter *Per Venerabilem* (1202) was incorporated into the decretal *Qui filii sint legitimi*. (Gregory IX, *Decretales*, IV.17.13: 1401-17 at 1411-15.)

55. See *supra*, ch. 1, p. 149.

56. Nussbaum, *Law of Nations*, pp. 17-23.

57. ". . .nam ipsa respublica maiestatem habet ad instar populi Romani, cum libera et ius habeat creandi regem." (Baldus, *Consilia*, Vol. III, 159, n. 6, fol. 46. Cited by Kantorowicz, *Two Bodies*, p. 298.) See also Ullmann, "Baldus' conception of law," pp. 386-99; and E.M. Meijers, "Balde et le droit international privé," *Etudes IV* (1966), pp. 132-41. Las Casas drew heavily on Baldo.

58. This line of reasoning has been traced back, through Cino, to the French jurist Pierre de Belleperche (d. 1308). See Ullmann, "Medieval Idea of Sovereignty," pp. 8-10 and p. 8, n. 1.

59. For the temporal aspect, see Ullmann, *Political Thought*, pp. 198-99.

60. Belch, *Paulus Vladimiri*, Vol. I, p. 24.

61. Ruddy, "Origin and Development," p. 242.

62. Ockham's synthesis of natural law with a relativist approach to specific situations is well presented by Max Shepard in "William of Occam and the Higher Law," *American Political Science Review* XXVI (1932), pp. 1005-24, and XXVII (1933), pp. 24-39.

63. Figgis, *Gerson to Grotius*, p. 21.

64. Ullmann, *Papacy and Political Ideas*, p. 366.

65. Figgis, *Gerson to Grotius*, p. 41. As Brian Tierney points out, however, the issue of unified versus divided sovereignty had roots that went back at least to the thirteenth century. (*Church Law and Constitutional Thought*, ch. 9, pp. 238-56.)

66. Oakley, *Political Thought of Pierre d'Ailly*, pp. 212-16, 226-30.

67. ". . .abhorrere prorsus et fugere tenemur absolutae potestatis mentionem. . ." (J.H. Parry, *The Spanish Theory of Empire in the Sixteenth Century*, (Cambridge: Cambridge University Press, 1940), p. 3, n. 1, citing *Variarum ex jure pontificio, regio et caesareo resolutionum*, bk. III, ch. VI.) See also Wyrwa, *Pensée politique polonaise*, pp. 327-35.

68. A.P. D'Entrèves, *Aquinas. Selected Political Writings* (Oxford: Basil Blackwell, 1965), p. xvii.

69. Figgis, *Gerson to Grotius*, pp. 68-70. Nikolaus wrote the book at the Council of Basle, 1432; according to Figgis, it was almost the last to treat Christendom as an organic unity. Diversity within the unity of faith and charity had been a favorite theme of Gregory I (the Great, pope, 590-604). Today, the theme had been picked up in its liturgical ramifications by Hans Küng, *The Council and Reunion*, tr. Cecily Hastings (London: Sheed, 1961).

70. Edmond Vansteenberghe, *Le Cardinal Nicolas de Cues* (Paris: 1920; reprint, Frankfurt am Main: Minerva MGMBH, 1963), p. 41; Tierney, *Religion, law*, p. 66.

71. Lewis, *Medieval Political Ideas*, Vol. I, pp. 192. Later, missionaries in the New World would be taken aback to find leadership operating on these principles among hunting and gathering Amerindians.

72. "Unde cum natura omnes sunt liberi, tunc omnis principatus sive consistat in lege scripta sive viva apud principem. . .est a sola concordantia et consensu subiectivo. (*De Concordantia Catholica*, ed. Gerhard Kallen, (Leipzig: 1941), bk. II, ch. XIV, p. 161); Yves Congar, "Quod omnes tangit, ab omnibus tractari et approbari debet," *Revue historique de droit français et étranger*, fourth series, XXXV (1958), pp. 210-59. The maxim would be used later by Las Casas to argue the right to self-determination, which was the theme of his *De Regia Potestate*, written in 1552-1553, but first published in Frankfurt, 1571.

73. Tierney, *Religion, law*, pp. 66-71.

74. Others also advocated this idea. See, for example, Belch, *Paulus Vladimiri*, Vol. I, p. 21. The discussion of Althusius's ideas is based on Tierney, *Religion, law*, pp. 71-79.

3   CROSSING THE ATLANTIC

1. Nussbaum, *Law of Nations*, pp. 61-63.

2. Muldoon, *Popes, Lawyers*, pp. 54-56, 103-4.

3. Henry Folmer, *Franco-Spanish Rivalry in North America 1524-1763* (Glendale, Calif.: Arthur H. Clark, 1953), p. 20; Nys, "Les publicistes espagnols," p. 538. Juan Antonio Llorente briefly summarized papal territorial grants in *Oeuvres de Don Barthélemi de Las Casas*, 2 vols. (Paris: Eymery, 1822), Vol. I, pp. 320-24; and Luis Weckmann examines papal claims to supremacy over islands in general in *Las Bulas Alejandrinas de 1493 y la Teoría Política del Papado Medieval* (Mexico: Editorial Jus, 1949). Papal policy toward the Canaries was not consistent, caught as it was between the claims of Portugal and Spain, as well as between the ideal of peaceful conversion and the expediencies of conquest. See Silvio Zavala, "Las Conquistas de Canarias y América," pp. 7-94, in *Estudios Indianos* (Mexico: Edición de el Colegio Nacional, 1948).

4. Ian Brownlie, *Principles of Public International Law* (Oxford: Clarendon Press, 1973), pp. 150-51.

5. "Quamvis enim infidelium loca propria auctoritate plerique debellare et occupare nitantur, nichilominus, quia Domini est terra et plenitudo eius, qui et Sanctitati Vestre plenariam orbis tocius potestatem reliquit, que de auctoritate et permissu Sanctitatis Vestre possidebuntur de speciali licencia et permissione omnipotentis Dei possideri videntur." (Letter from Duarte to Eugenius IV, in Charles-Martial de Witte, "Les Bulles Pontificales et l'Expansion Portugaises," *Revue d'Histoire Ecclésiastique*, 48 (1953), pp. 715-17. The letter is reproduced in English by James Muldoon in *The Expansion of Europe* (Philadelphia: University of Pennsylvania Press, 1977), doc. 10, pp. 54-56.

6. "Has indomiti silvestres fere homines inhabitant qui nulla religione coagulati, nullis denique legum vinculis irretiti, civili conversacione neglecta, in paganitate veluti pecudes vitam agunt. Iis navale comercium, literarum exercicium, genus aliquod metali aut numismatis nullum est. Habitacio denique nulla et amictus corporis nullus, set velut quedam perizomata de palmarum foliis aut caprarum pellibus ad operimentum dumtaxat verendorum circuncingentes, nudi pedes per ascabra, saxosa et abrruta moncium celerime transiliunt et in magnis yatibus et abditis antris terre latitant." (Letter from Duarte to Eugenius IV, in De Witte, "Les Bulles Pontificales," p. 715.) English version from Muldoon, *Expansion*, p. 54. For a modern description of early native Canarians, see Felipe Fernández-Armesto, *The Canary Islands After the Conquest* (Oxford: Clarendon Press, 1982), pp. 5-12. According to Fernández-Armesto, Canarians generated the same kind of controversy as did Amerindians as to their humanity. This work was brought to my attention by Dr. Nicholas Wickenden.

7. The similarities between the two peoples were not lost on Columbus, who on his first view of the Tainos of Guanahani, noted that they were "the colour of the Canarians, neither black nor white." (*The Journal of Christopher Columbus*, ed. Clements R. Markham (London: Hakluyt Society Publications, 1893); reprint, New York: Burt Franklin, n.d.), entry for 11 October 1492. Compare the description of Canarians running on rocky ground with that of French army officer Louis-Armand de Lom d'Arce, Baron de Lahontan (1666-c. 1716), who wrote that Amerindians of New France were inured "to jumping from rock to rock, being pierced by brambles and underbrush as they race through thickets as if in open country." (*Voyages du Baron de La Hontan dans l'Amérique Septentrionale*, 2 vols. (Amsterdam: Honoré, 1705; facsimile, Montreal: Editions Elysées, 1974) Vol. I, p. 47.)

8. Muldoon, *Popes, Lawyers*, p. 104. Zavala compares the conquests of the Canaries and the Americas in "Conquistas de Canarias y América."

9. Genesis 16.12. Oldrado da Ponte identified Christians with sheep and Moslems with oxen and wild animals. "Per oves enim intelligemus Christianos, quorum in tempore Salvator dicit se esse pastorem, et fuit pastor bonus, quia animam suam posuit pro ovibus suis. . . .Sed per boves et pecora campi intelligimus Saracenos, qui tanquam bestiae. ratione carentes relicto Deo vero

colunt idola. . . ." ("For by sheep we may understand Christians, of whom in this world the Saviour says he is the shepherd, and he was a good shepherd, since he laid down his life for his sheep. . . .But by the cattle and beasts of the field we understand the Saracens, who like beasts lacking reason, having abandoned the true God, worship idols.") (*Consilia* (Venice: Franciscus Zilettus, 1571), consilium 72, fols. 72-73.)

10. Juan Friede, "Las Casas and Indigenism," p. 154, in Juan Friede and Benjamin Keen eds., *Bartolomé de Las Casas in History* (DeKalb: Northern Illinois University Press, 1971). See also Dominik Josef Wölfel, "La Curia Romana y la Corona de España en la defensa de los aborigenes Canarios," *Anthropos* XXV (1930), pp. 1011-83.

11. ". . .un Perro vale para los Indios como diez hombres." (Andrés Bernáldez (d. 1513?), *Historia de los reyes católicos, D. Fernando y Da Isabel*, 2 vols. (Granada: Zamora, 1856), Vol. I, p. 311.) Columbus brought over dogs from the Canaries for use in the Indies. (G.V. Scammell, *The World Encompassed* (London and New York: Methuen, 1981), pp. 305, 338.) He is reported to have used 20 against the natives of Hispaniola upon his return in 1495.

12. See Llorente, *Oeuvres*, Vol. I, p. 311-12, for examples of subsequent bulls. Paul III issued a brief in 1544 authorizing missionary enterprises in the Orient without, however, conferring civil jurisdiction as Alexander VI's bull had done. (Silvio Zavala, *Las Instituciones Jurídicas en la Conquista de América* (Mexico: Editorial Porrúa, 1971), pp. 400-401.)

13. Frances Gardiner Davenport, *European Treaties Bearing on the History of the United States and Its Dependencies to 1648* (Washington: Carnegie Institution, 1917), p. 62. For a study of the bulls, see H. Vander Linden, "Alexander VI and the Demarcation of the Maritime and Colonial Domains of Spain and Portugal, 1493-1494," *American Historical Review* XXII, no. 1 (1916), pp. 1-20; Alfonso García-Gallo, "Las Bulas de Alejandro VI y el ordinamiento jurídico de la expansión portuguesa y castellana en Africa e Indias," *Anuario de Historia del Derecho español*, 27-28 (1957-1958), pp. 461-829; Luis Weckmann-Muñoz, "The Alexandrine Bulls of 1493: Pseudo-Asiatic Documents," *First Images* I, pp. 201-9; and idem, *Las Bulas Alejandrinas*. Weckmann-Muñoz's thesis that the pope was acting under the authority of the Donation of Constantine is challenged by Muldoon, *Popes, Lawyers*, p. 55.

14. Davenport, *European Treaties*, p. 77. The following year (1494) the Portuguese won Spain's agreement to move the line 270 leagues further west, thus securing for Portugal the route to India and, as it turned out, Brazil. In 1506 Julius II (pope, 1503-1513) confirmed this revised line in the bull *Ea Quae* (1506), after Vasco da Gama had rounded the Cape. (Ibid., pp. 84-100, 107-11; J.H. Parry, *The Age of Reconnaissance* (New York: New American Library, 1964), pp. 168, 175.) The Spanish view of the line is depicted in the *mappemonde* (1500) of Juan de la Cosa, owner and captain of the *Santa*

Maria who had sailed with Columbus in 1493-94, and the Portuguese view in the Cantino chart (1502). (Leslie F. Hannon, *The Discoverers* (Toronto: McClelland and Stewart, 1971), pp. 65-67.)

15. Davenport, *European Treaties*, p. 64.

16. Ibid., 77.

17. Bartolomé de Las Casas, *Apología*, tr. and ed. Angel Losada (Madrid: Editora Nacional, 1975), ch. 59-63, 69-70, 382-392; Stafford Poole, *In Defense of Indians*, (DeKalb: Northern Illinois Press, 1974), pp. 12, 15, 349-62; Muldoon, *Popes, Lawyers*, p. 138; Manuel Giménez Fernández, "Nuevos considerationes sobre la historia, sentido y valor de las bulas alejandrinas de 1493 preferentes a las Indias," *Anuario de Estudios Americano* I (1944), 171-429.

18. Lewis Hanke, *The Spanish Struggle for Justice in the Conquest of America* (Boston and Toronto: Little Brown, 1965), p. 26. See also Zavala, *De las Islas del mar Océano*, p. 8. In 1512, Palacios Rubios had written: ". . .las Islas que nos ocupan no son las Indias. . . .Hasta ahora ningún geógrafo ni cosmógrafo las ha mencionado y, por tanto, puede llamárselas con propriedad Islas nuevas o recientemente descubiertas." The Maya of Yucatan connected the bulls with their subjection. (*The Book of Chilam Balam of Chumayel*, tr. and ed. Ralph L. Roys (Norman: University of Oklahoma Press, 1967), p. 122.)

19. Among his other kingships, Fernando was king of Aragon, 1479-1516; and king of Castile (as Fernando V), 1474-1516. Isabel was queen of Castile, 1474-1504. Concerning Fernando's pragmatism, see Francisco Javier de Ayala, "El Descubrimiento de América y la Evolución de las Ideas Politicas," *Arbor* III, no. 8 (1945), pp. 304-21. Francis Bacon (1561-1626) classed Fernando as one of the "three wise men" among European monarchs whose policies pointed to the future. The others were Louis XI of France (reign, 1461-1483) and Henry VII of England (reign, 1485-1509). (Nys, "Les publicistes espagnols," p. 535.) Fernando also served Machiavelli as a model for his "new" prince.

20. ". . .primeque earum diri Salvatoris nomen imposui: cuius fretus auxilio tam ad hanc: quoque ad ceteras alias pervenimus. Eam vero Indi Guanahanin vocant."(Cristoforo Colombo, *Epistola de Insulis Nuper Inventis*, tr. Frank E. Robbins (Ann Arbor, Michigan: University Microfilms, 1966), p. 8.) This was the letter Columbus had sent in 1493 to Spanish officials announcing his discoveries.

21. ". . .toutes pleines de gens, comme une formiliere de formies. . .il semble que Dieu a mis en ces pays-là le gouffre ou la plus grande quantité de tout le genre humain." Gabriel Sagard, *Histoire du Canada et voyages que les Frères Mineurs Recollects y ont faicts pour la conversion des infidèles depuis l'an 1615*, 4 vols. (Paris: Tross, 1866; based on the 1636 edition), Vol. III, p. 576. Pierre Chaunu estimates that the Americas accounted for 20% of the world's population at the end of the fifteenth century. (*Conquête et exploitation des nouveaux mondes* (Paris: Presses Universitaires de France, 1969), p. 376.)

22. Las Casas understood this reciprocity. See his second memoir to Charles V in

Llorente, *Oeuvres*, Vol. I, pp. 165-68. In this connection, it is interesting to note that the Council of Toledo, which in effect acted as a parliament for Spain, counted more ecclesiastics than laity as members. At these assemblies, the king prostrated himself before the bishops and asked for their counsel. (Henry Thomas Buckle, *History of Civilization in England*, 3 vols. (London: Oxford University Press, 1903; first published 1857), Vol. II, p. 359. See also Nys, "Les publicistes espagnols," p. 534.) In European countries generally, the king's advisers included men of the church. (Ibid., p. 541 n. 1.)

23. The trend toward national sovereignty culminated in the "family of nations" concept which emerged from the Treaty of Westphalia, 1648. (J.L. Brierly, *The Law of Nations, an Introduction to the International Law of Peace* (Oxford: Clarendon Press, 1963), p. 5.)

24. Protection of Amerindians was the particular responsibility of bishops. This was considered a matter for ecclesiastical administration, for which the bishops were responsible to the king as patron of the Church in the Indies. See Nys, "Les publicistes espagnols," pp. 539-40. It occasionally happened that individuals appealed directly to the pope over the heads of their own monarchs, as when the aging Columbus, upset with devious court politics, sought the pope's intervention on his behalf. There is speculation that this led to the commissioning of his fourth voyage (1502-1504). (Friede, "Las Casas and Indigenism," p. 204.) He died two years later.

25. Parry, *Age of Reconnaissance*, pp. 320-21.

26. Those were Columbus's words, as recorded in his journal for 11-12 October 1492. (Markham, ed., *Journal of Christopher Columbus*, p. 38.)

27. By the seventeenth century, the term "savage" was being generally used in French and English to designate Amerindians; Spanish and Portuguese used the hardly less pejorative term "indios." The Portuguese used "selvagens" to indicate nomadic hunters and gatherers, peoples whom the Spaniards referred to as "indios bravos." For a sampling of sixteenth-century opinions on the "lack of capacity" and "bestiality" of Amerindians, see Henry Raup Wagner and Helen Rand Parish, *The Life and Writings of Bartolomé de las Casas* (Albuquerque: University of New Mexico Press, 1967), pp. 9-10. The authors err when they assert that Spanish settlers were the first to say that Amerindians were like animals. That opinion began to be heard from the first encounters, was already a stereotype by the time Spanish colonization began, and was destined to continue until well into the twentieth century. (Hanke, *Spanish Struggle*, passim, but particularly ch. 4.) Some authors have recently attempted to explain away such terms as "animales," "apartados de razón," etc., which appear in early Spanish colonial documents in reference to Amerindians. See Lewis Hanke, "More Heat and Some Light on the Spanish Struggle for Justice in the Conquest of America," *The Hispanic American Historical Review* 44, no. 3 (1964), p. 296, n. 13. Also, idem, *Aristotle and the American Indians* (London: Hollis & Carter, 1959), pp. 23-24. Similar attempts have been made in connection with the French use of

"sauvage." (Olive Patricia Dickason, *The Myth of the Savage and the Beginnings of French Colonialism in the Americas* (Edmonton: University of Alberta Press, 1984), pp. 63-65.)

28. Montesquieu, *The Spirit of the Laws*, tr. Thomas Nugent (New York: Hafner, 1949), I. bk. XVIII, s. 13, p. 276.

29. Loys Le Roy, *Exhortation aux français pour vivre en concorde, et jouir du bien de la paix* (Paris: Frederic Morel, 1570), 113v.

30. Wilks, *Sovereignty*, p. 27.

31. Dickason, *Myth of the Savage*, p. 50; Denys Hay, ed., *The Age of the Renaissance* (London: Thames & Hudson, 1967), p. 365.

32. Pietro Martire d'Anghiera, *De Orbe Novo*, 2 vols., tr. and ed. Francis Augustus MacNutt (New York: Putnam's, 1912), Vol. I, pp. 102-3. Something of the general attitude was expressed by Augustino Trionfo, when he observed that man needs government in the same natural way he needs clothes. (*Summa de potestate ecclesiastica*, Rome: 1584), XXXVII.2 ad 3, pp. 220-21.)

33. Luis Aznar, "Las etapas iniciales de la legislación sobre indios," *Cuadernos Americanos* XLI (1948), pp. 185-86.

34. "Et videtur, quod eis volentibus in pace, et quiete vivere non sint molestia inferenda." (Oldrado da Ponte, *Consilia*, consilium 72, fols. 72-73.)

35. In the words of Michel de Montaigne (1533-1592), "Our world has first discovered another. . .so new and so infantile that it is still being taught its ABC." *The Complete Works of Montaigne*, tr. Donald M. Frame (Stanford, Calif.: Stanford University Press, 1957), III.6, p. 693, in the essay "Of Coaches"; Vitoria, *De Indis*, III.18.

36. "Carent ii omnes (ut supra dixi) quocumque genere ferri: carent et armis utpote sibi ignotis nec ad ea sunt apti: non propter corporis deformitatem cum sint bene formati: sed quia sunt timidi ac pleni formidine. . . ." (Colombo, *Epistola*, pp. 10-11.)

37. *Journal*, entry for 14 October 1492.

38. *L'Histoire de la Terre-Neuve du Pérou en l'Inde Occidentale, qui est la principale mine d'or du monde, naguere descouverte et conquise et nommé la Nouvelle-Castile* [tr. Jacques Gohorry] (Paris: Vincent Sertenas, 1545), preface.

39. Francisco López de Gómara, *Historia de la Conquista de Mexico* (Caracas, Venezuela: Biblioteca Ayacucho, 1979), ch. 79, pp. 128-29. This edition comprises the second part of *Historia General de las Indias y Conquista de Mexico*, first published in 1522. These attitudes on the part of Amerindians continued to intrigue Europeans for a long time. Such an eminent figure as the Scots economist Adam Smith (1723-1790) thought that Amerindians were "much more ignorant than the Tartars of the Ukraine are at present. Even the Peruvians, the more civilized of the two, though they made use of gold and silver as ornaments, had no coined money of any kind." (*An Enquiry into the Nature and Causes of the Wealth of Nations* (New York: Random House, 1937), p. 203.) Concerning differences between Amerindian and European attitudes toward gold and silver, see *infra*, ch. 8, p. 247-8.

41. R.H. Major, ed., *Four Voyages to the New World: Letters and Selected Documents* (London: Hakluyt Society, 1847; reprint, New York: Corinth Books, 1961), p. 201. Las Casas estimated that Spain had conquered New World territories three times the size of the total extent of Christendom.

4 INTO A STRANGE WORLD

1. Parry, *Spanish Theory*, pp. 1-11.
2. Benjamin Keen, "The Black Legend Revisited: Assumptions and Realities," *Hispanic American Historical Review* 49, no. 4 (1969), pp. 705-6; Sverker Arnoldsson, *La leyenda negra, estudios sobre sus orígenes*, tr. Mateo Pastor-López et al. (Göteborg: Almquist & Wiksell, 1960).
3. See ch. 5.
4. *Colección de documentos inéditos relativos al descubrimiento, conquista, y organización de las antiguas posesiones españoles de América y Oceanía*, 42 vols. (Madrid: 1864-1884), Vol. VIII, p. 11; *Documentos inéditos relativos al descubrimiento, conquista, y organización de las antiguas posesiones españoles de ultramar*, 25 vols. (Madrid: 1885-1932), Vol. V, pp. 110-13; Antonio de Herrera y Tordesillas, *The General History of the Vast Continent and Islands of America, commonly call'd the West-Indies*, 5 vols., tr. Capt. John Stevens (London, Wood and Woodward, 1740; reprint New York: AMS Press, 1973), Vol. I, pp. 304-5; Llorente, *Oeuvres* Vol. I, pp. 260-62; 271-86.
5. Herrera, *General History*, Vol. I, passim; Llorente, *Oeuvres*, Vol. I, pp. 256-57. See also Friede, "Las Casas and Indigenism," pp. 142-46.
6. "Mandado que los yndios vecinos e moradores de la *Isla Española*, fuesen lybres e non suxetos a servidumbre." However, she then went on to say that Amerindians should be required to work for the Spaniards. (*Documentos inéditos relativos al. . .América y Oceanía*, Vol. XXXI, pp. 209-12, Real Cédula para que los vecinos de "La Española" sirvan a los cristhianos en labranza e granxeria e les ayuden a sacar oro, pagandoles sus xornales. Medina del Campo, Diciembre 20 de 1503.) According to Venancio D. Carro, in the matter of Amerindian rights, Isabel anticipated Vitoria. ("The Spanish Theological-Juridical Renaissance," *Las Casas in History*, eds. Friede and Keen, p. 242.)
7. This was appreciated by royal advisers as early as the 1550s, who observed that if the *encomenderos* were "confirmed in their authority, they will be united in a single body, which since it will be the nerve and strength of these Kingdoms, can rise easily and not obey the kings of Castile, hating, as is natural, to be governed by a foreign kingdom, as they will then view Spain." *Nueva colección de documentos inéditos para la Historia de España y de sus Indias*, 6 vols. (Madrid: 1896), Vol. VI; p. 63. Cited by Karen Spalding, *Essays in Political, Economic and Social History of Colonial Latin America* (Newark: University of Delaware, 1982), p. xiv.
8. See, for example, the *cédulas* sent to Diego Colón in 1511, arranging for Amerindians to be brought in from other islands for work in the gold fields

because the local ones were dying off so fast. (*Documentos inéditos relativos al. . .ultramar*, Vol. I, pp. 1-14, Réal cédula al virrey D. Diego Colón, el 6 de Junio 1511; ibid., pp. 15-26, Réal cédula al D. Diego Colón el 15 de Julio 1511.)

9. Hanke, *Spanish Struggle*, pp. 17-18. The only contemporary account extant is that of Bartolomé de Las Casas, *Historia de las Indias*, eds. Juan Perez de Tudela Bueso and Emilio Lopez Oto, 5 vols. (Madrid: Biblioteca de Autores Españoles, 1956-1958), Vol. II, bk. III, ch. 4, pp. 176-78. (Begun in 1527, and worked on off and on until his death in 1566, this work was first published in Madrid, 1875-1876.). See also Arthur Helps, *The Spanish Conquest in America*, 4 vols. (London: John Lane, 1900), Vol. I, pp. 175-81. Today a monument to Montesinos dominates the Santo Domingo harbor front.

10. Ricardo Levene, *Introducción a la historia del derecho indiano* (Buenos Aires: Librería Jurídica, 1924), pp. 199-200.

11. Francis Oakley, "Almain and Major: Conciliar Theory on the Eve of the Reformation," *The American Historical Review* 70, no. 3 (1965), pp. 681-82. See also idem, "On the Road from Constance to 1688: The Political Thought of John Major and George Buchanan," *The Journal of British Studies* I, no. 2 (1962), pp. 14-18.

12. Major's ready acceptance of the bestiality of Amerindians would later draw a stinging rebuke from Las Casas. See Losada, *Apología*, ch. 56, pp. 373-75.

13. John Major, *In Secundum Librum Sententiarum* (Paris: 1510), dist. 44, quest. 3.

14. Parry, *Spanish Theory*, pp. 18-19; Zavala, *Political Philosophy of the Conquest*, pp. 45-46; idem, "Las doctrinas de Palacios Rubios y Matías de Paz ante la Conquista de America," pp. LXXXIV-LXXXV, in *De las Islas del mar Océano*. However, the principle of the superior ruling the inferior had enjoyed wide support long before the discovery of the New World. Nikolaus von Kues, for one, supported it.

15. Losada, *Apología*, ch. 53-56, pp. 363-75; Poole, *Defense*, pp. 330-40; Hanke, *All Mankind*, pp. 100-3.

16. Burrus, ed., *Writings of Alonso de la Vera Cruz*, II.X.713-716, p. 371.

17. The subtleties of the term *servus* are dealt with by Anthony Pagden, *The Fall of Natural Man* (Cambridge: Cambridge University Press, 1982), pp. 115-16. See also Robert E. Quirk, "Some Notes on a Controversial Controversy: Juan Ginés de Sepúlveda and Natural Servitude." *The Hispanic American Historical Review* 34 (1954), pp. 357-64. Ayala used the idea of natural superiority/inferiority to argue that a people could not pass judgment on their prince, no matter how cruel and unjust, "for the inferior cannot bind the superior by a judgment." It was up to the pope, as keeper of both swords, to deal with an erring prince. (*De Jure et Officiis bellicis*, bk. i, ch. 2, s. 25-27, pp. 18-19.) One of the best known of the works arguing the natural servitude of Amerindians is that of the eminent jurist Juan de Solórzano Pereira (1575-1655), *Política Indiana*, published in 1648; it was a condensation of his *De Indiarum jure disputationes: sive de justa Indiarum occidentalium inquisitione* (1629-1639).

Solórzano served in high official capacities in Peru and on the Council of the Indies.

18. Quevedo, although opposed to Las Casas on the question of servitude, was not in favor of *repartimiento*. See *infra*, 245; and Las Casas, *Historia*, Vol. II, bk. III, ch. 72, p. 347; ch. 106, p. 430; ch. 147, pp. 530-38. Also, Hanke, *All Mankind Is One* (DeKalb: Northern Illinois University Press, 1974), p. 11.

19. Wagner and Parish, *Life and Writings*, p. 8.

20. Only two of the opinions produced by the junta itself are known to still exist, in second-hand versions. They are those of Bernardo de Mesa and Gil Gregorio, both of which were reported by Las Casas. See Pagden, *Fall of Natural Man*, pp. 47-50; Hanke, *Spanish Struggle*, pp. 27-29, 147; Beltrán de Heredia, "Un precursor del Maestro Vitoria," pp. 3-20; and idem, ed., "Matías de Paz, 'De dominio regum Hispaniae super Indos,'" *Archivum Fratrum Praedicatorum*, III (1933), pp. 133-81.

21. In popular terms, this was translated to mean that refusal to recognize the Catholic faith was sufficient to justify war. See Levene, *Derecho indiano*, p. 54.

22. On the Spanish view of slavery, see Friede, "Las Casas and Indigenism," pp. 146-47.

23. Las Casas, *Historia*, Vol. II, bk. III, ch. 8, p. 187. See also Wagner and Parish, *Life and Writings*, p. 9.

24. Las Casas, *Historia*, Vol. II, bk. III, ch. 8, p. 188. The principle of restitution was strongly supported by Vera Cruz, particularly on the part of the *encomenderos* who had illegally appropriated Amerindian lands. (Burrus, ed., *Writings of Alonso de la Vera Cruz* II.III.114, p. 139).

25. Las Casas, *Historia*, Vol. II, bk. III, ch. 57, p. 309. As Muldoon sees it, Las Casas did not understand the full import of Innocent IV's position, which did allow for invasion of infidel territory under certain conditions, differing from Hostiensis only on the grounds that would justify such an action. (*Popes, Lawyers*, p. 141.)

26. Zavala, ed., *De las Islas de la Mar Océano*, ch. 3, pp. 39-69; James Youngblood Henderson, "The Doctrine of Aboriginal Rights in Western Legal Tradition," in *The Quest for Justice*, eds. Menno Boldt and J. Anthony Long (Toronto: University of Toronto Press, 1985), pp. 187-88.

27. *Supra*, ch. 1, pp. 151-52. Innocent IV was often cited in defence of this stand.

28. Hanke, *Spanish Struggle*, p. 35; Las Casas, *Historia*, Vol. II, bk. III, ch. 57-58, pp. 308-12. For contemporary doubts as to its efficacy in practice, see Gonzalo Fernández de Oviedo y Valdés, *Historia general y natural de las Indias*, ed. Juan Perez de Tudela Bueso, 5 vols. (Madrid: Biblioteca de Autores Españoles, 1959), Vol. III, bk. XXIX, ch. 7, pp. 227-228. An English translation of the document is in Helps, *Spanish Conquest*, Vol. I, pp. 264-67, and in Lewis Hanke, "The 'Requerimiento' and its Interpreters," *Revista de Historia de America*, no. 1 (1938), pp. 26-28. In its original form, it is in *Documentos inéditos relativos al. . .ultramar*, Vol. XX, pp. 311-14.

29. *Documnetos inéditos relativos al. . .América y Oceanía*, Vol. IX, pp. 268-80; Losada, *Apología*, ch. 25, p. 237.
30. This version can be found in *Documentos inéditos relativos al. . .América y Oceanía*, Vol. III, pp. 369-77.
31. Hanke, *Spanish Struggle*, pp. 111-12. On the 1573 ordinances, see Benjamin Keen, "The White Legend Revisited: A Reply to Professor Hanke's 'Modest Proposal,'" *Hispanic American Historical Review* 51, no. 2 (1971), pp. 349-51.
32. Friede, "Las Casas and Indigenism," p. 205.
33. Tzvetan Todorov, *La Conquête de l'Amérique* (Paris: Editions du Seuil, 1982), p. 178. The English translation, by Richard Howard, was published by Harper & Row, 1985.
34. Despite their identification, the terms had different meanings. *Repartimiento* derives from *repartir*, to allot; *encomienda* from *encomendar*, to entrust as a charge. *Repartimiento* referred to both persons and land; *encomienda* was a form of tribute, or tax, to be paid in labor, which the state could reserve for itself or give out to individuals it wished to reward. See Kirkpatrick, *Conquistadors*, p. 353. A good explanation of how the system worked is in James Lockhart and Stuart B. Schwartz, *Early Latin America* (Cambridge: Cambridge University Press, 1983), pp. 69, 94-97, 138-40. On the establishment of Spanish administration in the Americas, see Levene, *Derecho indiano*, pp. 99-147; on the legal status of Amerindians as it finally became in Mexico, see Woodrow Borah, "The Juridical Status of Indians in New Spain," *América Indígena* XLV, no. 2 (1985).
35. Herrera, *Historia General de los Hechos de los Castellanos en las Islas y Tierra Firme*, ed. Angel de Altolaguirre y Duvale, 17 vols. (Madrid: 1934-1957), Vol. II, bk. V, ch. 9, pp. 451-53; Llorente, *Oeuvres*, Vol. I, pp. 256-58. See also Lesley Byrd Simpson, *The Encomienda in New Spain* (Berkeley: University of California, 1966); Robert S. Chamberlain, "Simpson's *The encomienda in New Spain* and recent encomienda studies," *Hispanic American Historical Review*, no. 2 (1954), pp. 238-50; Chamberlain's "The pre-conquest tribute and service system of the Maya as preparation for the Spanish repartimiento-encomienda in Yucatan," *University of Miami Hispanic American Studies*, no. 10 (1951); and Silvio Zavala, *La encomienda indiana*, 2nd ed. (Mexico: Porrua, 1973). Concerning the Canaries, see Alonso de Espinosa, *Del Origen de la Santa Imagen de Nuestra Señora de Candelaria* (Seville: 1594), bk. III, ch. 12 (in English, *The Guanches of Tenerife*, tr. and ed. Sir Clements Markham, (London: Hakluyt Society, 1907), pp. 116-120); and Roger Bigelow Merriman, *The Rise of the Spanish Empire in the Old World and in the New*, 4 vols. (New York: Macmillan, 1918), Vol. II, p. 187; John Francis Bannon, ed., *Indian Labor in the Spanish Indies* (Boston: Heath, 1966); C.M. Stafford Poole, "The Church and Repartimiento in the light of the Third Mexican Council, 1585," *The Americas XX*, no. 2 (1963), pp. 115-37.
36. The Augustinian professor maintained that the Spaniards had no right to exact tribute in the first place, as even if their conquest could be accepted as just (which was doubtful), it still did not give them the right to dispose of the

persons and property of Amerindians. (Burrus, ed., *Writings of Alonso de la Vera Cruz* II.IV.156-240, pp. 159-89.)

37. Lockhart and Schwartz, *Early Latin America*, pp. 128-29, 281-82; Scammell, *World Encompassed*, pp. 321-23. A contemporary opinion against *repartimiento/encomienda* as expressed by Dominican Juan Ramírez (1595) is reproduced in Lewis Hanke, ed., *Cuerpo de documentos del siglio XVI* (Mexico: Fondo de Cultura Económica, 1943), pp. 271-292.

38. Rafael Altamira, "El Texto de las Leyes de Burgos de 1512," *Revista de Historia de América*, no. (1938), pp. 5-79. Altamira also compares various versions of the laws, such as the one published in *Documentos inéditos relativos al. . .América y Oceanía*, Vol. I, pp. 237-41, and as analysed by Las Casas, *Historia*, Vol. II, bk. III, ch. 13-16, pp. 201-11. An English version of the laws by Roland D. Hussey of the University of Califoria (Los Angeles), "Text of the Laws of Burgos: 1512-1513, concerning the treatment of the Indians," appeared in *Hispanic American Historical Review* XII, no. 3 (1932), pp. 301-26.

39. Fernando's political ideal, for example, was exclusively Mediterranean. (Javier de Ayala, "El Descubrimiento de América," pp. 319-21.)

40. Levene, *Derecho indiano*, pp. 9-12, 33-42. An example of the kind of detail in which Spanish legislators became ensnarled was their attempt to determine rations for workers in the mines, in which they equated "cassava bread" with European bread. (Ph. André-Vincent, *Bartolomé de Las Casas, prophète du Nouveau Monde* (Paris: Taillandier, 1980), pp. 240-41.

41. Gierke, *Natural Law* p. 85. See also Parry, *Spanish Theory*, pp. 20-23. This is based on the *Digest* I.1.1.4, which says that *jus gentium* is universal to all human beings.

42. Vitoria, *De Indis*, III.4.

43. ". . .quod lex naturae quantum ad prima principia communia, est eadem apud omnes. . .sed quantum ad quaedam propria, quae sunt quasi conclusiones principiorum communium. . .sed ut in paucionibus potest deficere, & quantum ad rectitudinem, propter aliqua particularia impedimenta. . . .& etiam quantum ad notitiam. . ." (Aquinas, *Summa Theologiae*, Ia IIae, q. 94, art. 4. English version from Lewis, *Medieval Political Ideas*, Vol. I, p. 55.) Isidore of Seville had expressed the same idea in his *Etymologiae* in more sweeping terms: "All laws are either divine or human. Divine laws are based on nature, human laws on customs; and so the latter differs, since different laws please different people." ("Omnes autem leges aut divinae sunt, aut humanae. Divinae naturae, humanae moribus constant; ideoque haec discrepant, quoniam aliae aliis gentibus placent." (*Isidori Hispalensis Episcopi Etymologiarum sive Originum*, 2 vols., ed. and ann. W.H. Lindsay (Oxford: Clarendon Press, 1962; reprint of first edition, 1911, Vol. I bk. 5.2.)

44. ". . .possessionum & servitus non sunt inductae a natura, sed per hominum rationem ad utilitatem humanae vitae." (*Summa Theologiae* Ia IIae, q. 94, art. 5 ad. 3um.) See also D'Entrèves, *Natural Law*, pp. 42-44.

45. Roys, ed., *Book of Chilam Balam*, p. 75, n. 5. On the reoccurrence, hence inevitability, of events, see ibid., pp. 183-84. The Maya also had their own way of ascertaining the right to rule: they held an annual interrogation of chiefs to evaluate their continuing capacities for their positions. (Ibid., pp. 88-98.)

46. ". . .satis videtur esse consensus maioribus partis totius orbis. . . .certe hoc habere vim, etiam aliis repugnantibus." (*De Indis* III.4.)

47. Todorov, *Conquête de l'Amérique*, pp. 149-51; 256.

48. See *supra*, ch. 3, p. 181. The Hieronymite friars' instructions are in *Documentos inéditos relativos al. . .América y Oceanía*, Vol. XI, pp. 256-83; Las Casas, *Historia*, Vol. II, bk. III, ch. 88, pp. 376-83. Commissions, reports, letters, and other documents relating to the enquiry have been reproduced by Manuel Serrano y Sanz in *Origines de la Dominacíon Española en América* (Madrid; Casa Editoríal Bailly/Ballíere, 1918), pp. 536-612.

49. These ventures are described by Hanke, *Spanish Struggle*, pp. 42-53; and by Wagner and Parish, *Life and Writings*, pp. 20-34. A document dealing with Las Casas's plan is reproduced in *Documentos inéditos relativos al. . .América y Oceanîa*, Vol. VII, pp. 14-65.

50. There is some doubt as to when the first of the lectures were delivered. See Muñoz, *Vitoria and the Conquest of America*, pp. 62-63 and n. 30.

51. Antonio Rodríguez de Léon Pinelo (1594/5-1660), writer and an official of the Council of the Indies, thought that Amerindian cities had been constructed by a vanished race of giants. (*El paraîso en el Nuevo mundo* (2 vols., Lima: Torres Aguirre, 1943; first published in 1650).) The attraction of this type of speculation was vividly illustrated when Erich von Däniken brought out his space age version in 1968, which appeared in English under the title *Chariots of the Gods?*, tr. Michael Putpam (1970).

52. Losada, *Apología*, p. 382; Burrus, ed., *Writings of Alonso de la Vera Cruz* II.X.707:369. In this both Las Casas and Vera Cruz were going against majority opinion, as references to the prevalence of "hermaphrodites" were frequent in colonial accounts. For one example, see René Goulaine de Laudonnière, *L'Histoire notable de la Floride* (1586) in Paul Gaffarel, *Histoire de la Floride française* (Paris: Firmin-Didot, 1875), pp. 351-52. A recent study of berdachism among pre-columbian Amerindians distinguishes it from the homosexuality of Europeans. The berdache was classed as a third gender, male/female, and was forbidden by the strict taboo against same-sex relations from having liaisons with other berdaches, but only with heterosexual men. Berdaches were believed to have special spiritual powers, and had accepted roles in the communities. (Walter L. Williams, *Sexual Diversity in American Indian Culture* (Boston: Beacon Press, 1986).)

53. ". . .entre los bárbaros todo es al revés, porque es tiránico su gobierno y tratan a sus súbditos como a bestias, y quieren ser ellos tratados como dioses." (José de Acosta, *História Natural y Moral de las Indias*, ed. Edmundo O'Gorman (Mexico: Fondo de Cultura Económica, 1962), bk. V, ch. 11, p. 293. This work was first published in Seville in 1590. The English translation

is that of Edward Grimston (1604), *The Natural and Moral History of the Indies*, in the edition edited by Sir Clements R. Markham, 2 vols. (London: Hakluyt Society, 1880), Vol. II, p. 410. See also Gómara, *Historia de la Conquista de Mexico*, pp. 3-4, 62.

54. Vitoria, *De Indis* III.8.

55. Ibid., III.15. It was recognized that similar rites and sacrifices had been practised in Old World antiquity. See, for example, Samuel Rachel, *De Jurae Naturae et Gentium Dissertationes* (1676), tr. John Pawley Bate (Washington: Carnegie Institution, 1916), Vol. II, bk. I, s. XXII, p. 13.

56. *De Indis*, III.2, 3, 8, 9, 12, 13.

57. Vitoria appears to have been moved by concern for welfare of Amerindians when he stated that cases concerning their *dominium* should be judged by theologians, and not by jurists. (*De Indis* I.3.)

58. Ibid., III.16, 17, 18.

59. Compare, for instance, his position in *De Indis* II.16 with III.15. See also Muldoon, *Popes, Lawyers*, pp. 147-49; and Dickason, *Myth of the Savage*, pp. 130-31. Muñoz holds that the contradiction is more apparent than real. (*Vitoria and the Conquest*, pp. 188-89.)

60. The emperor's rebuke on the "prejudicial and scandalous" stand taken by Vitoria is summarized in Pagden, *Fall of Natural Man*, p. 106. The rebuke was addressed to Vitoria's superior, and does not name the professor.

61. Losada, *Apología*, ch. 56, pp. 375-76; Poole, *Defense*, p. 341; Hanke, *All Mankind*, pp. 104-5. See also Wagner and Parish, *Life and Writings*, p. 106; and Juan Perez de Tudela Bueso's preliminary critical study in Las Casas, *Historia*, Vol. I, pp. CXXXVI-CXL. Vitoria's prestige is indicated by the fact that when Henry VIII of England sought a second opinion from European universities on the question of annulment of marriage, the University of Salamanca professor was consulted by the empress on the subject, and his views were published in *De Matrimonio*, 1531. (Hamilton, *Political Thought*, p.174.)

62. *De Indis* III.18.

63. Cum iam non indigeant tutores Rex Hispaniarum debet relinquere indos in sua prima et propria libertate. ("Incipiunt annotationes in 2a 2ae D. Thomae per reverendum patrem fr. B.M. magistrum meritissimum," f. 35r, BV, MS Lat. 4645. In Pagden, *Fall of Natural Man*, p. 107 and n. 279.)

64. *Opera Omnia*, Vol. I, p. 671.

65. *Los Tesoros*, p. 131; Bradford W. Morse, ed., *Aboriginal Peoples and the Law: Indian, Metis and Inuit Rights in Canada* (Ottawa: Carleton University Press, 1985), p. 23.

66. Alberico Gentili, *De Jure Belli* (1612), trans. John C. Rolfe (Washington: Carnegie Institution, 1933), bk. 1, ch. 25, p. 122.

67. Grotius, *Law of War and Peace*, bk. 2, ch. 20, s. XL, p. 506.

68. Gentili, *De Jure Belli*, bk. I, ch. 9, s. 60-66, pp. 38-41; Grotius, *Law of War and Peace*, bk. II, ch. 20, s. XLVIII-LI, pp. 517-21.

69. Burrus, ed., *Writings of Alonso de la Vera Cruz*, II.X.718, pp. 371-73. This

concern about the rationality of Amerindians had been a factor which had led Pope Paul III to issue his bull *Sublimis Deus*. Only if Amerindians were rational could they be fit subjects for conversion.

70. Ibid., II.XI.812-13, p. 411.

71. The first publication of Vera Cruz's manuscript, in 1898, was confused with inaccurate interpretations. (Ernest J. Burrus, "Alonso de la Veracruz's Defence of the American Indians (1553-54)," *The Heythrop Journal* IV, no. 3 (1963), pp. 252-53.

72. Ayala, *De jure et officiis bellicis*, Vol. I, ch. 2, s. 6, p. 8.

73. Ibid., ch. 2, s. 29-30, p. 21.

74. Belli, *A Treatise on Military Matters and Warfare (De Re Militari et Bello Tractatus*, 1563), tr. Herbert C. Nutting (Washington: Carnegie Institution, 1936), pt. II, ch. 12, s. 5, p. 85.

5 IS ALL MANKIND ONE?

1. "Por donación de la Santa Sede Apostólica y otros justos y legítimos títulos, somos Señor de las Indias Occidentales, Islas y Tierra Firme del Mar Océano, descubiertas y por descubrir. . ." (Levene, *Derecho indiano*, pp. 56-57. See also Hanke, *Spanish Struggle*, p. 147.) The empire presided over by Charles was Europe's largest since that of Charlemagne. He abdicated his various positions 1555-1556.

2. Claudio Guillén, "Un padrón de conversos sevillanos (1510)," *Bulletin Hispanique* LXV, no. 1 & 2 (1963), pp.79-80. *Conversos* was the term for Jews who had converted to Christianity. The 1484 date for the birth of Las Casas, rather than the previously accepted one of 1474, is that established by Helen Rand Parish with Harold E. Weidman in "The Correct Birthdate of Bartolomé de Las Casas," *Hispanic American Historical Review* 56, no. 3 (1976), pp. 365-403. An excellent short biographical sketch of Las Casas is that of Manuel Giménez Fernández in *Las Casas in History*, eds. Friede and Keen, pp. 67-125. Giménez Fernández rejects out of hand the claim that Las Casas was scion of a noble family (Casaus) of the Canaries that had originated in France. See, for instance, Nys, "Les publicistes espagnoles," p. 543. Las Casas became a Dominican in 1522, but had received the tonsure before his first trip to America, in 1502, and was ordained a priest at Vega, Hispaniola, in 1510, where his was the first inaugural mass to be "sung in all those Indies." (Las Casas, *Historia*, Vol. II, bk. II, ch. 54, p. 136.) In 1513, he was chaplain and adviser to Pánfilo Narváez in Cuba.

3. See Pennington, "Bartolomé de Las Casas," p. 151. Some reservations as to the completeness of Las Casas's legal knowledge were expressed by Stafford Poole, in his preface to his translation of Las Casas's *Apología*: "He is at home in the law, both civil and canon, but. . .he cites the same sources again and again. . . .It would be difficult to say, on the evidence of the *Defense* alone, how truly complete his legal knowledge is." (*Defense*, p. xvii.) Pennington

presents a different picture. In *De Thesauris* written in 1565, the year before his death, to demonstrate the illegality of Spain's seizure of Peruvian treasures, Las Casas cited over twenty different canon and civil jurists from Gratian to Panormitanus. (Pennington, "Bartolomé de Las Casas;" p. 151.) His inaccuracies in quotations and citations have not helped his reputation in this regard.

4. Bartolomé de Las Casas, *Opúsculos, cartas y memoriales*, ed. Juan Pérez de Tudela Bueso (Madrid: Biblioteca de Autores Españoles, 1958), carta al Consejo de Indias, pp. 43-55; and Friede, "Las Casas and Indigenism," p. 159. See also Manuel M. Martínez, "Las Casas on the Conquest of America," pp. 337-38 in *Las Casas in History*, eds. Friede and Keen.

5. Nys, "Les publicistes espagnols," pp. 543-44. Las Casas's claim to have studied law for thirty-four years would mean that he had begun about the time of his "conversion" in 1514. His period of retreat after becoming a Dominican, which lasted until 1531, would have given him the time for his legal studies. (Llorente, *Oeuvres*, Vol. I, p. xii.) That he was self-taught has been used by some to question his authority in legal matters.

6. Lewis Hanke, *Las Teorías Políticas de Bartolomé de Las Casas* (Buenos Aires: Casa J. Peuser, 1935), p. 60; Pennington, "Bartolomé de Las Casas," pp. 151, 156-57. Las Casas's father, Pedro, had sailed with Columbus on his second voyage (1493), and with Ovando in 1502, when he was accompanied by Bartolomé.

7. Vera Cruz also held that restitution should be made, particularly in the cases of excessive tribute and illegal seizure of lands. See *supra*, ch. 4, p. 197. There were some gestures in that direction, such as at the second Council of Lima (1567-1568), which decreed that "those who have gravely injured the Indians must cease their oppression and restore what has been unjustly taken from them, since the sin continues if restitution is not made." The decree outlined the procedure for such restitution. (Martínez, "Las Casas on the Conquest of America," p. 344.)

8. Wagner and Parish, *Life and Writings*, pp. 236-37; Hanke, "More Heat," p. 301.

9. Las Casas, *Opúsculos*, Memorial de Fray Bartolomé de Las Casas y Fray Rodrigo de Andrada al Rey (1543), pp. 181-203 at 191a-93a.

10. Friede, "Las Casas and Indigenism," p. 204.

11. A Franciscan statesman-cardinal, Cisneros acted as regent following Fernando's death, and was a founder of the University of Alcalá de Henares.

12. Hanke, "More Heat," p. 338. In 1551-1553 alone Las Casas published nine treatises in Seville, keeping two presses busy. While his writing style can be difficult for modern readers in its closely reasoned (and sometimes tedious) argumentation, it can also be forceful in its forthright polemical approach. His style in Spanish was admired by his contemporaries. For an unflattering nineteenth-century evaluation, see Llorente, *Oeuvres*, Vol. I, p. iii.

13. Keen, "Black Legend Revisited," pp. 703-4. Once it became dominant,

antilascasian sentiment prevailed in Spain until the struggle against the Napoleonic invasion of 1808-1814. It was not confined to the colonists, as the letter of Fray Toribio de Motolinía (1495/9-1565) to Charles V in 1555 attests. (Toribio de Motolinía, *Memoriales e Historia de los Indios de la Nueva España* (Madrid: Atlas, 1970), pp. 334-45.)

14. Las Casas was behind the opposition to the book on moral grounds, but left the actual attack to the universities of Salamanca and Alcalá. The Rome version was entitled *Apologia pro libro de justis belli causis*. *Democrates secundus* in its original form was finally published in an analytical study by the Academía de Madrid in 1780. Sepúlveda's first *Democrates*, published in 1533, defended the doctrine of natural servitude.

15. Giménez Fernández, "A Biographical Sketch," p. 110.

16. The gap between legislation as enacted and as realized in practice in the colonies, while far from being unique to Spanish imperial administration, was striking because of the court's dedication in principle to social justice. See Levene, *Derecho indiano*, pp. 30-33; and Charles Gibson, *Spain in America* (New York: Harper & Row, 1966), pp. 94, 109-11. Papal policies were similarly handicapped. (Stickler, "Concerning the Political Theories," p. 450.)

17. ". . .que averiguasen si eran verdaderas todas aquellas atrocidades que le habían sido delatadas y propusiesen el oportuno remedio para hacer frente a tan grave mal, de manera que se restituyese a los indios su primitiva libertad, y al mismo tiempo aquel Nuevo Mundo fuese gobernado en el futuro, dotándosele de saludables leyes y prudentes instituciones." (Losada, *Apología*, p. 105; in English, Poole, *Defense*, p. 7. The original manuscripts are in Latin.)

18. According to Manuel Giménez Fernández, *Bartolomé de Las Casas*, 2 vols. (Seville: Escuela de Estudios Hispano, 1953, 1960), most members of the council favored Las Casas. However, their recommendations were not adopted. See also George Sanderlin, *Bartolomé de Las Casas. A Selection of his Writings* (New York: Knopf, 1971), p. 19.

19. Bartolomé de Las Casas, *Tradados*, 2 vols., tr. Agustín Millares Carlo and Rafael Moreno (Mexico: Fondo de Cultura Económica, 1965), Vol. I, p. 377.

20. This summary is drawn from Losada, *Apología*, pp. 109-13; the English version is by Poole, *Defense*, pp. 11-16. See also Nys, "Les publicistes espagnols," pp. 548-51; and Hanke, *Spanish Struggle*, p. 120. For other arguments favoring war against Amerindians, see Hanke, ed., *Cuerpo de documentos*, particularly the depositions of Franciscan Fray Miguel de Arcos (c. 1551), pp. 2-9; Dominican Vicente Palatino de Curzola (1559), pp. 12-37; Dominican Reginaldo de Lizárraga (1959), pp. 293-300; and Augustinian Juan de Vesconte (1559), pp. 301-12.

21. Gonzalo Fernández de Oviedo y Valdés, *Historia General y Natural de las Indias*, ed. Juan Perez de Tudela Bueso, 5 vols. (Madrid: Gráficas Orbe, 1959), Vol. I, bk. III, ch. 6, pp. 67-69. This work was first published in sections in Seville beginning in 1526 under the title *De la natural historia de las Indias.* . . .

The historian Gómara, who also had never been to the Indies himself, referred his readers to Sepúlveda to learn why Ameridians should be conquered. (Hanke, "More Heat," p. 297.)

22. Losada, *Apología*, p. 63.

23. Suárez later argued in great detail against Sepúlveda's position (*Three Theological Virtues: On Faith*, disp. XVIII, s. IV.3, p. 769; *Three Theological Virtues: On Charity*, disp. XIII, s. V, pp. 823-27, in *Selections from Three Works*, Vol. II), as did Ayala (*De jure et officiis bellicis*, Vol. I, ch. 2, s. 29, p. 21.)

24. Hanke, *Teorías Políticas*, pp. 27-28. Vitoria had made the same point. (*De Indis* II.4: "Secundo propositio: Dato quod summus Pontifex haberet talem potestatem saecularem in toto orbe, non posset eam dare principibus saecularibus. Hoc patet, quia esset annexa Papatui. Nec potest eam Papa separare ab officio summi Pontificis nec potest privare successorem illa potestate, quia non potest esse sequens summus Pontifex minor praecessore suo; et, si unus Pontifex dedisset hanc potestatem, vel nulla esset talis collatio vel sequens Pontifex posset auferre.")

25. Las Casas, *Los Tesoros*, pp. 279-87; Losada, *Apología*, ch. 40, pp. 308-9; Poole, *Defense*, pp. 260-61.

26. Pennington, "Bartolomé de Las Casas," pp. 156-58; Las Casas, Third Memoir, Eleventh Proposition, in Llorente, *Oeuvres*, Vol. I, p. 294. Suárez also argued strongly that non-Christian princes could not be deprived of their power and position solely on the ground of their unbelief; nor did he see idolatry as a just cause for war. (*Three Theological Virtues: On Faith*, disp. XVIII, s. 5.3-5, pp. 777-80; *Three Theological Virtues: On Charity*, disp. XIII, s. 5.1-4, pp. 823-25, in *Selections from Three Works*, Vol. II.) St. Thomas had even maintained that under certain conditions Christian rulers could tolerate pagan rituals within their jurisdictions. (*Summa Theologiae*, IIa IIae, q. 10, art. 11.)

27. Las Casas, in applying the arguments of Thomas Aquinas and Innocent IV to the New World, in effect modified them. (Losada, *Apología*, ch. 54-55, pp. 332-37; Poole, *Defense*, pp. 332-37.)

28. In Losada's version: "La potestad del Papa concierne exclusivamente al pueblo cristiano y no a las sectas de los demás, ya que de ningún modo nos corresponde juzgar a aquellos que están fuera."(Losada, *Apología*, ch. 20, p. 217. Zabarella was commenting on *Clementinis*, a body of laws promulgated in 1317 by John XXII (pope, 1316-1334) largely based on the constitutions of Clement V (pope, 1305-1314) at the Council of Vienne (1311-1312). (Poole, *Defense*, p. 148, n. 29 and xix.) Even such an ardent papalist as Agostino Trionfo had conceded that non-Christian princes held legitimate authority within their own domains. (Gwynn, *English Austin Friars*, p. 64.) Other authorities cited by Las Casas in support of this position were Antonio de Butrio, Panormitanus, and Pietro d'Ancarano.

29. Losada, *Apología*, ch. 25, p. 236; Poole, *Defense*, p. 173.

30. Losada, *Apología*, ch. 52, pp. 359-62; Poole, *Defense*, pp. 321-25; Gierke, *Political Theories*, pp. 73-75.
31. Hanke, *Teorías Polítícas*, p. 33; Hamilton, *Political Thought*, p. 4.
32. Losada, *Apología*, ch. 3: pp. 132-33; Poole, *Defense*, pp. 39-41. According to Pagden, Vitoria had opened up this line of reasoning for Las Casas, which the latter exploited more fully than the professor had done. (*Fall of Natural Man*, p. 106.)
33. Losada, *Apología*, ch. 40, p. 306; Poole, pp. 257-59. A good summary of this aspect of the thought of Las Casas is that of André-Vincent, *Bartolomé de Las Casas*, pp. 242-45. In taking this stand, Las Casas was representative of his order, the Dominicans, which had maintained a similar position in connection with the Mongol Mission of 1245.
34. Losada, *Apología*, ch. 59, pp. 382-85; Poole, *Defense*, pp. 349-52.
35. As Las Casas told the king, "yo soy de los más antiguos que a las Indias pasaron y ha mucho años que estoy allá, en los cuales he visto por mis ojos, no leído en historias que pudiesen ser mentirosas, sino palpado, porque así lo diga, por mis manos. . . ." (*Historia*, Vol. II, bk. III, ch. 49, p. 534.) See also Juan Friede, "Las Casas y el movimiento indigenista en España y América en la primera mitad del siglo XVI," *Revista de História de América*, no. 34 (México: 1952), pp. 339-411.
36. Todorov, *Conquête de l'Amérique*, pp. 170-71.
37. Hanke, *All Mankind*, p. 79. See also Bartolomé de Las Casas, *Del Unico Modo de Atraer a Todos los Pueblos a la Verdadera Religión* (Mexico: Fondo de Cultural Económica, 1975), p. 131; and idem, *Apologética Historia Summaria*, ed. Edmundo O'Gorman, 2 vols. (Mexico: Instituto de Investigaciones Históricas, 1967), bk. III, ch. 42, 43. Las Casas argued that the process of civilization was a voluntary one, based on a slowly developing education and the use of reason. (*Unico Modo*, pp. 131-37.) According to Giménez Fernández, this work, which Las Casas originally wrote in Latin under the title *De unico vocationis modo* (1539), presents the basic principles of modern missionary science so well that they were reaffirmed as such by the Second Vatican Council (1962-1965).
38. Hanke, *All Mankind*, pp. 83-84; Poole, *Defense*, pp. 25-41; Las Casas, *Unico Modo*, pp. 320-26; idem, *Apologética História*, Vol. I, bk. III, ch. 48, pp. 256-60. Loys Le Roy seconded that stand: ". . .n'y a nation, ou peuple tant barbare & rude, qui ne consiste de comandans & obeissans, & partant ne retienne quelque forme de police. . ." ("there is no nation or people so barbarous and rude that they do not have leaders and followers, and moreover do not have some form of polity"). (*De l'origine, antiquité, progres, excellence et utilité de l'art politique* (Paris: Frederic Morel, 1567), p. 19.) Montesquieu would later concur: "All countries have a law of nations, not excepting the Iroquois themselves, though they devour their prisoners: for they send and receive ambassadors, and understand the rights of war and peace." Their problem, he thought, lay in the fact that their law was "not founded on true princi-

ples." (*Spirit of the Laws*, Vol. I, bk. I, s. 3, p. 5.) He defined "savages" as hunters and "barbarians" as herdsmen and shepherds. (Ibid., bk. XVIII, s. 11, p. 276.)

39. Poole, *Defense*, pp. 42-43; Losada, *Apología*, ch. 4, pp. 134-35. Verá Cruz reported from his own observations during seventeen years as missionary that Amerindians "have their own form of government and customs by which they live; they also have through oral tradition from their forefathers laws by which they judge and plan rationally; they carry on enquiries, they consult with each other; all of which are actions not of fools and insane but of sagacious persons." (". . .suum tamen modum habent gubernandi et suas consuetudines quibus vivunt, habent et ore tenus a suis maiorbus leges per quas iudicant, discurrunt, ratiocinantur, inquirunt, consultant: quae sunt non fatuorum aut insanorum sed prudentum." Burrus, ed., *Writings of Alonso de la Vera Cruz* II.X.740, pp. 379-81.) This was endorsed by Roger Williams, who founded Providence colony (Rhode Island) in 1635 with the co-operation of the local Narragansetts. As he saw it, "their civil and earthly governments be as lawful and true as any governments in the world." (Cited by Perry Miller, *Roger Williams, His Contribution to the American Tradition* (New York: Atheneum, 1970), p. 148.)

40. Hanke, *All Mankind*, p. 99; Poole, *Defense*, pp. 321-25.

41. ". . .no solo se mostraron ser gentes muy prudentes y de vivos y señalados entendimientos, teniendo sus repúblicas (cuanto sin fe y cognoscimiento de Dios verdadero pueden tenerse) prudentemente regidas, provéidas y con justicia prosperadas, porque a muchas y diversas naciones que hobo y hay hoy en el mundo, de las muy loadas y encumbradas, y gobernación, política y en las costumbres, se igualaron, y a las muy prudentes de todo él, como eran los griegos y romanos, en seguir las reglas en la natural razón con no chico exceso sobrepujaron." (*Apologética Historia*, Vol. I, p. 4. Cited in English by Hanke, *All Mankind*, p. 77.)

42. Burrus, ed., *Writings of Alonso de la Vera Cruz* II.V.241-277, pp. 191-205.

43. *Apologética Historia*, Vol. II, bk. III, ch. 161, 162, pp. 140-50.

44. Losada, *Apología*, ch. 35-37, pp. 279-93; Poole, *Defense*, pp. 226-43. See also Hanke, *All Mankind*, pp. 93-95.

45. Losada, *Apología*, ch. 33, pp. 274-75; ch. 37, pp. 290-93. Poole, *Defense*, pp. 219-20; 240-43. Vera Cruz, in line with Vitoria, strongly disagreed; he saw the defence of innocent victims not only as lawful, but as a duty. Those who indulged in human sacrifice in any form should be deprived of their *dominium* and reduced to servitude. (Burrus, ed., *Writings of Alonso de la Vera Cruz* II.XI.825-839, pp. 417-23.)

46. *De Triplici Virtute Theologica, Fide, Spe, et Charitate (The Three Theological Virtues: On Charity, 1621), disp. XIII. s. 5, pp. 823-27, in *Three Selections*, Vol. II. Acosta also opposed Vitoria on this point. (*De Procuranda Salute*, tr. and ed. Francisco Mateos (Madrid: Magerit, S.A., 1952), pp. 163-65. This work was first published in 1588.

47. Losada, *Apología*, ch. 39, p. 302; Poole, *Defense*, pp. 253-54. Vitoria upheld

this argument in *De Indis* II. 16, but modified his position to allow for intervention in ibid., III. 15, when he maintained that Innocent IV's stand had been sound. He left unresolved the contradictions this change of position entailed. (See *supra*, ch. 4, p. 194.) Ayala strongly supported Las Casas, basing his position on St. Paul, 1 Corinthians 5.12: "For what have I to do to judge them that are without?" (*De jure et officiis bellicis*, bk. I, ch. 1, s. 29, p. 21.)

48. Poole, *Defense*, p. 97; Losada, *Apología*, ch. 11, p. 177. Las Casas also cited the bull *Sublimis Deus* to support this contention. (Losada, ibid., ch. 12, pp. 179-82; ch. 62, pp. 390-91; Poole, ibid., pp. 100-103, 179-82.)

49. ". . .que han sacrificado los españoles a su diosa muy amada y adorada dellos, la cudicia, en cada un aña de los que han estado en las Indias después que entraban en cada provincia, que en cien años los indios a sus dioses en todas las Indias sacrificaban." Las Casas, *Tratados*, Vol. I, p. 397. For Montaigne's thoughts, see his essays "Des Coches" and "Des Cannibales."

50. Losada *Apología*, ch. 28 [bis], pp. 252-53; Poole, *Defense*, pp. 191-92.

51. Losada, *Apología*, ch. 26, p. 242; Poole, *Defense*, p. 181.

52. ". . .la divina Providencia instituyó un solo, mismo y unico modo de enseñarles a los hombres la verdadera religión en toda la tierra y en todo tiempo, que es un modo que persuade al entendimiento por medio de razones y que atrae suavement la voluntad. . . ." (Las Casas, *Del Unico Modo*, pp. 326-27.) In this Las Casas was basing himself solidly on St. Thomas, who came out categorically against the use of force for evangelization. (*Summa Theologiae* IIa IIae, q. 10, art. 8.)

53. "Ergo [summus pontifex] potest compellere [eos] ad hoc." Burrus, ed., *Writings of Alonso de la Vera Cruz* II.XI.797-799, p. 405.

54. Losada, *Apología*, ch. 42, pp. 315-20; ch. 49, pp. 343-48. Poole, *Defense*, pp. 267-73, 304-312. Hanke, *All Mankind*, pp. 96-97.

55. Poole, *Defense*, p. 298.

56. Southern, *Western Views*, pp. 56-57; Russell, "Paulus Vladimiri's Attack"; *supra*, ch. 1, p. 158.

57. The Laws of Burgos (1512-1513) also had been largely of the Dominicans' doing. On Vitoria's influence, see Hamilton, *Political Thought*, pp. 175-76. Levene holds that Las Casas's *Brevíssima Relación de la destrucción de las Indias* "dictated" the New Laws. (*Derecho indiano*, pp. 209-14.) See also Hanke, "More Heat," p. 307; idem., *Spanish Struggle*, pp. 150-52; Nys, "Les publicistes espagnols," passim. On the influence of Las Casas, see Juan Pérez de Tudela Bueso, "La gran reforma carolina de las Indias en 1542," *Revista de Indias* XVIII, no. 73-74 (Madrid, 1958), pp. 463-509. Tudela considers the New Laws to be the crowning achievement of the reign of Charles V.

58. Friede, "Fray Bartolomé de Las Casas," pp. 99-100. According to Arthur Scott Aiton, the publication of the New Laws in the colonies resulted in business coming to a standstill, prices rising, and the return to Spain of 600 settlers with the first fleet to sail after the proclamation. (*Antonio de Mendoza, First Viceroy of New Spain* (New York: Russell & Russell, 1927), p. 98.)

59. Hanke, *Spanish Struggle*, pp. 91-105; Scammell, *World Encompassed*, p. 332; Lockhart and Schwartz, *Early Latin America*, p. 285.

60. Marcel Bataillon, *Etudes sur Bartolomé de Las Casas* (Paris: 1965); Lewis Hanke, "A Modest Proposal for a Moratorium on Grand Generalizations: Some Thoughts on the Black Legend," *The Hispanic American Historical Review* LI, no. 1 (1971), pp. 117-18. According to Burrus, Felipe II held Vera Cruz in high regard.

61. Woodrow Borah, *Justice by Insurance* (Berkeley and Los Angeles: University of California Press, 1983), pp. 48-51. I am indebted to Dr. David C. Johnson, University of Alberta, for bringing this work to my attention.

62. Stafford Poole, "'War by Fire and Blood'—the Church and the Chichimecas 1585," *The Americas* XXII, no. 2 (1965), pp. 115-37; Philip Wayne Powell, *Soldiers, Indians, and Silver* (Berkeley and Los Angeles: University of California Press, 1952).

63. *Supra*, ch. 4, p. 195 and n. 63.

64. Hanke, *Spanish Struggle*, p. 156.

65. Giménez Fernandez, "Fray Bartolomé," p. 115. Two petitions from Amerindians of Mexico City, both dated 1574, are reproduced by Burrus in *Writings of Alonso de la Vera Cruz*, Vol. V, pp. 291-300. They are asking for an amelioration of their lot.

66. Francisco del Paso y Troncoso, comp., *Epistolario de Nueva España 1505-1818*, 16 vols. (Mexico: Antigua Libreria Robredo, 1940). Petitions are scattered through the various volumes; for example, Vol. IX, pp. 1-49.

67. Todorov, *Conquête de l'Amérique*, pp. 197-98.

6   ROUTES OF CHALLENGE: TRADE AND LAND

1. H.P. Biggar, ed., *A Collection of Documents Relating to Jacques Cartier and the Sieur de Roberval* (Ottawa: Public Archives of Canada, 1930), p. 170, the Spanish Ambassador in France to the Emperor, 27 December 1540.

2. Ibid., p. 404, the Spanish Ambassador in France to the Emperor, 3 November 1541. See also ibid., p. 426, Sarmiento to the Emperor, 15 January 1542.

3. Fernand Braudel and Ernest Labrousse, *Histoire économique et sociale de la France*, 4 vols. (Paris: Presses Universitaires de France, 1977-79), Vol. I, pp. 246-54; idem, *La Méditerranée et le monde méditerranien à l'époque du Philippe II* (Paris: Armand Colin, 1949), p. 167. In English, *The Mediterranean and the Mediterranean world in the age of Philip II*, tr. Seân Reynolds (London: Collins, 1972).

4. Both of these rights had long been seen as arising from natural law, that of freedom of the seas directly and that of trade indirectly through *jus gentium*. Justinian's *Institutes* (2.1.1) had also included freedom of access to the sea shore. France used the "natural right" to navigate the seas and to trade during the negotiations for the Treaty of Cateau-Cambrésis, 1559. (Davenport, *European Treaties*, Vol. I, p. 220 and n. 9.) Vitoria had used them to argue

Spain's right to be in the New World. (*De Indis*, pp. 151-52.) For a later formulation of the doctrine that the sea cannot be lawfully occupied, see Grotius, *Law of War and Peace*, bk. II, ch. 2, s. 3-10.

5. This doctrine of consent had been very useful to such monarchs as Philippe IV (reign, 1285-1314) and Edward I (reign, 1272-1307) in their struggles to establish national sovereignty. Concerning Edward, see Gaines Post, "A Romano-Canonical Maxim, 'Quod Omnes Tangit,' in Bracton," *Traditio* IV (1946), pp. 197-251. The invocation of the Roman legal maxim in relation to the New World may have been suggested by comparisons between Amerindians and peoples of European antiquity, which were frequent during the sixteenth century. For one, Le Roy, *L'Origine*.

6. Dickason, *Myth of the Savage*, pp. 213-17.

7. Paul Gaffarel, *Histoire du Brésil français au seizième siècle* (Paris: Maisonneuve, 1878), p. 87. The shipowner's statement, tardily dated 1538, is reproduced on pp. 366-72.

8. A 1525 map clearly places Labrador and Baccalaos (Newfoundland) and adjacent fishing grounds on the Portuguese side of the line. (Armando Cortesão and Avelino Teixeira da Mota, eds., *Portugaliae Monumenta Cartographica*, 6 vols. (Lisbon: 1960), Vol. I: "Anónimo-Diogo Ribeiro," plate 37; see also Lawrence C. Wroth, *The Voyages of Giovanni da Verrazzano 1524-1528* (New Haven: Yale University Press, 1970), plate 37.)

9. Wroth, *Verrazzano*, p. 142, and Carli letter, p. 157. Brian Slattery, "French Claims in North America, 1500-59," *Canadian Historical Review* LIX, no. 2 (1978), pp. 139-69, makes a strong point of the fact that Verrazzano's primary purpose was to find a route to the Orient; however, that had been the primary purpose of all the voyages of exploration, including those of Columbus, Giovanni Caboto, the Corte-Real brothers, and later, of Jacques Cartier. Even such late arrivals as Samuel de Champlain, who came to Canada expressly to colonize, had not given up the idea of finding the elusive route.

10. Marcel Trudel, *Histoire de la Nouvelle-France I. Les vaines tentatives 1524-1603,* (Montreal: Fides, 1963), pp. 46-47, 49.

11. Slattery, "French Claims," pp. 141-42; also, Keller et al., *Creation of Rights of Sovereignty*, pp. 100-105.

12. Sebastian Münster and François de Belleforest, *La Cosmographie universelle de tout le monde,* 2 vols., Paris, Sonnius, 1575, II: pp. 2036, 2115; André Thevet, *La Cosmographie universelle,* 2 vols., Paris, L'Huillier, 1575 II: pp. 964-65, 1009v-1010. See also Thevet's *Les Singularitez de la France antarctique* (Paris: La Porte, 1557), 148v-49, where he says that the English initiative that resulted in Caboto's voyage of 1497 had no consequence, and that in any event he had not got as far as the Gulf of St. Lawrence and the river, which had been "discovered" by Cartier.

13. Wroth, *Verrazzano*, p. 159.

14. Ibid., Carli letter, p. 158.

15. Ibid., p. 264, citing Ramusio, *Navigationi et Viaggi*, III (Venice, 1556), pp. 417-19.

16. Wroth, *Verrazzano*, pp. 160-62.

17. A good short account of Verrazzano's voyages is that of Samuel Eliot Morison, *The European Discovery of America* (New York: Oxford University Press, 1971), pp. 277-325.

18. Wroth, *Verrazzano*, plates 19 and 22, and pp. 248-49. On earlier Portuguese maps of the region, see Paul Gaffarel and Charles Gariod, *Découvertes des Portugais au temps de Christophe Colomb* (Paris: Ernest Leroux, 1892), p. 16.

19. William F. Ganong, *Crucial Maps* (Toronto: University of Toronto Press, 1964), p. 124.

20. Cortesão and Teixeira da Mota, *Portugaliae Monumenta*, Vol. I, plate 80.

21. Ganong, *Crucial Maps*, pp. 105-6, 126-27. Ganong examines the effects of Verrazzano's voyage on mapmakers in some detail, pp. 99-133. See also Wroth, *Verrazzano*, pp. 297-305, for a listing of primary and derivative maps.

22. In this connection it is interesting to note that France did not attempt to establish a colony on the Carolina coast until 1562, after the Treaty of Cateau-Cambrésis, 1559, in which France and Spain had reached a verbal agreement that the actions of their nationals in the New World would not be considered a cause for war between the two countries in the Old.

23. Cornelius J. Jaenen, "Sovereignty and Ancestral Rights During the French Regime," paper presented in the Native Studies Lecture Series, University of Saskatchewan, 4 October 1984 (typescript), p. 12.

24. As Slattery observes, "these royal symbols would clearly lend themselves to invocation in establishing a territorial claim, should this prove useful at some later stage." ("French Claims," p. 152.) See also Münster and Belleforest, *Cosmographie* II: p. 2184. Belleforest wrote of the Amerindians that they understood very well that the European action of raising a cross on their territory was an act of usurpation. (". . .ils voioyent bien que cela estoit une signe d'usurpation que faisyent les nostres sur leur terre.")

25. Biggar, ed., *Cartier and Roberval*, pp. 447-67.

26. André Thevet, "Le Grand Insulaire et Pilotage," Bibliothèque Nationale, Paris, Departement de Manuscrits, Fonds Français, MS 15452; Münster and Belleforest, *Cosmographie* II, p. 2184; *The Voyages of Jacques Cartier*, ed. H.P. Biggar (Ottawa: Acland, 1924), pp. 66, 100.

27. Biggar, ed., *Cartier and Roberval*, pp. 140-42, the Emperor to the Cardinal of Toledo, 11-13 November 1540.

28. Keller et al., *Creation of Rights of Sovereignty*, pp. 23-25.

29. ". . .au parachevement de la navigation des terres par vous jà commancées à descouvrir oultre les Terres Neufves. . . ." (Biggar, ed., *Cartier and Roberval*, pp. 44-45.)

30. "aller venir esdits pays estranges, de descendre et entrer en iceulx et les mectre en nostre main, tant par voye d'amictié, ou aymables compositions, si

faire se peult, que par force d'armes, main forte et toutes autres voyes d'hostilité, de assaillir villes, chasteaulx fortz et habitacions et d'en construyre et en ediffier ou faire construyre et edifier d'aultres esdits, pays, et y mectre habitateurs. . .desmectre. . .cappitaines, justiciers et generallement tous autres officiers que bon luis semblera de par nous et qui luy semblera estre necessaires pour l'entretenement, conqueste et tuition desdits pays et pour atraire les peuples d'iceulx à la congnoissance et amour de Dieu, et iceulx mectre et tenir en notre obeissance. . . ." (Biggar, ed., *Cartier and Roberval*, pp. 178-185 at p. 180.) Since Roberval was a Huguenot, the king was inclusive as to his religious intentions, and referred to building "temples et eglises pour la communicacion de notre saincte foy catholique et dotrine crestienne. . . ." (Ibid., 178). The English version is that of James Phinney Baxter, ed., *A Memoir of Jacques Cartier* (New York: Dodd Mead, 1906), pp. 317-18.)

31. Ganong, *Crucial Maps*, p. 363. "Et pource que Ilz na este possible (Avec les gentz dudict pays) faire trafique a raison de Leur austerite intemperance dudict pays et petit proffit sont retournes en France esperant y retourner quand il plaira au Roy."

32. Bibliothèque Nationale, Paris, Cartes et plans, 87682. Illustrated in Hannon, *The Discoverers*, pp. 70-71. Le Testu's report did much to encourage the Brazilian colonial enterprise of Chevalier Nicolas Durand de Villegaignon (c. 1510-1571).

33. Cortesão and Teixeira da Mota, *Portugaliae Monumenta*, Vol. I, plate 74.

34. Marc Lescarbot, *History of New France*, 3 vols., tr. and ann. W.L. Grant (Toronto: Champlain Society), 1907, Vol. I, p. 17.

35. Vera Cruz, for one, had been very clear on this point, citing Ezeckiel 46.18: "At no time shall he rob the people by violence of their rightful patrimony; if he will endow the sons of Israel let him do it out of his own patrimony." (Burrus, ed., *The Writings of Alonso de la Vera Cruz* II.458-63, pp. 275-77.) As late as 1927, Quebec was refusing to make treaties with the Amerindians of Ungava (a territory which had been turned over to the province in 1912), on the grounds that the province had never recognized Amerindian title to land.

36. W.J. Eccles, "Sovereignty-Association, 1500-1783," *Canadian Historical Review* LXV, no. 4 (1984), pp. 485, 496.

37. Nicolas Perrot, *Memoire sur les moeurs, coustumes et relligion des sauvages de l'Amérique septentrionale*, ed. J. Tailhan (Montreal: Editions Elysées, 1973), pp. 126-28, 292-94; Reuben Gold Thwaites, *The Jesuit Relations and Allied Documents*, 73 vols. (Cleveland: Burrows Bros. 1896-1901), LV, pp. 105-15. A Spanish example of such a procedure in 1593 on the Orinoco in Guiana was reported by Richard Hakluyt: after raising a cross and doing homage before it, Domingo de Vera, "master of the campe, tooke a bowle of water and dranke it off, and took more and threw abroad on the ground: he also drewe his sworde and cut the grasse off the ground, and the boughes off the trees saying, I take this possession in the name of King Don Philip our master, and

of his Governour Antonio de Berreo: and because some make question of this possession, to them I answere, that in these actions was present the Cassique, or principall Don Antonio, otherwise called Morequito, whose land this was, who yeelded consent to the said possession, was glad thereof, and gave his obedience to our lord the king. . . .and all the Captaines and souldiers said, that the possession was well taken, and that they would defend it with their lives. . ." (*The Principal Voyages Traffiques and Discoveries of the English Nation*, 12 vols. (Glasgow: MacLehose, 1903-1905; based on the second edition, 1598-1600), Vol. X, p. 435.)

38. William W. Warren, *History of the Ojibway People* (St. Paul, Minn.: Minnesota Historical Society Press, 1984), p. 131.
39. For example, the English had behaved similarly in Virginia. (Olive Patricia Dickason, "Europeans and Amerindians: Some Comparative Aspects of Early Contact," *CHA Historical Papers 1979*, p. 195.)
40. See also Slattery, "French Claims," pp. 168-69.

7   JUS GENTIUM TAKES ON NEW MEANINGS

1. Keller et al., *Creation of Rights of Sovereignty*, pp. 33-34. Also, John Howard Clinebell and Jim Thomson, "Sovereignty and Self-Determination: The Rights of Native Americans under International Law," *Buffalo Law Review* 27 (1978), pp. 685-88.
2. Biggar, ed., *Precursors*, pp. 41-59.
3. Richard Hakluyt, *The Principall Navigations Voiages and Discoveries of the English Nation* (London, 1589), 2 vols. (Cambridge: Cambridge University Press, 1965), Vol. II, pp. 509-11; Nys, "Les publicistes espagnols," p. 540. In the same vein were letters patent issued by Henry VII to a group of English and Portuguese merchants in 1501. (H.P. Biggar, ed., *Precursors of Jacques Cartier 1497-1534* (Ottawa: Public Archives of Canada, 1911), pp. 41-59; Gaffarel and Gariod, *Découvertes des Portugais*, pp. 14-15.)
4. Biggar, ed., *Precursors*, pp. 31-32.
5. Ibid., pp. 32-37, Letters patent by Manoel of Portugal to Gaspar Corte-Real 12 May 1500.
6. *Supra*, ch. 6, p. 222; M. Michelant & M. Ramé, eds., *Relation originale du voyage de Jacques Cartier* (Paris: 1867), Vol. II, pp. 6, 8, 41-42. See also *Edits, ordonnances royaux, déclarations et arrêts concernant le Canada*, 3 vols. (Québec: 1854-1856), Vol. III, pp. 8-9, letters patent for Troilus de La Roche de Mesgouez, 1598.
7. Biggar, ed., *Precursors*, p. 110; Estevão Gomes (1483/4-1538) was similarly instructed for his voyage to discover the Northwest Passage. (Ibid., pp. 145-53.)
8. "Nec alio quopiam iure quam quod Hispani hinc illinc oppulerint, casulas posuerint, flumen aut Promontorium denominaverint, quae proprietatem acquirere non possunt." (William Camden, *Annales rerum anglicarum et hibernicarum regnante Elizabetha ad annum MDLXXXIX* (London: Guilielmus

Stansbij, 1615), p. 309. A French edition appeared in 1624, which was translated and published the following year in English under the title *Annales of all the most remarkable things that happened during her blessed Raigne over the Kingdomes of England and Ireland*, tr. from the French (London: Benjamin Fisher, 1625).)

9. ". . .praescriptio sine possessione haud valeat. . . ." (Camden, *Annales*, p. 309; Biggar, ed., *Cartier and Roberval*, p. 141, the Emperor to the Cardinal of Toledo, 11-13 November 1540).

10. A.L. Rowse, *The Elizabethans and America* (New York: Harper, 1959), pp. 31-32.

11. ". . .quo minus caeteri Principes commercia in illis regionibus excerceant, & Colonias ubi Hispani non incolunt. . .necnon Oceanum illum vastum libere navigent cum maris & aës usus omnibus sint communis, he ius in Oceanum, populo, aut privato cuipiam possit competere, cum nec natura, nec usus publici ratio occupationem permittat." (Camden, *Annales*, p. 309.) See also Edward P. Cheyney, "International Law under Queen Elizabeth," *The English Historical Review* XX, no. 80 (1905), pp. 659-72.

12. *De Indis* III.3, 7, 12.

13. *De jure belli*, bk. I, ch. 19, s. 145:90.

14. H.P. Biggar, *The Early Fur Trading Companies of New France* (Toronto: University of Toronto Library, 1901; reprint, New York, Argonaut Press, 1965), pp. 19, 32.

15. *Thomas Gage's Travels in the New World*, ed. J. Eric S. Thompson (Norman: University of Oklahoma Press, 1985), p. 5. Gage eventually renounced Catholicism and returned to England. Encyclopaedist Denis Diderot (1713-1784) would later use similar points to those raised by Gage to argue against rights of discovery and colonization (Yves Benot, *Diderot, de l'athéisme à l'anticolonialisme* (Paris: 1970), pp. 196-97.)

16. Vitoria, *De Indis* III.16, 17.

17. ". . .que no querían consejo de gente que no conocían, ni menos acogerlos en sus casas, porque les parecían hombres terribles y mandones. . . ." (Gómara, *Historia*, ch. 18, p. 33.)

18. Roys, ed., *Book of Chilam Balam*, p. 83.

19. Fernández de Enciso, *Summa de geografia que trata de todas las partidas y provincias del mundo: en especial de las Indias*, (Seville: Jacob Kromberg, 1519; reprint, Madrid: 1948), pp. 220-21.

20. Geoffrey Atkinson, *Les Nouveaux horizons de la Renaissance française* (Paris: Droz, 1935), p. 26. See Gómara, *Histoire generalle des Indes occidentales & Terres neuves qui jusques à present ont esté descouverte*, tr. M. Fumée (Paris: Michel Sonnius, 1569), p. 233, and such French writers as Nicolas Le Chaleux, André Thevet, and Henri Lancelot-Voisin, Sieur de La Popelinière. (Dickason, *Myth of the Savage*, p. 134 and n. 47.)

21. Herrera, *General History*, Vol. II, pp. 125-26.

22. Biggar, tr. and ed., *Voyages of Jacques Cartier* pp. 64-67; *supra*, ch. 6, p. 220.

23. *Narratives of early Virginia, 1606-1625*, ed. Lyon Gardiner Tyler (New York: 1907), p. 425. Cited by Alden T. Vaughan, "'Expulsion of the Salvages': English Policy and the Virginia Massacre of 1622," *William and Mary Quarterly*, third series, XXXV, no. 1 (1978), p. 72.

24. *Hernán Cortés: Letters from Mexico*, tr. and ed. A.R. Pagden (New York: Grossman, 1971), pp. xv-xvi, xx, 6-9.

25. *Supra*, ch. 3, p. 180.

26. Vitoria, *De Indis* II.7; Grotius, *Law of War and Peace*, bk. II, ch. 2, s. 4-5, pp. 191-92; ibid., ch. 8, s. 6, p. 298.

27. Robert Gray, *A Good Speed to Virginia* (1609), ed. Wesley F. Craven (New York: Scholar's Facsimile, 1937), B1 verso, C3 verso passim. Gray urged, however, that the English obtain possession of the land by legal means, adding that a war for the purposes of evangelization would be within the law. Wilcomb Washburn surveys attitudes and legal issues in "The Moral and Legal Justification for Dispossessing the Indians," *Seventeenth-Century America*, ed. James Morton Smith (New York: Norton, 1959), pp. 15-32. Also, *supra*, ch. 6, p. 220.

28. Samuel Purchas, *Hakluytus Posthumus or Purchas His Pilgrimes*, 20 vols., (Glasgow: MacLehose, 1905-1907), Vol. XIX, pp. 222-23.

29. *More's Utopia and a Dialogue of Comfort* (London: Dent, 1951) p. 70.

30. Vera Cruz distinguished between public and private property; in the latter case, avaricious individuals should not be allowed to accumulate a superfluity to the detriment of the poor. Burrus, ed., *Writings of Alonso de la Vera Cruz* II.III.106-155, pp. 137-57.

31. Textor, *Synopsis of the Law of Nations (Synopsis Juris Gentium, 1680)*, tr. John Pawley Bate (Washington: Carnegie Institution, 1916), ch. 8, p. 67. See also *Digest* 41.1.5.

32. Gentili, *De Jure Belli*, bk. 1, ch. 17, s. 131, p. 81.

33. Grotius, *Law of War and Peace*, bk. II, ch. 2, s. 17, p. 202.

34. Hanke, ed., *Cuerpo de documentos*, p. xxix. Juan Velásquez de Salazar, an official of the city of Mexico, in 1575 wrote that while an argument could be made that Amerindians held title as the first inhabitants of the New World, in fact it did not hold "porque sin el apoyo de la ley o del derecho ninguna posesión es efectiva, y el derecho lo perdieron estos naturales al ser cautivados por la fuerza" (because without the support of law or right, no possession is effective, and what rights those nations have are lost when they are made captive by force). On the later English and American development of this train of thought, see *infra*, ch. 8, pp. 246, 249 n. 29; and Gordon I. Bennett, "Aboriginal Title in the Common Law: A Stony Path Through Feudal Doctrine," *Buffalo Law Review* 27 (1978), 628-29. For the contrary view, that Amerindians were true owners of their lands, and that European monarchs had no legal right to assume that they could dispose of them without the consent of the peoples concerned, see Burrus, ed., *Writings of Alonso de la Vera Cruz* II.III.106-155, pp. 137-57; and VIII.436-79, pp. 267-83.

35. Francis Jennings, "Virgin Land and Savage People," *American Quarterly* XXIII, no. 4 (1971), pp. 521-26.

36. Jennings, "Virgin Land," p. 528. The fact that many of these "purchases" could not be considered legal, even in the terms of the day, is another issue. See Burrus, ed., *Writings of Alonso de la Vera Cruz* II.VI.278-341, pp. 207-27.

37. Hakluyt, *Principall Navigations*, Vol. II, p. 705. See also Kimmey, "Christianity and Indian Lands," *Ethnohistory* 7, no. 1 (1960), p. 48.

38. George Peckham, "A True Report of the late discoveries, and possession taken in the right of the Crowne of England of the Newfound Lands" (1583) in Hakluyt, *Principall Navigations*, Vol. II, pp. 705-6. See also Gray, *A Good Speed*, C2 verso; and Fred M. Kimmey, "Christianity and Indian Lands," pp. 44-61. Gómara, listing the benefits Amerindians received by being conquered, included being taught Latin and the sciences, "worth more than all the silver and gold taken from them, because with literacy they are truly men, which silver does not accomplish. Thus they were liberated through conquest, and were bettered by becoming Christian." ("Hanles enseñado latín y ciencias, que vale más que quanta plata y oro les tomaron; porque con letras son verdaderamente hombres, y de la plata no se aprovechaban mucho ni todos. Así que libraron bien en ser conquistados, y mejor en ser cristianos." (*Historia*, ch. 243, p. 367.)

39. Vaughan, "Expulsion of the Salvages," p. 73.

40. According to Vaughan, out of 1,240 settlers in the colony on the eve of the attack, almost 350 were killed in the initial raid, with another five to six hundred dying in the consequent famine and epidemic. The death toll among the colonists had been even worse before the raid: in six months during the winter of 1609, their numbers had dropped from 500 to 60. Opechancanough led a second attack in 1644 that was almost as destructive as the first. ("Expulsion of the Salvages," pp. 57-84.) He was captured, subjected to indignities, and eventually shot in the back by one of his guards.

41. Purchas, *Hakluytus Posthumus*, Vol. I, p. 42.

42. *The Original Writings and Correspondence of the Two Richard Hakluyts*. ed. E.G.R. Taylor, 2 vols. (London: Hakluyt Society, 1935), Vol. II, pp. 329-30.

43. This technique is mentioned by Vaughan, "Expulsion of the Salvages," p. 72.

44. Purchas, *Hakluytus Posthumus*, Vol. XIX, pp. 218-67.

45. Nancy Oestreich Lurie interprets the Amerindian side of these events in "Indian Cultural Adjustment to European Civilization," in *Seventeenth-Century America*, ed. Smith, pp. 33-60.

46. Purchas, *Hakluytus Posthumus*, Vol. XIX, p. 231; [John Bonoeil], *His Majesties Gracious Letter to the Earle of South-Hampton* (London: 1622). Cited by Vaughan, "Expulsion of the Salvages," pp. 79-80.

47. Gentili, *De Jure Belli*, bk. I, ch. 25, p. 126.

48. *Journall of the English Plantation at Plimouth* (London: 1622; facsimile: Ann Ar-

bor: University Microfilms, 1966), pp. 36-37; William Bradford, *Of Plymouth Plantation* (New York: Capricorn, 1962), p. 73. Bradford's work, probably written between 1630 and the 1650s, was not published in its entirety until 1856.

49. Through the years, the status of these early treaties between Amerindians and Europeans has been given various interpretations by the courts. It is an area that needs much more research.

50. *De Jure Naturae et Gentium Libri Octo* (Oxford, 1688) tr. C.H. and W.A. Oldfather, 2 vols. (Washington: Carnegie Institution, 1934) Vol. II, bk. IV, ch. 4, s. 367, p. 539, and s. 370, p. 542.

51. Textor, *Synposis*, ch. 8, p. 66; *Digest* 41.2.3.1. Cornelis van Bynkershoek (1673-1743) would later make the same point. (*Quaestionum Juris Publici Libri Duo* (1737), tr. Tenney Frank (Washington: Carnegie Institution, 1930), bk. I, ch. 6, s. 46, pp. 44-45.)

52. Emer de Vattel, *The Law of Nations or the Principles of Natural Law*, tr. Charles G. Fenwick (Washington: Carnegie Institution, 1902), bk. I, ch. 7, s. 81, pp. 37-38.

53. Ibid., bk. I, ch. 18, s. 208.

54. Vattel, *Law of Nations*, bk. I, ch. 1, s. 4, p. 11.

8   CONCLUSION

1. Brierly, *The Law of Nations*, p. 7. International law as it is known today is generally dated to the publication of Grotius's *The Law of War and Peace* (1625).

2. Cited by Le Bras, *L'Age classique*, p. 369.

3. "non solum potuit rex vel imperator sed quilibet, etiam privatus homo christianus." Burrus, ed., *Writings of Alonso de la Vera Cruz* II.X.629, p. 343.

4. Cited by Sir William Holdsworth, *A History of English Law*, London, Methuen, 1938, 234. This argument had long been heard in Spain. See, for instance *supra*, ch. 7, n. 34. Later, this point would be expanded even further before the Canadian courts when "settlement" would be defined as "conquest."

5. Alonso de Espinosa, *Guanches of Tenerife*, pp. 90-91.

6. Brierly, *Law of Nations*, p. 11. See also Calasso, *I Glossatori*.

7. "Domini, pro certo, ista nostra jura moralia variantur ex tempore secundum morum variatatem." (Cited by Woolf, *Bartolus*, p. 51.)

8. Frederick Bernays Wiener, *Uses and Abuses of Legal History: A Practitioner's View* (London: Quaritch, 1962), p. 15.

9. "De la monarchie et des choses requises à son establissement. . .," in *Exhortation aux français*, pp. 111-14.

10. For instance, León Pinelo used the medieval catch-phrase "as the Philosopher says" as proof for his statement that Amerindians were slaves by nature. Keen observed, with a note of wonder, that he apparently did not consider

further proof necessary. (Introduction, *Las Casas in History*, eds. Friede and Keen, p. 12.) On the effects of Aristotle's doctrine in the New World, see Hanke, *Aristotle and the American Indian*.

11. During the nineteenth century, the Aristotelian doctrine became romanticized as the "white man's burden." The fiction of the superiority of European colonizing nations over colonized peoples reached absurd heights at the turn of the nineteenth century into the twentieth.

12. Phelan, "Authority and Flexibility," pp. 58-60. Another maxim in a similar, but much more radical, vein was *Cuando no es justa la ley, no han obedecer al rey* ("When the law is not just, they do not have to obey the king").

13. Many Spaniards, Vera Cruz among them, regarded their king as the vicar of the pope. Burrus, ed., *Writings of Alonso de la Vera Cruz* II.II.62, p. 17; also, pp. 22-23.

14. *Complete Works of Montaigne*, bk. III, 6, p. 695, "Of Coaches."

15. Roys, ed., *Chilam Balam*, p. 112; Todorov, *Conquête*, p. 91.

16. See, for example, Nancy M. Farriss's study on the continuity of native social organization under the Spanish in *Maya Society Under Colonial Rule* (Princeton, N.J., Princeton University Press, 1984); Karen Spalding, *Huarochiri: An Andean Society under Inca and Spanish Rule* (Stanford: Stanford University Press, 1984); and Charles Gibson, *The Aztecs Under Spanish Rule* (Stanford: Stanford University Press, 1964).

17. Aspects of Stone Age technology are discussed by Jean-Pierre Protzen, "Inca Stonemasonry," *Scientific American* 254, no. 2 (1986), pp. 94-105; and James A. Marshall, "Geometry of the Hopewell Earthworks," *Early Man* (Spring 1979), pp. 1-5; and idem, "An Atlas of American Indian Geometry," *Ohio Archaeologist* 37 no. (1987), 36-49.

18. Lescarbot, *History of New France*, Vol. I, p. 17.

19. Gómara, *Historia*, p. 127.

20. Heather Lechtman, "Pre-Columbian Surface Metallurgy," *Scientific American* 250, no. 6 (June 1984), pp. 56-63. The research was done at the Massachusetts Institute of Technology Laboratory for Research on Archaeological Materials.

21. An analogy within Amerindian society existed on the Canadian Northwest Coast. The Haida of the Queen Charlotte Islands, aggressive traders and warriors, frequently raided for slaves among the Salishan peoples of southern Vancouver Island and the Fraser Valley, peoples who were renowned for their spiritual leadership and expertise in spirit travel, but whose material and martial resources were no match for those of the northerners.

22. *Of Plymouth Plantation*, p. 75.

23. A provocative study of this aspect of the conquest is that of Todorov, *Conquête*.

24. William S. Simmons, "Cultural Bias in New England Puritans' Perception of Indians," *William and Mary Quarterly*, third series, XXXVIII, no. 1 (1981), pp. 56-72. Also Robert F. Berkhofer, Jr., *The White Man's Indian* (New York: Knopf, 1978).

25. This sentiment has persisted into the twentieth century. See Sydney Olivier, *The League of Nations and Primitive Peoples* (London: Oxford University Press, 1918), p. 10.

26. "Ius descendit, id est, nascitur, a iusticia." *Commentarius ad Digestum vetus*, Venice 1616, titulus *De Justitia et iure*, lex *Iuri operam daturum*, no. 3. Cited by Ullmann, "Baldus's Conception of Law," p. 388. See also d'Entrèves, *Natural Law*, p. 42.

27. Scott, *Spanish Conception*, p. 95.

28. *Digest* 41.3.4.22; Bennett, "Aboriginal Title," p. 619. Roman law paid considerable attention to property rights, as did ecclesiastical law.

29. Alpheus Henry Snow, *The Question of Aborigines in the Law and Practice of Nations* (New York and London: Putnam's, 1921), pp. 34–35.

30. Sverker Arnoldsson, *La conquista española de América según el juicio de la posteridad* (Madrid: Instituto Ibero-Americano Gotemburgo Suecia, 1960), p. 10.

Index